Software Maintenance and Computers

Edited by David H. Longstreet

SOFTWARE MAINTENANCE AND COMPUTERS

David H. Longstreet

IEEE Computer Society Press Tutorial

 IEEE Computer Society Press The Institute of Electrical and Electronics Engineers, Inc.

Software Maintenance and Computers

Edited by David H. Longstreet

IEEE Computer Society Press
Los Alamitos, California

Washington ● Brussels ● Tokyo

```
Software maintenance and computers / [edited by] David H. Longstreet.
      p.   cm.
   Includes bibliographical references.
   ISBN 0-8186-8898-X
   1. Software maintenance.  2. Electronic digital computers.
QA76.76.S64S63  1990
005.1'6--dc20                                         90-33579
                                                         CIP
```

Published by IEEE Computer Society Press
10662 Los Vaqueros Circle
P.O. Box 3014
Los Alamitos, CA 90720-1264

Cover designed by Jack I. Ballestero

Printed in the United States of America

IEEE Computer Society Order Number 898
Library of Congress Number 90-33579
IEEE Catalog Number 90EH0302-0
ISBN 0-8186-5898-3 (microfiche)
ISBN 0-8186-8898-X (case)

Additional copies can be ordered from:

IEEE Computer Society Press	IEEE Computer Society	IEEE Computer Society	IEEE Service Center
Customer Service Center	13, Avenue de l'Aquilon	Ooshima Building	445 Hoes Lane
10662 Los Vaqueros Circle	B-1200 Brussels	2-19-1 Minami-Aoyama,	P.O. Box 1331
P.O. Box 3014	BELGIUM	Minato-Ku	Piscataway, NJ 08855-1331
Los Alamitos, CA 90720-1264		Tokyo 107, JAPAN	

Preface

This tutorial is directed at managers of information systems, programmers, and researchers. The managers of information systems should begin to realize the importance of software maintenance. This tutorial will help managers understand the basic concepts of software maintenance. Furthermore, once they begin to understand the "real" costs of software and how these costs can and do affect their budgets, they will begin utilizing software maintenance.

This tutorial will familiarize the programmer with some of the basic concepts of software maintenance and then they can begin to understand its importance. Once they begin to understand and apply these techniques, they will be able to reap some of the benefits.

For the researcher, this tutorial, as all tutorials, collects a substantial amount of literature. Because the book cannot contain all known works on software maintenance, an annotated bibliography (50 entries) has been included. The bibliography contains articles from Australia, USSR, West Germany, Great Britain, Japan, Canada, and the United States. This should provide a researcher with a view of world-wide research being conducted. I have included a listing of companies that will provide copies (in English) of any of the articles in the bibliography for a nominal fee.

Tutorial Organization

Part 1, the introduction, contains several articles that will introduce the reader to the basic concepts of software maintenance. Articles are presented that describe the current state of software maintenance, and questions and answers dealing with software maintenance.

Part 2 on management issues deals with how managers address the maintenance problem. The topics range from managers' attitudes regarding maintenance to solutions through configuration management. It is broken into several subsections: managerial issues, personnel issues, controlling costs, outside help, and solutions through configuration management.

In Part 3, maintenance, repair, and testing is broken into four subsections: metrics, repair, preventative maintenance, and documentation.

Part 4, on case studies, presents some actual problems and their solutions.

Part 5, on automated tools, provides an overview of the current research into automated techniques of software maintenance.

The tutorial concludes with an annotated bibliography.

I would recommend that anyone interested in studying software maintenance review the other tutorials available from the IEEE Computer Society Press. In particular, I would recommend the following tutorials, *Software Restructuring* by Robert Arnold and *Software Reusability* by Peter Freeman.

Acknowledgments

I would like to thank David Card at Computer Sciences Corporation, and David Gustafson at Kansas State University, who provided some valuable suggestions.

Table of Contents

Part 1: Introduction

If builders built buildings the way programmers wrote programs, then the first
woodpecker that came along would destroy civilization.

Gerald Weinberg, Computer Scientist

Reports on Computer Science and Technology

The National Bureau of Standards has a special responsibility within the Federal Government for computer science and technology activities. The programs of the NBS Institute for Computer Sciences and Technology are designed to provide ADP standards, guidelines, and technical advisory services to improve the effectiveness of computer utilization in the Federal sector, and to perform appropriate research and development efforts as foundation for such activities and programs. This publication series will report these NBS efforts to the Federal computer community as well as to interested specialists in the academic and private sectors. Those wishing to receive notices of publications in this series should complete and return the form at the end of this publication.

National Bureau of Standards
Special Publication 500-130

Background

This Guide provides answers to sixty-four key questions about software maintenance. It is designed for Federal executives and managers who have a responsibility for the planning and management of software projects. It is also intended for Federal staff members affected by, or involved in, making software changes and who need to be aware of steps that can reduce both the difficulty and cost of software maintenance.

Issues addressed in the Guide include the feasibility and applicability of software reuse, the development of maintainable software, as well as the improvement of existing software, achieving programmer and software productivity, and the three key attributes of maintainable software: correctness, understandability, and reliability. Finally, it discusses software tools that can aid in making existing code more maintainable. The question and answer format is used to organize the material in a concise manner that represents a general approach for evaluating software maintenance problems and alternative workable solutions.

Understanding Software Maintenance

1. WHAT IS SOFTWARE MAINTENANCE?

Software maintenance is the performance of those activities required to keep a software system operational and responsive after it is accepted and placed into production. It is the set of activities which result in changes to the originally accepted (baseline) product set. These changes consist of modification created by correcting, inserting, deleting, extending, and enhancing the baseline system.

2. WHAT ARE THE TYPES OF SOFTWARE MAINTENANCE?

The three types of software maintenance are perfective, adaptive, and corrective.

3. WHAT IS PERFECTIVE MAINTENANCE?

Perfective maintenance includes all changes, insertions, deletions, modification, extensions, and enhancements which are made to a system to meet the evolving and/or expanding needs of the user. They are generally performed as a result of new or changing requirements, or in an attempt to augment or fine tune the software. Activities designed to make the code easier to understand, such as restructuring or documentation updates (often referred to as "preventive" maintenance), are considered to be perfective. Optimization of code to make it run faster or use storage more efficiently is also included in the perfective category. Estimates indicate that perfective maintenance comprises approximately 60% of all software maintenance effort.

4. WHAT IS ADAPTIVE MAINTENANCE?

Adaptive maintenance consists of any effort which is initiated as a result of changes in the environment in which a software system must operate. It accounts for about 20% of all the software maintenance efforts. The environmental changes are normally beyond the control of the software maintainer and consist primarily of changes to the:

1. rules, laws, and regulations that affect the system;
2. hardware configurations, e.g., new terminals, local printers;

Reprinted from *NBS Special Publication 500-130*, October 1985. United States Government work not protected by United States copyright.

3. data formats, file structures; and

4. system software (e.g., operating systems, compilers), utilities.

5. WHAT IS CORRECTIVE MAINTENANCE?

Corrective maintenance refers to changes necessitated by actual errors (induced or residual "bugs") in a system. It accounts for 20% of all the software maintenance efforts and consists of activities normally considered to be error correction required to keep the system operational. The key causes for corrective maintenance are design errors, logic errors, and coding errors. Design errors are generally the result of incorrect, incomplete, or unclear descriptions of the system change being requested, or a misunderstanding of the change request. Logic errors are the result of invalid tests and conclusions, faulty logic flow, incorrect implementation of the design specifications, or unusual combinations of data, which were not thoroughly tested. Coding errors are generally caused by the programmer and are the result of either incorrect implementation of the detailed logic design, or the incorrect use of the source code logic.

6. WHAT IS MAINTAINABILITY?

Maintainability refers to the effort required to find and fix or modify an error in operational software. Maintainability examines the effects of software failure, and ways to minimize those effects. In order to maintain control over the software maintenance process, and to ensure that the maintainability of the system does not deteriorate, it is important that software maintenance be anticipated and planned. The quality and maintainability of a software system often decrease as the system grows older. This is the result of many factors which, taken one at a time, may not seem significant but become cumulative and often result in a system which is very difficult to maintain. Quality programming capabilities and techniques are readily available. However, until a firm discipline is placed on how software maintenance is performed, and that discipline is enforced, many systems will be permitted to deteriorate to the point where they are impossible to maintain. It is likely that as the software maintainability is improved, the capacity to handle additional changes will increase.

7. WHAT IS THE "REQUIREMENTS TO RELEASE" CONCEPT?

Generally, changes are made in order to keep the system functioning in an evolving, expanding user and operational environment. When software maintenance is performed as an iterative development process, the concept of requirements to release can be applied. This concept presumes that whenever a modification is made to the software system, a function review is made to determine if a corresponding change is needed anywhere else in the system. This review should, as a minimum, include an assessment of the software design, code, test data, and associated documentation products.

8. HOW CAN "REQUIREMENTS TO RELEASE" HELP TO IMPROVE THE SOFTWARE MAINTENANCE PROCESS?

A significant portion of the activities performed in software maintenance environments is reactive. As a result, there is often a tendency to zero in on the immediate problem, fix it and wait for the next problem to arise. If an examination is made of the functional requirements, there is a likelihood of gaining a better perspective on the problem, and its solution.

9. HOW IS SOFTWARE MAINTENANCE CURRENTLY PERFORMED?

In many organizations, software maintenance is still performed with second generation tools, using second generation techniques. There are indications, however, that managers are adopting and enforcing the use of improved techniques and practices. Standards and guidelines which provide guidance on how to improve software quality have been published by NBS, IEEE, and the DOD.

10. WHAT IS THE RELATIONSHIP BETWEEN SOFTWARE QUALITY AND SOFTWARE MAINTENANCE?

Software quality can be characterized by such attributes as reliability, understandability, testability, modularity, and expandability, all of which make the software more maintainable. Thus, software quality and maintainability are inextricably bound together. The greater the number of quality attributes engineered into the software during development, the higher the degree of confidence in its maintainability.

Although it is significantly easier to build quality into the software, it can also be improved during maintenance. The cost of adding quality to existing software, however, is considerably more expensive.

11. WHAT IS THE RELATIONSHIP BETWEEN SOFTWARE TESTING AND SOFTWARE MAINTENANCE?

Testing is performed to find errors and omissions. It is also performed to ensure that the logic and structure of the software are appropriate. The more thorough the unit, integration, and system testing, the more likely the software will be reliable and correct. Consequently, testing provides assurance that the activities of software maintenance have been performed correctly.

Cost

12. WHAT IS THE COST OF SOFTWARE MAINTENANCE?

Software maintenance represents 60%-70% of the total cost of software which runs into the tens of billions of dollars each year. Perfective maintenance (changes, enhancements, extensions, etc.) comprises approximately 60% of the software maintenance costs. Adaptive maintenance and corrective maintenance are each approximately 20% of the total.

13. CAN SOFTWARE MAINTENANCE COSTS BE REDUCED?

While total software costs have risen rapidly, the ratio of development to maintenance costs has remained relatively constant. This is a result of the growing dependency of many organizations on software, the extended life of software, and the increasing complexity and size of many applications.

Continued advances in modern programming technology (e.g. modern software engineering tools and methods, fourth generation languages, application generators, etc.) will permit more sophisticated systems to be built at less cost. The dichotomy of this situation is that the more useful a system, the longer it will be used and the more it will cost over its lifetime. Thus, for some software, the cost over the total software lifetime may actually rise, but the cost per year will decrease.

14. WHAT CAN BE DONE TO BRING SOFTWARE MAINTENANCE COSTS UNDER CONTROL?

The most important piece in the puzzle of controlling total software costs is strong, effective management of the entire process. The greater the discipline invoked in the software maintenance process, the higher the quality of software which will result.

The Federal Government continues to custom develop more than 90% of its software. Reuse of existing software, including the use of off-the-shelf packages, can help hold down costs. Other solutions, such as the use of non-procedural languages, greater use of modern software engineering technology, tools and methods, and the institution of more effective management control also offer opportunities to bring the cost of software maintenance under control.

15. SHOULD AN ORGANIZATION HAVE A SOFTWARE MAINTENANCE POLICY?

Yes, a software maintenance policy is a vital step in controlling software maintenance costs. The policy should describe in broad terms the responsibilities, authorities, functions, and operations of the software maintenance organization.

Personnel

16. WHAT TYPE OF PERSON IS NEEDED FOR SOFTWARE MAINTENANCE?

The person needed in a software maintenance environment should be highly skilled and able to perform all of the functional activities that occur during the software lifecycle. The person should be experienced, and have good analytical capabilities. Above all, these people should be disciplined and thorough in their approach to analysis, coding, debugging, testing, and documentation.

17. WHAT SPECIFIC EXPERIENCES ARE NEEDED FOR SOFTWARE MAINTENANCE?

It is essential that software maintainers have experience working on tasks individually, as well as in teams. The person should have had a major responsibility for the completion of some of these tasks. It is important that the person have a breadth of knowledge about software management since in a maintenance environment, anything that can go wrong usually does. As a minimum, the person should have a number of years experience working:

- independently,
- as part of a team,
- with specific languages and computers,
- with modern programming practices,
- on various types of application.

18. WHY DO SOFTWARE MAINTAINERS HAVE A HIGHER RATE OF TURNOVER THAN OTHER ADP PERSONNEL?

Maintainers tend to change jobs at a higher rate than other ADP professionals primarily because of the image of maintenance. In many organizations, the traditionally held view that maintenance requires less aptitude than development is quite common. As a result, working conditions, including renumeration, tends to be less for maintainers than for developers. Within the next few years, this situation should change as increasing numbers of managers recognize the value of the maintainer to the daily operation of the organization.

Software Reuse

19. WHAT IS REUSABLE SOFTWARE?

The popular notion of software reuse focuses on the software's source and object code. While source and object code can be reused, software consists of more than just code. Research has shown that greater benefits can be accrued through the use of the requirements, specifications, design, documentation test data and other elements of the software.

20. CAN SOFTWARE REUSE IMPROVE SOFTWARE MAINTENANCE?

Yes. In fact, software reuse should be at the heart of the strategy for software maintenance. Research has shown that the quality of software deteriorates when the only elements of the software that are reused are the sources and object code. By effectively reusing the requirements, specifications, design, documentation, test data, and other elements on which the code is based, the quality of the software can be maintained or even enhanced during the repeated modifications which occur after the software has been developed and placed into operational use.

21. HOW DO I RECOGNIZE THE OPPORTUNITIES FOR REUSE?

Any time a new application is developed, or enhancements are planned for existing software, the first question which should be addressed is "Do software elements (requirements, specification, etc.) exist which can be reused in this application?" The type of software reuse that is practical in each situation varies. If a new application is being developed, the opportunity to reuse elements from existing similar application and subsystems should be examined. When enhancements are made to an existing application, existing software elements should be used as the baseline whenever possible. Only when it is clear that reuse of existing software elements is inappropriate, should the decision be made to create brand new software elements.

Management

22. HOW CAN THE IMAGE OF SOFTWARE MAINTENANCE BE IMPROVED?

Upper management must be kept informed of the overall success of the software maintenance effort and how software maintenance supports and enhances the organization's ability to meet its objectives. Software maintenance is an important effort which supports and contributes to the ability of the organization to meet its goals. Too many of the problems encountered in software maintenance are the result of the negative attitude that it is a function which exists because the software support staff can "never do it right." Rather, the emphasis should be on the concept that software maintenance enables an organization to improve and expand its capabilities using existing systems.

The software maintenance manager has the responsibility for keeping the maintenance staff happy and satisfied. Software maintenance must be thought of as the challenging, dynamic, interesting work it can be.

23. WHAT ARE SOME OF THE ACTIONS THAT MANAGEMENT CAN TAKE TO DETERMINE WHEN TO CONSIDER REDESIGN?

A system which is in virtually constant need of corrective maintenance is a prime candidate for redesign. As systems age and additional maintenance is performed on them, many become increasingly fragile and susceptible to changes. The older the code, the more likely frequent modifications, new requirements, and enhancements will cause the system to break down.

When a decision has been reached to redesign or to stop supporting a system, the decision can be implemented in a number of ways: support can simply be removed and the system can die through neglect; the minimum support needed to keep it functioning may be provided while a new system is built; or the system may be rejuvenated section by section and given an extended life. How the redesign is affected depends on the individual circumstances of the system, its operating environment, and the needs of the organization it supports.

24. HOW DO YOU DETERMINE WHEN TO ACQUIRE NEW SOFTWARE?

Although maintenance is an ongoing process, there comes a time when serious consideration should be given to acquiring new software. If there are requirements for which the existing system is totally inadequate or if the existing software is sufficiently outdated that the viability of the organization is affected, then consideration should be given to the acquisition of new software.

A major concern of managers and software engineers is how to determine whether a software package will satisfy all of the existing requirements. In most cases, the software package handles only a part of the requirements. Thus, the acquired software package often will either have to be modified, or additional software will be needed.

25. WHAT ARE THREE KEY QUESTIONS TO BE ANSWERED WHEN ACQUIRING A SOFTWARE PACKAGE?

Organizations are acquiring software packages at an increasing rate. There are a number of questions that should be answered, however the three that are perhaps the most crucial are:

- How well can I use the software as it is?
- How easy is the software to maintain?
- Will I be able to use it if I change the processing environment?

26. WHAT ARE SOME OTHER FACTORS TO CONSIDER WHEN SELECTING A SOFTWARE PACKAGE?

- Does the purchase or lease agreement permit the purchaser to make modifications?
- If not, are there adequate assurances that the seller of the package will make needed modifications?
- Will the staff require training in order to understand, modify or test the software package?
- If so, will the training be provided free or at an additional cost to the purchaser?

27. HOW DO YOU DECIDE WHETHER TO CONTINUE MAINTENANCE OR TO REDESIGN?

The costs and benefits of the continued maintenance of software which has become error-prone, ineffective, and costly must be weighed against those of redesigning the system. While there are no absolute rules on when to rebuild rather than maintain the existing system, some of the conditions that might lead to a decision to redesign include:

- Frequent failures
- Code over seven-to-ten years old

- Overly complex program structure and logic
- Code written for outdated hardware
- Running in emulation mode
- Very large modules or unit subroutines
- Excessive resource requirements
- Hard-coded parameters that must be changed
- Difficulty in keeping maintainers
- Seriously deficient documentation
- Missing or incomplete design specification

The estimated life cycle of a major application system is seven-to-ten years, although 15 to 20 year-old software systems are not uncommon. Software tends to deteriorate with age as a result of numerous fixes and patches. However, if the system was designed and developed in a systematic, maintainable manner, and if maintenance was carefully performed and documented using established standards and guidelines, it may be possible to run it efficiently and effectively for many more years.

28. WHY SHOULD THERE BE A CENTRAL APPROVAL POINT FOR SOFTWARE CHANGES?

A central approval point is essential to ensure that the desired changes are made to the appropriate software. One of the key problems in many software maintenance environments is inadequate control over the change process.

29. SHOULD DOCUMENTATION BE A CRITERION FOR PRODUCT COMPLETION/DELIVERY? (PAY NOW OR PAY LATER)

It is essential that the documentation be delivered as part of the completed software product. Without the documentation, there is little assurance that the software satisfies stated requirements or that the organization will be able to maintain it. The cost of software maintenance is proportional to the effectiveness of the documentation which describes not only what the system does, but the logic used to accomplish its tasks.

30. WHY SHOULD AN ORGANIZATION HAVE A SOFTWARE MAINTENANCE STANDARDS POLICY?

A software maintenance standards policy helps to ensure software quality. Such standards describe in broad terms the responsibilities, authorities, functions, and operations of the software maintenance organization. The policy should be comprehensive enough to address any type of change to the software system and its environment, including changes to the hardware, software and firmware. To be effective, the policy should be consistently applied and must be supported and promulgated by upper management to the extent that it establishes an organizational commitment to software maintenance. When supported by management, the standards and guidelines help to direct attention toward the need for greater discipline in software design, development, and maintenance.

31. WHAT ARE SOME OF THE KEY ELEMENTS WHICH SHOULD BE INCLUDED IN A SOFTWARE PRODUCT RFP TO ADDRESS SOFTWARE MAINTENANCE?

Too often, Federal managers are forced to accept software products which, in addition to being delivered late, do not perform as required. An examination of the RFP usually reveals that:

- performance clauses were omitted;
- software quality assurance plans were not required; and
- software configuration management plans were left to the discretion of the contractor.

These are just a few of the elements that could help to prevent the delivery of defective, incomplete software products.

32. HOW CAN MAINTAINABILITY BE BUILT INTO EXISTING SOFTWARE?

There must be a program which has achieving maintainable software as its sole objective. It should include:

- a plan for ensuring the maintainability requirements are specified into the software change design.
- a measurement procedure to verify that maintainability goals have been met.
- a performance review to provide feedback to managers, users, and maintainers on the effectiveness of the maintainability program.

33. WHAT ARE SOME STEPS THAT CAN BE TAKEN TO HELP IMPROVE SOFTWARE MAINTENANCE?

- Use high level languages
- Use standard coding conventions (variable names, structures, etc.)
- Use modular structures
- Use meaningful comments
- Use only standard compiler options

34. WHAT CAN BE DONE TO TURN EXISTING SPAGHETTI CODE INTO UNDERSTANDABLE, RELIABLE SOFTWARE?

Software maintenance is a labor intensive activity. Consequently, automated tools should be used whenever possible. There are a number of structuring tools available that are designed specifically for reformatting and restructuring code. Some of these have been around for several years and thus, have a track record. For further details see [NBS88].

35. WHAT IS THE BEST MEASURE FOR DETERMINING IF THE QUALITY OF THE SOFTWARE IS DEGRADING?

If changes to specific areas begin to occur more frequently, and require increasingly more effort to correct or modify, the software is probably degrading. This is particularly true if someone familiar with the code is making the changes.

36. WHAT ARE METRICS?

A metric is a measure of the extent or degree to which a product possesses or exhibits a certain characteristic for determining the value or level of effort required to perform a given function.

37. HOW CAN METRICS BE USED TO IMPROVE THE SOFTWARE MAINTENANCE PROCESS AND PRODUCTS?

Currently, there are a number of metrics used to determine productivity. Of these, Lines of Code is the most commonly used. The complexity metrics can also be useful for determining how difficult a software change will be. Other metrics that can be employed include automated completeness and consistency checkers. Not only can they be used to measure programmer productivity, they can aid in understanding how software changes affect the overall software system from a maintainability standpoint.

38. WHAT ARE THE KEY CONTRIBUTORS TO SOFTWARE MAINTENANCE COMPLEXITY?

- Deeply nested DO loops
- Excessive IF statements
- Excessive use of global variables
- Excessive GOTO statements

- Embedded parameters, literals, constants
- Self-modifying code
- Excessive interaction between modules
- Multiple entry-exit modules
- Redundant modules

39. WHAT ARE THE "DRIVERS" OF SOFTWARE MAINTENANCE?

The primary drivers of software maintenance are requests for enhancements. Other drivers include the poor condition of the code, scheduling, budget constraints, use of ineffective or outdated programming techniques, and tools.

40. WHAT ARE SOME SOFTWARE MAINTENANCE TECHNIQUES WHICH HAVE PROVEN TO BE USEFUL?

- Top down programming
- Stepwise refinement
- Regression testing
- Code walkthroughs
- Code audits/reviews
- Peer reviews

41. IS DOCUMENTATION NECESSARY IN A MAINTENANCE ENVIRONMENT?

Documentation is valuable in both development and maintenance environments. The level of documentation needed is a function of both the application and the maintenance environment. For further information on documentation, see [FIPS38], [FIPS64], and [FIPS106].

42. AT WHAT POINT SHOULD DOCUMENTATION BE REQUIRED?

Documentation should be required for each product deliverable, intermediate as well as final.

43. HOW SHOULD TEST DATA BE HANDLED?

There should be a well-defined policy for generating and storing test data. In some instances, it is preferable to use actual data rather than generated data. In either case, the user should help develop the test data. For further information on testing, see [NBS56], [NBS93], and [FIPS106].

44. WHEN SHOULD FORMAL LIBRARY PROCEDURES BE USED?

Microcomputers, especially when linked to mainframe computers, are making software systems increasingly accessible. One method of ensuring that the production or operational systems are not altered intentionally or unintentionally is to enforce formal library procedures. This usually can be accomplished by permitting adequate access to essential software and limited (read only) or no access to the operational software.

Users

45. SHOULD USERS BE INVOLVED IN DEFINING OBJECTIVES OF THE SOFTWARE PRODUCT?

The days of casting off the users as uninformed are past. In todays' environment, there is a general recognition that user input is essential. Whether it is as a member of the configuration control board or the audit and review team, the key to producing a correct product is early user involvement.

46. WHY SHOULD USERS BE INVOLVED IN THE CHANGE PROCESS?

Users have as much at stake as anyone in wanting the change to be implemented correctly. Therefore, their input should be solicited.

47. SHOULD USERS, MANAGERS, AND MAINTAINERS BE INVOLVED IN DECISIONS REGARDING SOFTWARE CHANGES?

Yes. Too often the cause of software failure is due to inadequate communication between those who must use or are affected by the software change. A number of techniques can be employed to facilitate interface between users, maintainers, and managers. They include walkthroughs, configuration management control boards, audit and review teams, etc.

48. WHY SHOULD USERS BE INVOLVED IN GENERATING TEST DATA?

The users are more familiar with the data than the maintainer. While generated test data is useful, user generated, or live user data, is always preferable.

49. AS USERS ACQUIRE MORE AND MORE MICROCOMPUTERS AND ATTEMPT TO DO THEIR OWN PROGRAMMING, WILL THE SOFTWARE MAINTENANCE BURDEN INCREASE?

Users do not always know in detail what they want until they see a version of it, and then they want to modify. Unless there is close interaction between users and data processing personnel, the gap between these two groups will widen as users seek to handle more of their application development and maintenance. In the short term, the burden will be somewhat lessened, but as users experiment with more sophisticated packages, the maintenance burden on the traditional data processing departments is likely to increase.

50. WHAT ARE SOME SUCCESSFUL SOFTWARE MAINTENANCE TOOLS?

Tools that have been found to be effective include: automated restructurers, debuggers, documenters, test and program generators, editors, cross referencers, software configuration management, and tracing tools.

SOFTWARE CONFIGURATION MANAGEMENT (SCM)

51. WHAT IS SOFTWARE CONFIGURATION MANAGEMENT?

Software Configuration Management (SCM) refers to the control of software changes. It helps to ensure that:

- all software change requests are handled accurately and completely;
- the resulting products satisfy the specified requirements;
- key software maintenance considerations, responsibilities, and requirements are identified; and
- the processing of software change requests (SCR) is facilitated.

52. WHAT ARE THE SCM RESPONSIBILITIES?

SCM is responsible for configuration identification, configuration control, configuration status accounting, auditing, records retention, disaster recovery, library activities, and coordinating the various activities with the users, management, and the staff.

53. DOES SCM APPLY TO THE SOURCE CODE AND DOCUMENTATION?

SCM should be applied to the baseline documentation, as well as the source and object code.

54. WHAT TOOLS SUPPORT SCM?

There are a number of tools that are effective for SCM. Most of these tools provide version control and/or library and archival functions. However, there is a wide range in the price of this class of tools. For more specific information, see [NBS88].

55. ARE TOOLS ESSENTIAL FOR IMPLEMENTING SCM?

Manually tracking software changes back to the requirements and to other changes is a very labor-intensive process. In a large application environment, with frequent changes, performing SCM manually can prove to be quite difficult, if not impossible.

56. WHAT IS A CONFIGURATION CONTROL BOARD (CCB)?

The primary role of the configuration control board (CCB) is to facilitate software changes into the system. The CCB should be comprised of representatives who are involved in, or affected by, the software changes.

57. WHAT ARE THE SPECIFIC DUTIES OF THE CCB?

- Evaluate, assign, prioritize, and schedule software maintenance work requests.
- Set the meeting time.
- Establish the agenda to consider proposed software changes plans, procedures, and interfaces.
- Inform the initiator of the software change request on the actions taken.
- Track progress of all maintenance tasks and ensure that they are on or ahead of schedule.
- Adjust schedules when necessary.
- Communicate progress and problems to the user.
- Communicate progress and problems to upper management.
- Establish and maintain maintenance standards and guidelines.
- Enforce standards and make sure that the software maintenance is of high quality.

58. WHAT LEVEL OF FORMALITY IS NEEDED TO IMPLEMENT AN SCM PROGRAM?

The level of formality depends on the environment. There may be a CCB or an individual who functions as a CCB. The key is to assign the responsibility for ensuring that the software changes satisfy the stated requirements before they are released for production.

Tools

59. WHAT STEPS SHOULD BE TAKEN PRIOR TO SELECTING TOOLS FOR SOFTWARE MAINTENANCE?

- There should be an inventory of the existing tools.
- Current and potential use of the tools should be examined.
- An attempt should be made to acquire tools that are compatible with the existing environment.
- Training should be planned for everyone who will either use tools or be affected by their use.

60. WHAT SHOULD BE CONSIDERED WHEN SELECTING TOOLS?

Many tools have been developed in a research environment and used as prototypes to demonstrate concepts. They were never engineered as production products though they are being used as such. Such tools are generally not well documented, not efficiently coded, seldom portable, and often not adequately supported.

61. WHAT IS AN INTEGRATED TOOL?

An integrated tool generally refers to one that uses a common data base and/or a common command language for controlling and using a set of tools. The use of such tools may help to enforce uniformity within a software maintenance environment.

62. HOW ARE SOFTWARE MAINTENANCE TOOLS CATEGORIZED?

Software maintenance tools fall into seven categories:

- Configuration management
- Monitoring/evaluation
- Redesign
- Code production/analysis
- Verification/validation/testing (VVT)
- Testing/integration
- Documentation

63. WHAT ARE SOME EXAMPLES OF SOFTWARE MAINTENANCE TOOLS IN EACH CATEGORY?

Configuration management:
   support library, status reporting

Monitoring/evaluation:
   performance analyzers, automatic recovery tools

Redesign:
   requirements analyzers

Code production/analysis:
   structurer, debugger, comparator

VV&T:
   static analysis, path analyzer

Testing:
   test data generator

Documentation:
   automatic documentor

64. CAN SOFTWARE MAINTENANCE BE CONTROLLED?

In order to maintain control over the software maintenance process, and to ensure that the maintainability of the system does not deteriorate, it is important that software maintenance be anticipated and planned for. The quality and maintainability of a software system often decrease as the system grows older. This is the result of many factors which, taken one at a time, nay not seem significant but become cumulative and often result in a system which is very difficult to maintain. Quality programming capabilities and techniques are readily available. However, until a firm discipline is placed on how software maintenance is performed, and that discipline is enforced, many systems will be permitted to deteriorate to the point where they are impossible to maintain.

Software maintenance must be performed in a structured, controlled manner. It is not enough to get a system "up and running" after it breaks. Proper management control must be exercised over the entire process. In addition to controlling the budget, schedule, and staff, it is essential that the software manager control the system and the changes to it. Systems must not only be developed with maintenance in mind, they must be maintained with maintainability in mind. If this is done, the quality and maintainability of the code actually can improve.

Supporting ICST Documents

[FIPS38]   "Guidelines for Documentation of Computer Programs and Automated Data Systems,"
           FIPS PUB 38, 1976.

[FIPS64]	"Guidelines for Documentation of Computer Programs and Automated Data Systems for the Initiation Phase," FIPS PUB 64, 1979.
[FIPS99]	"Guideline: A Framework for the Comparison of Software Development Tools," FIPS PUB 99, 1983.
[FIPS101]	"Guideline for Lifecycle Validation, Verification, and Testing of Computer Software," FIPS PUB 101, 1983.
[FIPS105]	"Guideline for Software Documentation Management," FIPS PUB 105, 1984.
[FIPS106]	"Guideline on Software Maintenance," FIPS PUB 106, 1984.
[NBS56]	NBS Special Pub 500-56 "Validation, Verification, and Testing for the Individual Programmer," M. Branstad, J. Cherniavsky, and W. Adrion, 1980.
[NBS78]	NBS Special Pub 500-78, "NBS Programming Environment Workshop Report," M. Branstad and W.R. Adrion, eds., 1978.
[NBS87]	NBS Special Pub 500-87 "Management Guide to Software Documentation," A. Neumann, 1982.
[NBS88]	NBS Special Pub 500-88 "Software Development Tools," R. Houghton, Jr., 1982.
[NBS93]	NBS Special Pub 500-93 "Software Validation, Verification, and Testing Technique and Tool Reference Guide," P. Powell, Editor, 1982.
[NBS106]	NBS Special Pub 500-106 "Guidance on Software Maintenance," R. Martin and W. Osborne, 1983.
[NBS114]	NBS Special Pub 500-114 "Introduction to Software Packages," Sheila Frankel, editor, 1984.

Suggested Additional Reading

[BOEH81]	B. Boehm, *Software Engineering Economics*, Prentice Hall, 1981.
[COUG82]	D.J. Couger and M.A. Colter, "Effect of Task Assignments on Motivation of Programmers and Analysts," research report, Univ. of Colorado, 1982.
[GLAS81]	R.L. Glass and R.A. Noiseux, Software Maintenance Guidebook, Prentice Hall, 1981.
[MART83]	J. Martin, C. McClure, *Software Maintenance--The Problem and Its Solutions*, Prentice Hall, 1983.
[MCCL81]	C.L. McClure, *Managing Software Development and Maintenance*, Van Nostrand Reinhold, 1981.
[PARI80]	G. Parikh, editor, *Techniques of Program and System Maintenance*, Ethnotech, 1980.
[PARI83]	G. Parikh, N. Zvegintov, *Tutorial on Software Maintenance*, IEEE Computer Society Press, 1983.
[PERR81]	W.E. Perry, *Managing System Maintenance*, Q.E.D. Information Sciences, Inc., 1981.

ANNOUNCEMENT OF NEW PUBLICATIONS ON COMPUTER SCIENCE & TECHNOLOGY

Superintendent of Documents
Government Printing Office
Wasington, DC 20402

Dear Sir:

Please add my name to the announcement list of new publications to be issued in the series: National Bureau of Standards Special Publication 500-.

Name_____

Company_____

Address_____

City _____ State ____ Zip Code _____

(Notification key N-503)

The State of Software Maintenance

NORMAN F. SCHNEIDEWIND, SENIOR MEMBER, IEEE

Abstract—A state of software maintenance survey is presented, indicating the incongruity of the simultaneous existence of importance and neglect in this field. An overview is given of selected developments and activities covering the following topics:

- The "Maintenance Problem."
- Models.
- Methods for improving maintenance.
- Metrics.
- Maintenance information management.
- Standards.
- Maintenance of existing code.
- Surveys.

The paper concludes with a prognosis of what is ahead in maintenance: a battle and tradeoff between the forces for maintaining the base of existing software and the forces for the evolution of new systems. An Appendix is provided for the reader who desires information about a software maintenance conference and a special interest group.

Index Terms—Metrics, models, software maintenance.

I. INTRODUCTION

TO gauge the state of software maintenance, ask yourself these questions:

- How many articles have appeared in this TRANSACTIONS on the subject of maintenance in the last couple of years? Answer: none between August 1985 and November 1986, inclusive, and few prior to this period in the history of the TRANSACTIONS. However, before rushing to judgement about the "guilt" of TSE, realize that it is not unique in this regard among technical journals.

Some additional questions to ponder:

- How many computer science departments have a course in maintenance?
- How many doctoral dissertations have there been in maintenance?

To work in maintenance has been akin to having bad breath. Yet, examine the "Problem" below and ask yourself whether there is any justification for this neglect. But, first, a disclaimer, followed by some definitions so that we may proceed from a common reference point.

The information which follows represents a selected overview of the state of the software maintenance field. Since this is a survey paper, it is difficult to cover every aspect of the field, given time and page limitations. We apologize for any significant work which may not be covered.

Manuscript received October 31, 1986.
The author is with the Naval Postgraduate School, Monterey, CA 93943.
IEEE Log Number 8612830.

A. Definitions

Maintenance: Modification of a software product after delivery to correct faults, to improve performance or other attributes, or to adapt the product to a changed environment [1].

Maintainability: The ease with which a software system can be corrected when errors or deficiencies occur, and can be expanded or contracted to satisfy new requirements [2].

B. Why Is There a Maintenance Problem?

There is a maintenance problem because [3]:

- 75–80 percent of existing software was produced prior to significant use of structured programming.
- It is difficult to determine whether a change in code will affect something.
- It is difficult to relate specific programming actions to specific code.

The main problem in doing maintenance is that we cannot do maintenance on a system which was not designed for maintenance. Unless we design for maintenance, we will always be in a lot of trouble after a system goes into production.

In addition, there is the very significant personnel problem concerning the myth that there is no challenge for creative people in maintenance.

According to Zvegintzov, most software is immortal (immoral?). He says that all surveys of the distribution of effort between new systems and present systems show about a 50–50 split [4]. This is the case because of the following important considerations:

- Functions are added, not replaced.
- Every new function must be tied into the present system.
- Systems are not totally replaced, except for overriding economic or technical reasons.
- Organizations strive for compatibility in systems, not perfection.

Specifically, Lientz and Swanson report from a survey of data processing managers in 487 data processing organizations that: departments spend about half of their application staff time on maintenance; over 40 percent of the effort in supporting an operational application system is spent on providing user enhancements and extensions; the average application system is between three and four years old, consists of about 55 programs and 23 000 source statements, and is growing at a rate of over 10 percent a year; and about one-half man-year is allocated annually to maintain the average system [5].

If all programs to be maintained were well documented and cleanly structured, and used third-normal form data models and data dictionaries for generating the programmer's data, the task of the maintainer would be much easier. The problem for most maintainers is that they have to maintain ill-documented code that is covered with patches with no comprehensible structure and that has data representations buried in the program code. It is a major detective operation to find out how the program works, and each attempt to change it sets off mysterious bugs from the tangled undergrowth of unstructured code [2].

C. Why Is Maintenance Hard?

Maintenance is hard because [6]:
• We cannot trace the product nor the process that created the product.
• Changes are not adequately documented.
• Lack of change stability (See Metrics Section below).
• Ripple effect of making changes.
• Myopic view that maintenance is strictly a postdelivery activity.

One consequence of this lack of attention to maintainability requirements during design is loss of traceability. This is defined as the ability to identify the technical information which pertains to a software error detected during the operational phase (or other postrequirements phase) and thereby trace the error to the applicable design specifications and user requirements statements [7].

D. Why Is Maintenance Expensive?

In the early days of programming, when programmers' salaries were an almost insignificant percentage of the data processing budget, when programmers spent most of their time writing new programs, and when machine resources were expensive, the mark of a well written program was efficiency. Twenty years later, when programmers' salaries consume the majority of the data processing budget, when programmers spend most of their time maintaining programs, and when hardware is cheap, a new standard for well written programs has emerged: how maintainable are they, especially for future generations of programmers [8]?

E. Should Existing Code Be Discarded?

If existing code is so bad, why should it be retained? Belady believes that we cannot and should not declare "old" software obsolete or not worth studying [9]. This collection of functions is an important asset, embodying a wealth of experience, and constitutes an inventory of "ideas" for identifying the building blocks of future systems. Even if the code itself is inelegant and possibly not reusable, a study of the specifications and identification of the most frequently used components could reveal a set of generic classes of algorithms and functions which could be usable in future systems.

II. Models

A. Do We Have the Wrong Model for Maintenance?

Since the software industry does not seem to have a good understanding of and model for maintenance, it is worthwhile to consider some proposed models which provide insight into the maintenance process. Lehman suggests that change is intrinsic in software, and must be accepted as a fact of life, and since software undergoes change throughout its life, there is no reason to distinguish maintenance from initial development. Evolutionary development is inevitable [10], [11]. Furthermore, the very act of installing software changes the environment; pressures operate to modify the environment, the problem, and technological solutions. Changes generated by users and the environment and the consequent need for adapting the software to the changes is unpredictable and cannot be accommodated without iteration. Programs must be more alterable and the resultant change process must be planned and controlled. According to Lehman, large programs are never completed, they just continue to evolve. In other words, with software, we are dealing with a moving target and that, in effect, "maintenance" is performed continuously. Lehman suggests that the word "maintenance" not be used and that the term "program evolution" be used instead. If this model of the software process is correct, it suggests that change activity and change management should be an integral part of development and all other phases of the life of software. In this view, a change would be no more associated with "maintenance" than with development.

B. Do Requirements End in the Requirements Phase?

Lehman's view seems to be supported by Lientz and Swanson [12]. They state that the approach which is in vogue of getting requirements right before starting the design may be based on the fallacious assumption that requirements are fixed. The reality is that requirements change continually, often in response to organizational change. These changes are more likely to emanate from experience in the use of the system than from an abstract specification in the early design of the system. The major problem in requirements assessment may not be the development of a complete, consistent and unambiguous specification, prior to design, but, rather, the evolution of requirements which allow a timely response of the software to organizational change. Requirements assessment during maintenance may be as demanding as during development.

C. Is the Life Cycle Model Appropriate for Maintenance?

The traditional view of the software life cycle has done a disservice to maintenance by depicting it solely as a single step at the end of the cycle. In fact, it would be more accurately portrayed as 2nd, 3rd, ⋯ , nth round development [13]. The traditional view also fosters the idea that structured techniques are best applied to development, whereas their application to maintenance is equally valid.

In contrast, the traditional view of maintenance is that it is an activity confined to the postdelivery phase, is not directly related to development, and has its own special requirements.

III. METHODS FOR IMPROVING MAINTENANCE

Software maintenance authors have made many suggestions for improving the maintainability of software. These suggestions can be classified into three categories: design approach, maintenance practices, and management.

A. What Design Approaches Are Needed?

Software design practices should include criteria for maintainability [14]. These criteria are the following:
• Design software with maintainability in mind.
• Develop design criteria for achieving maintainability.
• Simplicity should outweigh completeness.
• Change management should be used to:
 —Limit the effects in the maintenance phase of a change made in the design phase.
 —Determine ripple effects on other modules of making a change to a common module:
  • global variables.
  • modules which invoke or are invoked by a common module.
 —Determine the effect on a module of making a change to a local variable.
• Evaluate the design for excessive complexity.

Another design approach to aid maintenance describes the design in terms of parts and the interconnections of those parts [15]. With parts interconnections as the focal point of the design and documentation, the system maintainer can more readily judge the possible ripple effect of change. Three levels—system, assembly, and component—are shown in list and graphical form, where each succeeding level provides a more detailed description of the previous level. A parts list and connections list is shown for each level. The parts list shows functions and the data associated with the functions. The connections list shows the input/output relationships between functions and data.

B. What Maintenance Practices Are Needed?

Maintainability can be significantly improved if the following practices are used [16], [14], [17], [18]:
• Change Management:
 —Make easiest changes first.
 —Change one module at a time.
 —Inspect proposed changes for each type of side effect.
 —Run regression tests after every change.

• Produce guidelines for modifying and retesting software.
 —Provide information to support assessment of the impact of a change in various parts of the software.

C. What Other Practices Are Needed?

• Identify source statements which have been changed with a number which is associated with the change request.
• Learn to *read* programs (alien code).
• Keep diaries of bugs and maintenance issues.
• Centralize variable declarations in a program.
 —Use abstract data types to define the legitimate types and values which objects of a type may assume and a set of operations which may be performed on that type.
• Centralize symbolically defined and referenced database definitions in a computer processible data dictionary.
• Since it can be taken for granted that software will evolve and change, each programmer in the process should give consideration to the next programmer in the life cycle.

One of the major sources of error in making maintenance modifications arises when neither the program nor the documentation reveal that sections of a program that are far apart are related. As suggested by Letovsky and Soloway, this may cause the programmer to make assumptions about the plans of a program which are based purely on local information. This can lead to an inaccurate understanding of the program as a whole [19]. Their solution to this problem is to provide answers to the two questions:

What information needs to be provided to the reader of the program?
When and how should this information be provided?

Easily accessible information is needed to form correct interpretations of delocalized plans. What is needed is to move from documenting the code itself to documenting the plans in the code. A tool which may provide this capability is under development.

D. What Management Policies Are Needed?

Some guidelines offered by McClure [14] for improving the management of maintenance are the following:
• Involve maintainers in design and testing.
• Put the same emphasis on the use of standards in maintenance as in design.
• Rotate personnel between design and maintenance.
• Make design documentation available to maintainers at design time.
• Carry over the use of design tools into maintenance.
• Use configuration management and change request procedures.
• Establish a liaison between users and maintenance.

Boehm suggests the following for maximizing the motivation and, hence, productivity of maintenance personnel [20]:

- Couple software objectives to organizational goals.
- Couple software maintenance rewards to organizational performance.
- Integrate software maintenance personnel into operational teams.
- Create a discretionary perfective maintenance budget.
- Create the perquisites of software ownership.
  —Participation by maintenance personnel in: development standards creation, development reviews, and acceptance test preparation.
- Rectify the negative image of software maintenance.

The reader can see that the objective of these guidelines is to *integrate* design and maintenance—to reverse the current procedure of considering and managing these activities in disparate and separate functions.

E. What Tools Are Needed?

Tools are needed in maintenance to look for (and hopefully find) structure [2]:
- Looking for structure. Several types of structure need to be understood:
  —Procedural structure.
  —Control structure.
  —Data structure.
  —Input/output structure.
- Understanding data aliases:
  —Data may be referred to by several names.
- Following data flow:
  —Where do data originate? Where are they used?
- Following control flow:
  —The consequences of executing each path must be understood.
- Understanding versions of a program:
  —How does a change affect different versions of a program?

Tools are available which address the above areas. These consist of displaying the following [2]:
- Structure Chart: Shows hierarchy and call/called relationships.
- Data Trace: Origins, uses, and modifications of variables.
- Control Trace: Shows control flow statements and indicates how a destination can be reached from a given origin.
- Version Comparisons: Statements which differ between two versions of a program are highlighted.

Additionally, the following tool capabilities are useful for maintenance [21]:
- Stored test execution information giving dynamic behavior of a program.
- Test cases to exercise modified sections of a program.
- Symbolic and actual execution information.

An interesting tool is one designed to restructure unstructured code. One tool of this type is called structured retrofit, involving the restructuring of Cobol programs [22]. The application of this kind of tool rests on the premise that with 7 out of 10 programmers involved in maintenance, and costs for this activity soaring, maintenance must be made easier and, hence, less costly. Furthermore, the argument is made that even if the code is bad, the logic of the design may not be bad. In other words, the design concept was good but its implementation was poor. Since this poor code is meeting user requirements but is difficult and costly to maintain, it should be salvaged, where feasible.

The structured retrofit procedure consists of the following steps:
- Scoring: Programs are evaluated as candidates for restructuring by scoring them against the following criteria:
  —Degree of structure.
  —Level of nesting.
  —Degree of complexity.
  —Breakout of verb utilization.
  —Analysis of potential failure modes.
  —Trace of control logic.

However, even if a program scores low on the above criteria but still runs with little time required for maintenance, it will not be retrofitted.
- Compilation: Programs which are to be retrofitted are compiled. Programs which do not compile cleanly are referred to others for resolution. Programs continue in the retrofit process only if they compile cleanly.
- Restructuring: Programs that are unstructured are put through this process to make them structured. The resulting program will produce the same transformation on the same input data as the original program.
- Formatting: Programs are made more readable through the formatting process. They are then recompiled to pick up possible syntax errors.
- Validation: The same inputs are applied to the original and restructured programs and the outputs are compared on a bit-by-bit basis by a file-to-file compare utility.
- Optimization: The code is optimized to reduce overhead which may have been introduced by the restructuring process.

It is claimed that structured retrofit has been able to restructure 60 percent of programs offered automatically, another 20 percent with some manual intervention, and 20 percent cannot be restructured cost-effectively.

IV. METRICS

In order to perform maintenance effectively, we must be able to measure the effects of design approaches on maintenance and, especially important, be able to measure the effects of maintenance approaches on future maintenance!

Ideally, we want maintenance to improve software. Our minimum objective is that maintenance should have a neutral effect. Unfortunately, too often, maintenance makes software worse, due to unforseen ripple effect. In order to minimize ripple effect, software must be stable. Stability must be achieved at design time, not during the maintenance phase. Stability in design is achieved by minimizing potential ripple effect caused by interaction between modules (i.e., a change to a module causes undesirable changes to other modules). The definitions and concepts applicable to achieving design stability were developed by Yau and Collofello [23]; these are the following:

• Program stability: Quality attribute indicating the resistance to the potential ripple effect which a program would have when it is modified.

• Module stability: A measure of the resistance to the potential ripple effect of a modification of the module on other modules in the program.

• Logical stability: Measure of resistance to impact of modification on other modules in terms of logical considerations.

• Performance stability: Measure of resistance to impact of modification on other modules in terms of performance considerations.

• "Maintenance activity" is a change to a single variable.

• Intramodule change propagation involves flow of changes within the module as a consequence of a modification.

• Intermodule change propagation involves flow of changes across modules as a consequence of a modification.

• Intramodule change propagation is utilized to identify the set of interface variables which are affected by logical ripple effect as a consequence of a modification to a variable definition in a module. This requires an identification of which variables constitute the module's interfaces and the potential intramodule change propagation among the variables in the module.

• Once an interface variable is affected by a change, the flow of changes may cross module boundaries and affect other modules. Interface change propagation is used to identify the set of modules involved in intermodule change propagation as a consequence of affecting an interface variable in a module.

• Measure the complexity of affected modules to analyze the possible relationship between complexity and vulnerability to ripple effect.

• Compare stability of alternate versions of module for the purpose of making a design choice. (However, there may be no time available to design alternatives.)

• Use as predictor of amount of maintenance required.

• Reject request for maintenance if it involves modifying unstable modules.

• Restructure modules with poor stability.

The measure of design stability of a module, proposed by Yau and Collofello [23], [24], is the reciprocal of the total number of assumptions made by other modules about the given module. If the given module has poor design stability and it is modified, it is likely to produce undesirable effects on other modules, which either invoke, share global data with, or are invoked by the given module. The rationale of this metric is that modules which cause large ripple effects, if modified, are among the modules with poor design stability. This definition of sta-

bility only applies to modular software. This point illustrates one of the difficulties in trying to improve maintenance: much of the existing software which must be maintained is not modular!

More information needs to be captured in a metric than just the effects of a change to a single variable or the effects of changes to a set of variables. What is needed is the effects of changes on other aspects of a program, such as documentation. Also, since all assumptions are not equally important, this metric could possibly be improved by weighting the assumptions. Although this metric addresses an important aspect of maintainability dealing with assumptions that are made about interfaces between modules, it is silent on the subject of intramodule design characteristics. Despite these limitations, this metric would be very useful, primarily, for deciding among design alternatives for *new* software.

An approach to assessing the difficulty of *maintaining* a program is to quantify program difficulty as the sum of the difficulties of the constituent parts [25]. A Maintainability Analysis Tool was developed to analyze the difficulty of understanding and maintaining Fortran programs by assigning weights, which represent relative difficulty of understanding, to various program attributes, such as syntactic elements (e.g., parameter) and syntactic attributes (e.g., name in COMMON). The numeric weights and factors are summed for a program to yield a measure of difficulty. Obviously, there can be a lot of subjectivity involved in assigning weights and measures.

A strategy for determining whether to continue to *maintain* software is to focus on modules which may be candidates for rewriting. These error prone modules need to be identified. One method for identifying error prone modules is to have maintenance personnel record information about: 1) which modules were changed, 2) how much effort was involved in making the changes, and 3) reasons for making the changes [26].

Another aspect of applying metrics to maintenance is the establishment of criteria for determining whether maintenance is being *performed* effectively. Arnold and Parker [27] established the following criteria for 40 telemetry processing projects at the NASA/Goddard Space Flight Center:

• Desired effort distribution: Distribution of maintenance effort between enhancements/restructurings and fixes.

• Desired frequency distribution: Distribution of reports approved for action between enhancements/restructurings and fixes.

• Completion rates: Rates for enhancements/restructurings and fixes.

• Effort per change: Labor time limits for enhancements/restructurings and fixes.

V. MAINTENANCE INFORMATION MANAGEMEENT

Since maintenance usually involves having to understand what someone else did to the code, information about the characteristics of the code and specifications (if they exist) are essential to doing an effective job of maintenance. Important elements of the information base are: control flow information, data flow information, and declaration information [28]. This information base should be established as part of every *design* and *maintenance* activity.

VI. STANDARDS

In general, development standards have been inappropriate for use in maintenance [29]. Of greater concern is the fact that standards efforts have not addressed maintenance.

Although no standards exist for maintenance, management guides are available from the National Bureau of Standards, which provide methodologies and procedures for conducting an effective maintenance program [30], [31]. Among the recommendations of [30] are the following:
- Develop a software maintenance plan.
- Recognize improvement of maintainability.
- Elevate maintenance visibility in the organization.
- Reward maintenance personnel; provide a career path and training.
- Establish and enforce standards.

The major conclusion of [31] is that, in addition to developing software with maintenance in mind, software must also be maintained with maintenance in mind!

VII. MAINTENANCE OF EXISTING CODE

This activity involves maintaining software which has not been modularly designed. It dominates maintenance work.

A. Restructuring

As reported above, in the description of the structured retrofit system, unstructured code can be converted to a structured format. Due a proof by Jacopini and Bohm, any computable algorithm in any language, can be represented by a structured graph. This result is the basis for restructuring programs. Unstructured programs typically have graphs whose nodes are so connected that the graph cannot be effectively partitioned into independent regions. However, by means of a graph simplification process, an unstructured program can be rendered into a structured form. The original unstructured program is parsed into an abstract syntax tree. Several tree to tree transformations are performed to reduce the tree to a few simple control flow expressions. When the tree is sufficiently simple, it is transformed into a control flow graph. This simplification process terminates when the topology of the graph represents a structured algorithm.

Although the method sounds impressive there are problems in restructuring when the program has GOTO's. In addition, an enormous amount of machine time may be required to develop new control graphs representing the new structure [8]. However, if it is determined that restructuring is more economical than rewriting, it is clear that restructuring is only feasible when an automated method such as this is used.

It is not always feasible to make unstructured code look like structured code and more readable by using structured documentation. In a study conducted by Schneidewind [32] to analyze the effectiveness of documentation for maintenance purposes, where the documentation had been created with the intent of making the software more readable and understandable by showing a 'hierarchical structure' of unstructured code, it was found that the new documentation did not always tell the truth about the code logic as represented by the program listing. The reason for this was that the hierarchical documentation could not faithfully describe software which was unstructured. Lesson learned: the code must also be restructured.

B. Recovering the Design with Abstract Specifications

For situations in which no specifications exist, a technique called Maintenance by Abstraction is claimed to allow one to recover the design by using the following steps [33]:
- Inspect the code.
- Propose a set of abstractions (directed graph representations of the code).
- Choose the most suitable set of abstractions.
- Construct a specification from the abstractions.

The recovered design (i.e., the specification derived above) is then applied to the Transformation-based Maintenance Model. The directed graph representation of the code is examined to find nodes representing design decisions such that the order of design decisions can be reversed—for the purpose of making maintenance changes—in a way that will not affect the final implementation. It appears that this complex procedure would only be cost effective on large programs.

The IBM Federal Systems Division is upgrading the Federal Aviation Administration National Airspace System, 20 year old, 100 000 line, en route software by modeling programs as either function abstractions (transforms a value in input domain to output range) or data abstractions (class of data objects and the set of operations performed on them) [34]. Function abstractions can also be regarded as entities which do not retain data across invocations and data abstractions as entities which do retain data. The abstractions were used by the designer to determine the required change (added, deleted, and updated functions as needed).

VIII. SURVEYS

To provide a feel for the characteristics of maintenance as practiced in various organizations, results from several surveys are presented briefly below.

In a survey of 487 data processing organizations, it was found that most maintenance is perfective (55 percent): performed to enhance performance, improve maintainability, or improve executing efficiency. This is followed by adaptive maintenance (25 percent): performed to adapt software to changes in the data requirements or processing environments. Lastly, there is corrective maintenance (20 percent): performed to identify and correct software failures, performance failures, and implementation failures [12].

Chapin [35] reports that from a limited survey of users of fourth generation languages that although these languages are beneficial for development, their use may make maintenance more difficult and expensive. One reason he cites for this situation is that interprogram and intersystem communication of data with these languages is often obscure, thus rendering the effect of a maintenance action unclear.

In another survey by Chapin [36], he reports on information collected from supervisory personnel closest to software maintenance work. The survey consisted of 260 questionnaires collected from 123 data processing installations; there were 769 responses across the various questions. The biggest problems identified were poor documentation and inadequate staff. With regard to the latter, there is a problem in matching the characteristics of the software to be maintained with appropriate personnel.

IX. PROGNOSIS

Much of the problem will remain of being condemned to maintain existing, nonstructured code for a long time into the future—perhaps 20 years. This situation will only change when two things happen: 1) software development environments become so effective and programmer productivity becomes so great that it will be more economical to develop new systems than to maintain old systems; 2) organizations want to do business in *new* ways. Thus the decision will not be over the cost of reprogramming or redesign, but about whether organizations will adapt their information systems to support the organization's survival in a changing world. In the interim, restructuring techniques will be an important tool for attempts to convert a "sow's ear into a silk purse." In making the restructuring decision, only relevant costs should be considered. The fact that a lot of money has been spent in the past is irrelevant to making a decision about the future. These are sunk costs; only future costs should be considered. The cost to rewrite, redesign, or develop a new system *are* relevant costs.

On the personnel front, there is hope. Software engineers are being sensitized to the need for considering maintainability in their designs. More academics will do research in maintenance when academic administrators recognize the importance of maintenance. Computer science programs will contain a course on maintenance when academics themselves recognize the importance of maintenance!

APPENDIX

The following lists some information about an important conference and a special interest group in the field of software maintenance:

A. Conference

The first conference in software maintenance, sponsored by technical societies, was the Software Maintenance Workshop, held at the Naval Postgraduate School, Monterey, CA, December 6–8, 1983 [37]. It was sponsored by the IEEE Technical Committee on Software Engineering of the IEEE Computer Society, National Bureau of Standards, and the Naval Postgraduate School, and in cooperation with the ACM Special Interest Group on Software Engineering.

The second conference was the Conference on Software Maintenance–1985, held at the Sheraton Inn Washington–Northwest, Washington, DC, November 11–13, 1985. It was sponsored by the same organizations as above, minus the Naval Postgraduate School, and with the addition of the Data Processing Management Association, and in cooperation with the Association for Women in Computing, and the Software Maintenance Association.

The next conference, Conference on Software Maintenance–1987, will be held in Austin, TX, September 21–24, 1987. For information contact:

Roger J. Martin, General Chair
National Bureau of Standards
Bldg. 225, Rm B266
Gaithersburg, MD 20899
(301) 921-3545

B. Special Interest Group

The Software Maintenance Association (SMA) is a special interest group in the field. For information about this organization and a maintenance newsletter, contact:

Nicholas Zvegintzov
141 Marks Place, #5F
Staten Island, NY 10301
(718) 981-7842.

REFERENCES

[1] *An American National Standard IEEE Standard Glossary of Software Engineering Terminology*, ANSI/IEEE Standard 729, 1983.
[2] J. Martin and C. McClure, *Software Maintenance: The Problem and Its Solutions*. Englewood Cliffs, NJ: Prentice-Hall, 1983.
[3] D. P. Freedman and G. M. Weinberg, "A checklist for potential side effects of a maintenance change," in *Techniques of Program and System Maintenance*, Girish Parikh, Ed. Ethotech., Inc., 1980, pp. 61–68.
[4] N. Zvegintzov, "Nanotrends," *Datamation*, pp. 106–116, Aug. 1983.
[5] B. P. Lientz and B. E. Swanson, "Problems in application software maintenance," *Commun. ACM*, vol. 24, no. 11, pp. 763–769, Nov. 1981.
[6] N. F. Schneidewind, "Quality metrics standards applied to software maintenance" (Abstract), in *Proc. Comput. Standards Conf. 1986* (Addendum), IEEE Comput. Soc., May 113-15, 1986.
[7] M. B. Kline and N. F. Schneidewind, "Life cycle comparisons of hardware and software maintainability," in *Proc. Third Nat. Rel. Conf.*, Birmingham, England, Apr./May 1981, p. 4A/3/1–4A/3/14.
[8] E. Bush, "The automatic restructuring of COBOL," in *Proc. Conf. Software Maintenance–1985*. Washington, DC: IEEE Comput. Soc. Press, Nov. 1985, pp. 35–41.
[9] L. A. Belady, "Evolved software for the 80's," *Computer*, vol. 12, no. 2, pp. 79–82, Feb. 1979.
[10] M. M. Lehman, "Programs, life cycles, and laws of software evolution," *Proc. IEEE*, vol. 68, no. 9, Sept. 1980.

[11] ——, "Program evolution," Dep. Computing, Imperial College of Science and Technology, London SW7 2BZ, England, Res. Rep. DoC 82/1, Dec. 1982.

[12] B. P. Lientz and E. B. Swanson, *Software Maintenance Management.* Reading, MA: Addison-Wesley, 1980.

[13] J. R. McKee, "Maintenance as a function of design," in *AFIPS Conf. Proc.*, vol. 53, 1984 Nat. Comput. Conf., pp. 187–193.

[14] C. L. McClure, *Managing Software Development and Maintenance.* New York: Van Nostrand, 1981.

[15] J. Silverman, N. Giddings, and J. Beane, "An approach to design-for-maintenance," in *Proc. Software Maintenance Workshop*, R. S. Arnold, Ed. Washington, DC: IEEE Comput. Soc. Press, Dec. 1983, pp. 106–110.

[16] R. L. Glass and R. A. Noiseux, *Software Maintenance Guidebook.* Englewood Cliffs, NJ: Prentice-Hall, 1981.

[17] J. B. Munson, "Software maintainability: A practical concern for life-cycle costs," *Computer*, vol. 14, no. 11, pp. 103–109, Nov. 1981.

[18] E. Yourdon, "Structured maintenance," in *Techniques of Program and System Maintenance*, Girish Parikh, Ed. Ethotech, Inc., 1980, pp. 211–213.

[19] S. Letovsky and E. Soloway, "Delocalized plans and program comprehension," *IEEE Software*, vol. 3, no. 3, pp. 41–49, May 1986.

[20] B. Boehm, "The economics of software maintenance," in *Proc. Software Maintenance Workshop*, R. S. Arnold, Ed. Washington, DC: IEEE Comput. Soc. Press, Dec. 1983, pp. 9–37.

[21] Z. Kishimoto, "Testing in software maintenance and software maintenance from the testing perspective," in *Proc. Software Maintenance Workshop*, R. S. Arnold, Ed. Washington, DC: IEEE Comput. Soc. Press, Dec. 1983, pp. 166–117.

[22] M. J. Lyons, "Salvaging your software asset (tools based maintenance)," in *AFIPS Conf. Proc.*, 1981 Nat. Comput. Conf., pp. 337–341.

[23] S. S. Yau and J. S. Collofello, "Some stability measures for software maintenance," *IEEE Trans. Software Eng.*, vol. SE-6, pp. 545–552, Nov. 1980.

[24] ——, "Design stability measures for software maintenance," *IEEE Trans. Software Eng.*, vol. SE-11, pp. 849–856, Sept. 1985.

[25] G. M. Berns, "Assessing software maintainability," *Commun. ACM*, vol. 27, no. 1, pp. 14–23.

[26] H. Schafer, "Metrics for optimal maintenance management," in *Proc. Conf. Software Maintenance-1985.* Washington, DC: IEEE Comput. Soc. Press, 1985, pp. 114–119.

[27] R. S. Arnold and D. A. Parker, "The dimensions of healthy maintenance," in *Proc. 6th Int. Conf. Software Eng.* Washington, DC: IEEE Comput. Soc. Press, Sept. 1982, pp. 10–27.

[28] J. S. Collofello and J. W. Blaylock, "Syntactic information useful for software maintenance," in *AFIPS Conf. Proc.*, vol. 54, 1985 Nat. Comput. Conf., pp. 547–553.

[29] N. F. Schneidewind, "Usability of military standards for the maintenance of embedded computer software," in *Advisory Group for Aerospace Research & Development Conf. Proc. 330, Software for Avionics*, North Altantic Treaty Organization, The Hague, Netherlands, Sept. 6–10, 1982, pp. 21-1-21-6.

[30] J. A. McCall, M. A. Herdon, and W. M. Osborne, "Software Maintenance Management," Nat. Bureau Standards, NBS Special Publ. 500-129, Oct. 1985.

[31] R. J. Martin and W. M. Osborne, "Guidance of software maintenance," Nat. Bureau Standards, NBS Special Publ. 500-106, Dec. 1983.

[32] N. F. Schneidewind, "Evaluation of maintainability enhancement for the TCP/TSP Revision 6.0 Update .20," Naval Postgraduate School, Rep. NPS54-82-004, Feb. 1982.

[33] G. Arango, "TMM: Software maintenance by transformation," *IEEE Software*, vol. 3, no. 3, pp. 27–39, May 1986.

[34] R. N. Britcher and J. J. Craig, "Using modern design practices to upgrade aging software systems," *IEEE Software*, vol. 3, no. 3, pp. 16–24, May 1986.

[35] N. Chapin, "Software maintenance with fourth-generation languages," *ACM Software Engineering Notes*, vol. 9, no. 1, pp. 41–42, Jan. 1984.

[36] ——, "Software maintenance: A different view," in *AFIPS Conf. Proc. 54*, Nat. Comput. Conf., 1985, pp. 509–513.

[37] R. S. Arnold, N. F. Schneidewind, and N. Zvegintzov, "A software maintenance workshop," *Commun. ACM*, vol. 27, no. 11, pp. 1120–1121, 1158.

Norman F. Schneidewind (A'54–M'59–M'72–SM'77), for a photograph and biography, see this issue, p. 301.

Software Maintenance Models

David A. Gustafson, Austin C. Melton, Kyung Hee An, and IeHong Lin

Department of Computing and Information Sciences
Kansas State University, Nichols Hall, Manhattan, KS 66506

Abstract

This paper discusses two models of the software maintenance process; these models are based on the changes that occur in software as it is maintained. These changes define objective measures of the maintenance process. One model, the macro model, can be used to evaluate some aspects of the maintenance process; this model was based on a version of Unix written in C.

The other model, a classification system for software maintenance activities, could be used to identify the type of activity that is occurring during a specific maintenance action. This model is based on a revision of Swanson's classification scheme for software maintenance. The proposed classification system was objectively determined by analyzing the changes that occurred between different versions of COBOL programs that were produced in commercial environments.

Keywords

software maintenance, models, changes, C, COBOL, classification system

Introduction

The development of models for the software maintenance phase is essential if software maintenance is to become a science. There are many types of models that would be useful for software maintenance, including macro models of maintenance, models of maintenance activities, and detailed models of maintenance tasks. Models of the maintenance process would help us to understand the process, to evaluate maintenance efforts, to improve the management of maintenance and eventually to improve the maintenance process itself.

This paper reports on research activities aimed at developing models of software maintenance. We believe that a good approach to use when developing a model of a process is to study and analyze the changes that occur during that process.[2] Our basic assumption is that many changes that occur during a process are objective indicators that can tell us much about the process itself. Our work involves a combination of research in program changes (compare Dunsmore)[5] and research in maintenance. The use of dynamic program process data (e.g., changes) should complement the use of static program data (for example, Crawford).[4] We feel that our present and future research will confirm that dynamic program data does, in fact, tell us much about various maintenance activities.

Our early work on modeling the integration process[6,8,9] demonstrated the usefulness of analyzing changes. We define a macro maintenance model as that which is based on changes used to define a macro measure of the overall maintenance process in source code during maintenance.

The macro model gives a manager a standard with which to evaluate his current maintenance efforts. The model can be used to identify bad maintenance practices, such as not updating comments, and it can be used to distinguish corrections from rewrites. In fact, the model might also be used to determine which modules are most likely to be modified during maintenance. Although a specific maintenance task may influence where changes may take place, there is often flexibility about where a change actually occurs. Some places are more likely to change than others. Work performed by Kafura and Reddy[7] indicates that there is flexibility and, unfortunately, that changes are often made in the wrong place.

As the macro model is refined, many additional capabilities may be added: The ability to distinguish good practices from bad practices should improve; the ability to quantify the complexity of a maintenance change may be developed; and the ability to quantify the effect of maintenance on the quality of the program may be developed. These additional capabilities would improve our ability to decide when programs should be rewritten; they would be of tremendous help in managing a maintenance effort and in understanding the maintenance process.

We also define a model of maintenance activities,[11,12] which classifies each change as one or more maintenance-type activities; the possible types are corrective, adaptive, retrenchment, retrieving, prettyprinting, and documentation. Knowing the type of maintenance activity that is actually occurring should make it easier to manage the maintenance process.

Initial Investigations

We initially investigated[6] the changes in the source code between system3 and system5 of Unix[TM].* System5 was created from system3. The investigation was to analyze the differences between modules changed in the two versions. The differences were studied as changes to the older version. Figure 1 shows the percentage of change of each type with respect to the total number of changes. Using several statistic packages, the changes were analyzed for the relationships. The results supported the development of a macro model of maintenance.

In our investigations of the changes in the source code between the Unix system3 and system5 C modules, 123 modules, consisting of 35,464 lines of code in system3 and 46,023 lines of code in system5, were analyzed. Programs were written to collect all the information, and definitions were developed to organize the analysis of the data.

Some of these definitions are given below:

- *change[type]:* number of statements of the specified type that have been changed.
- *percent change[type]:* percentage of changes of specified type; note: percent change[type] = (change[type]/change[all]) * 100.
- *average nesting level:* the average level of nesting for the statements in a module.
- *weight[type]:* the percent change[type] in the original experiment (Figure 1). (This weight was originally proposed as a predictor of which statement type was most likely to change.)
- *weight:* this is the sum of weight[type] for each statement in the module.
- *LOC:* the number of lines of code (including comments) in a module.
- *weight/LOC:* the average weight per line.

The average level of nesting for the statements in a module is determined by the indented tabs of each line. The weight[type] represents the change percentage for that type of program statement. The change percentage of each statement from our initial investigation is presented in Figure 1; this percent gives the likelihood of the statement being changed in the changed modules. The weight of a module is the sum of the weight[type] of each statement in the module, therefore the weight is usable as a measure for predicting further changes. The lines of code measure show how many lines a module has or how big it is.

Development vs. Maintenance

The percent change[type] measure appears to be significant. The pattern of this measure is very different during successful development than during maintenance. The pattern of percent change[type] during maintenance and the pattern of percent change[type] during development are presented in Figure 2.[8,9] These two patterns, the one for the maintenance phase and the other for the development phase, differ most radically for function calls and declarations. At first, the percent changes[declarations] for maintenance seem strange. However, adaptive maintenance cannot occur without the addition or alteration of declarations; if the data items remain unchanged, there can be little increase in the functionality. Thus, a significant value for percent change[declarations] is a good indicator of adaptive maintenance. But corrective and perfective maintenance should not have significant changes to declarations. The percent change[function calls] should be higher in developmental environments where the interfaces between units are not as stable as in working systems that are undergoing maintenance. Thus, the ratio of percent change[function calls] to percent change[declarations] should be useful in identifying the current lifecycle phase. A high ratio implies a development type activity, and a low ratio should indicate an adaptive maintenance environment. Additionally, a low percent change[declaration] should indicate corrective or perfective maintenance.

---

*UNIX is a trademark of AT&T Bell Laboratories, Inc.

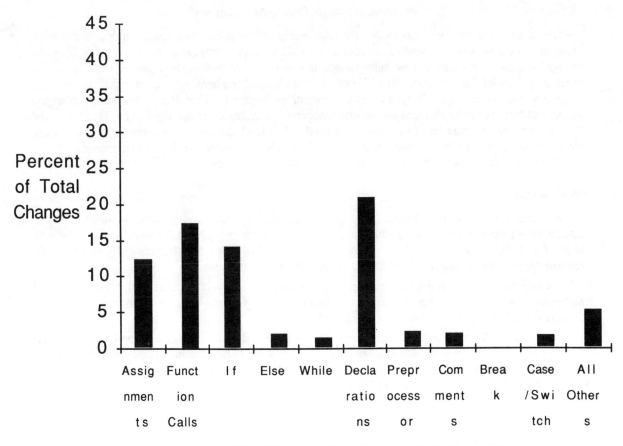

Figure 1: Percent of Total Changes That Were Each Statement Type

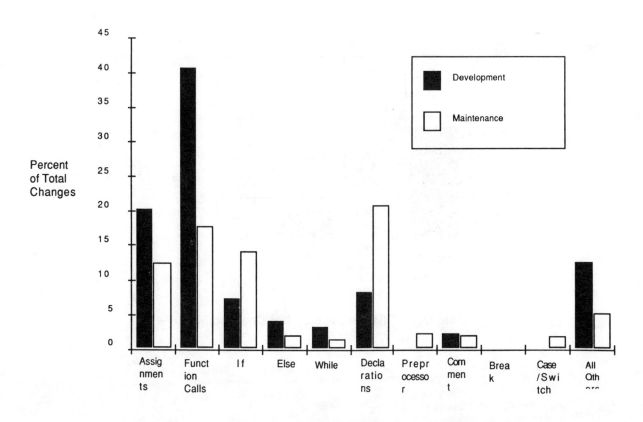

Figure 2: Changes During Maintenance and Development

Predicting Changes During Maintenance

In analyzing the data, we also looked for relationships between the data and the modules that were changed. The goal was to develop a measure that would identify which modules were most likely to be changed during maintenance. One surprise was that most of the unchanged modules were big. The average number of lines of code (417.125) of the unchanged modules was greater than the average number of lines of code (279.365) of the changed modules (Figure 3). Thus, if a module size is relatively big, it will tend not to be changed during maintenance. The average nesting level (68.643) of changed modules was greater than the average nesting level (51.943) of unchanged modules (Figure 3). Thus, modules with relatively low nesting levels will tend to remain unchanged during maintenance. These results seem to suggest that size and average nesting level may be two predictors for maintenance.

Relationships

We further analyzed the changes that occurred between system3 and system5 to understand the maintenance process better. The modules in system3 were sorted by size and the sizes of the modules in lines of code (LOC) were plotted for system3 and system5 (Figure 4). The data are fairly regular. The relative orders of the modules in system3 and system5 are almost the same.

Similarly the modules in system3 were ordered by weight and the weights of the modules from system3 and system5 were plotted (Figure 5). Again the modules with higher weights increased more in weight and the relative ordering of the modules was maintained.

Finally, the modules in system3 were ordered by average nesting level and these levels and the levels for the system 5 modules were plotted (Figure 6). Although the relative ordering appears to be maintained, the increases in average nesting level occurred in the modules with lower average nesting level. In fact, some of the modules (around module 11) decreased in average nesting level.

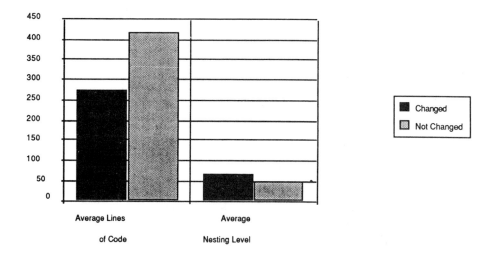

Figure 3: Changed Versus Not Changed Modules

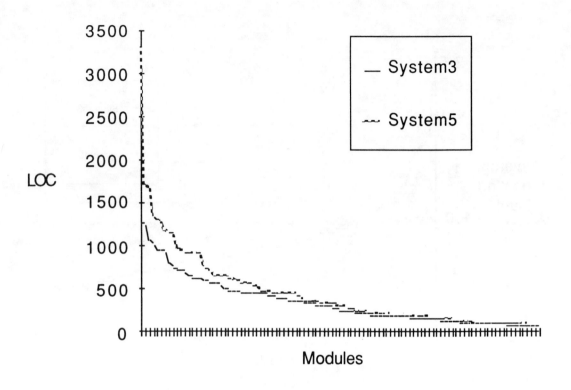

Figure 4: LOC in System3 and System5

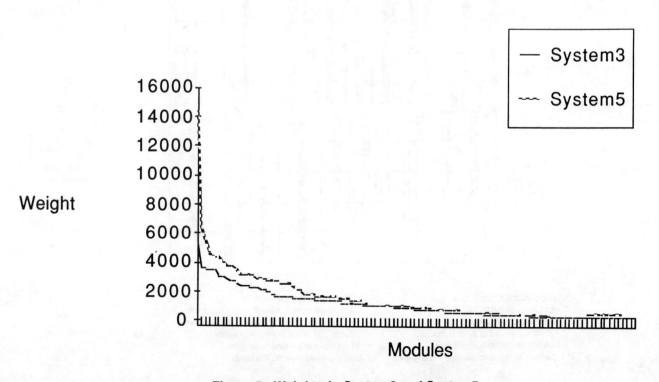

Figure 5: Weights in System3 and System5

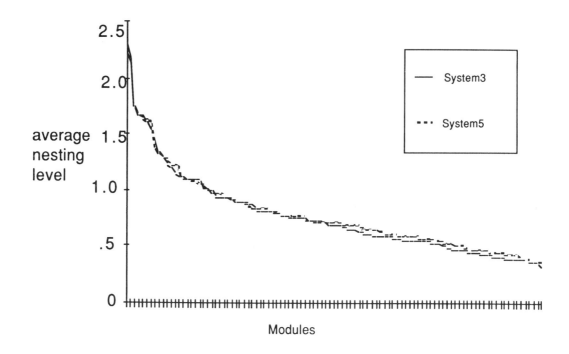

Figure 6: Average Nesting Levels

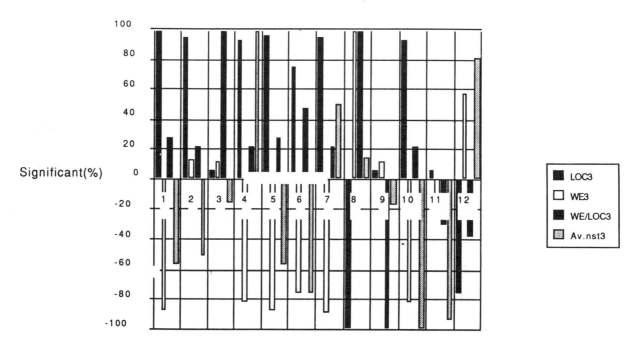

1. Lines of code in system5
2. weight of system5 modules
3. weight of system5 modules/LOC
4. average nesting level of sytem5 modules
5. increase in size of modules
6. percent increase in size of sytem3 modules
7. increase in weight of sytem3 modules
8. percent increase in weight of system3
9. increase weight per line of code
10. increase in average nesting level
11. percent increase in average nesting level
12. binary (increase or no increase)

Figure 7: Significance of Predictors

The data were analyzed by using several statistical packages. The technique of the regression analysis was used to check on relationships between variables and also to assist in determining the best set of predictor variables. The confidence level and significant level (75%) were used to determine whether or not a variable was reliable. A negative value of the t-test implies a negative correlation between variables and a positive value implies a positive correlation between variables.

Figure 7 presents some of the results of the multiple regression tests. The dependent variables are listed at the bottom of the figure; the independent variables are lines of code, weight, weight per line, and average nesting level of the system3. The increased number of lines of code (dependent 1) in system5 is highly correlated with the lines of code (96.2%) and weight (88.6%) of system3. The positive relationship for lines of code implies that the larger modules (if changed) will have larger increases in lines of code. But the significant levels of the weight per line (28.4%) and average nesting level (57.4%) of system3 are below the standard cutoff point. The relation between the updated lines and weight is surprising. The negative relation implies that the modules with higher weights have fewer additional lines of code.

The seventh dependent variable is the difference in weights between the two systems; Figure 8 shows how weight changes are related to the lines of code, weight, weight per line, and average nesting level of system3. The difference in weights between the two systems was correlated with the lines of code (95.7%) and weight (88.9%) of system3 because the significant levels are higher than the standard cutoff point. But we did not consider the relations for the weight per line (23.6%) and average nesting level (50.7%) of system3 because of the low confidence levels. The positive relation for the lines of code implies that larger modules tend to have larger increases in weights. The negative relation for the weight implies that modules with higher weights tend to have decreases in the weights; that is, if the weight of a module is relatively high, it will tend to decrease during maintenance.

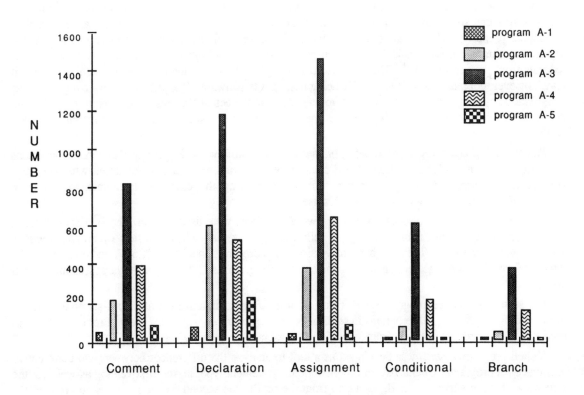

Figure 8: Statement Types on Program Set A

The tenth dependent variable is the difference of the average nesting levels between system3 and system5. The significant levels of the lines of code (93.4%), weight (82.2%), and average nesting level (99.9%) are very high, but the weight per line (23.3%) of system3 is not a predictor because of the low significant level. The relation between the difference of average nesting levels and lines of code is positive, which implies that the larger modules will tend to have larger increases in nesting level. In other words, if the size of code is increasing, the nesting levels will tend to increase during maintenance or enhancement. The negative relation involving the weight implies that modules with higher weights will decrease in average nesting level. The other negative relation involving the average nesting level implies that modules with higher nesting levels tend to decrease in nesting levels. In other words, if the nesting levels are high, they will tend to be reduced during maintenance.

Conclusions for the Macro Model

We have proposed a macro model of the maintenance process based on objective measures of the changes that occur during the maintenance process. We have performed preliminary data analysis on one maintenance effort and have found some interesting patterns that have intuitive support. With these patterns, a manager could use the model to help determine the type of maintenance that is being done.

As more data collection and analysis are done, the model will be refined, will allow for more evaluation of the quality of the maintenance process, and will also lead to more understanding of maintenance itself. A major problem in this area is the lack of sufficient data to analyze; it would be helpful if more companies would or could make their software available for analysis.

Model of Maintenance Activities

To understand the maintenance phase better, it is important to be able to differentiate various types of maintenance activities. We need to develop methods to classify different types of maintenance activities. Proper methods of classifying types of maintenance activities should help to understand the maintenance phase and eventually should help to manage the maintenance effort.

A classification consisting of three types of maintenance activities has been proposed by Swanson.[8] The three types are corrective, adaptive, and perfective. Corrective maintenance is performed to correct errors that are uncovered after the software is brought into use. Adaptive maintenance is applied to obtain a proper interface with a changed external processing environment. Perfective maintenance is applied to eliminate inefficiencies, to enhance performance, or to improve maintainability based on the requests from the user group.[10] This classification system is based on the intention of the maintainer; it may, however, not relate to what is actually being done to the software. It would be an improvement to the classification system to modify or extend it to one based on the actual changes being done to the software. Any system based on a maintainer's intentions can not be automated and may not tell the manager what is really being done.

The method of analyzing changes is a good method for identifying what types of maintenance activities are really occurring, and the resulting classification scheme should give information about what activities are actually occurring during maintenance. Further, measuring the changed statements will give an objective indication of the maintenance process itself.

Two sets of COBOL programs, each with several versions, were used as data. The first set, from an organization involved in manufacturing, is called program set A, which consists of all the versions available for 5 programs. The numbers of versions of these programs are 4, 5, 6, 7, and 11, giving 33 total versions. The average version size for the shortest program is -270 and for the largest is more than 4650.

The second set, called program set B, came from a different organization and consists of the last 20 versions of 8 programs. All programs in set B have been operational for many years. Program set B was used to verify the results obtained from analyzing the programs in program set A.

A shell program, *count*, was developed as a tool to analyze the differences between two consecutive versions of a program. *Count* lists the counts of each statement type in the first version as well as the statements that are altered, deleted, or added from the first to the second version. We have grouped the statements into 8 categories: comment, declaration, assignment, conditional, branch, input-output, label, and other statements.

TYPE represents a type of statement, and ALL stands for the collection of all statement types.

```
TYPE ::= ALL | comment | declaration |
assignment | conditional | branch | input-output |
label | other
comment ::= spacing purposes | textual
assignment ::= MOVE | ADD | SUBTRACT | COMPUTE
conditional ::= IF | ELSE | ON | AT END
branch ::= CALL | PERFORM | GOTO | NEXT | EXIT
input-output ::= DELETE | DISPLAY | OPEN | READ |
WRITE | REWRITE
other ::= EXAMINE | INSPECT | SEARCH | SORT |
SET | EXEC CICIS | GOBACK
```

The three types of statement changes are altered, deleted, and added. Altered statements, although existing in both versions, are different in the second version. Deleted statements are in the original version but are missing from the second version. Added statements are in the second version but not in the first.

For the convenience of notational representation, let

```
Changes      ::= Altered | Deleted | Added
Altered[TYPE] : Number of specified TYPE that has
been altered
Deleted[TYPE] : Number of specified TYPE that has
been deleted
Added[TYPE] : Number of specified TYPE that has been
added
Changes[ALL] = Altered[ALL] + Deleted[ALL] +
Added[ALL]
Changes[TYPE] = Altered[TYPE] + Deleted[TYPE] +
Added[TYPE]
```

Count invokes several Unix utilities, such as diff and grep, to analyze the COBOL programs. Six modules are included in *count*; they are *checking, preprocessing, distinguishing, difference, calculation,* and *report*. Details of the processing can be found in earlier papers.[11,12]

Program set A, consisting of 5 different programs with 33 versions, was analyzed using the *count* shell program. Figure 8 illustrates the characteristics of program set A. Of the 8 types of statements, the results for input-output, label, and other statements are not shown because the quantity of their data was relatively small when compared to the data for the other five types of statements. From the graph, it is easy to see that assignment statements and comment statements play an important role in program set A.

The program *count* runs two sequential versions of a program. The results of the analysis on program set A are 28 deltas. The contents of a delta include Number[TYPE] of each statement in the first version and Altered[TYPE], Deleted[TYPE], and Added[TYPE] between the original and new versions. In addition to these numbers, the statements being changed are also listed as part of the content of a delta.

Types of Maintenance

From reading the original COBOL programs and checking the 28 deltas, six distinct types of maintenance activities were identified; they are corrective, adaptive, retrenchment, retrieving, prettyprinting, and documentation. As more investigations are conducted, we expect that more specialized types of maintenance activities may be identified.

Compared with the three types of maintenance proposed by Swanson,[8] this new classification system does not include perfective maintenance. The reason for excluding perfective maintenance from the classification is caused by the difficulty of inferring the intention of the maintainer. The possible reasons for the maintainer to update source code are too complicated to identify simply from the changed statements. Thus, the perfective and corrective activities have been combined into the corrective activity.

The distinction between adaptive and corrective can also be hard to make. The size of the change is used to distinguish these types in questionable cases.

The six types of maintenance activities are described below in terms of the probable purpose of the activity. Rules for classifying changes into these types are given in the next section.

Corrective

The corrective activity is maintenance for minor revisions of the original version. Correcting errors or failures in source codes is corrective maintenance, which causes some statements to be altered as well as a few statements to be added and/or deleted.

Adaptive

The adaptive activity concerns the addition of new functions or the deletion of old functions from the original codes to meet changes in the requirements. In this type of activity, there are a lot of statements added or deleted in addition to possibly changing a few statements.

Retrenchment

Retrenchment maintenance temporarily removes a function from executable code by adding asterisks in front of the appropriate statements (commenting out the statements). This activity was not expected when we started our analysis. An example of retrenchment maintenance is the following:

Statements in original version:

```
IF MAORD = 'A'
GO TO 0530-READ-MATLDESC-PURCHSPECS
IF MAORD = 'N'
GO TO 0530-READ-MATLDESC-PURCHSPECS
```

Statements in new version:

```
* IF MAORD = 'A'  GO TO 0530-READ-MATLDESC-PURCHSPECS
* IF MAORD = 'N'  GO TO 0530-READ-MATLDESC-PURCHSPECS
```

The result of retrenchment increases the Number[comment] from the original version to the new version. It also decreases the number of statements, but it usually leaves the LOC unchanged. Although some companies may require programmers to comment-out code instead of deleting old code, this was not the case here. It is interesting to note that the commented-out code was often retrieved in a subsequent version.

Some companies may prohibit retrenchment and then it might be reasonable to remove retrenchment from the classification system. However, it may still be very useful to retain retrenchment to enforce the prohibition.

Retrieving

The retrieving activity removes asterisks from commented-out code or documentation statements and thus brings the statements back into executable service. Retrieving is the reverse of retrenchment maintenance.

Prettyprinting

Prettyprinting simply adds asterisks for spacing purposes. There is no functionality added or deleted. The objective of prettyprinting is to allow the program to be more easily read. The prettyprinting maintenance increases Number[comment] in a new version.

Documentation

Documentation is the addition of comment statements to the program. This is different from prettyprinting; the documentation activity puts descriptions or explanations just before a block of source codes. The number and type of statements changed in documentation maintenance is similar to the prettyprinting maintenance.

Rules for Classification

The rules for classifying types of maintenance were developed from the empirical data obtained from executing the program *count* on program set A. These rules were derived from correlation analysis between the *count* output and the human classification of the activity type. The numerical threshold values may be altered as more programs are analyzed. The rules are built into the shell program *classify*. The input for the *classify* program is the output from the *count* program. The discussion of the rules for corrective and adaptive activities are grouped together because of their similarity. Similarly, retrenchment is grouped with retrieving and prettyprinting is grouped with documentation.

Corrective and Adaptive

A modified block of statements is defined as a series of altered statements. If there are more than three blocks of statements in which the lines of codes are modified or if the addition and deletion of statements other than comment statements is greater than 10, the delta is classified as adaptive maintenance. Otherwise, it is said to be corrective maintenance. Formally, the term "modified block" is defined as "a block where the ratio of Number[TYPE] in both versions is greater than 2 if Number[TYPE] in two versions is more than 10, or the ratio is greater than 5 if one of Number[TYPE] is less than 10.

Retrenchment and Retrieving

In both activity types there are some altered statements and no deleted or added statements. The altered statements are changed to or from comments. Number[comment] is increased from the original version to the new version in retrenchment; the value, however, is decreased in retrieving maintenance. These types are identified by checking that only an asterisk was added/deleted from a non-blank altered line.

Prettyprinting and Documentation

For both activity types the increase or decrease of Number[comment] is caused by the addition or deletion of comment statements. If the goal of an added or deleted comment statement is for spacing purposes only, the type of maintenance is classified as prettyprinting; otherwise, it belongs to documentation maintenance. The shell program *classify* can distinguish between these two types of maintenance by checking if there is text in the added comment. These types are identified by checking that comment lines are added/deleted with or without other text on the lines.

Results for Program Set A

The results of types of maintenance in the 28 deltas from program set A are illustrated in Figures 9 and 10. Of the 28 deltas, single types and combinations of two or three types of maintenance exist. For example, the combination of corrective and documentation maintenance is expressed as corrective and documentation maintenances.

Classification of Program Set B

Program set B, which includes 8 programs, was obtained from a data processing environment. Some of these programs have been in use for more than 10 years. For each program, 20 versions were received and analyzed with the shell programs *maintain* and *classify*; we wanted to verify the classification rules proposed in the previous section. The results generated 19 deltas on each program for a total number of 152 deltas (see Figure 11).

In the results collected from the 152 deltas on program set B, the combination of corrective and documentation types was the most frequently occurring maintenance; 81 deltas belong to this combination of types of maintenance. Added comment statements in the identification division contribute to documentation maintenance and the changed statements result in corrective maintenance. It was concluded that most maintainers explained what they modified in the identification division and then made the actual changes in the procedure division. The percentages of occurrence of each type of maintenance for program set B are represented in Figure 11.

In contrast to the same representation from program set A, prettyprinting maintenance happened at a lower percentage.

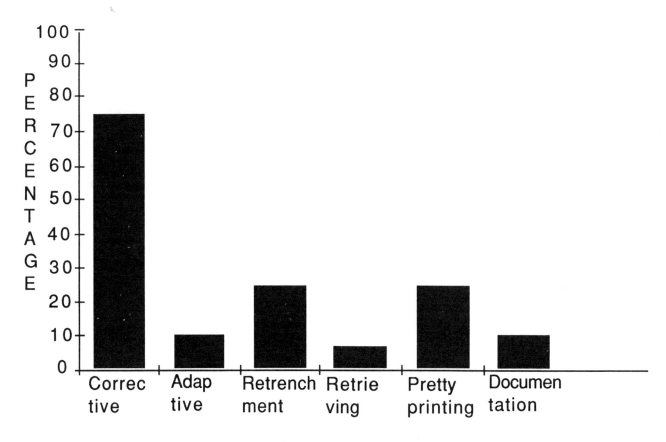

Figure 9: Percentages of Occurrence of Each Type of Maintenance

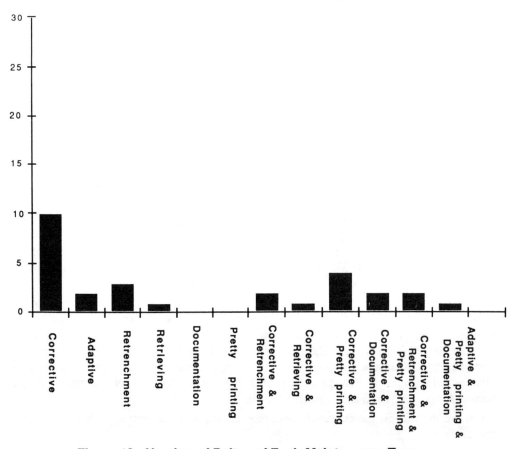

Figure 10: Number of Deltas of Each Maintenance Type

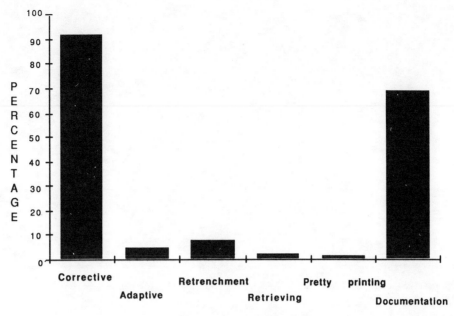

Figure 11: Percentage of Each Type of Maintenance In Program Set B

Validation

The classifications were checked against the explanations for the changes; these explanations were given by the maintainers as comments in the environment section. None of the explanations contradicted the classifications made by the classify program. However, our classifications give a better indiction as to what type of activity actually occurred. Thus, we feel that our rules were successful and useful in classifying the maintenance activities.

Conclusions for Model of Maintenance Activities

Six types of maintenance activities were identified from the analysis of the changes on sequential versions of the programs. As more programs are analyzed these types may be refined and/or more types may be identified. This effort is viewed as an initial step in establishing an objective classification for types of maintenance activities.

Classification rules were presented to distinguish various types of maintenance. The rules were developed on program set A and were used to classify the activities on program set B, which came from another environment. The classifications agreed with the maintainers comments that were recorded in program set B.

Future effort in this area needs to include verifying the present classification scheme with more (COBOL) programs from different sources to check the effectiveness of classifying types of maintenance from these tools.

Conclusions

Two models for software maintenance have been presented, the macro model and the model of maintenance activities. These models are a starting point for developing better understanding of the maintenance process. With these models, objective evaluations of software maintenance should be possible. These models should be useful in improving the maintenance process. Maintainers should be better able to understand the maintenance process; managers should be better able to evaluate the actual maintenance process; and objective studies of maintenance should have a better basis for arriving at conclusions.

Further work is necessary to develop more detailed models of the maintenance tasks. These models will be more challenging to develop if they are objective models that will be related to the mental activities of the maintainers.

Part 2: Management Issues

Adding manpower to a late software project makes it later.

Frederick P. Brooks, Jr., *The Mythical Man-Month: Essays on Software
Engineering*,
Addison-Wesley, 1974.

In order to keep engineers and scientists cognizant of the importance of progress, load them down with forms, multiple reports, and frequent meetings.

Richard F. Moore, The National Cash Register

Anyone having supervisory responsibility for the completion of the task will invariably protest that his staff is too small for the assignment.

Andrew Hack, *The End of the American Dream*,
Atheneum, 1970

Reprinted from *IEEE Software*, Volume 4, Number 9, September 1987, pages 35-45. Copyright ©1987 by The Institute of Electrical and Electronics Engineers, Inc. All rights reserved.

Measuring and Managing Software Maintenance

Robert B. Grady, *Hewlett-Packard*

An effective way to improve software quality is to set measurable goals and then manage your projects to achieve those goals. Hewlett-Packard has developed some methods to do just that.

Why does it take so many people to support software systems? Software development has evolved rapidly in the short time that computers have existed. With most products, such evolution is accompanied by the creation of replacement products and the obsolescence of old ones. However, the nature of software products is that they change and evolve *frequently*. Today, better design and implementation methods lead to higher initial software quality than in the past, but the quality of older products that have undergone continuous change is often poor. Because we cannot economically replace all our old software, we must find better ways to manage needed changes. Until we do, software maintenance will continue to represent a large investment — and software quality will *not* improve.

Management patterns

Many organizations responsible for the evolution of software systems seem to operate constantly in a reactive mode, fighting the flames of the most recent fire. Behind the visible sense of urgency, though, three primary strategic elements appear to control the actions of managers:

- minimizing defects,
- minimizing engineering effort and schedule, and
- maximizing customer satisfaction.

In a broad sense, the ultimate objective of all three approaches is customer satisfaction. This article specifically discusses their relationships to the maintenance of delivered software. Maintenance includes fixing defects, enhancing product features or performance, and adapting to new hardware or external software. Of course, the items above are not unique to the maintenance phase. Managers know that a consolidated strategy must be pursued, although shifting priorities among the items is sometimes more frequent during maintenance than during initial product development. The following examples illustrate this argument.

Minimizing defects: (1) Besides fixing defects, engineers investigate the causes of defects. (2) Before a major new enhancement is attempted, the number of defects in the part of the product to be enhanced is reduced to a minimum. (3) The original development engineers continue to be responsible for fixing defects and making product enhancements for at least six months after product release and before moving on to other product development.

Minimizing engineering effort and schedule: (1) Resources are removed from maintaining/enhancing activities and assigned to new-product development (minimize effort). (2) Resources are removed from development to perform maintaining/enhancing activities (minimize schedule). (3) Extended work times are used to complete an enhanced version in an unalterable schedule. (4) The amount of time taken to make fixes or run tests becomes so critical that shortcuts become necessary.

Maximizing customer satisfaction: (1) After initial product deliveries, development-team members visit customer sites to train, observe operations, and isolate defects. (2) Special patches and workarounds are quickly found for defects and installed for individual customer installations. (3) Work on some defects is deferred to create an enhancement for one key customer.

Business pressures. If you look at an organization that is starting to get involved with software products, it frequently will try to capture a market by working closely with customers to define their product needs completely and correctly the first time and by following up with quick responses to problems. Its initial success depends heavily on customer satisfaction. As its products become accepted in the market, it tries to increase its advantage by maximizing the quality of all its product releases and by gradually improving them with enhancements and improved hardware and software connections.

On the other hand, when competitive products exist, pressures build to create unique features or new products. Organizations are forced to balance engineering effort and schedules between new development and maintenance, and trade-offs are often made to decrease the maintenance effort in favor of new development.

Thus business pressures encourage organizations to emphasize different strategic elements to remain competitive. These pressures influence product features, product quality, timeliness, and the ability to satisfy all these needs more economically than the competition. Table 1 summarizes the major characteristics of these strategic elements.

Metrics. Project measurements are a powerful way to track progress toward goals. Such metrics are frequently displayed in high-level management presentations. For example, the number of defects outstanding or the time to respond to defects are frequently cited when discussing postrelease software. The rate of generating code or product features is often tracked for prerelease software. Without such measures for managing software maintenance, it is difficult for any organization to understand whether it is successful, and it is difficult to keep from frequently changing strategy. It is in the best interests of both managers and engineers responsible for software maintenance to help provide the data needed to choose the best balance among available strategies.

The metrics included in this article were summarized by Hewlett-Packard's Software Metrics Council at its October 1986 meeting using a measurement and evaluation paradigm described by Victor Basili, Dieter Rombach, and David Weiss.[1-3] (The four-year-old council has 20 software managers and engineers from 15 HP divisions and supports many types of software. They identify key software metrics and promote their use through HP's divisions.) The complete HP list contains five goals, 31 questions, and 35 metrics (see the box on p. 38).

Collection and analysis of this metric data does *not* depend on any specific process of maintenance or development.

Minimizing defects

The following graphs and methods are successfully used to minimize defects. They help identify how many defects exist, what the trend is, where and when defects occur, and what the defects' underlying causes are. Although their thrust is fixing defects during maintenance, the information they provide also helps managers when making decisions about enhance-ments and adaptive changes (to surrounding hardware and software). The metrics are

- count of prerelease defects,
- count of postrelease defects,
- count of remaining critical and serious defects,
- count of defects sorted by module and cause,
- noncomment source-code statements (NCSS),
- percentage of branches covered during test, and
- calendar time by phase.

Defect categories. Figure 1 shows a bar chart that addresses three important questions about postrelease quality and how to maximize engineers' effectiveness during maintenance.[4] In this example (and in later ones), the questions' numbers are the same as those in the box on p. 38. Defect analysis indicated that three of the 13 modules (24 percent of the code) accounted for 76 percent of the defects reported before release. This could have meant that these modules had simply been tested more thoroughly than the others. Six months after release, though, a similar analysis was performed using data reported by customers, and the results were that the same three modules accounted for a similar portion of the defects.

This information helped managers formulate a more thorough plan to test the three modules and long-term plans to rewrite the error-prone modules. Until then, the team was wise to exercise caution when considering enhancements to those modules, since their design was relatively unstable or complex. Defect categorization is a powerful tool to help identify where work must be done and to predict where you can expect more defects to appear.

Another effective way to examine defect data is to analyze causes of defects. By identifying common causes of defects, you can take steps to limit the possibility of these problems occurring again.

One organization at HP performed such an analysis[4] and found that more than one third of their defects were caused by a poor understanding of their users' interface requirements. They responded by

Table 1.
Major strategic elements of software maintenance.

	Minimize defects	Minimize engineering effort and schedule	Maximize customer satisfaction
Major business factor	Hold/increase market share	Competitive pressures forcing new-product development or cost control	Attempt to capture market share
When least effective	When product features are not competitive or reasonable market is not held	When single product is primary source of revenue	Late in the life of a product
Characteristic features	Analysis and removal of sources of defects	Focus on balancing resources between maintenance and new development	Customer communication, quick response
Most visible metrics	Defect categorization by module, cause, type, and severity; size; branch coverage	Calendar time, engineering effort, defects	Product metrics, defects, time
Group most likely to drive strategy	Lab or quality organization; customer support as catalyst	Division or company management	Lab during initial development, customer support later
Potential drawbacks if focus is too restricted	Defects may be fixed that are not cost-effective; modules may not be rewritten that should be	Defect backlog can become unmanageable	Process of developing products may not improve

changing their process to focus more specifically on user-interface design (such as technical design reviews and evolutionary prototypes reviewed by representative customers; Grady and Caswell[4] give a more complete discussion of their analysis).

Figure 2 shows three categories of defects before and after release for four successive releases of the same product after the organization had changed its user-interface design process. It shows that the organization now has few design errors. The percentage of defects found after release also dropped from 25 percent of the total for the first two releases to less than 10 percent in the third and to zero in the fourth. While they were not completely successful in removing all sources of defects, they did improve their process so that the defects did not reach customers.

Another way to monitor defects is to plot a weekly graph that shows cumulative defect and enhancement requests along with similar graphs of the unresolved defects. Such trends help indicate project

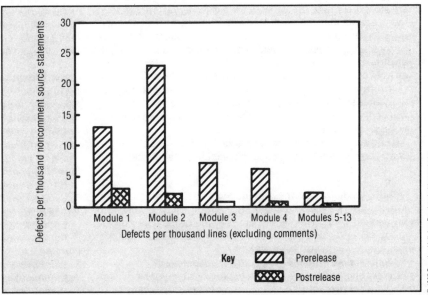

Figure 1. Defect analysis by code module. Addresses questions 13 (what are high-leverage opportunities during preventive maintenance?), 16 (what is the postrelease quality of each module?), and 26 (what can I predict will happen after release based on prerelease metrics?). (The questions are detailed in the box on p. 38.)

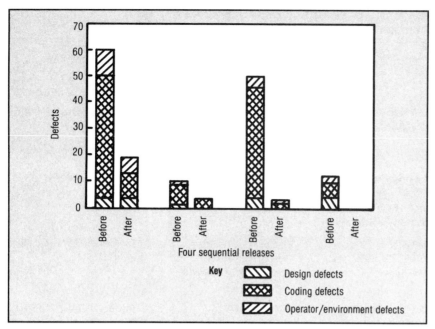

Figure 2. Number of defects found before and after release. Addresses questions 18 (what are we doing right?) and 28 (what defects are getting through?).

progress and expected completion. For large systems, the rate of change in these trends may be more important than the trends themselves because it shows the product's stability. Figure 3 shows the rates of change of both the incoming defects and the defects fixed for part of one large HP system. HP's experience has proven that products whose defect-status slopes did not decline had poor quality after release.

The defect data can also be combined with a weekly staffing profile to calculate the average time needed to fix a defect.

Branch coverage. During a product's maintenance cycle, one primary concern is

Maintenance goals, questions, and metrics

The metrics defined by the HP Software Metrics Council were derived using a measurement and evaluation paradigm that says that goals lead to questions that lead to metrics that supply answers to the questions (see references 1-3 in the main text). To the extent that the questions are a complete set, and to the extent the metrics satisfactorily answer the questions, you can learn if the goals are met.

This section is organized by the primary goals that must be accomplished. With each goal, there is a brief discussion of who is most likely to ask the questions. While discussing these metrics, the council identified four major individuals or groups who are most likely to ask the questions in their areas: top management, project management, customer engineers (this category includes all individuals responsible for dealing directly with customers), and process managers. While "process manager" is not an official job title at HP, someone at most divisions is identified as holding that responsibility for software maintenance.

A fifth group likely to ask these questions is the quality-assurance staff. Because they frequently act as the voice of a conscience, they are likely to ask questions in all areas, so they are not explicitly noted in the following list.

The metrics listed here are not precisely defined and should be considered general approaches to measurable feedback.

Goal: Maximize customer satisfaction. The group most likely to ask questions about customer satisfaction is that responsible for dealing with customers. There is some overlap with other groups. For example, question 6 concerns everyone, and project managers usually will ask question 7.
1. *What are the attributes of customer satisfaction?*
2. *What are the key indicators of customer satisfaction?*
3. *What are the factors resulting in customer satisfaction?*
4. *How satisfied are customers?*
5. *How do you compare with the competition?*
   • Survey data.
6. *How many problems are affecting the customer?*
   • Incoming defect rate.

• Open critical and serious defects.
   • Break/fix ratio.
   • Postrelease defect density.
7. *How long does it take to fix a problem (compared to customer expectation and compared to commitment)?*
   • Mean time to acknowledge problem.
   • Mean time to deliver solution.
   • Scheduled versus actual delivery.
   • Customer expectation (by severity level) of time to fix.
8. *How does installing the fix affect the customer?*
   • Time customer's operation is down.
   • Customer's effort required during installation.
9. *How many customers are affected by a problem? And how much are they affected?*
   • Number of duplicate defects by severity.

Goal: Improve the maintenance/enhancement process. This goal is almost equally shared by project managers and process managers. The primary difference between the two groups lies in the scope of the questions. Project managers will ask the questions with a much narrower view, with the emphasis on optimizing the performance of their particular project.
10. *Where are the resources going? Where are the worst rework loops in the process?*
   • Engineering months by product/component/activity.
11. *What are the total life-cycle maintenance and support costs for the product (and how distributed by time and organization)?*
   • Engineering-months by product/component/activity.
   • Engineering-months by corrective, adaptive, and perfective maintenance.
12. *What development methods affect maintenance costs?*
   • Prerelease records of methods and postrelease costs.
13. *What are high-leverage opportunities for preventive maintenance?*
   • Defect categorization.
   • Code stability.
14. *Are fixes effective? Are unexpected side effects created?*
   • Break/fix ratio.

to ensure that new defects are not introduced. An effective way to check this is to maintain suites of test programs that are continually updated as products change and improve. Figure 4 illustrates one of several ways needed to verify the tests' completeness. It shows two levels of branch-coverage limits and the data for one part of an HP product.

Branch coverage is measured by using a program that automatically inserts statements into the product's precompilation source code. These statements increment counters during testing to provide a histogram of what code parts were executed and what parts were not. In the example, you

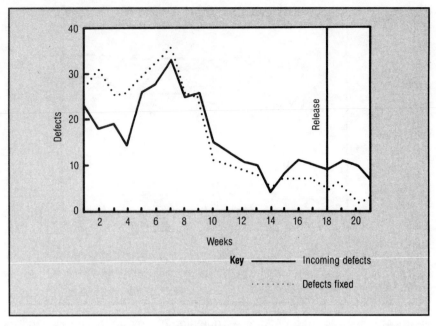

Figure 3. Project defect status. Addresses questions 20 (how do we know when to release?) and 22 (how long does it take to fix a defect?).

15. *How maintainable is the product as changes occur? When do I give up and rewrite?*
- Incoming problem rate.
- Defect density.
- Code stability.
- Complexity.
- Number of modules changed to fix one defect.
16. *What is the postrelease quality of each module?*
- Defect density, critical and serious defects.
17. *What will process monitoring cost and where are the costs distributed?*
- Engineering-hours and cost.
18. *What are you doing right?*
- Error-detection effectiveness (ratio of prerelease defect density to postrelease defect density).
- Break/fix ratio.
19. *What are key indicators of process health, and how are you doing?*
- Release schedules met, trends of defect density, and serious and critical defects.

Goal: Make maintenance more predictable. Everyone is interested in schedules. Other than question 20, though, every group has its own view of what is important.
20. *How do you know when to release?*
- Predicted defect detection based on prerelease records and postrelease defect densities.
- Branch coverage.

21. *What will the maintenance requirements be?*
- Code stability, complexity, and size.
- Prerelease defect density.

22. *How long does it take to fix a defect historically? With new processes? With resource changes? With complexity and severity variations? For each activity in process?*
- Calendar time and process and module records.
23. *Where are the bottlenecks?*
- Queue time.

24. *How can you predict cycle time, reliability, and effort?*
- Calendar time.
- Engineering time.
- Defect density.
- Number of defects to fix.
- Break/fix historical averages.
- Code stability.
- Complexity.
- Number of lines to change.

Goal: Improve prerelease development. This goal belongs to the process manager.
25. *How effective is the development process in preventing defects?*
- Postrelease defect density.
26. *What can I predict will happen after release, based on prerelease metrics?*
- Correlations between prerelease complexity, defect density, stability, FURPS, and postrelease defect density; ability to easily make changes; and customer survey results.
27. *What practices yield the best results?*
- Correlations between prerelease practices and customer satisfaction metrics.
28. *What defects are getting through? What caused those defects?*
- Defect categorization.

Goal: Minimize maintenance cost. This goal belongs to top management, although the questions are sometimes indirectly heard from other groups.
29. *How much do the maintenance-phase activities cost?*
- Engineering time and cost.
30. *What are the major cost components? What factors affect the cost?*
- Engineering-months by product/component/activity.
31. *How do costs change over time?*
- Track cost components over entire maintenance life cycle.

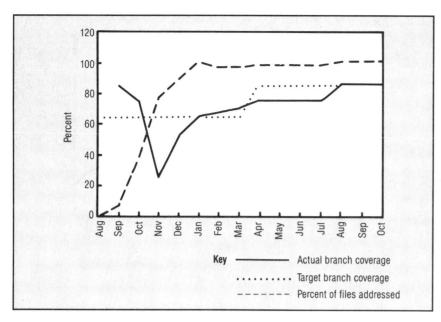

Figure 4. Branch coverage. Addresses question 20 (how do we know when to release?).

can see how the goals for coverage and the actual coverage get higher over time. This graph represents composite data during integration-level testing of all components. Unit-level testing is performed earlier in the process, and the goal for unit-level coverage is 100 percent.

Top-management presentation. The graphs presented so far are most useful for project managers. The next two help summarize the status of product maintenance for top managers. The first graph deals with measuring customer satisfaction. Figure 5 is an example of data that receives monthly management attention in HP because it summarizes how many unfixed critical and serious problems customers see.[4] (The data shown is not current, and it is normalized so the actual number of defects is not reflected.)

The second graph (Figure 6) shows the postrelease defect density for the first 12 months after release for one division's products. Better than any other visual representation, this graph summarizes whether all the other efforts to reduce defects are having a permanent, positive

effect. The figure shows some progress toward higher quality at release in the past year and a half for product line 2. There are no recent data points for the other two product lines that would indicate whether they made such progress.

You can see how these last two graphs complement the earlier graphs by providing top-management views that are consistent with the focus of minimizing defects.

These six illustrations came from different projects, entities, and times. Measuring any one or two of them is useful, but the best results are achieved by tracking them all. Fortunately, the amount of data to collect is not a great burden. Many managers track such data as numbers instead of graphs, and on a daily basis this minimizes their effort. On the other hand, graphs are helpful when it is important to *see* a trend.

Minimizing engineering effort and schedule

A common management focus is minimizing engineering effort and completion time. For many projects, this focus is the most effective way to serve all the customers' needs. One set of metrics particularly applies to this focus in the maintenance phase. Like some defect-categorization examples in the previous section, the effort and time data in the following examples must be supplemented by analysis of detailed data and specific actions to make improvements in costly areas. The metrics here are

• engineering-months by product/component/activity,

• engineering-months by defects/enhancements,

• defect and enhancement request counts,

• counts of remaining critical and serious defects,

• calendar time by phase and activity, and

• code stability (percent of code changed).

Completion rates. Figures 7 and 8 illustrate two views of engineering and calendar time in the maintenance of two products. The first shows the actual times to fix various defects versus the estimated

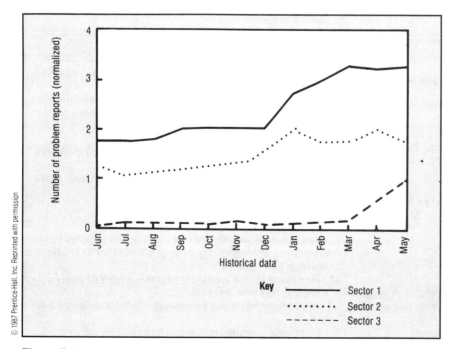

Figure 5. Unresolved critical and serious problem reports (software quality by sector). Addresses question 6 (how many problems affect the customer?).

times.[4] The advantage of this type of representation over the one shown in Figure 3 is that it gives you some feel for the data dispersion (calculating average fix times from the data in Figure 3 doesn't). This figure shows the average time it takes to respond to defects in engineering-hours. It also shows that the predicted time to fix defects was reasonably accurate for estimates of six hours or under, but higher estimates were not as accurate.

One important variable not included in Figure 7 is the percentage of *effective* hours available (not including non-project-related efforts). In this case, the average number of effective hours available pushed the estimated time to fix closer to 4 than to 2.71. The manager of this product line uses this data to estimate schedules more accurately, to measure how effective new tools or training are, and to shorten schedules by providing an environment with a higher percentage of effective hours (even if only temporarily).

On the other hand, Figure 8 shows fix times in calendar time (from when an engineer is first assigned to a defect until the corrected code is tested and returned to a control library) rather than in engineering-hours. This form of tracking is useful during maintenance as a mechanism to focus on the release schedule for a product update. The figure shows the results of a concentrated effort at one HP division to drastically reduce the time to get product updates through the release process.

The steps that they took (and are still taking) are a model for process improvement. First, they set a fixed cycle time for updates that went to customers. The order in which defects were fixed was set by the marketing group that dealt with customers. Next, they created a sign-off form that specified the steps needed to fix each defect (quick fixes and workarounds were handled separately from this process). This form also captured the amount of engineering time spent for each step. From this data, they learned what the breakdown of time was for each task. These times were compared to each task's effectiveness. Last, they introduced one major process change per update cycle so they could monitor their overall effectiveness.

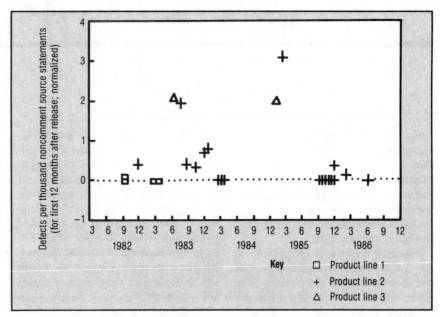

Figure 6. Software quality (postrelease defect density). Addresses question 25 (how effective is development in preventing defects?).

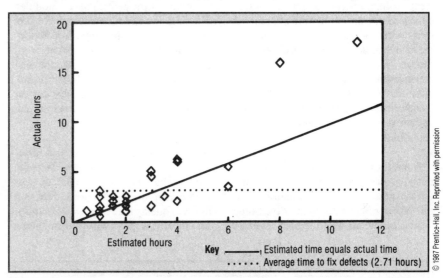

Figure 7. Defect fix times (estimated versus actual time). Addresses questions 22 (how long does it take to fix a defect?) and 24 (how can we predict cycle time, reliability, and effort?).

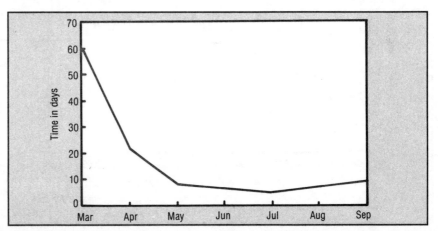

Figure 8. Average time to fix a service request for one product. Addresses questions 22 (how long does it take to fix a defect?) and 24 (how can we predict cycle time, reliability, and effort?).

For example, it may have taken an engineer half a day to unit-test a change. They found that few defects turned up during unit test if design reviews were conducted before the changes were made and that these defects were successfully caught by defect-specific tests. As a result, they eliminated the unit tests.

When you use the approaches shown in the Figures 7 and 8, remember that not all maintenance activities are corrective. The effort and time characteristics of changes made to improve products can be quite different from the those for defect fixes. For tracking purposes, it is convenient to treat enhancements either as major changes (in terms of time and effort) with most of the characteristics of new designs or as minor changes to be grouped with defect fixes. Generally, only minor enhancements are allowed for some period after initial product release, and major enhancements begin to become a predominant cost only after incoming defects have stabilized.

Complexity. For large software systems, a strategic focus on minimizing effort and schedule must take into account the effect of overall complexity. Some years ago, Belady and Lehman proposed

a law of software development that said, "The entropy of a system increases with time unless specific work is executed to maintain or reduce it."[5] Figure 9 shows increasing entropy for one large software product, OS/360, in the form of the fraction of modules handled for each new release over almost 10 years' time. The larger the percentage of modules changed, the greater the probability that new defects will be introduced and that more testing will be required to complete the job. At the 3000-day point, it appears that a major effort was undertaken to control the number of modules changed for an update.

Looking at the percentage of modules affected is just one of several metrics that characterize maintainability. It is important to also look at incoming defect rates, individual module stability and complexity, test coverage, and other factors to isolate the areas of the product that are the largest contributors to overall maintenance costs.

Cost trade-offs. Managers seek information on cost trade-offs between methods that might be applied to new development or maintenance. HP has improved quality in recent years by applying effective software-engineering

methods to products during initial development. These methods include structured analysis and design, the use of prototypes for products with extensive user interactions, design and code inspections, branch-coverage analysis, testing-prediction models, and statistical quality-control techniques.

The next example, analysis of engineering time, demonstrates the potential value of these methods, whether they are used during initial development or during maintenance. Table 2 shows the relative amounts of time needed to fix defects as a function of when the defects were introduced for two products.

The first thing you can see is that the average times to find and fix defects are substantially more than the four hours discussed in the Figure 7 example. That example represented the early maintenance records of a relatively small product (10,000 noncomment source-code statements). The data in Table 2 is from two very large, mature software products. The effects of defects on their maintenance is also very large.

When you become aware of the potential downstream costs of as much as two engineering-months for each design defect, the motivation to train engineers to use design reviews effectively becomes high. Similarly, the motivation to use other defect-prevention methods also becomes high. Only by tracking and analyzing engineering costs by different activities can you learn the facts to make the most cost-effective decisions for your maintenance situation.

The most common top-level graphic view that supports a focus on minimizing engineering effort and schedule is the project PERT chart. The primary metric it tracks is time. Some automated PERT packages also allow input of engineering-hours and associated work-breakdown reports. Another metric graphed at HP is the mean time to fix critical and serious known problems. It is similar to Figure 8, but it includes all the time seen by customers — not just the time used by the lab.

A major goal in the maintenance phase is to *balance* responsiveness to customer needs against the need to minimize overall engineering resources that do not create new sources of revenue.

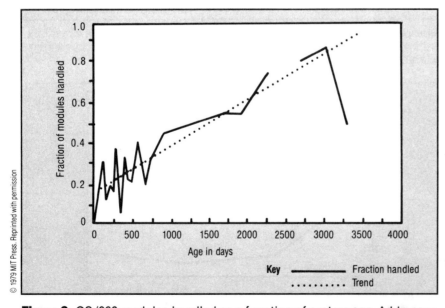

Key ——————— Fraction handled
·········· Trend

Figure 9. OS/360 modules handled as a function of system age. Addresses question 15 (how maintainable is the product as changes occur? when do I give up and rewrite?).

Maximizing customer satisfaction

Maximizing customer satisfaction is easiest to pursue when the product team has close ties to customers. Examples are small-volume products or products used only by customers in the same company. For other products, it is necessary to provide very efficient communication links from the customers through the various layers of a sales and support organization to get the data and feedback needed.

In some ways, overemphasizing this focus can result in a short-term viewpoint if the following examples are not supplemented by other measures to make more permanent process and product changes. On the other hand, the effective use of surveys on which this strategic focus depends is a very powerful tool to positively affect later product generations. The metrics here are

- survey data,
- counts of unresolved critical and serious defects,
- calendar time by phase and activity (emphasis on times customers experience problems),
- defect and enhancement request counts, and
- break/fix ratio (count of defects introduced versus count of defects fixed).

Quality attributes. Figure 10 shows how one Japanese company displays quality. It combines a view of defect status (correctness) with a stronger product (as opposed to process) focus[6] than in the previous figures. This diagram was used during the initial development of a product, and several metrics were selected for each product attribute to derive the percentages.

For products in the maintenance phase, you can learn effective measures for some of these attributes through well-constructed customer surveys. By responding to these customer needs with product enhancements, a company not only improves its market position, it also makes an important statement to customers of ongoing commitment to serving their needs.

One HP group has developed several guidelines for creating such surveys:

- Define what the goals are for the survey, what questions must be answered, how the data will be analyzed, and how results will be presented. State or graph sample conclusions.
- Test the survey and your method of data analysis before sending it out.
- Ask questions that require simple answers, preferably quantitative or yes/no.
- Keep surveys short (preferably one page).
- Don't send surveys with other material so they won't get lost in the shuffle.
- Make them very easy to return (for example, a fold-and-seal, prestamped form).

Product-quality attributes that should

Table 2. Engineering-time versus defects for two software projects.

Phase introduced	Project 1 % defects introduced	Average fix time*	Project 2 % defects introduced	Average fix time*
Investigation	—	—	3	575
Design	20	315	15	235
Implementation	75	80	65	118
Test	5	46	17	74
Total	100	125	100	140

*Time includes finding and fixing (units are engineering-hours). Defects were fixed mainly during implementation and test phases.

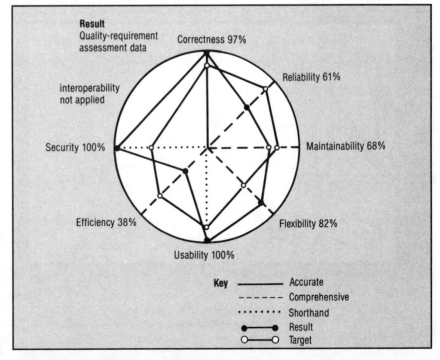

Figure 10. Example of displaying quality. Addresses question 3 (what are the factors resulting in customer satisfaction?).

be considered are contained in a model of quality features, called FURPS, which is commonly used in HP.[4] (The letters stand for the categories modeled: functionality, usability, reliability, performance, and supportability.) Each category contains several measurable attributes. You should formulate at least one question from each category when preparing customer surveys. The presentation method in Figure 10 is useful because it allows all the major FURPS components to be displayed in one chart. This helps raise awareness of the importance of balance and completeness when setting goals and measuring progress against the goals.

Other sources of quality-attribute measurements are sales followups, direct visits by designers to customer sites, and direct measurements of a product in the labs.

Responsiveness. Another key factor of customer satisfaction is responsiveness to concerns. For example, the two categories of HP defect reports that represent the problems of most concern to customers are "serious" and "critical." When customers experience these problems, they expect a timely response. Figure 11 shows how one division at HP has represented data and weighted it to ensure that activities' priorities are rated appropriately. A site is placed on "alert" status when a serious or critical problem is encountered. If no workaround is found quickly, the site is placed on "hot" status by the field organization. The graph in Figure 11 shows the results of improved responsiveness by the division.

Similar graphs help control maintenance activities for a product line or customer relationship. For example, a goal can be set for response time to resolve critical and serious problems with any key customer account. This provides a much tighter coupling between setting customer expectations and achieving customer satisfaction. The key point is to establish the desired metric and consistently measure the appropriate part of the process.

While Figure 11 addresses the most important defects visible to customers, it is also important to deal with all the other defects that are day-to-day nuisances (not serious or critical, just annoying). The graph of the average time to fix service requests in Figure 8 is a useful way to monitor all the defects. Optimizing the average time to fix a service request, as well as minimizing the problem resolution indexes in Figure 11, helps ensure that there is some balance between responsiveness to problems that have no workarounds and those that do.

Focusing on customer satisfaction can lead to well-accepted, successful products. On the other hand, managers will be most successful in the long term by supplementing this focus with some of the process-related methods from the other emphases (minimizing defects and minimizing engineering effort and schedule).

Controlling software maintenance costs requires that an organization have a strategy for maintenance (whether or not it is explicitly stated) and that the primary characteristics of the strategy and the most effective measures of its success be understood. Software metrics provide measurable pictures of progress in meeting the organization's goals.

Figure 12 shows a simplified dataflow diagram of maintenance that summarizes relevant data for three strategic elements. The metrics mainly involve detailed defect information. They also include size and complexity data from automated counters, engineering effort and time information collected manually, and information from customer surveys performed mainly by marketing and support personnel. Because the model only addresses data sources, it does not depend on any particular process for maintenance. On the other hand, evaluating the data provides useful checks against any of the three focuses, and the model provides a framework for data that supports better decisions. Conscientious use of this model will help achieve a proper balance between the equally important goals of customer satisfaction and development control.

There are several factors to remember when considering which focus you might emphasize. Software metrics can only be *part* of a successful overall plan for development improvement. The metrics selected will help manage a business for many years, so they must be carefully cho-

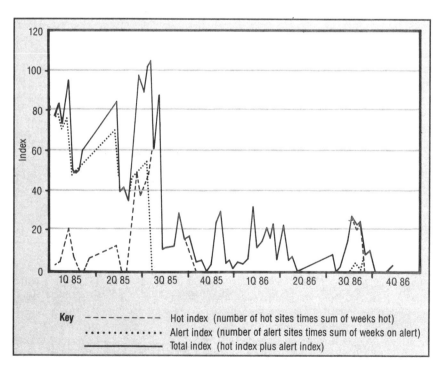

Figure 11. Division software-problem resolution index. Addresses question 19 (what are key indicators of process health and how are we doing?).

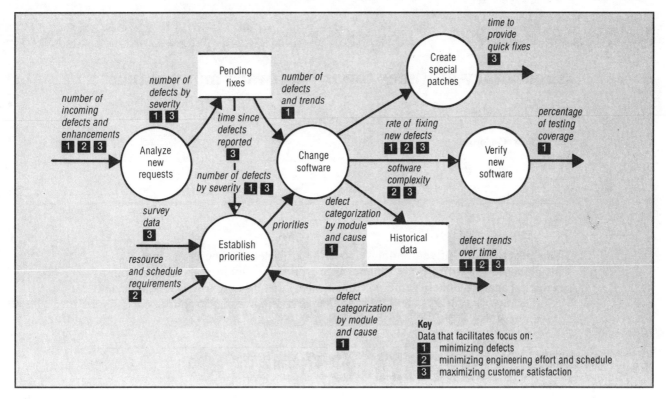

Figure 12. Sources of software maintenance-management information.

sen. No matter what strategy you pursue, you can effectively execute that strategy only if you understand the necessary product and process attributes. That understanding *requires* software metrics.

The focus on minimizing defects is directed most completely to long-term improvement. The focus on maximizing customer satisfaction and the focus on minimizing engineering effort and schedule both serve important purposes driven by immediate business needs. If the initial set of metrics is selected carefully, you can start with a short-term focus and evolve into a long-term strategy.

Project managers today seldom take the time to analyze data for more than one or two of the views presented here. And yet they could make better decisions if they did spend the time. There is a strong need for more complete automation of the data collection, analysis, and presentation process than is generally available. Such automation would include comparison of data against preset limits and automatic generation of exception reports, as well as many of the views shown earlier. Until such a complete system is available, subsets of the methods described here are effective and can be used immediately by software managers to achieve higher quality software. ◇

Acknowledgments

I would like to express my continued appreciation to the HP Software Metrics Council for its commitment and efforts that formed the basis for the successes of our program. Chuck Sieloff, Brian Sakai, Ken Oar, Bob Horenstein, Vic Langford, Dick Levitt, and Susan Muldoon all provided valuable data for this article. I particularly thank Jan Grady, Debbie Caswell, and John Burnham for their patience and helpful suggestions regarding this article's development.

References

1. V. Basili and H.D. Rombach, "Tailoring the Software Process to Project Goals and Environments," *Proc. Ninth Int'l Conf. Software Eng.*, CS Press, Los Alamitos, Calif., 1987, pp. 345-357.
2. V. Basili and D.M. Weiss, "A Methodology for Collecting Valid Software Engineering Data," *IEEE Trans. Software Eng.* Nov. 1984, pp. 728-738.
3. H.D. Rombach, "Using Maintenance Management in an Industrial Environment," presentation incorporated into Tech. Report TR-1764, Computer Science Dept., Univ. of Maryland, College Park, Md., 1987.
4. R. Grady and D. Caswell, *Software Metrics: Establishing a Company-Wide Program*, Prentice-Hall, Englewood Cliffs, N.J., 1987, pp. 88, 110, 123, 124, and 159.
5. L. Belady and M. Lehman, "The Characteristics of Large Systems," in *Research Directions in Software Technology*, P. Wegner, ed., MIT Press, Cambridge, Mass., 1979, pp. 106-142.
6. T. Sunazuka, M. Azuma, and N. Yamagishi, "Software Quality Assessment Technology," *Proc. Eighth Int'l Conf. Software Eng.*, CS Press, Los Alamitos, Calif., 1985, pp. 142-148.

Robert B. Grady works in Hewlett-Packard's Software Development Technology Lab. He previously managed the HP Software Engineering Lab and was responsible for establishing a company-wide software metrics program. He has managed development projects for compilers, measurement and control systems, firmware, and manufacturing automation and information systems. His research interests include software tools, development environments, and metrics.

Grady received a BS in electrical engineering from the Massachusetts Institute of Technology and an MS in electrical engineering from Stanford University. He is a member of the Computer Society of the IEEE.

Grady can be contacted at Hewlett-Packard, PO Box 10350, Palo Alto, CA 94303-0867.

Supervisory attitudes toward software maintenance

by NED CHAPIN

InfoSci Inc.
Menlo Park, California

ABSTRACT

This paper reports fifteen findings about the attitudes of supervisors of software maintenance toward software maintenance work. The findings are drawn from a statistical analysis of data gathered from a survey of 158 supervisors. Relationships to other reported surveys are noted. The paper offers five conclusions drawn from the findings.

INTRODUCTION

In the past five years, several surveys have reported attempts to take the measure of application software maintenance. The largest of these, as reported by Lientz and Swanson,[1] gave very little coverage to the attitudes held by personnel doing the maintenance work, and no coverage to the attitudes held by personnel who supervise computer software personnel in the actual performance of application software maintenance. The important survey conducted by the Controller General of the U. S. Federal Government[2] provided no coverage on this matter. The National Bureau of Standards maintenance survey[3] passed over this topic. The IBM survey[4] of maintenance at 25 computer sites did not touch on this subject. Even the survey of supervisors of software maintenance reported by Chapin[5] at last year's National Computer Conference was silent about supervisory attitudes.

On a prima facie basis, the attitudes of supervisory personnel can be expected to be important in affecting the quantity of work assigned subordinates achieve, the quality of that work, and the way that work is accomplished. Positive attitudes are associated with higher effectiveness and negative attitudes with lower effectiveness.[6] Supervisory attitudes are recognized as being affected in turn by many factors,[6] including the work situation and the actions of higher-level managers. The relevance of supervisory attitudes in software maintenance has been noted elsewhere.[7]

The interplay of the work situation and supervisory attitudes in the area of application software maintenance is the focus of the survey reported in this paper. The contributing role of management objectives has been discussed elsewhere.[8] Although some of the findings are as expected, other findings are surprising and offer new insight into the performance and management of application software maintenance. Before launching into those findings and drawing some conclusions, however, a short description of the survey and a few definitions are in order to lay the groundwork.

DEFINITIONS

The term *application software maintenance* is used in this paper to refer to the combination of four main kinds of activities involved in servicing existing application programs and systems. An alternative phrase sometimes used for this combination is *application software support*. These definitions differ in detail from some others in the field[3,9] but preserve a useful degree of congruence with the most popular definitions[1] while correcting for some possible oversights.

One kind of activity included in the combination is making enhancements or modifications to the capability of existing application software to meet user requests.[5] Usually, this activity arises from users' changed views of their requirements (e.g., a user wants to add a new profit center to reflect the production and marketing of a new product).

A second kind of activity included in the combination is making adaptations in existing application software to work in a changed data processing environment.[5] An example of such adaptation is altering existing application programs and systems to fit with the features of newly introduced communication systems software.

A third kind of activity is making corrections and routine form changes in existing application software to preserve its current functionality.[5] Two examples of this activity are: (1) to return to a running state an application program which has abnormally terminated during execution and (2) to change the spelling of a data name to be consistent among all the programs within a system.

A fourth kind of activity is providing consultative assistance to help individuals use the application program or system.[5] For example, assistance might be provided to a user who asks why a computer is producing totals on one report which do not reconcile with the totals shown on another report produced by the computer as an output from the same system.

In this paper, *supervisor* means any person who makes work assignments to the personnel assigned to do application software maintenance and who receives the results of those work assignments. A supervisor may have other duties, including in some instances, actually doing some maintenance work. In the survey reported here, job title was not the criterion; the exercise of supervisory responsibility was. Job titles commonly encountered were supervisor, project leader, lead analyst, lead programmer, programming manager, and data processing manager.

SURVEY

The survey was carried out by personal contact with supervisory personnel in software maintenance, providing them with a questionnaire, and then follow-up with personal contact to secure return of the completed form. At only one installation were more than one-half of the supervisory personnel solicited; higher-level supervisors or managers generally designated the personnel to respond to the questionnaire. No compensation or consideration beyond verbal thanks was offered to those who completed and returned questionnaires. The sites included in the survey are predominantly in the Boston to Atlanta area of the United States. A wide range of industries and government facilities was included in the survey sites.

The last part of the questionnaire was optional, asking in a very open-ended manner for comments. Comment responses were obtained from 158 supervisory personnel employed at 71 different data processing installations. Because the respondents used their own words to express their comments, the result was a great diversity of wording. The diversity did not make the classification of the comments easy, even though the emphasis in the classification was on the attitudes expressed by the survey respondents. An independent check was conducted on the classification as a validation.

Table I gives a tabulation of the survey, together with a breakdown based on whether the respondent had identified documentation as a problem at the site. The documentation factor was included because of the attention it received in relation to supervisors in work reported previously.[5] The three categories of attitude shown are favorable, neutral, and unfavorable. A favorable attitude is noted if a respondent commented positively about software maintenance; for example: "Fun work with lots of user contact." An unfavorable attitude is noted if a respondent commented on an unpleasant aspect of software maintenance or in a negative manner; for example: "Dull and boring." A neutral attitude is noted if a respondent commented in neither a positive nor negative manner; for example: "More people work on maintenance than on development here." Some respondents offered multiple comments. The preponderance of the respondents' comments in such cases was the basis for assignment to a category.

FINDINGS

Null hypothesis 1: Supervisory attitudes are equally distributed among favorable, neutral, and unfavorable.

An equal distribution of attitudes would be rectangular in shape at a height of about 52 or 53 respondents. A chi square test[10] of this null[10] hypothesis yielded a chi square of 19.91 with two degrees of freedom (19.91, 2 df). This magnitude of chi square is significant[10] at the one percent level for this number of degrees of freedom, and hence this null hypothesis is rejected.[10] The finding is that supervisory attitudes are not equally distributed among favorable, neutral, and unfavorable but are biased to more than expected unfavorable attitudes.

Null hypothesis 2: Supervisory attitudes cluster in the neutral area with non-neutral attitudes expressed less frequently.

For testing null hypothesis 2, some distribution is needed that reflects on a reasonable theoretical basis, a central clustering and that is appropriate for a sample size in excess of 150 cases. The binomial distribution can serve where the expected proportion of frequencies are 0.25, 0.50, and 0.25.[11] A chi square test (33.65, 2 df) showed significance at the one percent level, and hence the hypothesis is rejected. The finding is that supervisory attitudes are not clustered in the neutral area, but are biased to more than expected unfavorable attitudes.

TABLE I—General tabulation of the survey

Documentation	Favorable	Neutral	Unfavorable	Total
Yes a problem	10	30	37	77
Not a problem	17	30	34	81
Totals	27	60	71	158

Null hypothesis 3: Supervisory attitudes are normally distributed among favorable, neutral, and unfavorable.

For null hypothesis 3, the stanine[10] categories based on the normal distribution can serve admirably with stanines one, two, and three forming one category; stanines four, five, and six forming the middle category; and stanines seven, eight, and nine forming the remaining category. A chi square (42.97, 2 df) showed significance at the one percent level, and hence the hypothesis is rejected. The finding is that supervisory attitudes are not normally distributed, but are biased to more than expected unfavorable attitudes.

Null hypothesis 4: Supervisory attitudes have the same distribution whether documentation is regarded as a problem by the supervisors.

Several options can be explored for hypothesis 4 of various combinations and breakdowns of the data. The most deviant of the data are for the documentation seen as a problem. With the total distribution taken as the expected distribution, a chi square test (3.10, 2 df) accepted the hypothesis. Since the distribution within the favorable and unfavorable attitude groups is different from the neutral and from each other, each of these distributions can be explored. A chi square test of favorable and neutral attitude responses (1.82, 1 df) accepted the hypothesis. A chi square test of unfavorable and neutral attitude responses (0.11, 1 df) also accepted the hypothesis. A chi square test of favorable and unfavorable attitude responses (2.46, 1 df) narrowly accepted the hypothesis. The finding is that supervisory attitudes have the same distribution whether or not documentation is regarded as a problem by the supervisors but supervisors who hold favorable attitudes tend to see documentation as less of a problem.

Null hypothesis 5: Supervisors see documentation as a problem just as much regardless of whether their attitudes include evidence of having taken positive action.

This hypothesis breaks the favorable attitude category into two subcategories, action–favorable and passive–favorable, with the "yes" documentation responses being 2 and 8 respectively (total of 10) and the "no" documentation responses being 6 and 11 respectively (total of 17). A chi square test of the "yes" observed with the subcategory totals (8 and 19 totaling 27) accepted the hypothesis (1.02, 1 df). A chi square test of the "yes" with the "no" (3.80, 1 df) narrowly missed being rejected at the five percent level. A chi square test of all of the "yes" attitudes but with the favorable broken into the two subcategories accepted (1.28, 3 df) the hypothesis when the expected distribution was the total distribution, and only narrowly accepted (3.73, 3 df) the hypothesis when the expected distribution was the "no" responses. The finding is that supervisors see documentation as a problem just as much when their attitudes include evidence of having taken positive action as not, but there is a tendency for the positive-action group to see documentation as less of a problem.

Null hypothesis 6: The average age of the software being maintained has no relationship with supervisory attitudes.

The average age reported of the software the staff was maintaining was tallied by years up through nine years, then in three groups of 10–11, 12–14, and 15 or more years (see Table II). A no-response group was also tallied for missing data about the average age of the software. The tallies in-

TABLE II—Tabulation of the average estimated age of software maintained

ID**	1	2	3	4	5	6	7–9	10+	12+	15+	NoRsp	Total
					Estimated age in years of the software maintained							
F	0	1	1	2	5	4	3	1	3	2	5	27
N	2	2	2	5	9	7	7	12	2	1	11	60
U	1	1	6	8	13	11	8	4	8	2	9	71
Sum	3	4	9	15	27	22	18	17	13	5	25	158
Y	2	1	4	8	12	11	12	6	5	2	14	77
N	1	3	5	7	15	11	6	11	8	3	11	81

**Notes: F–favorable, N–neutral, U–Unfavorable, Y–"yes" documentation status, N–"no" documentation status, NoRsp–no response, and ID–identification of category.

cluded breakdowns by attitudes and by "yes" and "no" documentation problem reported. A chi square test of attitudes for the extreme ages (less than 4 years and more than 11 years) with the non-extreme ages (4 through 11 years) of the software, accepted the hypothesis (2.85, 2 df). A chi square test of attitudes for old (more than 11 years) with not-old (up through 10 years) software, weakly accepted the hypothesis (4.93, 2 df). A chi square test of attitudes for new (less than 4 years) with old (more than 11 years) software also weakly accepted the hypothesis (4.94, 2 df). A chi square test of attitudes for any specified response with no response on the average age of the software accepted (1.13, 2 df) the hypothesis. All null hypotheses tested for documentation as a problem in relation to the average age of the software were also accepted. The finding is that the average age of the software being maintained has no relatinship with supervisory attitudes, but with a tendency for more polarization of attitudes away from neutral as the software was younger or older than an average of 5 to 6 years, and with no relationship with reporting documentation as a problem.

Null hypothesis 7: The average size of the software programs being maintained has no relationship with supervisory attitudes.

A tally was made of the reported average size in terms of lines of source code of the programs being maintained by the staff (see Table III). As reported sizes increased, the reported precision of the sizes decreased. Hence, tallies of attitudes were made for categories in 500 line intervals through 3,500 lines, in 1,000 line intervals from 4,000 through 10,000 lines, and one category included 11,000 or more lines. Missing size data also were tallied by attitude. Also, tallies were grouped by specific response (such as "2K") and general response (such as "average"). A similar set of tallies was made for size

and documentation. A chi square test for favorable attitude responses by specific, general, and unreported size accepted (0.39, 2 df) the hypothesis. Similar tests for neutral (0.50, 2 df) and unfavorable (0.35, 2 df) attitudes also accepted the hypothesis. All tests involving the specific sizes reported and all tests involving documentation also accepted the null hypothesis. A chi square test for the three attitudes when specific software sizes were reported accepted (0.16, 2 df) the hypothesis, as did tests when general sizes were reported (0.50, 2 df) and when no size response was made (3.57, 2 df). A chi square test for attitudes accepted the hypothesis (1.51, 2 df), for the combination of general and no size responses. The finding is that the average size of the software programs being maintained has no relationship with either supervisory attitudes or reporting documentation as a problem.

Null hypothesis 8: The proportion of corrective maintenance done has no relationship with supervisory attitudes.

Tallies of attitudes and documentation problem status were made by the amount of corrective maintenance reported as a percentage of total software effort (see Table IV). These data were grouped in categories of five-percent increments which centered on percentages ending in zero or five through 50%; the 55%–up category included all items in that category and higher, and the 5% category extended down to include 0%, instead of the expected 3% through 7%. All tests involving attitudes accepted the null hypothesis. Breaking the observed distribution on "yes" and "no" documentation problem reported between the 15% and 20% categories, a chi square test for "yes" with the total distribution of cases taken as the expected, accepted the hypothesis (1.30, 1 df), as did a test for "no" (1.24, 1 df). The finding is that the proportion of corrective maintenance done has no relationship with either supervisory attitudes or reporting documentation as a problem.

TABLE III—Tabulation of the average estimated size of the programs maintained

ID**	<1	1	2	3	4	5	6	7–9	10	11+	N-C	Total
					Estimated size in thousands of lines of source code							
Sum	22	22	35	11	7	4	7	5	4	7	34	158
Y	10	12	19	6	3	1	5	1	2	4	14	77
N	12	10	16	5	4	3	2	4	2	3	20	81

**Notes: F–favorable, N–neutral, U–unfavorable, Y–"yes" documentation status, N–"no" documentation status, N-C–Not enough information to classify, and ID–identification of category.

TABLE IV—Tabulation of the estimated percentage of corrective maintenance done

	Estimated percentage of corrective maintenance done											
ID**	0–7	8–12	13–17	18–22	23–27	28–32	33–37	38–42	43–47	48–53	54–+	Total
F	6	6	3	3	2	3	1	1	0	1	1	27
N	9	20	3	8	7	4	3	3	0	2	1	60
U	11	18	8	13	7	6	2	3	1	1	1	71
Sum	26	44	14	24	16	13	6	7	1	4	3	158
Y	10	22	4	12	7	9	4	5	0	2	2	77
N	16	22	10	12	9	4	2	2	1	2	1	81

** Notes: F–favorable, N–neutral, U–unfavorable, Y–"yes" documentation status, N–"no" documentation status, and ID–identification of category.

Null hypothesis 9: The proportion of development work done has no relationship with supervisory attitudes.

Tallies of attitudes and documentation problem status were made by the amount of development work reported as a percentage of total software effort. These data were grouped by categories of 10-percent increments which centered on percentages ending in two and one-half percent with boundaries from 18% through 87%; the 88%–up category included all items in that category and higher, and the 17% category extended down to include 0%. All tests involving attitudes accepted the null hypothesis. Breaking the observed distribution on "yes" and "no" documentation problem reported between the 57% and 58% categories, a chi square test for "yes" with the total distribution of cases taken as the expected, accepted the hypothesis (1.48, 1 df), as did a test for "no" (1.42, 1 df). The finding is that the proportion of development work done has no relationship with either supervisory attitudes or reporting documentation as a problem.

Null hypothesis 10: The experience level of the personnel doing the maintenance work has no relationship with supervisory attitudes.

Tallies were made of the supervisory attitudes and documentation "yes" or "no" for the reported average levels of staff experience in years (see Table V). The data were grouped in one-year experience categories from 1 through 6 years and in three additional categories: 7–9 years, 10 or more years, and no experience level reported. All tests involving documentation accepted the null hypothesis. For example, a chi square test for "yes" and "no" documentation with experience levels of less than 3 years and 6 or more years of experience accepted the hypothesis (1.24, 1 df). This was also true for tests involving attitudes. For example, a chi square test for attitudes of experience levels of less than 3 years and 6 or more years weakly accepted the hypothesis (4.14, 2 df). The finding is that the experience level of the personnel doing the maintenance work has no relationship with supervisory attitudes, but there is a mild tendency for more polarization of attitudes away from neutral when personnel are more experienced. Also, there is no relationship between experience level and reporting documentation as a problem.

Null hypothesis 11: Supervisor comments concerned with users have no relationship with supervisory attitudes.

An example of supervisor comments received is: "Users set our priorities." The responses were grouped by the dominant content of the responses, the attitudes expressed, and the "yes" or "no" status of the view of documentation (whether or not documentation was reported as a problem). In testing this hypothesis, the expected distribution was taken as the total distribution of the sample—that is, the subgroup was expected to be like the entire group. All tests for documentation status accepted the null hypothesis. A chi square test for attitudes of the comments dealing with users accepted the hypothesis (0.18, 1 df). The finding is that supervisor comments concerned with users have no relationship with either supervisory attitudes or reporting documentaion as a problem.

Null hypothesis 12: Supervisor comments concerned with tools and methods used in maintenance work have no relationship with supervisory attitudes.

TABLE V—Tabulation of the estimated experience level of maintainers

	Estimated experience level in years for the staff									
ID**	1	2	3	4	5	6	7–9	10+	NoRsp	Total
F	4	2	5	6	7	2	1	0	0	27
N	0	11	8	8	11	3	2	10	7	60
U	9	15	9	8	11	8	3	7	1	71
Sum	13	28	22	22	29	13	6	17	8	158
Y	8	11	9	10	16	9	3	8	3	77
N	5	17	13	12	13	4	3	9	5	81

** Notes: F–favorable, N–neutral, U–unfavorable, Y–"yes" documentation status, N–"no" documentation status, NoRsp–no response, and ID–identification of category.

The responses were grouped by the dominant content of the responses, the attitudes expressed, and the "yes" or "no" status of the view of documentation (whether or not documentation was reported as a problem). In testing this hypothesis, the expected distribution was taken as the total distribution of the sample—that is, the subgroup was expected to be like the entire group. All tests for documentation status accepted the null hypothesis. A chi square test for attitudes of the comments dealing with tools and methods accepted the hypothesis (1.85, 1 df). The finding is that supervisor comments concerned with tools and methods used in maintenance work have no relationship with either supervisory attitudes or reporting documentation as a problem.

Null hypothesis 13: Supervisor comments which had no dominant content have no relationship with supervisory attitudes.

An example of a comment with no dominant content is: "Maintenance is here to stay." The responses were grouped by the dominant content of the responses, the attitudes expressed, and the "yes" or "no" status of the view of documentation (whether or not documentation was reported as a problem). In testing this hypothesis, the expected distribution was taken as the total distribution of the sample—that is, the subgroup was expected to be like the entire group. All tests for documentation status accepted the null hypothesis. A chi square test for attitudes of the comments having no dominant content rejected the hypothesis (6.05, 1 df). The finding is that supervisor comments which had no dominant content are associated with neutral supervisory attitudes (a trivial finding) but show no relationship with whether documentation is reported as a problem (a non-trival finding).

Null hypothesis 14: Supervisor comments concerned with personnel motivation have no relationship with supervisory attitudes.

The responses were grouped by the dominant content of the responses, the attitudes expressed, and the "yes" or "no" status of the view of the documentation. In testing this hypothesis, the expected distribution was taken as the total distribution of the sample—that is, the subgroup was expected to be like the entire group. All tests for documentation status accepted the null hypothesis. A chi square test for attitudes of the comments concerning personnel motivation rejected the hypothesis (9.54, 2 df) at the one percent level. The finding is that supervisor comments concerned with personnel motivation showed a lower than expected relationship with neutral attitudes, a higher than expected relationship with negative attitudes toward software maintenance, and no relationship with reporting documentation as a problem.

Null hypothesis 15: Supervisor comments concerned with personnel qualifications have no relationship with supervisory attitudes.

The responses were grouped by the dominant content of the responses, the attitudes expressed, and the "yes" or "no" status of the view of the documentation. In testing this hypothesis, the expected distribution was taken as the total distribution of the sample—that is, the subgroup was expected to be like the entire group. All tests for documentation status accepted the null hypothesis. A chi square test for attitudes of comments concerning personnel qualifications rejected the hypothesis (9.82, 2 df) at the one percent level. The finding is that supervisor comments concerned with personnel qualifications showed a higher than expected relationship with neutral attitudes, a lower than expected relationship with negative attitudes toward software maintenance, and no relationship with reporting documentation as a problem.

CONCLUSIONS

The findings lead to a number of interesting conclusions. In this discussion, *supervisory attitudes* refer to attitudes toward application software maintenance ranging from unfavorable through neutral to favorable. *Documentation status* refers to whether ("yes" or "no") supervisors reported documentation as a problem in application software maintenance. The support for the conclusions offered is the analysis presented in the section on Findings.

One conclusion is that supervisory attitudes have surprisingly little relationship to some of the major factors characterizing the software maintenance environment. Much wailing has been done about how maintenance is made harder by having old code to maintain, by not having good tools and methods, by not having good documentation, by having big programs to maintain, by having users who are hard to work with, by having a high load of corrective maintenance to handle, and by having inexperienced staff to do the maintenance work.[12] Yet, this survey shows these particular factors have no significant relationship with supervisory attitudes. Sharply put, the conclusion means that whether, for instance, old code or new code must be maintained, supervisors appear to be unaffected in their view (favorable or unfavorable) of application software maintenance. Generally, the major factors in the environment which commonly have been regarded as associated with favorable to unfavorable supervisory attitudes are not significant factors. Put in the vernacular, those factors do not get to the supervisor. But if these common factors do not, what does?

A second conclusion is that although documentation status in this sample has no significant association with supervisory attitudes, a tendency appears for favorable supervisory attitudes to be associated with the "no" status, especially when supervisors regard themselves or their organizations as actively doing anything to change the way application software maintenance is handled in their organizations. Although this conclusion supports work that has been reported elsewhere,[5] it raises some interesting questions, such as: Is documentation one of the things supervisors take action on, or is simply doing anything a morale booster so that problems such as the documentation do not loom as large? Are documentation problems a symptom of some less obvious and underlying factors, untapped in this survey, which might be actual determinants of supervisory attitudes?

A third conclusion is that, though not significant in this sample, two factors are associated with a tendency to polarize supervisory attitudes, thereby decreasing the proportion of neutral attitudes. One factor was maintaining application software which was either young or old. The other factor was having experienced staff available for doing maintenace work.

Yet, in both cases, there was no significant relationship with more favorable attitudes, only a tendency to be less neutral. The character of these polarizations suggest that some supervisors may simply be displaying a passive reaction to what they perceive as intractable reality.

A fourth conclusion is that two factors had significant relationships with supervisory attitudes. Negative attitudes were higher and neutral attitudes lower when the supervisory comments concerned personnel motivation. Negative attitudes were lower and neutral attitudes higher when the supervisory comments concerned personnel qualifications. While this conclusion supports work reported elsewhere,[13] both motivation and personnel qualifications are factors over which supervisors actually have substantial influence. Because the relationships here have significance, it may be that some factor unseen in the analysis of this survey is operating in the personnel area and influencing supervisory attitudes.

A fifth and final conclusion is that supervisory attitudes are significantly and far more strongly negative than expected. Such negativity has major effects on managing application software maintenance and on the expectations of higher level and user management. Subordinates are sensitive to and influenced by the attitudes of their supervisors toward the work.[14] When such attitudes are unfavorable, personnel productivity, work quality, morale, motivation, and esprit de corp all typically suffer.[6] If we seek to improve application software maintenance in our organizations, the attitudes held by supervisors demand attention. The findings in this paper offer a groundwork for action.

REFERENCES

1. Lientz, Bennet P., and E. Burton Swanson. *Software Maintenance Management*. Reading Mass: Addison-Wesley, 1980.
2. *Federal Agencies Maintenance of Computer Programs: Expensive and Undermanaged*. Washington DC: Comptroller General, U.S. General Accounting Office, 1981.
3. Martin, Roger J., and Wilma M. Osborne. *Guidance of Software Maintenance*. Washington DC: National Bureau of Standards, 1983.
4. Fjeldstad, R. K., and W. T. Hamlen. "Application program maintenance study." In Parikh and Zvegintzov (eds), *Tutorial on Software Maintenance*. Los Angeles: IEEE-Computer Society, 1983, pp. 13–27.
5. Chapin, Ned. "Software Maintenance: A Different View." *AFIPS, Proceeding of the National Computer Conference* (Volume 54), 1985, pp. 507–513.
6. Drucker, Peter F. *Management: Tasks, Responsibilities, Practices*. New York: Harper and Row, 1974.
7. Tinnirello, Paul C. "Improving Software Maintenance Attitudes." *AFIPS, Proceedings of the National Computer Conference* (Vol. 52), 1983, pp. 107–112.
8. Chapin, Ned. "Software Maintenance Objectives." *AFIPS, Proceedings of the National Computer Conference* (Vol. 52), 1983, pp. 779–784.
9. Parikh, Girish, and Nicholas Zvegintzov. "The World of Software Maintenance." *Tutorial on Software Maintenance*, Los Angeles: IEEE Computer Society Press, 1983, pp. 1–3.
10. Ary, Donald, Lucy Chester Jocobs, and Asghar Razavieh. *Introduction to Research in Education*. New York: CBS College Publishing, 1985.
11. Hopkins, Kenneth D., and Julian C. Stanley. *Educational and Psychological Measurement and Evaluation*. Englewood Cliffs, New Jersey: Prentice-Hall, 1981.
12. Parikh, Girish (ed.). *Techniques of Program and System Maintenance*. Lincoln, Neb: Ethnotech, Inc., 1980.
13. Couger, Daniel J., and Mel A. Colter. *Maintenance Programming*. Englewood Cliffs, New Jersey: Prentice-Hall, 1985.
14. Chapin, Ned. "Productivity in Software Maintenance." *AFIPS, Proceedings of the National Computer Conference* (Vol. 50), 1983, pp. 349–352.

Reprinted from *IEEE Transactions on Software Engineering*,
Volume SE-13, Number 3, March 1987, pages 311-323.

Understanding Software Maintenance Work

SALAH BENDIFALLAH AND WALT SCACCHI, MEMBER, IEEE

Abstract—Software maintenance can be successfully accomplished if the computing arrangements of the people doing the maintenance are compatible with their established patterns of work in the setting. To foster and achieve such compatibility requires an understanding of the reasons and the circumstances in which participants carry out maintenance activities. In particular, it requires an understanding of how software users and maintainers act toward the changing circumstances and unexpected events in their work situation that give rise to software system alterations. To contribute to such an understanding, we describe a comparative analysis of the work involved in maintaining and evolving text-processing systems in two academic computer science organizations. This analysis shows that how and why software systems are maintained depends on occupational and workplace contingencies, and vice versa.

Index Terms—Articulation work, computing milieux, maintenance work, primary work, social analysis of computing, software evolution, software maintenance, software productivity, text-processing.

I. Introduction

SOFTWARE maintenance is complex and costly. Maintenance activities are estimated to take up more than half of the life-cycle cost of software systems [7], [25]. Yet software maintenance remains the least understood and most problematic part of the software process.

Reducing the cost of software maintenance entails understanding the various kinds of alterations that people make to software systems and providing tools for carrying out these alterations. But more importantly, we believe it entails understanding the circumstances that give rise to why alterations are made, how they are performed, and how these circumstances are tied to the evolution of the *work arrangements* in the setting: the organization and distribution of productive resources (computers, software tools, skills, time, money, computer facility staff, etc.) committed to supporting current work activities, the constraints upon use of these resources, and how people work within these constraints to transform the resources into finished products or services [11], [30], [10].

A common classification of alterations [40], [27], [13], [28], [1], [41] distinguishes *corrective, adaptive, perfective, and preventive* alterations according to their *immediate* causes, the evolution of system requirements or the inadequacy of the current system. Adaptive, perfective, and preventive activities are typically considered en-

Manuscript received September 2, 1985; revised February 11, 1986. This work was supported by AT&T Information Systems, TRW Defense Systems Group, and IBM through Project Socrates at USC.

The authors are with the Department of Computer Science, University of Southern California, Los Angeles, CA 90089.

IEEE Log Number 8610901.

hancement activities. They are the major share of maintenance work, consuming as much as 75 percent or more of maintenance time [25]. This is especially true in cases where maintenance is *an afterthought* and an explicitly separate phase of the software life-cycle, completely independent from development. The recognition of enhancement as the dominant maintenance activity has given rise to a new approach to software engineering, where incremental system enhancement is deemed the main software activity and hence tools and methods are devised which reclaim maintenance into the realm of development activities [2], [33], [3].

However, further emphasis on tools cannot alone solve the problems of software maintenance. Merely mobilizing technical means cannot suffice to solve what appear to be more fundamental problems concerning the reasons systems are altered and the conditions under which they are altered. Maintenance activities are labor intensive and involve programming as well as nonprogramming tasks. Enhancement activities, in particular, depend on work arrangements in the organizational setting. Thus, following the introduction of the new enhancement tools, demands on work arrangements must be shifted for assuring that these tools can be effectively utilized, in particular for assuring that such tools can be successfully *fit* into the routine work practices of the setting [30].

Our purpose in this paper is to contribute to a better understanding of the fundamental aspects of software maintenance *work*. Specifically, we want to understand *the ways local circumstances in the workplace affect how and why people perform software maintenance tasks*, and conversely, *how maintenance work affects workplace arrangements*. Local circumstances include the incentives and constraints for *why* people alter their software systems, and indicate *when* people act to maintain their systems. The workplace specifies *where* maintenance work is performed and the ways it is organized. *How* people order and perform their maintenance work also entails *who* does this work, and *what* kind of maintenance activity is performed.

We present an empirical analysis of two cases of comparable software systems in similar organizations. The case studies concern the evolution of text-processing systems in two academic computer science organizations, CSD and CSRO.[1] CSD [5], [6] is the computer science department of a major university, and CSRO [17], [30], [18] is the computer science research organization at-

[1]We use pseudonyms throughout.

tached to another major university. Our choice to examine the evolution of similar software systems in similar settings is an attempt to mitigate the influence of many potentially confounding variables.

We use the CSD and CSRO cases to illustrate the kind of analytical detail needed to understand why and how software maintenance work is accomplished. These two cases alone cannot represent how software maintenance work is performed in every organization. However, our research design (presented in Appendix) provides an analytical framework for generalizing our findings and assessing findings from related research. Subsequently, insofar as any model or systematic account of software maintenance work can be assessed in terms of our research design, it should also be able to account for the kind of activities and situations we describe.

The thrust of our analysis is to explicitly consider the work situation in which a software system evolves. Rather than examining maintenance work by focusing on the features of the system itself, we explicitly consider the co-evolution of the participants' work tasks with their local work arrangements.

We start our investigation in Section II by examining what the people who use software systems do as their *primary work*. Their involvement in particular tasks typically matches either some current occupational or career interest, or some circumstantial commitment which must be met in order to pursue other work activities. Primary work includes all the tasks for which a person is explicitly responsible and rewarded. Ideally, these tasks are in line with each person's interests in the organization (e.g., professional advancement) and are tasks each person would rather concentrate on if given full discretion. At CSD and CSRO, most participants are computing specialists whose primary work includes computer science research work. Research publications and related technical documents are an important, professionally recognized product of this kind of work (cf. [19]). The use of a text-processing system is central to the production of these reports.[2]

We examine how CSD and CSRO participants use the text-processing systems to accomplish their primary work. Each text-processing task at CSD and CSRO has some relationship to tasks performed or controlled by other participants. At any time, the successful coordination of these interlocking tasks depends on a variety of social and technical arrangements. The work required to coordinate and align these arrangements to accomplish the tasks at hand is called *articulation work* [39], [10], [37], [9]. This is the focus of our investigation in Section III. In particular, we investigate the participants' activities when their primary work tasks get *dis*-articulated. In both settings, different kinds of *re*-articulation work emerge in response to unexpected breakdowns in the organization of primary work. Participants choose one of two alternatives. The first is to take the system as a *fait accompli* and *accom-*

modate the way they work to the way the system operates within local computing arrangements. The other is to make changes in the system as well as in the work arrangements, i.e., negotiate the appropriate maintenance alteration to be performed and who will carry out the work. Consequently, *how and why software maintenance work is performed depends on how the related articulation work is accomplished.*

We develop this conclusion in Section IV by examining the similarities and differences between the two cases. The evolutionary courses of the two systems diverge. At CSRO, the text-processing system evolves into multiple user-personalized configurations, and all maintenance work on the system is performed by the users themselves in a loosely coupled manner. At CSD, the text-processing system evolves so that a dominant configuration emerges. The original user/maintainer of this configuration develops a reputation of expertise, and maintenance work on the system thereby becomes this person's primary work through an opportune career option. For us, the divergence between the two evolutionary courses indicates a relationship of *mutual influence* between the circumstances of maintenance work, the participants' strategies for prioritizing the demands of their work, and the incentives for and constraints on these demands.

Last, in Section V, we discuss related research and then conclude in Section VI with a summary of our findings and their implications for understanding software maintenance work.

II. PRIMARY WORK

We first examine a primary work activity at CSD and CSRO, the production of research publications. Next, we survey the work arrangements which supported this activity. Then, we examine the text-processing tasks which CSD and CSRO participants performed and coordinated in carrying out this activity.

A. Primary Work at CSD and CSRO

Users of the text-processing systems at CSD and CSRO were typical of those found in academic computer science organizations: faculty, project managers, research associates, graduate assistants, systems support staff, and administrative and clerical staff. At the outset of each academic term, faculty, graduate students, and research associates might join or leave. Systems support staff as well as members of the managerial, administrative, and clerical staff could, on the other hand, leave or join at any time.

At CSD and CSRO, the process of producing a research publication emerged from the shared construction of an idea or alternate work arrangement (hereafter, *concept*) deemed a departure from practices described in related publications (cf. [19]). The concept would pass through several stages of development. From stage to stage, it took on forms such as conversational conjectures, informal debates and clarifications, notes, memoranda, overhead projection transparencies, group presentations, preliminary

---

[2]In fact, regular use of most computing applications leads to the production of reports, listings, and formatted displays of one kind or another.

drafts, and polished technical reports. In addition, some researchers constructed software systems and related documentation in pursuing their concept, often to a point where their software development work would dominate the effort they would commit to producing research publications.[3] At any stage, any number of participants could (un)knowingly collaborate in the process of constructing the publication. Similarly, at any stage, the process could be put off when unexpected circumstances arose that sidetracked or derailed the participants' interest in the concept.

The actual manner in which a concept was investigated was bound to the career contingencies of the computing participants involved. A junior researcher could adopt a concept and work on it to solve a particular problem at hand, often in connection with an ongoing project and a senior researcher. For example, a graduate student decided to develop a knowledge-based program explanation system to further his interest in advancing knowledge-based systems technology, as part of the reknown FOO project. In such cases, the concept might evolve no farther than an internal report, technical memoranda, or other related artifacts (e.g., a concept demonstration system) unless the researchers believed their research findings were substantial enough to further develop, publish, and circulate. What followed was an explicit collaboration and commitment between the researchers to "get the machine out the door" (cf. [14]) by producing a professional-quality report that could be disseminated to colleagues.

Initial dissemination took place among local research and discussion groups, where the potential publication was circulated, critiqued, debated, and revised. Researchers could utilize available networks (social, professional, and electronic) to announce an emergent publication "in press" or "in preparation," or otherwise bring the attention of prospective readers to the emergence of the publication. Public distribution occurred when the publication was circulated through the appropriate marketplace of ideas as a technical report, an article in a professional journal, or a monograph. This marketplace included other academic organizations where participants strove to stay abreast of research developments by colleagues pursuing similar research and publications.

When a publication was distributed and cited in the professional literature and among cohorts, the resulting recognition enabled new professional opportunities for the publication's authors, and contributed to furthering their reputations and that of their organization. These outcomes carved out a rather pivotal role for the text-processing systems used at CSD and CSRO. These systems encompassed the computational resources used to produce intermediate and final versions of emerging professional

publications. We describe them next as we review the work arrangements in each setting.

B. The Work Arrangements and Text-Processing Systems

We first examine the incentives which sustained the participant's primary work at CSD and CSRO, then describe the computing infrastructure which both facilitated and constrained accomplishment of this work.

Participants' Incentives: The focal incentives of most participants at CSD and CSRO were shaped by shared commitments to create and publish valuable research results. These commitments were renewed through the actions of individual researchers, collegial reference groups, academic units/universities, professional associations, and research funding agencies. Through carefully prepared and revised publications of research results, participants could:

- experience the self-satisfying accomplishment of a job well done, a new entry in their curriculum vita, and the pride in personally distributing copies to friends and colleagues;
- increase their professional status and reputation when recognized as making a significant contribution, and in turn, increase their influence in their academic community;
- establish or reinforce their identity with an invisible college of scholarly cohorts via cocitation and joint authorship;
- help gain promotion, salary increases, and a larger share of resources allocated within their academic unit, or job offers elsewhere;
- achieve widespread reproduction of the publication, increase their professional visibility, make public conference presentations, receive ceremonial awards (for special accomplishments), and achieve bibliographic archival all through the sustaining publication activities of professional associations (e.g., ACM, IEEE); and
- establish and maintain a conduit for resources flowing from funding agencies that in turn were acknowledged for their support and stimulation of the work leading to research publications.

Accordingly, participants regularly assessed which ensemble of these outcomes motivated their effort to produce a research publication.

Computing Facilities: CSD's and CSRO's participants used local computing resources in a manner commensurate with their level of research funding and their position in the organization. Not all users had computer terminals and high-quality printers readily accessible, nor did they all have the same allocation of system resources such as computing cycles and on-line disk storage space.

At CSD, all participants had free use of local computing facilities managed by the department. There was a terminal in an office for each faculty member and systems

---

[3]While participants at both CSRO and CSD might normally develop software systems as part of their primary work, at the time of our studies, researchers would more often receive professional rewards and promotions based on the publication of their concepts, rather than on only their demonstration of a concept by a software system.

programmer, and a shared terminal in each office for graduate students or research associates. Additional computing resources were available elsewhere within the university on a "pay as you go" basis to those who could afford it (mostly faculty with research grants and their research assistants). One such resource was a large time-shared system dedicated to text-processing, which we call the "pay" machine, in contrast to CSD's own "free" machine.

The communication facilities available to CSD participants for automatically distributing their documents or messages included three major electronic mail components. ZIP, the local mail system and NZIP, which handled nationwide network mail, were acquired from outside vendors. CEDEX, an integrated mail system, was later developed locally by Dr. T., a junior faculty member who wanted an integrated mail handling system. Because he sent and received mail on both the local area and the national computer network, he found separate mail burdensome and decided, after consulting with a few regular users, to unify the functions of ZIP and NZIP into a single software system.

At CSRO, computer terminals were provided by individual research projects according to thier funding arrangements; bigger projects had a larger staff and more terminals than smaller projects. Users in small or unfunded projects were often particularly pressed when many users in the large projects were also computing. Use of disk storage space and computing cycles on CSRO's single time-sharing machine was regulated by an allocation scheme enforced by a dedicated MONITOR program and an automatic file ARCHIVE facility.

Four other system components supported text-processing tasks at CSRO. NETMAIL, an integrated mail handling system, was acquired from another organization. BB, a bulletin board facility used as a repository of project communications and other public notices, was developed locally by users. The ARCHIVE utility was developed by local computer facility programmers to automatically store unused computer files (e.g., old documents or source program codes). Last, the MONITOR program was developed by the computer facility manager as a means to keep users from exceeding their allocated amounts of computer time or storage space and to invoke ARCHIVE whenever these amounts were exceeded.

These computing arrangements formed the backbone of the text-processing system in each setting. We now describe how the text-processing system components became part of each setting's work arrangements to support the participants' primary work, the production of research publications.

The Text-Processing Systems: The text-processing systems used at CSD and CSRO were distinguished mainly by the fact that they had evolved over different periods of time. Both systems had originally been developed outside of their setting of use. In both settings, the adoption of text-processing system components, communication components, and other supporting facilities was straightfor-

ward. Some parts came bundled with the computer system (from the system's manufacturer), while other parts were bought or brought in and adapted by eager users. At CSD, the text-processing system had been acquired from outside for local use and maintenance only one year prior to the time of study. In contrast, at the time of the study, some components of the text-processing system used at CSRO had a five-year history in the setting, during which they had undergone substantial in-house redevelopment for local use and maintenance.

The TEPS text-processing system we investigated at CSD had two major components: a screen-oriented text-editor (TEDS) and a text-formatter (TEFS). Both were developed at another academic computer science organization and were user-modifiable in order to fit into different patterns of use. TEDS was an extensible system, but had many idiosyncratic features which made it complex for some to learn. Installed on CSD's free machine in March 1984, TEDS had since been revised to mitigate its complexity. Nevertheless, CSD users still faced a tradeoff between its extensibility and its idiosyncratic features. TEFS was developed for computing users who produce technical academic manuscripts. It was first developed in 1978, and began to reach a broader community of users during 1979. By September 1984, TEFS was installed on CSD's free machine. Participants who had to access the pay machine primarily to use TEFS could then migrate to the free machine, with the prospect of continuing their established patterns of text-processing at a lower cost. Within a year, many CSD participants were using TEDS and TEFS on the free machine with sufficient frequency as to often bog down system performance during office hours.

The text-processing system components at CSRO were operational and in routine use at the onset of our inquiry in 1978. The most used components of the text-processing system included screen-oriented text-editors and the NEAT text-formatter. The text-processing components formed an eclectic ensemble of user-specific configurations developed locally in an *ad hoc* and fragmented manner. When the main computer system was installed at CSRO, it came with two line-oriented text-editors and one text-formatter supplied by the vendor. Different users imported screen-oriented text-editing, text-formatting, and other text-processing programs from other compatible computing facilities. The design history of these various text-processing tools was fragmented and hard to reconstruct. Also, there was no overall system design to coordinate the use of different system components. Consequently, the efforts to implement and modify the text-processing system at CSRO followed an unplanned trajectory based on individual participants' needs, interests, and dispositions.

The researchers' primary work with these text-processing systems at CSD and CSRO was typically organized into sequences of small tasks or *task chains* involving the computing resources available in the setting [30]. We examine task chains next.

C. Task Chains

A researcher's primary work with the text-processing system did not always require using the text-formatter. The text-editor alone would be used to produce documents intended for limited distribution within the working group of the author(s). Such documents required no more than an ''acceptable'' quality presentation. The text-formatter was usually used when it was necessary or desired to produce a document with ''nice'' quality presentation intended for outside distribution. The chains of text-processing tasks involved in a researcher's primary work mobilized a number of other computing resources, such as terminals, printers, and electronic mail systems. Depending on the current work arrangements, a text-processing task chain could materialize in different forms [30]. The following is an example of such a task chain:[4]

1) get access to a computer terminal;
2) gain access to the system;
3) create or alter text files with a text-editor;
4) format the text files;
5) obtain a formatted and printer-ready version of the files and verify that formatting/type setting is as desired;
6) gain access to a suitable printer and get the document printed;
7) verify that the formatting obtained is as expected; and
8) repeat any appropriate subchain until satisfaction or bottleneck.

Users of the text-processing systems at CSD and CSRO usually expected to perform and complete these tasks without any problem. However, should a system bug or any other interruption[5] arise in the current work arrangements, each user was responsible for bringing about whatever actions were necessary to carry out her/his task chain to completion. The more familiar the path down a task chain and the fewer the interruptions which *dis*-articulated the task chain, the less the amount of articulation work a user had to commit to doing in order to produce a document in the desired form. We examine this articulation work in the next section.

III. ARTICULATION WORK

In a routine excursion down a document-preparation task chain, users knew the various system operations and other actions to be performed. Otherwise, when unforeseen problems disarticulated the task chain, users consulted system documentation or other system users for cooperation in completing the task chain. We examine first

---

[4]Other examples of text-processing task chains can be found in [10], [18], [30].
[5]Such interruptions included running out of printer paper, jamming of the printer and consequent destruction of the current document copy, accidental deletion of the current document file, errant editor keystrokes that deleted emerging text, retrieving files that were automatically archived, encountering a high level of demand for shared computing resources, printer hardware failure, or an operating system crash.

how the successful completion of a primary work task chain gave rise to articulation activities and then examine the different forms of these articulation activities.

A. Task Chain Breakdowns Spawn Articulation Work

Completing a primary work task chain successfully is inherently nontrivial. Even though the task chain may be readily described and understood at some appropriate level of abstraction (e.g., our earlier description of a text-processing task chain), it is more accurately an *emergent* process. It is enacted somewhat differently in each particular work instance as the involved participant(s) may see fit to respond to contingencies in work arrangements [10].

At CSD and CSRO, whenever the excursion down a text-processing task chain became problematic—such as when the commitments of resources (including people) to some task chain were not met, when interruptions or bottlenecks were encountered—some articulation work had to be performed before the task chain could be resumed (either where it was stopped or as befitted the work arrangements resulting from the interruption). As the user of the text-processing system or the cooperative participants acted to resume the task chain, further problems could arise, leading to the emergence of more articulation work.

To understand the consequences of this emergent process for the eventual completion of a text-processing task chain and the subsequent effect on the user's primary work, let us consider a typical scenario of breakdown of a task chain and consequent emergence of articulation work at CSD. This scenario is summarized in Fig. 1, where the annotations in italics (corresponding to the underlined parts of the description) represent examples of articulation work.

Typically, a user's first response to a bottleneck was to try to accommodate to the new situation by initiating a quick remedial action. However, this response was not always successful. The user would then seek appropriate help from other nearby participants (e.g., another researcher, a member of the clerical staff, a member of the official maintenance staff). Getting help, however, required some negotiating since most participants were preoccupied with their own tasks. In the unfortunate circumstance where the user ended up being left to her own means, she would attempt to work around the difficulty. When this was not possible or not successful, the user would try some other means to work toward a solution by a reasonable deadline. In turn, this often resulted in postponing completion of the current task chain and switching to another, depending on the user's schedule and dispositions. Working around the problem often required further unexpected accommodation activities and sometimes even gave rise to some other (sub-)task chain. Moreover, getting someone to devote what could amount to a substantial effort to obtain a solution by a particular deadline required negotiation. If none of the above alternatives could be achieved, the user's last resort was to completely restructure the task chain—if possible, so as to bypass the

Example: The printer paper box is empty on the evening before the research report must be submitted to meet a publication deadline.

Can I do something quickly about the bottleneck?
If so then do it and resume the (sub)task chain;
  (*load more printer paper, then print the report*)
  if not can I get immediate help from someone who knows what to do?
    (*find someone who knows how to load more printer paper*)
  if so then do it and resume the (sub)task chain;
    (*print the report*)
  if not can I afford to postpone work on this task chain?
    (*can the report be delivered late without much hassle*)
  if not then immediately attempt a work-around
    (*the report must be sent out the next day by Express mail; so find another printer, move the document files to a backup system, or move to a typewriter*)
    and resume the task chain;
  if so can I get someone else to work on it by a reasonable deadline?
    (*ask a graduate student to retrieve and load printer paper, and then make sure the printer is operating correctly*)
  if so then postpone the rest of the task chain until the fix is made and switch to an alternate task chain;
    (*e.g., update a bibliography file*)
  if not can I fix it myself by some reasonable deadline?
    (*procure enough printer paper and install it right away*)
  if so then postpone the rest of the task chain until the fix is made;
  if not attempt to restructure the task chain
    (*send a letter explaining the delay*)
    and propose to routinize the handling of the interruption via a software enhancement.
    (*modify the system to keep track of the number of pages printed since previous refill, and to notify users when queued paper is running low.*)

Fig. 1. A summary description of articulation activities emerging from a resource bottleneck in a task chain.

interruption and render it ineffectual. Then, if office support or maintenance support was available, the user would try to negotiate with the support participant(s) an appropriate enhancement to the text-processing system itself or the work arrangements in the setting, depending on the nature of the bottleneck in the text-processing task chain.

The foregoing scenario highlights the nature of articulation work and its relationship to maintenance work at CSD and CSRO. It illustrates the cooperative activities necessary to deal with unforeseen problems in a person's primary work task chain, i.e., to *re*-articulate the report production task chain. In particular, it underscores the accommodations and negotiations inherent in bringing about commitments to accomplish maintenance activities in a setting. At CSD and CSRO, we found these two basic types of articulation activities:

1) Accommodation activities, whereby participants readily attempt to adapt their patterns of work to the constraints imposed by the current behavior of the text-processing system and other resources involved in the task chain;

2) Negotiation of maintenance activities, whereby participants seek to alter the text-processing system and other resources involved in the task chain to perform according to their expectations or desires.

We next describe each of these two types of articulation activities in turn.[6]

---

[6]These two types of articulation activities can also be viewed as special kinds of *fitting* work, whereby participants seek to establish a good fit between their patterns of work and the work arrangements in the setting [30], [10].

B. Accommodation Work

Accommodation work emerged when users faced contingencies in their primary work, and responded by doing their work in a way compatible with these contingencies. Researchers at CSD and CSRO considered the production of professional documents an important goal. They sought efficient resources arrangements and effective patterns of work to achieve this goal. Therefore, they eagerly adopted text-processing software tools and resources that could reduce their work. They also preferred to adapt and reshape the way they did their work rather than invest more time, skill, and effort to correct system flaws such as design errors and maintenance inadequacies. Similarly, as shown in the example of the previous section, users accommodated resource contingencies by restructuring their patterns of work.

New CSD and CSRO participants did a good amount of accommodation work when they arrived. They had to adjust their prior patterns of work to fit the local computing arrangements and learn to utilize the available resources as they prepared their reports. Yet there often was no single source of information or documentation which described the use of these systems in a manner adapted to their level of knowledge. Thus they learned to work with these facilities and to (re)structure their work patterns by interactive use (exploration) of the system, or through interaction and negotiation with other computer users.

Both experienced and new users saw their accommodation work as a component of their productivity. Their concern for productivity was reflected in the strategy that guided their accommodation work: they naturally sought to minimize their effort at restructuring their patterns of work while maximizing the contribution of this restructuring to their primary work activities and purposes.

Accommodation Work at CSD: A common accommodation activity at CSD, which entailed a minimal restructuring of work patterns, was to copy a configuration from an experienced user, especially if it seemed to take care of "just about everything you would want to do for the moment" as one user put it.

Some users went a long way in restructuring their patterns of work. As they became more knowledgeable about the work arrangements, in particular about system limitations and resource constraints, they created their own TEFS configurations. Some participants did so because they believed this would also result in less articulation work thereafter. Others did so to simply avoid the hassle of learning many features that may turn out to be of little use. Still other users engaged in extensive accommodation work in response to compelling institutional constraints, such as the constraint to format their publications according to a particular journal's guidelines. For example, a junior faculty member, Dr. T., brought in files of his unfinished dissertation when he joined CSD. He had to reformat this document with TEFS in order to take advantage of the facility, but needed at the same time to create his own document configuration tailored to the dissertation publication format appropriate to his university of origin.

As newcomers established or restructured their work patterns to take advantage of TEPS, they typically invested as little time as possible in learning useful TEPS features. Instead, they would usually ask an experienced user, but preferably a user who had been at CSD only a short time. This kind of experienced user usually could relate to the new participant's frustrations with more sympathy than an "older" user. More often than not, she/he knew a sufficient yet not overwhelming number of useful features.

Accommodation Work at CSRO: An accommodation activity common to most users was simply to chart out the location of system deficiencies (including "traps," "mazes," and "black holes") as they discovered them and to structure the content of text-processing tasks so as to avoid the charted features.[7]

CSRO participants who were more knowledgeable about system limitations and resource constraints (re)structured their patterns of work by developing their own combinations of NEAT macro routines. After that, they often believed the additional work of maintaining their individual configuration was worth the savings in articulation work avoided. Some participants also developed their own NEAT configurations to satisfy specific formatting needs by using suitable versions of appropriate programs.

Newcomers at CSRO and other new users of NEAT often preferred to treat NEAT as a black box and rely on the help of experienced users to manage, minimize, or avoid NEAT hassles. As one participant remarked, "NEAT can be nice. But there are a lot of idiosyncracies that are a pain . . . As I use it more, I run into more of them. If you want to do something exotic, you have to find somebody who knows it. For example, there are some hassles to using special characters. You have to know how to use them. They're not in the manual." This know-how was available only from experienced users.

CSRO participants also engaged in cooperative accommodation activities when dealing with other resources involved in text-processing task chains. For example, unexpected bugs transpired at some point in the behavior of the NETMAIL system. Many of its regular users tried to figure out what had gone wrong with it. Eventually, their cooperation led to a common diagnosis of the problem. However, rather than relying on expectedly lengthy negotiations with the computer facility maintainers and delaying the use of the facility until maintenance work could be performed, users chose instead to continue to use it as it was and accommodated themselves to its erratic, mysterious, and sometimes frustrating performance.

Among the variety of accommodation activities at CSD and CSRO, the most common sought to avoid, circumvent, or undo adverse system effects due to bugs and idiosyncracies in the text-processing system. However, users might eventually believe they simply could not get satisfaction from the system as it was. They would then negotiate system repairs and enhancements. This was a more resource-consuming kind of articulation work, as we show next.

C. Negotiation of Maintenance Work

Use of the text-processing system at CSD and CSRO generated maintenance activities both on the text-processing system itself and on the other computing facilities involved in a document production task chain. We describe in turn the two kinds of maintenance and related negotiations in each setting in turn.

Maintenance Work at CSD: At CSD, maintenance work on the text-processing system itself was performed by one of the researchers, Dr. T. As we saw in looking at participants' accommodation activities, many users started off with TEPS by adopting and adapting another user's configuration as a way of creating their own. These users subsequently maintained these configurations privately and separately from other users. This meant they would spend time and effort on activities that would distract or contribute little to the production of their research publications.

As an illustration, Dr. T. needed to handle the work-in-progress he had brought in from the computer science department from which he was trying to graduate.[8] How-

---

[7]The development of such accommodation experience and skill is coincidentally a strategy often practiced by users of computer games such as *Adventure*, *Zork*, and other fantasy exploration games.

[8]He would eventually spend more than one year revising his dissertation without completing any other research publications in the interim.

ever, his documents were formatted in macro-routines that did not work on the CSD system, and he did not know how to use either TEDS or TEFS. With the encouragement of two senior colleagues who were enthusiastic users of TEFS on the pay machine, he decided to "bring up" TEFS on the free machine and use it to reformat his documents. He spent much of his time during the Summer of 1984 in reading the manual "from beginning to end." He then realized that he needed to increase the character set supplied by the vendor and that the only way to do so was to augment the TEFS database. He thus had to read the manual for database administrators. Before long, he had learned just about everything there was to learn concerning TEFS. Literally, he had made himself the "resident expert" in TEFS, and had come to be perceived, for all practical purposes, as its *de facto* maintainer. Later, he also came to be considered the expert maintainer of TEDS, the text-editing component of TEPS, through what he saw as his other "contribution to the (research) lab" at CSD. He had developed CEDEX, the integrated mail handling system, by extending TEDS to unify the functions of ZIP and NZIP, respectively, the local mail system and the national network mail system.

As a result of his work, Dr. T.'s expertise in system maintenance was often taken as evidence of official responsibility for enhancement activities. Nevertheless Dr. T. did not consider himself totally bound to maintaining the text-processing system. In the face of too many users' requests for fixes or enhancements, he pinpointed the fact that "most of the work is actually done by a few people." As he put it, "now, I would still give away the knowledge . . . but after all, this is not what I am getting paid to do." He had to balance competing career demands and current work contingencies—i.e., teaching and research (his official primary work) versus maintenance activities. However, he was ready for the right opportunity to engage in a radical enhancement to TEDS, including a complete redesign, which he saw as the prime modification to TEPS really worth making. In the meantime, in negotiating other user requests for a modification, he considered whether there was a general need for the modification, how easily it could be accomplished and, often above all, "how people asked."

Meanwhile, work on the local computing facilities at CSD was the primary work of a resident systems programmer. His primary work included making sure that the facilities were always operational by maintaining the machine, its peripherals, the operating system, and other computing equipment such as personal workstations. In addition, he was officially in charge of maintaining the mail system. He maintained CEDEX (the TEDS-based component of the mail system) in consultation with Dr. T. The systems programmer's decisions on fixes and enhancements were "not based on a vote by the user community" and not very likely to be influenced by negotiating. He would typically make an enhancement on his own initiative, most likely "when it is easy to do, for even the enhancement aspect of maintenance work is often

nuisance work." He would then make the enhancement available to the participants who could, at their discretion, either exploit it or do without it. Rarely, he would make an enhancement in response to users' demands, also depending, in his words, on "how people ask and how easy it is to do."

As a rule, neither the resident systems programmer nor Dr. T. would implement a proposed enhancement if it were not intended to compensate for a flaw in the system. Flaws in the system included things such as unintended side effects of a TEDS command or unforeseen consequences of a previous enhancement decision. Both maintainers accorded the lowest priority to flaws which were more readily controllable by the users. The examples of such flaws they cited included patterns of use which did not accommodate the way the system actually worked and proposed enhancements which corresponded to a system "behavior which the user could achieve by some workaround." From the perspective of both maintainers, making enhancements selectively helped prevent the system from going beyond the bounds of manageable complexity.

Eventually, Dr. T. was asked by the senior researchers at CSD to become the main person responsible for the maintenance of the TEPS and all other research support systems at CSD. As he was increasingly spending more of his time and effort in modifying systems that helped him and others produce their research publications, this change of position from faculty to research staff was agreed to after he received assurances from the senior researchers as to CSD's long-term commitment to his new position.

Maintenance Work at CSRO: In contrast to CSD, maintenance activities on the text-processing system at CSRO were distributed across the user community. Maintenance work on NEAT, the dominant text-formatter, was performed solely by the users themselves, with no one in particular having the official responsibility for maintaining the whole system. According to one participant, "actually, it's not maintained at all." Different users indicated that no one at CSRO really knew everything about how the original program worked. Nearly all users reported that NEAT was rife with bugs. Some readily pointed out what they considered to be system design flaws: system bugs, missing features, irrelevant system features, awkward stylistic conventions, and poor system performance characteristics. Some of the system flaws may have resulted from the method of implementation (e.g., insufficient testing) by the system builders. Bugs and idiosyncracies were not fixed, but the system was somehow being used. Most bugs were found through testing with real data. Users attempted an action they believed to be correct, as indicated by someone else or by the system documentation, and found that some unexpected system behavior resulted. The documentation for NEAT was roughly five years old and not updated to reflect maintenance alterations. This led to some problems for users who acquired an intermediate version of the

NEAT program that had been altered without the documentation being changed accordingly.

What resulted from the fact that no one was explicitly assigned to maintain NEAT was that many different sets of NEAT macros were implemented by capable users to get around the bugs they encountered. The resulting routines also had to be maintained. Furthermore, some users were willing to enhance versions of certain programs to satisfy their specific needs. These routines were likely to conform to the particular needs of some, but not all, users. Multiple versions of the NEAT text-formatting system were in use, and their users became system maintainers in order to keep their running version up to date with their patterns of use. In addition, many of the added NEAT macro routines were incompatible or redundant. This gave rise to new system maintenance demands, such as the upkeep of NEAT bug-avoidance macro libraries. Yet, most users felt that the more time and other resources they could avoid spending on support activities, the better. They saw maintenance activities as only a necessary burden, distinguished from "real" computing work, i.e., system use or development.

Maintenance work on the local computing facilities at CSRO was the primary work of a specific support group. The group's official responsibility included maintenance work on the resources supporting test-processing task chains—e.g., machine and operating system, terminals, printers, mail system (NETMAIL), bulletin board (BB), file archiving facility (ARCHIVE), and computer use monitoring system (MONITOR). But the members of this group did not assume responsibility for maintaining NEAT, nor were they involved in acquiring or developing it.

D. Articulation Work Can Become Primary Work

At both CSRO and CSD, we observed that recurring accommodation and negotiation activities could lead to these activities becoming a regular part of someone's primary work. At both CSRO and CSD, a number of users (although not a majority) developed software systems in pursuing the development of their research concepts. For these people, software development work was a form of their primary work, much like their production of research publications. This was no surprise, for in academic computer science organizations such as CSRO and CSD, many of the research publications produced emerged as a result of the development of a software system concept that in turn would be documented in related research publications. However, not all software development work was done to develop research concepts suitable for publication.

At CSRO, a number of junior researchers developed NEAT macro routines to better customize the text processing system to fit both their style of work and the idiosyncracies of this system. In turn, these software routines were usually undocumented, but normally within the immediate comprehension of their user-developers. Accordingly, the circumstances at CSRO were such that devel-

oping and maintaining one's own NEAT macro routines became an infrequent, but otherwise regular part of the work researchers would perform in developing their concepts. But no publication we examined mentioned the development of NEAT macros as an essential part of their research concept. Thus, the development of NEAT macros represented a necessary but undocumented part of these researchers' primary work.

At CSD, the circumstances were different. Here we observed that the primary work of Dr. T. grew from his efforts to produce a publishable form of his research results (his dissertation). In order to produce this publication, he had to both modify his source documents and TEPS so that he could format his publication according to another institution's guidelines. He acquired extensive knowledge of TEPS, as well as other electronic mail system components. As it seemed that he was predisposed to modifying these software systems as a major part of his work, then work on these publication support systems was a natural extension to this line of work. When senior researchers recognized Dr. T.'s expertise with TEPS, his disposition towards spending more effort in modifying software systems over the development of research publications, and their need to find someone to maintain the system that supported their primary work, they acted to create a new research staff position that Dr. T. would then occupy. This action reinforced Dr. T.'s preference to develop software over publications, and reduced the senior researchers effort to continually negotiate and accommodate to quirks and features of TEPS. Thus, in this regard, what started as accommodation work for Dr. T. eventually became a regular part of his primary work, via an opportunity to change his job position at CSD.

IV. DISCUSSION

Given the data and analysis for the two cases, we return to our focal interests: understanding the ways local circumstances in the workplace affect how people perform software maintenance work, and the ways maintenance work affects workplace arrangements. We see that local circumstances include the professional incentives that encourage people to recognize opportunities to fulfill occupational or career goals. Maintenance work is performed when bugs are encountered, resource bottlenecks arise, task chains break down, new functionality is desired, related computing innovations are adopted, or personal customizations are sought. The workplace can be described in terms of kinds of problems solved and computing applications used to accomplish primary work, as well as the task chains through which this work is performed. How people perform maintenance work can be characterized according to how they undertake 1) accommodation activities to live with the system as it is, and 2) negotiations with others to alter the system. Last, who performs what maintenance tasks can depend not only on a job title, but also on users' desire to be compatible with other systems to which they are bound through technological, organizational, and professional constraints.

Participants' incentives evolve in response to constraints and opportunities in their computing workplace. The strong emphasis on publishing in academic organizations affects the patterns of use of the text-processing system and the participants' efforts at balancing primary work and articulation work. As we saw at both CSRO and CSD, participants naturally evolve accommodation patterns in response to the day-to-day contingencies which affect their primary work task chains. However, participants sometimes develop patterns of accommodation in a dedicated fashion, such as in the form of a new concept for text-processing system development or modification, in connection with the timely recognition of a pivotal career constraint or opportunity. In contrast to day-to-day accommodation patterns, these latter accommodation patterns can have a substantial impact on the coevolution of the text-processing system, its embedding work arrangements, and its users' patterns of work.

At CSRO, day-to-day accommodation patterns became commonplace, so that maintenance work on the text-processing system by users became an infrequent form of their primary work. Indeed, since members of the CSRO user community were not restricted to using only a single version of the numerous individual subsystems available, all these subsystems had to be maintained. The necessary maintenance activities were thus distributed across the user community throughout the organization.

In contrast, at CSD, the evolution of the text-processing system was intimately tied to accommodation activities that subsequently turned into maintenance activities for one particular user, Dr. T. His text-processing system configuration emerged as *the* TEPS system. Maintenance work on TEPS afforded him a reputation of expertise and eventually became part of his primary work. Dr. T.'s accommodation work on TEFS and his emergence as a *de facto* system maintainer resulted largely from interactions between his career constraints, his perspectives on career opportunities at CSD, and circumstantial computing work arrangements. This is shown by the chronology of his activities:

1) respond to a career constraint—the necessity to reformat his dissertation work-in-progress files with a special TEFS configuration—by investing a substantial amount of time in articulation work to learn TEFS;

2) become knowledgeable enough about TEFS to be considered a *de facto* resident expert;

3) perceive the necessity for an integrated mail handling system supported by TEDS and combining the features of ZIP, the local mail system, and NZIP, the system which separately handles network mail;

4) again, invest time in articulation work and produce CEDEX; in the process become very knowledgeable about TEDS, and be considered, as in the case of TEFS, a foremost authority;

5) balance productive effort between his *de facto* maintenance of TEPS and his primary activities as researcher in ways that often favor the former, fostering a new specialization; and

6) accept the offer of a new position at CSD as research staff, and thereby enable his primary commitment to further develop and maintain CSD's research support systems.

The dynamics of Dr. T.'s commitment to articulation work on TEPS, together with his career constraints and opportunities, created a major shift in the distribution of articulation efforts. His commitment to and routinization of maintenance work on TEPS encouraged other participants to adopt his text-processing system configuration as the common system. As a result, these participants were freed from the burden of doing maintenance work as a notable portion of their articulation work and from dealing with the attendant delays.

Thus, the negotiations and accommodation activities that participants employ to balance their primary and articulation work are mutually bound to how they evolve the systems they use. These activities are also mutually bound to the evolution of work arrangements and the patterns of work.

The participant's proportion of primary work output to articulation work input diminishes when a novel bottleneck in a task chain induces substantial articulation efforts. Eventually, either the bottleneck goes away or the necessary articulation work gets routinized and the participant's proportion of primary work output to articulation work input increases—at least until other kinds of bottlenecks arise in the task chain. However, in connection with the responses of some participants to career contingencies and patterns of system use in the setting, articulation work may also give rise to new primary work along with a centralized organizational unit officially responsible for performing it.

Last, the ratio of primary work to articulation work with a given software system can be viewed as an indicator of how well the system fits into circumstances in the workplace. When primary work dominates, the fit is appropriate, whereas, when articulation work dominates, the fit is poor. Thus, over the lifetime of a system, a high rate of articulation work points to not only a poorly fit system, but also a loss of productive work effort.

V. Related Work

In many ways, our analysis of software maintenance is a departure from established practice. In this regard, our research can be compared to both the approach and results of other studies. For example, the collection of papers appearing in the last two workshops on software maintenance [35], [36] address the applicability and appropriateness of various software tools, techniques, and empirical measures. By and large, these studies focus on *attributes of the software* being maintained, but not on who, how, why and when they are maintained. Nonetheless, these technologies can assist in reducing certain forms of articulation work. For example, tools for maintaining software system configurations and controlling the proliferation of system versions (e.g., [26]) could be employed at CSRO to reduce duplicated maintenance efforts.

However, no technology can completely eliminate or supplant the practical utility of software system articulation work. Instead, each new tool or technique is packaged in such a way that its users must accommodate and negotiate its fit into routine work arrangements.

Belady and Lehman [4], [20] derived through a series of studies a number of laws and dynamics of program evolution from measures of software alterations. Their provocative insights are primarily grounded in attributes of programs and in idealized models of the software development process they conjecture [21]. However, their results give only modest insight into how software maintenance activities vary with the type of organizational setting, the type of application in use, local computing resource availability, incentives and constraints that motivate participants to maintain their systems in idiosyncratic ways, and so forth.

Other studies of software maintenance substantiate the preponderance of the maintenance of existing systems over the development of new systems. Lientz and Swanson [40], [25], [23], [24], [22] document how different kinds of maintenance activities correlate with various organizational attributes and how user requests for system enhancements dominate maintenance activities. But their analyses rely upon data collected primarily from the DP managers' vantage point, and thus provide a restricted view of maintenance. However, in recent reports they recommend that attention be focused on users and their work environment to better understand the dynamics of software maintenance [24], [22].

Rockart and Flannery's [29] studies of end-user computing in large organizational settings find that certain maintenance tasks are frequently performed by functional support personnel in user departments (e.g., Dr. T. at CSD). But their reports do not account for the kinds of computing applications end-users employ to accomplish their routine (primary) work tasks or how these users convince, or otherwise negotiate with, the functional support personnel to get maintenance activities accomplished.

Last, as we found in this and related studies, software maintenance activities add to, or redistribute access to, the available supply of computing resources that systems users can mobilize to accomplish their primary work. Maintenance work of the kinds we describe is central to the ongoing use *and* innovation of local computing arrangements, and it has been observed across many types of organizations and computing applications studied [15], [17], [30], [18], [32]. This leads us to observe that software maintenance work is both a cause and consequence of how systems and work arrangements coevolve.

VI. Conclusions

Software maintenance is a complex and poorly understood phenomenon. Our interest is to better understand how local circumstances in the workplace affect the ways in which software maintenance work is performed. We presented a study of the maintenance of two comparable software systems in two similar organizations. We analyzed the evolution of a software system, its users' primary and articulation work activities, and the work arrangements in which the software system is embedded as three processes that are mutually dependent.

We found there exists a duality between what people want to use their system for versus what they have to do to get their work products out the door. This is what we distinguished as primary work and articulation work. On the one hand, articulation work emerges naturally from bottlenecks in the task chains people follow to accomplish their primary work. On the other hand, the accommodation activities and negotiations employed by system users and maintainers determine the successful completion of their primary work. The pivotal role of articulation work is, not surprisingly, implicit in the traditional distinction [28] between *productive* maintenance activities and "*wheel-spinning*" maintenance activities. The latter's toll increases with the lack of forethought for a software system's maintenance as well as the accommodation efforts imposed by unfamiliarity with the system. But it also increases with the articulation efforts imposed by changing circumstances in the workplace.

Finally, this work poses a number of interesting questions that require further investigation. For example, to what extent are the patterns of software maintenance work described in the cases similar to or distinct from those patterns in other kinds of settings with different software systems? To answer such a question implies a need to examine the primary and articulation work activities of system users, their incentives, computing facilities, and software systems used. In turn, this question further suggests that comparative studies of different kinds of software maintenance work are in order. Also, the kinds of questions we asked—who, what, where, when, why and how—suggest that a simple comprehensive framework for understanding software maintenance work can be developed and serve as a guide for analyzing how well different software tools fit into local circumstances in the workplace.

Appendix
Research Design

The CSRO and CSD case studies were conducted from 1978 to 1984. They are parts of a larger ongoing study of the process of innovation in computing, the routine use of computing systems, and the evolution of software systems in complex organizational settings [17], [30], [18], [31], [34].

Comparative case studies provide a useful way to study poorly understood phenomena [8]. Our research design for developing an understanding of software maintenance follows the methods of case study research. This entails the systematic collection of data about individual cases and the analysis of data to produce generalizable findings [30]. We use empirical data and seek to develop findings based on different levels of analysis to establish a grounded theory [12], [38] of software maintenance.

Our research design incorporates four elements of scientific inquiry: a mode of analysis, terms of analysis, a unit of analysis, and levels of analysis. The *mode of analysis* is the basic framework used to develop theoretical accounts of the phenomena under investigation. Our basic framework is the set of motivating questions presented in the introduction to this paper. The *terms of analysis* reflect the perspective and terminology used for characterizing the phenomena under investigation. Our vocabulary is derived from current research in the social analysis of computing and other forms of technical work [16], [15], [17], [30], [18], [32], [10], [37], [11], [19].

The *unit of analysis* is the subject of investigation used as the basis for theory development. It is the focal element in an individual case study and provides the dimensions of the problem space under investigation suitable for comparative analysis. The dimensions we use are *type of organizations* (academic computer science), *computing application* (automated text-processing), *regular work activities* (producing documents), *computing system in use or contention* (text-processing system), *relevant system life cycle activities* (use and maintenance) and *incentives and constraints on resource use*. In this paper, the focus of our analysis is the work involved in using and maintaining text-processing systems, at both CSRO and CSD.

The fact that both computing applications are text-processing applications and both CSRO and CSD are academic computer science organizations reflects the level of our analysis. The *level of analysis* varies with the dimensions across which the unit of analysis is examined and generalizations of findings are attempted. The unit of analysis (an individual case) stands at the base level of analysis and generalizability. Many choices are possible for the higher levels of comparison and generalizability: cases within the same organization, cases across organizations (our choice here), and cases within and across organizations [30], [8]. In this paper, we examine the maintenance of two computing applications of the same kind (text-processing) in two organizations of the same kind (academic computer science). Further generalization requires, for instance, comparison with similar case studies of different types of applications in different types of organizations [30], [8].

The mode, terms, unit, and levels of analysis chosen provide a framework for the collection and analysis of individual cases selected for comparison and the ongoing synchronization of the comparative analysis. This helps us maintain awareness of where the analysis may lead, how it is pursued, and what is being analyzed, as well as what is being neglected.

In collecting and analyzing data, we focus on the *interactional* nature of work in settings involving computing: how people interact with each other, their computing systems and their work arrangements [17], [30], [18], [10]. In the CSRO and CSD cases, we seek to understand how people in a work setting attempt to resolve unforeseen problems with software system use, such as anomalies in system behavior and other alterations in their computing work arrangements.

The data employed are collected through a sequence of structured interviews with local participants, by first-hand observation of people's activities in the work setting and by participant-observation. The grounded theory approach *emphasizes* collecting information prior to evaluating it, so that no particular theory is singled out to be espoused or discredited [12], [38]. This implies that interviews be started with general questions so as not to preclude any possible outcomes, then continued with more and more focused questions as warranted by the answers obtained.

The interviews we conduct are both structured and open-ended. They are structured by a set of common questions asked of all informants as well as a set of questions specific to each informant. They are open-ended in the sense that these questions are framed so as to elicit descriptive answers. Analysis of these descriptive answers may then lead to further interviews with specific follow-up questions.

At CSRO and CSD, the 50 or so interviews we conducted lasted from as little as 30 minutes to more than 3 hours, with an average of about 50 minutes. Topics covered by the general questions we asked each informant included: 1) how long they had been in the setting; 2) their occupational or professional interests and the nature of their work; 3) which systems they used, for what activities they used them and how they used them; 4) what could go wrong in using these systems to do their work and how they dealt with such contingencies; 5) which changes in the work arrangements had an impact on the way they used the systems to do their work; 6) whether they had any experiences of the ways in which changes actually occurred in the setting; 7) whether and why they would want any changes implemented and how they would go about having them implemented. Naturally, this provides us a wealth of data about many situations which are described in this paper and elsewhere [17], [30], [18], [5], [6].

Informants in each setting were selected because of their role with respect to the systems studied (e.g., users, maintainers, developers), their position in the organizational hierarchy (e.g., managerial staff, faculty, administrative staff), or a referral by another informant.

At CSRO, interviews were conducted with project managers, research faculty, administrative and clerical staff, research associates, research staff programmers, computer facility programmers, the computer facility manager, and graduate assistants. At CSD, interviews were conducted with faculty, administrative, and clerical staff, the systems programmer, and graduate assistants.

Additional data were obtained throughout the study by on-the-spot conversations with participants whenever they happened to encounter problems of system use in the presence of the observer. Moreover, our observation activities included hands-on use of the systems described, review of software system documentation and research publications of all kinds, administrative memoranda, and bulletin-board and other public electronic mail messages.

Acknowledgment

Helpful comments on an earlier draft were generously provided by D. Estrin, L. Gasser, E. Gerson, S. L. Star and A. Strauss. The referees also suggested important clarifications in our presentation.

References

[1] R. S. Arnold and D. A. Parker, "The dimensions of healthy maintenance," in *Proc. 6th Int. Conf. Software Eng.*, pp. 10–27, Sept. 1982.

[2] R. Balzer, T. E. Cheatham, and C. Green, "Software technology in the 1990's: Using a new paradigm," *Computer (Special Issue on The DoD STARS Program)*, vol. 16, no. 11, pp. 39–45, Nov. 1983.

[3] V. R. Basili and A. J. Turner, "Iterative enhancement: A practical technique for software development," *IEEE Trans. Software Eng.*, vol. SE-1, Dec. 1975.

[4] L. A. Belady and M. M. Lehman, "A model of large program development," *IBM Syst. J.*, vol. 15, no. 3, pp. 225–252, 1976.

[5] S. Bendifallah, "Management of computing: A case study," in *Case Studies in the Management of Computing*, W. Scacchi, Ed., Dep. Comput. Sci., Univ. Southern California, Los Angeles, Tech. Rep., 1983.

[6] S. Bendifallah and W. Scacchi, "Software evolution and articulation work: A comparative case study," in *Proc. Int. Workshop Development and Use of Computer-Based Systems and Tools*, Aarhus, Denmark, Aug. 1985, pp. 59–82.

[7] B. Boehm, "Software engineering," *IEEE Trans. Comput.*, vol. C-25, pp. 1226–1241, Dec. 1976.

[8] F. van der Bosh, J. R. Ellis, P. Freeman, L. Johnson, C. L. McClure, D. Robinson, W. Scacchi, B. Scheff, A. von Staa, and L. L. Tripp, "Evaluation of software development life cycle: Methodology implementation," *ACM SIGSOFT Software Eng. Notes*, vol. 7, no. 1, pp. 45–60, Jan. 1982.

[9] J. H. Fujimura, "The construction of doable problems in cancer research," *Social Studies of Sci.*, to be published.

[10] L. Gasser, "The social dynamics of routine computer use in complex organizations," Ph.D. dissertation, Dep. Inform. Comput. Sci., Univ. California, Irvine, 1984.

[11] E. M. Gerson and S. L. Star, "Analyzing due process in the workplace," *ACM Trans. Office Inform Syst.*, vol. 4, no. 3, pp. 257–270, 1986.

[12] B. Glaser and A. Strauss, *The Discovery of Grounded Theory: Strategies for Qualitative Research*. Chicago, IL: Aldine, 1967.

[13] R. L. Glass and R. A. Noiseux, *Software Maintenance Guidebook*. Englewood Cliffs, NJ: Prentice-Hall, 1981.

[14] T. Kidder, *The Soul of a New Machine*. New York: Avon, 1982.

[15] R. Kling, "Social analyses of computing: Theoretical perspectives in recent empirical research," *ACM Comput. Surveys*, vol. 12, no. 1, pp. 61–103, Mar. 1980.

[16] R. Kling and E. M. Gerson, "Patterns of segmentation and intersection in the computing world," *Symbolic Interaction*, vol. 1, no. 2, pp. 24–43, 1978.

[17] R. Kling and W. Scacchi, "Computing as social action: The social dynamics of computing in complex organizations," *Advances in Computers*, vol. 19, pp. 249–327, 1980.

[18] ——, "The web of computing: Computer technology as social organization," *Advances in Computers*, vol. 21, pp. 1–90, 1982.

[19] B. Latour and S. Woolgar, *Laboratory Life*. Beverly Hills, CA: Sage, 1979.

[20] M. M. Lehman, "Programs, life cycles, and laws of software evolution," *Proc. IEEE*, vol. 68, pp. 1060–1076, Sept. 1980.

[21] ——, "Program evolution," *Inform. Processing Management (Special Issue on Empirical Foundations of Information and Software Science)*, vol. 20, no. 1-2, pp. 19–36, 1984.

[22] B. P. Lientz, "Issues in software maintenance," *ACM Comput. Surveys*, vol. 15, no. 3, pp. 271–278, Sept. 1983.

[23] B. P. Lientz and E. B. Swanson, *Software Maintenance Management*. Reading, MA: Addison-Wesley, 1980.

[24] ——, "Problems in application software maintenance," *Commun. ACM*, vol. 24, no. 11, pp. 763–769, 1981.

[25] B. P. Lientz, E. B. Swanson, and G. E. Tompkins, "Characteristics of application software maintenance," *Commun. ACM*, vol. 21, no. 6, pp. 466–471, June 1978.

[26] K. Narayanaswamy and W. Scacchi, "An environment for the development and use of large software systems," in *Proc. Softfair II*, San Francisco, CA, Dec. 1985, pp. 14–25.

[27] G. Parikh, "The world of software maintenance," in *Techniques of Program and System Maintenance*, G. Parikh, Ed. Cambridge, MA: Winthrop, 1982, pp. 9–13.

[28] R. S. Pressman, *Software Engineering—A Practitioner's Approach*. New York: McGraw-Hill, 1982.

[29] J. F. Rockart and L. S. Flannery, "The management of end user computing," *Commun. ACM*, vol. 26, no. 10, pp. 775–784, Oct. 1983.

[30] W. Scacchi, "The process of innovation in computing: A study of the social dynamics of computing," Ph.D. dissertation, Dep. Inform. Comput. Sci., Univ. California, Irvine, 1981.

[31] W. Scacchi, Ed., "Case studies in the management of computing," Dep. Comput. Sci., Univ. Southern California, Los Angeles, 1983.

[32] ——, "Managing software engineering projects: A social analysis," *IEEE Trans. Software Eng.*, vol. SE-10, pp. 49–59, Jan. 1984.

[33] ——, "A software engineering environment for the system factory project," in *Proc. 19th Hawaii Int. Conf. Syst. Sci., Software*, vol. IIA, 1986, pp. 822–831.

[34] W. Scacchi, S. Bendifallah, P. Garg, A. Jazzar, J. Macias, *et al.*, "Modeling the software process: A knowledge-based approach," Dep. Comput. Sci., Univ. Southern California, Los Angeles, 1986.

[35] R. S. Arnold, Ed., *Rec. Software Maintenance Workshop*. Washington, DC: IEEE Computer Society Press, 1983.

[36] *Proc. Conf. Software Maintenance*. Washington, DC: IEEE Computer Society Press, 1985.

[37] A. Strauss, "Work and the division of labor," *Sociological Quart.*, vol. 26, no. 1, pp. 1–19, 1985.

[38] A. Strauss, *Qualitative Analysis*. New York: Cambridge University Press, 1987.

[39] A. Strauss, S. Fagerhaugh, B. Suzcek, and C. Weiner. *The Social Organization of Medical Work*. Chicago, IL: University of Chicago Press, 1985.

[40] E. B. Swanson, "The dimensions of maintenance," in *Proc. 2nd Int. Conf. Software Eng.*, 1976, pp. 492–497.

[41] W. K. Wiener-Ehrlich, J. R. Hamrick, and V. F. Rupolo, "Modeling software behavior in terms of a formal life cycle curve: Implications for software maintenance," *IEEE Trans. Software Eng.*, vol. SE-10, pp. 376–383, July 1984.

Salah Bendifallah received the Engineer diploma in engineering economy/informatics from the Polytechnic School of Algiers, University of Algiers, Algeria, in 1974; the M.S. degree in industrial engineering from Stanford University, Stanford, CA, in 1979; and the M.S. degree in engineering/computer methodology from the University of California, Los Angeles, in 1982.

He is completing work toward the Ph.D. degree in computer science at the University of Southern California, Los Angeles. His major research interests are in knowledge-based modeling and simulation of the software process, knowledge-based software engineering, and social analysis of software engineering work.

Mr. Bendifallah is a student member of the American Association for Artificial Intelligence, the Association for Computing Machinery, the Society for Computer Simulation, and the Society for General Systems Research.

Walt Scacchi (S'77-M'80) received the B.A. degree in mathematics, the B.S. degree in computer science in 1974, and the Ph.D. degree in computer science from the University of California at Irvine.

He is an Assistant Professor of Computer Science and Communications at the University of Southern California, Los Angeles. Since 1981, he has directed the System Factory Project at USC. His research interests include large-scale software engineering, knowledge-based systems, and social and organizational analysis of computing.

Dr. Scacchi is a member of the Association for Computing Machinery, the American Association for Artificial Intelligence, and the Society for the History of Technology (SHOT).

Making Software Visible, Operational, and Maintainable in a Small Project Environment

WILLIAM BRYAN AND STANLEY SIEGEL

Abstract—Practical suggestions are presented for effectively managing software development in small-project environments (i.e., no more than several million dollars per year). The suggestions are based on an approach to product development using a product assurance group that is independent from the development group. Within this check-and-balance management/development/product assurance structure, a design review process is described that effects an orderly transition from customer needs statement to software code. The testing activity that follows this process is then explained. Finally, the activities of a change control body (called a configuration control board) and supporting functions geared to maintaining delivered software are described. The suggested software management practices result from the experience of a small (approximately 100 employees) software engineering company that develops and maintains computer systems supporting real-time interactive commercial, industrial, and military applications.

Index Terms—Configuration control board, design review, product assurance, project management, testing.

Manuscript received November 5, 1981; revised October 1, 1982.
The authors are with CTEC, Inc., 6862 Elm Street, McLean, VA 22101.

I. INTRODUCTION

IN *The Mythical Man-Month* [1], Brooks asks, "Why is programming fun?" He then offers five reasons, the fifth one being the following (page 7):

Finally, there is the delight of working in such a tractable medium. The programmer, like the poet, works only slightly removed from pure thought-stuff. He builds his castles in the air, from air, creating by exertion of the imagination. Few media of creation are so flexible, so easy to polish and rework, so readily capable of realizing grand conceptual structures.

The tractability of the software medium that Brooks refers to is, we maintain, the basic challenge to software engineering project management. The purpose of this paper is to offer practical suggestions for taking on this challenge with a reasonable degree of confidence.

Our suggestions are *practical* because they are:

• derived from techniques successfully applied in the real world;

• applicable to the large range of projects that involve from a handful up to 30 or so people, or stated in other terms, whose budgets span from tens of thousands to millions of dollars;

• based on good business sense and therefore saleable to corporate management;

• grounded in common sense and therefore adaptable to other organizations. (We believe a philosophy of "try it, you'll like it" that appeals to basic reason and is tempered with patience—as opposed to a "do it because we tell you" philosophy—is an effective way to contain poetic license).

Our suggestions are geared to:

• *making software visible*, or transforming software into something that management and others can see (our notion of *software* emcompasses specification documentation as well as its resultant computer code—see [2, ch. 1]),

• *making software operational*, or producing software that performs according to stated customer needs,

• *making software maintainable*, or being able to modify software in response to revised customer needs or identify discrepancies with respect to these needs.

This paper does *not* relate a case study of one company's successful application of software engineering project management techniques to *one* particular project. Rather, it reflects a corporate attitude toward performing software engineering project management on *any* business endeavor. For this reason, we believe that our suggestions may be, at least in part, beneficial to others. We do not claim that these suggestions are all-encompassing (we have project management problems, too); nor do we claim that these suggestions are directly applicable to a corporate environment other than ours. [The dogmatic application of a successful technique in our company to the problems of another company—even one of similar size and structure—may fail for a variety of reasons, such as corporate politics and/or policies; for example, some company executives are simply willing to live with the pain of some problems (i.e., maintain the status quo) rather than subject themselves to the trauma of change that potential solutions might invite.]

This paper addresses the following topics:

1) An Independent Product Assurance Group (Section II).

2) Transitioning from a Statement of Customer Needs to Software Code—The Software Development and Change Control Process (Section III).

3) Determining that Operating Software Code is Consistent with Customer Needs—The Testing Cycle (Section IV).

4) Keeping the Customer Satisfied—The Configuration Control Board (CCB) and the Maintenance Process (Section V).

Section VI summarizes the key points. For easy reference, this summary is in the form of suggestions for organizing and managing a software project.

II. An Independent Product Assurance Group

We work for a firm, CTEC, Inc., that started as a one-person management consulting company in March 1974. In 1976, a client asked the company to pick up the pieces from a failing software development effort. Since that time, we have been in the business of developing, fielding, and maintaining operational systems with software content. The size of our software projects ranges from tens of thousands to hundreds of thousands of lines of programming language (higher order and/or assembler) source code; the types of software that we develop and maintain support real-time interactive commercial, industrial, and military applications. The company has grown steadily and has achieved a business base of just under $8 million. In 1978, the company reorganized into a matrix-managed organization (described later in this section). A software development process (see Section III) meshing with this organization has gradually become standardized. The process has even caused the extension of the matrix-managed organization to a third dimension: product assurance. The forces of this third dimension stabilize the software development process and manifest themselves primarily as peer reviews (see Section III). They impress visibility and traceability on the software development process.

Before looking more closely at this three-dimensional approach to matrix management, it is instructive to briefly consider the disciplines needed for making visible, operational, and maintainable software. Required is the interplay of three groups of disciplines—development, product assurance, and management—as illustrated in Fig. 1 and described in the following paragraphs.

• The *development discipline* shoulders the responsibility for creating the software during its various life cycle stages and doing what must be done to get the product into the hands of the customer, e.g., analysis, design, coding, and training.

• The *product assurance discipline* provides management with checks and balances with respect to the developer's activities. As Fig. 2 illustrates, these checks and balances help assure that product integrity is attained, and, ultimately, that the customer is satisfied. By product integrity we mean a product:

— that fulfills customer needs
— that can be easily and completely traced through its life cycle
— that meets specified performance criteria
— whose cost expectations were met
— whose delivery expectations were met (see [2, pp. 58-59]).

Fig. 2 also indicates that we view product assurance as the interplay of the functions of quality assurance (QA), configuration management (CM), verification and validation (V&V), and test and evaluation (T&E). The identifiers *QA*, *CM*, *V&V*, and *T&E* mean different things to different people, as evidenced by the wide variation of meaning associated with these terms in the literature (e.g., one person's QA is another person's T&E). For us, the world of product assurance is divided into the four processes shown in the far left of Fig. 2. We believe that these processes are necessary to help assure product integrity. We assign these processes the function labels shown in Fig. 2 to provide some linkage with extant, albeit nonuniform, terminology. The boundaries between these four processes are not distinct; their domains overlap (e.g., T&E can be viewed as a form of QA in which the "stand-

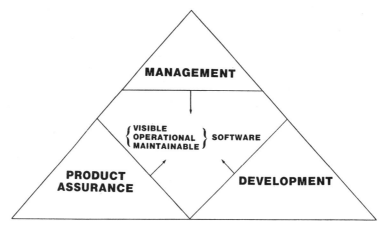

Fig. 1. Requisite disciplines for making visible, operational, and maintainable software.

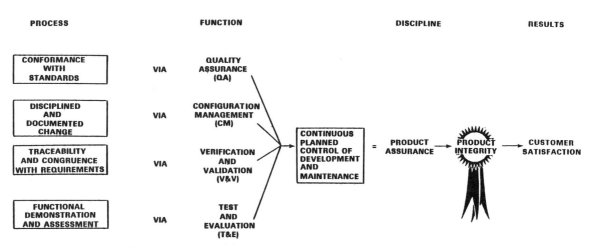

Fig. 2. Product assurance: Its functions and the results of its application.

ard" is a test plan or procedure against which the coded form of the software operating on hosting hardware is being compared). The function labels and process overlaps are not important here. What is fundamental is the integrated performance of all these processes.

• The *management discipline*, which can be divided into project management and general management, provides direction to development and product assurance activities to effect synergism. Project management provides this direction generally at the level of day-to-day activity associated with product development. General management provides this direction generally at the level above a particular project organization. Typically, this direction concentrates on sorting things out with respect to two or more projects that may be competing for corporate resources.

Fig. 3 depicts an organizational structure that we have used to develop and maintain software systems. This figure is a specific implementation of the philosophy represented in Fig. 1, where each discipline is depicted as an axis in a three-dimensional space. Along the "development axis" are three functional departments: 1) Systems Analysis and Design, 2) Systems Engineering, and 3) Software Engineering. The Systems Analysis and Design Department is concerned with defining customer requirements, developing solution approaches (in the big-picture sense, such as architectural level tradeoff studies), and designing algorithms for specific mathematical

problems associated with a system under development. This department is staffed with individuals trained in operations research, systems analysis, and computer science. The Systems Engineering Department is concerned with performing a top-level hardware/software functional allocation (i.e., specifying which system functions are to be carried out by hardware and which are to be carried out by software). This department is staffed with individuals trained in human factors analysis, hardware engineering, and communications engineering. The Software Engineering Department is concerned with detailed software design, software coding (programming), and program debugging. This department is staffed with individuals trained in computer program design and conversant with one or more programming languages.

Along the "management axis" in Fig. 3, there are project management offices that report to corporate management. A project manager is appointed for each project or set of related projects. Each project manager draws upon the resources of the three departments just described. However, the project manager does not assume authority over these resources. The staff continue to report to their respective department managers. [The row/column (i.e., matrix-like) organizational setup shown in Fig. 3 gives rise to the terminology *matrix management*.]

Along the "product assurance axis" in Fig. 3 is the Product Assurance Department. This department plays the role of the

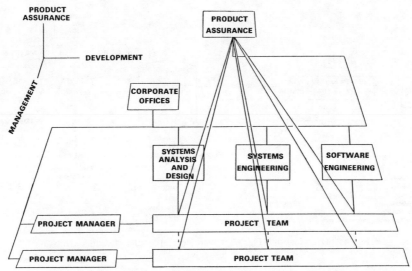

Fig. 3. A three-dimensional organizational structure for making visible, operational, and maintainable software—a "plane" of matrix management augmented by a "third dimension" of product assurance.

devil's advocate, providing each project manager (and corporate management) with an avenue to gain visibility into project progress other than through the three functional departments. Typically, these departments and the Product Assurance Department perceive project progress from different viewpoints—the three functional departments perhaps more optimistically and the Product Assurance Department perhaps more pessimistically. This department thus provides management with a potentially contrasting view of project progress so that management has the opportunity to make more intelligent decisions. To ensure its effectiveness, the Product Assurance Department is separated organizationally from the functional departments and the project managers. Thus, the department's objectivity is maintained which, in turn, maintains its effectiveness. This posture provides corporate management with an added measure of assurance that projects are proceeding on schedule, within budget, in a traceable manner, and in accordance with customer requirements and performance criteria (and, if projects are not proceeding in this manner, this department offers corporate management an opportunity to find out why). For example, through the configuration control board mechanism described in the following two sections, a visible trace of project activities is compiled and maintained by the Product Assurance Department, providing management with an essential input for making intelligent decisions regarding subsequent project evolution.

III. Transitioning from a Statement of Customer Needs to Software Code—The Software Development and Change Control Process

This section describes our software development and change control process in terms of the three-dimensional organizational structure portrayed in Fig. 3. This process aims at making software development and change control visible—and thus manageable—activities. The result is a software product that is operational (i.e., meets customer needs) and is maintainable once it is fielded.

Fig. 4 portrays the flow of our software development and change control process. The cyclic flow depicted in the figure is based upon the major release approach. This approach consists of periodically (i.e., approximately every 6 to 12 months) incorporating a group of enhancements into an existing operational baseline to create the subsequent operational baseline. This group of enhancements, when incorporated into an existing operational baseline and deployed, constitutes a *major release*. A major release is thus a controlled way of upgrading a deployed system in roughly uniform increments (in contrast to an approach that upgrades a deployed system each time a change is approved—regardless of the magnitude of the change). The primary advantage of the major release approach is that it permits changes to be more effectively integrated with one another and with capabilities in the current operational baseline. The primary disadvantage of the major release approach is that the customer generally has to tolerate system weaknesses and problems for a longer period of time.

The following is a walk-through of Fig. 4 (the numbers in circles are keyed to the paragraph numbers given below).

1) Customer requirements (as articulated in a contract) are translated into software code via a sequence of progressively more detailed specification steps with each step in the sequence formalized by a design review (coding does not begin until all design reviews are completed). This design review cycle (described in more detail in [3]) generally involves the development and review of the following three specification documents describing the enhancement to be incorporated into the next major release.

a) Preliminary Design Document (PDD), which translates the customer requirements into a functional approach to the solution. The document contains data flow descriptions and a top-level system concept incorporating the enhancement. The primary purpose of the PDD is to provide sufficient documentation for a more detailed design of the enhancement after top-level consideration of alternatives

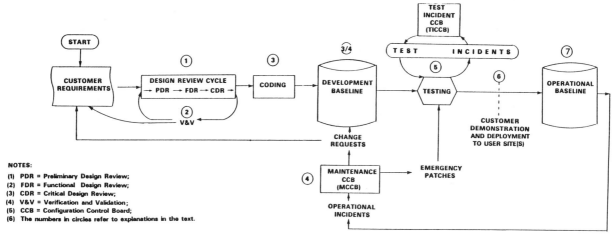

Fig. 4. Overview of CTEC's software development and change control process.

NOTES:
(1) PDR = Preliminary Design Review;
(2) FDR = Functional Design Review;
(3) CDR = Critical Design Review;
(4) V&V = Verification and Validation;
(5) CCB = Configuration Control Board;
(6) The numbers in circles refer to explanations in the text.

for implementing the enhancement. The PDD is generally prepared by the Systems Analysis and Design Department. It is presented for review, modification, and/or approval at a Preliminary Design Review.

b) Functional Design Document (FDD), which focuses on allocating the functions identified in the PDD to hardware and software, and explaining the functions and implications of the design. The FDD typically contains the syntax for command strings and formats for menus that comprise the interface between the user and the system. The FDD is generally prepared by the Systems Engineering Department. It is presented for review, modification, and/or approval at a Functional Design Review.

c) Critical Design Document (CDD), which describes the design of specific software modules needed to implement the commands, menus, and other functions described in the FDD. The CDD typically contains logic diagrams (e.g., Warnier-Orr diagrams) which are then transformed into software code (i.e., programming language statements) during the coding stage shown in Fig. 4. The CDD is generally prepared by the Software Engineering Department. It is presented for review, modification, and/or approval at a Critical Design Review.

Depending on the level of detail in the customer requirements, the PDD and/or the FDD may be omitted from the design review cycle. For example, a contract with a customer may already contain as an appendix a document comparable to an FDD developed, say, by another contractor. In such cases, a design review may be held at the outset of a project to determine if any changes need to be made to the customer-provided FDD (or PDD). The customer generally participates in the Functional Design Review and Critical Design Review and formally approves the associated design documentation. If necessary, the customer requests changes to this documentation (which may then be submitted for customer approval at a subsequent design review). The Preliminary Design Review is generally not attended by the customer, since this review is a formal brainstorming session on how to design for a customer requirement. The PDD may be made available to the customer as a progress report.

2) Throughout the design review cycle, the Product Assurance Department performs verification and validation (V&V)

of the design documentation. This department verifies that each document follows logically from its predecessor and validates that each document is consistent with customer requirements. As is explained in Section IV, the Product Assurance Department is also responsible for developing and executing procedures to test the development baseline (Fig. 2). The V&V activity of this department provides the department with early inputs for these procedures. (See [4] for a discussion of verification and validation for software design documentation and for all other software products developed during the life cycle.)

3) Once the CDD is approved, the Software Engineering Department prepares code in accordance with the CDD and FDD. This code is then integrated with the code from the existing operational baseline to form a development baseline.

4) Also added to the development baseline is code from change requests approved by a Maintenance Configuration Control Board (MCCB). The MCCB is a change control body that functions throughout the period between major releases (and, in particular, throughout the design review cycle). The MCCB is described in Section V. (See [2] and [5] for a more detailed discussion of the concepts of change control and CCB as presented in this paper.)

5) Once the development baseline is constructed, it is turned over to the Product Assurance Department for testing. The testing cycle and the associated activities of the Test Incident Configuration Control Board (TICCB) are described in Section IV.

6) At the end of the testing cycle, the operation of the development baseline is demonstrated to the customer. Generally, this operation is demonstrated at our facilities and then at the user sites. This demonstration consists of executing the test procedures used during the testing cycle referred to in 5 above. This demonstration also consists of excursions from these test procedures that the customer may select to satisfy himself that the software code is performing in accordance with specifications. Sometimes, the customer may choose to have the demonstration at the user sites conducted by an agent other than our company, using either our test procedures or other test procedures.

7) If the customer is satisfied with the onsite demonstra-

tion, the development baseline replaces the existing operational baseline and becomes the new operational baseline. The customer may accept the development baseline as the new operational baseline even if all test incidents have not been resolved. These outstanding test incidents are then considered operational incidents and submitted to the MCCB for resolution.

The preceding discussion completes the walk-through of Fig. 4. The next section focuses on the testing cycle and the activities of the TICCB shown in the figure.

IV. DETERMINING THAT OPERATING SOFTWARE CODE IS CONSISTENT WITH CUSTOMER NEEDS—THE TESTING CYCLE

The testing cycle begins with a turnover of the development baseline by the Software Engineering Department to the Product Assurance Department.[1] This turnover is formalized by a memorandum from the Software Engineering Department to the Product Assurance Department listing all the change requests and software modules that are being handed over. Before the conclusion of the turnover meeting, a date is agreed upon for returning the development baseline (and test incidents) to the Software Engineering Department. (This initial turnover meeting can be regarded as the first TICCB meeting in the testing cycle depicted in Fig. 4.) The Software Engineering Department also turns over the media containing the development baseline software code. The Product Assurance Department makes a copy of this code and places the copy under configuration control. This copy becomes the reference point against which subsequent changes to the development baseline are made as a result of test incidents.

With the establishment of a configuration-controlled development baseline, the Product Assurance Department begins executing its test procedures. The test procedures document typically consists of several hundred pages and generally grows with each major release. It contains tests developed for change requests and patches, tests developed for the new capabilities being incorporated as a result of the most recent design review activity, and tests developed for capabilities introduced in previous releases. Satisfactory execution of these procedures thus provides a level of confidence that 1) the new capabilities are performing in accordance with the specifications set forth in FDD's and CDD's, 2) incorporating these new capabilities has not introduced any problems in capabilities that were part of previous releases, and 3) correcting old problems has not introduced new problems or reintroduced other old problems previously fixed.

Each set of test procedures addressing a functional area is introduced by a brief description of the capabilities included in that functional area and the testing approach taken. The step-by-step test procedures are then presented using the five-column format shown in Fig. 5. This five-column format is particularly suited to the testing of interactive systems, where the user interface is via a keyboard input and the system response is via a display of information on one or more screens. The definition of each column is as follows.

1) Column 1, *Step*, provides an identifying number for each step in the test procedure.

2) Column 2, *Operator Action*, defines the action taken by the tester to perform a particular step of the test procedure.

3) Column 3, *Purpose*, explains why a particular step is being executed or a capability is being exercised.

4) Column 4, *Expected Results*, describes the system response or other result that is expected upon completion of the action described in the *Operator Action* column. The information in this column comes from FDD and/or CDD material, or modifications to this material as a result of MCCB-approved change requests (see Section V).

5) Column 5, *Comments*, contains information that may be helpful to the tester. Examples include a description of the rationale behind a particular sequence of test steps, boundary value information for the functions being tested, or commentary on possible problems or critical areas. This column may also contain references to particular change requests approved by the MCCB. These references provide a means for tracing specific test results back to software specifications which, in turn, provide a means for tracing back to customer requirements. In this manner, the customer can be shown during demonstration testing that the capabilities he asked for are indeed embodied in the executing software code.

As the test procedures are executed, the tester may notice a discrepancy between the results specified in the Expected Results column and the actual response of the system. When such a discrepancy occurs, the tester fills out the upper portion of the Test Incident Report (TIR) form shown in Fig. 6. The tester also attempts to recreate the discrepancy by re-executing the pertinent test steps. If he is successful, he checks YES on the TIR form; otherwise he checks NO. The tester may also attach additional information to the TIR form, such as a printer output or a hard copy of information appearing on a display screen at the time the discrepancy was encountered.

When all the test procedures have been executed, a TICCB meeting, which was scheduled at the first turnover CCB meeting, is convened. At this meeting, the Product Assurance Department formally returns the development baseline to the Software Engineering Department. The TIR's generated during the execution of the test procedures are discussed to clarify possible misunderstandings about the problems described on the TIR forms. Following the meeting, the Product Assurance Department writes a memorandum such as that shown in Fig. 7 that summarizes what happened at the meeting. This memorandum gives visibility to the testing process because it accomplishes the following:

1) Formally establishes that the development baseline is now back in the hands of the Software Engineering Department.

2) Gives pointers[2] to the problems discovered during

---

[1] It should be noted that the Software Engineering Department generally performs some testing on the development baseline before this turnover. This testing focuses on ensuring that source compilation and assembly errors are not present and that all necessary code is present. This testing also generally includes checking the operation of individual modules to ensure, for example, that inputs are properly accepted and outputs are properly generated.

[2] That is, the TIR *numbers* (in this case, #1 to #105).

TEST XX.Y — OBJECTIVE: This area contains a statement that defines the objective of Text XX.Y.

TITLE: This line contains the long title of the test procedures.

NOTES: This area provides general notes as required to execute the test procedures within a section.

STEP	OPERATOR ACTION	PURPOSE	EXPECTED RESULTS	COMMENTS
N	Describes the actions taken by the person who is executing the test procedures.	Describes the reason for the step.	Describes the expected response of the system to the action specified in the Operator Action column.	Contains additional information such as boundary data, a discussion of the rationale for the step or operator action, or the test strategy underlying the step. May also contain pointers to FDD, CDD, and/or change request documentation.

[Document No.]
[Release No.] [Page No.]

Fig. 5. Five-column format for specifying test procedures.

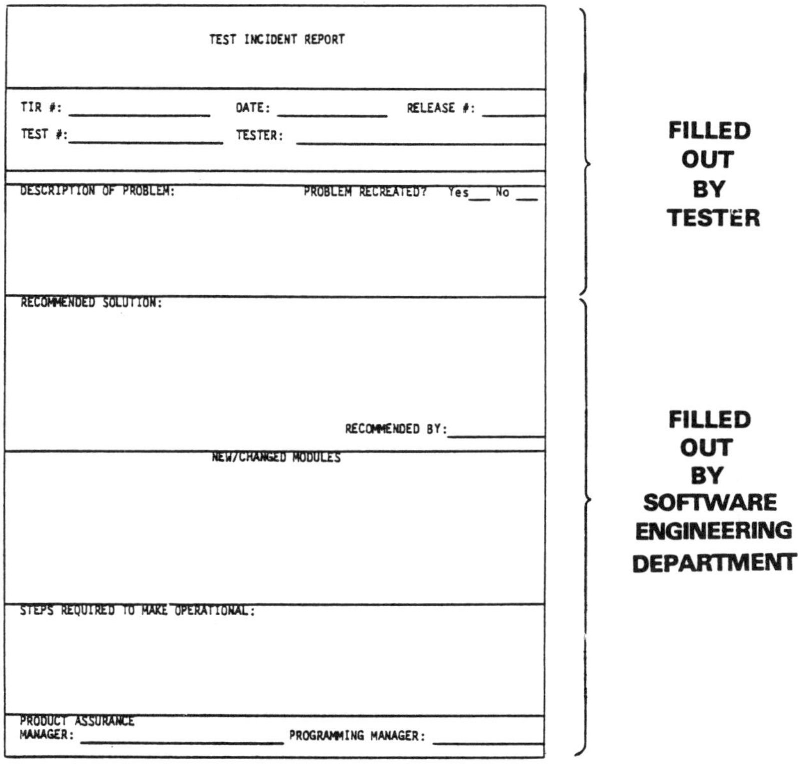
TEST INCIDENT REPORT

TIR #: ______ DATE: ______ RELEASE #: ______
TEST #: ______ TESTER: ______

DESCRIPTION OF PROBLEM: PROBLEM RECREATED? Yes__ No__

RECOMMENDED SOLUTION:

RECOMMENDED BY: ______

NEW/CHANGED MODULES

STEPS REQUIRED TO MAKE OPERATIONAL:

PRODUCT ASSURANCE MANAGER: ______ PROGRAMMING MANAGER: ______

Fig. 6. Test Incident Report (TIR) form.

testing. (It may be useful to attach copies of at least some of the TIR's to the memorandum because, for example, upper level management may wish to get a feeling for the nature of the problems encountered during testing.)

3) Highlights particularly significant problems (in this case, the problems defined in TIR's 37 through 45) and offers a starting point for the programming staff to seek solutions to these problems through a pointer to a specification document (in this case, CDD #1-C5).

Following the TICCB meeting, the Software Engineering Department begins developing solutions to the TIR's on its copy of the development baseline. These solutions are documented on the bottom part of the TIR form shown in Fig. 6. The Software Engineering Department completes its analysis of all of the TIR's prior to the scheduled date of the next TICCB meeting. The Software Engineering Department also makes coding changes to the development baseline that it believes will correct the problems (and performs tests to see if the problems have indeed been corrected). The Software Engineering Department completes as many of these changes as possible prior to the scheduled date of the TICCB meeting. (If too many changes are still not completed by that date, the Software Engineering Department may request a postponement of the TICCB meeting.) On the scheduled date, another TICCB meeting is convened and the Software Engineering Department formally returns the (updated) development baseline to the Product Assurance Department. The solutions to the TIR's presented at the previous TICCB meeting are discussed. The Software Engineering Department may also present new TIR's generated as a result of its attempt to fix the other TIR's. Following the meeting, the Product Assurance Department writes a memorandum such as that

```
MEMORANDUM

TO:     Distribution            DATE:   15 May 1995
FROM: Product Assurance Department   CHRON: 95-PAD-105
SUBJ:   Release XX Testing Meeting #1

1.0  Date of Meeting: 14 May 1995

2.0  Attendees: [Here, the name of each person who attended
                 the meeting and his organizational affiliation
                 are listed.]

3.0  CCB Action:

     a. Release XX was turned over to the programming staff.

     b. One hundred and five (105) TIR's were turned over and
        discussed. There was extensive discussion of TIR's 37
        through 45 which describe problems related to the new
        menus defined in CDD #1-C5. The manager of the Soft-
        ware Engineering Department indicated that he would
        have his staff give particular attention to this set of
        problems.

     c. It was agreed that the Software Engineering Department
        would return the Release XX software to the Product
        Assurance Department on 21 May 1995 for additional
        testing.

Distribution: [Here, the name of each person who is to receive
               a copy of the memorandum is listed. This list gen-
               erally includes all the meeting attendees and cor-
               porate management.]
```

Fig. 7. Sample TICCB minutes summarizing the turnover of the development baseline from the Product Assurance Department to the
Software Engineering Department.

shown in Fig. 8 that summarizes what happened at the
meeting.

The Product Assurance Department then repeats the
activities it performed when it first received the development
baseline. The cycle of turnovers between the Product Assurance
Department and the Software Engineering Department continues until no TIR's remain or until there is corporate agreement that any outstanding TIR's are not sufficiently serious
to prevent demonstration of the development baseline to the
customer. Each turnover is documented as indicated in Figs.
7 or 8.

As shown in Fig. 1, in-house testing (Step 5) is followed
by a demonstration t the customer (Step 6). This demonstration typically consists of execution of our test procedures by
the customer at our facility augmented by customer excursions from these procedures. As a result of this demonstration,
additional TIR's may be generated that the customer may
want fixed before the development baseline is deployed
for onsite testing. When the demonstration (which may last
several days or longer) has been completed to the satisfaction of the customer, he signs the test procedures. The development baseline is then deployed to the user sites. Testing by our
company and/or other customer agents is then performed on the
development baseline operating in a live environment. Additional test incidents that the customer may want corrected may
result from this testing. When the customer and the user
agree that the development baseline is operating satisfactorily
in accordance with our and/or the other customer agents'
test procedures minus any mutually acceptable discrepancies,
the user states in writing that the development baseline has
been accepted. At that point, the development baseline becomes the new operational baseline.

```
MEMORANDUM

TO:     Distribution            DATE:   22 May 1995
FROM: Product Assurance Department   CHRON: 95-PAD-129
SUBJ:   Release XX Testing Meeting #2

1.0  Date of Meeting: 21 May 1995

2.0  Attendees: [Here, the name of each person who attended
                 the meeting and his organizational affiliation
                 are listed.]

3.0  CCB Action:

     a. Release XX was returned to the Product Assurance De-
        partment.

     b. Of the one hundred and five (105) TIR's turned over at
        the 14 May meeting, one hundred (100) TIR's have been
        corrected via code changes (TIR's #1 through 87, and
        91 through 103).

     c. The manager of the Software Engineering Department
        stated that TIR #88 was the result of an improper op-
        eration of the system by the Product Assurance Depart-
        ment and therefore no corrective action was required.
        The manager of the Product Assurance Department
        said that he would correct the pertinent test procedures
        to provide appropriate clarification to the testers.

     d. The manager of the Software Engineering Department
        submitted TIR's 106 through 125. He indicated that
        solutions and associated code had been developed for
        TIR's 106, 119, and 122 through 125. He also indicated
        that solutions for the remaining new TIR's have not yet
        been developed. There was some discussion about TIR
        119 which the manager of the Software Engineering De-
        partment felt may not really be a problem because the
        specification, FDD #2-185, was vague in the area of con-
        cern. The manager of the Software Engineering Depart-
        ment stated that he wrote TIR 119 to obtain clarification
        on the matter. It was decided that the problem cited in
        TIR 119 was indeed a problem.

     e. It was agreed that the Product Assurance Department
        would return the Release XX software to the Software
        Engineering Department on 30 May 1995.

Distribution: [Here, the name of each person who is to receive a
               copy of the memorandum is listed. This list generally
               includes all the meeting attendees and corporate
               management.]
```

Fig. 8. Sample TICCB minutes summarizing the turnover of the development baseline from the Software Engineering to the Product
Assurance Department.

V. KEEPING THE CUSTOMER SATISFIED—THE
CONFIGURATION CONTROL BOARD (CCB)
AND THE MAINTENANCE PROCESS

Following the establishment of the new operational baseline, the user employs it in his live operational environment
until the next major release replaces it. During this operational phase, the user may require that maintenance be performed on the software. One cause of this maintenance
requirement may be the discovery of latent defects in the
software, i.e., software performance that fails to meet the
user's previously stated requirements. Other causes of maintenance action are a change in the user's needs or a desire to
enhance his system. Each maintenance requirement is documented in the form of an operational incident report. Operational incident reports are forwarded to the Maintenance
Configuration Control Board (MCCB) for processing.

The MCCB consists of CTEC and customer representatives. Jointly chaired by our project management and the

customer's project management, it meets regularly (typically weekly) to process operational incidents submitted by users of the currently deployed operational baseline. In response to these incidents, the MCCB takes one of the following actions:

1) Determines that the incident was the result of improper user operation of the system. In this case, the user is informed of the proper way to use the system, and the incident report is simply archived.

2) Determines that the incident was either 1) the result of proper user operation and therefore represents a system deficiency or 2) an operation not provided by the current system and therefore represents a system enhancement or a changed user need. In both cases, the MCCB approves a change request that, depending on the nature of the change, results in one of the following dispositions:

a) The change is within the scope of the existing maintenance contract. In this case, the change is submitted to the Software Engineering Department for coding and incorporation into the next release of the operational baseline.

b) The change is not within the scope of the existing maintenance contract. In this case, the change is filed for incorporation into a subsequent contract (i.e., customer requirements statement) for eventual incorporation into a future major release.

c) The change is needed to correct a problem that is making the operational baseline inoperative or unable to satisfactorily support operations. In this case, an emergency patch to the operational baseline is authorized by the MCCB. The Software Engineering Department prepares the patch code, which is then submitted to the Product Assurance Department for testing. If this testing indicates that the patch code corrects the problem, the patch code is sent to the affected user sites where it is incorporated into the operational baseline. This patch code is also incorporated into the development baseline.

Each MCCB meeting is documented by a set of minutes similar in nature and form to those of the TICCB (see Figs. 7 and 8). As was the case with the TICCB minutes, the minutes of the MCCB are recorded, archived, and reported by a member of the Product Assurance Department.

VI. Summary and Conclusions

In the preceding sections, an organization and procedures for making software visible, operational, and maintainable have been described. The organization emphasizes an independent product assurance group. During the software development and change control process, the transition from a statement of customer needs to software code is accomplished through a series of design reviews that provide visibility to the developing software and enhance its maintainability through the establishment of traceability. The testing cycle, which determines that operating software is consistent with customer needs, ensures that the software works. During the operational period, the Maintenance CCB ensures that the software as changed is visible, operational, and retains its maintainability.

The foregoing practices have been successful for our company, and we feel that they can be applied to problems faced by similar small organizations developing and maintaining software systems. Their adoption/adaptation can enhance the likelihood of successfully meeting the software engineering project management challenge. We feel that our experience is further confirmation of the hypothesis stated in [6] that "large-project software engineering procedures can be cost-effectively tailored to small projects."

References

[1] F. P. Brooks, Jr., *The Mythical Man-Month: Essays on Software Engineering.* Reading, MA: Addison-Wesley, 1975.
[2] E. H. Bersoff, V. D. Henderson, and S. G. Siegel, *Software Configuration Management: An Investment in Product Integrity.* Englewood Cliffs, NJ: Prentice-Hall, 1980.
[3] W. Stallings, "A matrix management approach to system development," in *Proc. 19th Annu. ACM/NBS Tech. Symp., Pathways to System Integrity,* June 1980, pp. 41–48.
[4] W. Bryan, S. Siegel, and G. Whiteleather, "Auditing throughout the software life cycle: A primer," *IEEE Computer,* vol. 15, pp. 57–67, Mar. 1982.
[5] ——, "An approach to software configuration control," in *Performance Evaluation Review* (1981 ACM Workshop/Symp. Measurement and Evaluation of Software Quality, Mar. 25–27, 1981), vol. 10, no. 1, Spring 1981, pp. 33–47.
[6] B. W. Boehm, "An experiment in small-scale application software engineering," *IEEE Trans. Software Eng.,* vol. SE-7, pp. 482–493, Sept. 1981.

William Bryan received the Ph.D. degree in computer science from George Washington University, Washington, DC, in 1976.

He is currently a senior staff member in the Intelligence Systems Division of CTEC, Inc., McLean, VA. He has been actively involved at CTEC in the application of software configuration management and other product assurance disciplines, including quality assurance, verification and validation, and test and evaluation. This activity has included detailed technical audits of software and documentation, disciplined control of changes to software and documentation, and acceptance testing of software systems, all for systems ranging in size from small to very large. He has lectured extensively on software product assurance, both nationally and internationally. His lecturing is based on his considerable experience in the actual practicing of software product assurance. He has over 23 years experience in the software engineering profession, and has worked in the specification, development, and maintenance of military command and control systems, industrial process control systems, and large database management systems.

Stanley Siegel received the Ph.D. degree in theoretical nuclear physics from Rutgers University, New Brunswick, NJ, in 1970.

He is currently the Technical Director of the Intelligence Systems Division of CTEC, Inc., McLean, VA. A 100-person company, CTEC develops software systems that support military and intelligence operations. CTEC also provides independent verification and validation (V&V) services which include application of the software life cycle management techniques described in his textbook on software configuration management. He has worked in the computer field in various areas, including systems programming and automated support for national level military command and control systems. During the past seven years, he has been at CTEC performing and teaching software product assurance. He lectures internationally on this subject, which includes configuration management, quality assurance, auditing, and testing.

Software productivity metrics: Some candidates and their evaluation

by JAI NAVLAKHA
Florida International University
Miami, Florida

ABSTRACT

Software productivity is one of the most important attributes of the software development process. No accepted standard exists to measure software productivity, although lines of code per man-month has become a de facto standard in the industry. This paper describes some properties that any productivity metric should exhibit and the advantages one expects to derive from its use. Three software complexity metrics—Halstead's effort, McCabe's cyclomatic complexity and Albrecht's function point—as well as lines of code per man-month are compared and evaluated with respect to the properties and advantages described.

"Software Productivity Metrics: Some Candidates and Their Evaluation" by J. Navlakha from *Proceedings of the 1986 National Computer Conference*, Volume 55, pages 69-76. Copyright ©1986 by AFIPS Press--reprinted with permission.

INTRODUCTION

Software engineering refers to the application of science and mathematics by which the capabilities of computer equipment are made useful to people via computer programs, procedures, and associated documentation.[1] The annual cost of software in the U.S.A. in 1980 was approximately $130 billion or about 5% of GNP. It is estimated to grow to 13% of GNP by the year 1990.[2] Over the past two decades or so, the cost of hardware has been decreasing steadily whereas the cost of developing software has been increasing consistently. In addition, the demand for software is increasing faster than our ability to supply it.

In such an economic atmosphere, it is extremely necessary to develop methods to measure various attributes of computer software in order to continually enhance our capabilities to increase productivity. The area of software engineering that deals with such measurements is called *software metrics*. Software metrics has evolved from a gradual recognition of the need and importance to measure and control the quality and developing cost of software products.

Measurement discipline is as fundamental to programming as it is to any other area of engineering. Boehm, Brown, Kaspar, Lipon, Macleod, and Merritt[3] define a software metric as a measurement of software, that is, a measure of the extent or degree to which a product possesses and exhibits a certain quality, property, or attribute. Software metrics can be used to measure many properties and attributes of software including its reliability, complexity, productivity, quality, correctness, availibility, maintainability, portability, and development effort. Software metrics also can be used to provide a precise definition of certain measurements to be used in a legal contract, to manage resources and, most of all, to evaluate the quality of a design and pinpoint potential problem areas of the design so that changes and improvements can be made at any stage during the software development process.

Thus, it is evident that software metrics is an important area of software engineering. However, it is also one of the most difficult research areas. Munson and Yeh[4] report that the attributes of software which materially affect cost, quality, and productivity are still unknown or, when known, are unmeasurable.

One of the most important attributes of the software development process that must be measured is the software productivity. No standard definition exists of productivity, and hence there is no standard metric which can be used to measure it. The importance of measuring productivity improvements in an organization can hardly be overemphasized. Accurate measurements help to:

1. Make good cost estimates which provides a competitive edge

2. Pinpoint productivity bottlenecks which helps in investment strategy for future improvements
3. Adapt tools and techniques to changing needs of projects
4. Compare different organizations

Many viewpoints exist about software productivity such as economic viewpoint, life-cycle viewpoint, and management viewpoint. The detailed differences among them are described by Navlakha.[5] All these viewpoints and the fundamental difficulty of measuring software make it extremely difficult to have a standard definition of software productivity. It is interesting to note that the IEEE standard glossary of software engineering terminology[6] defines many attributes of software including quality and reliability but does not define software productivity.

Although no standard metrics exist for measuring software productivity, industry has created a non-standard "standard" in the form of lines of code per man-month. Users of this metric include companies like Hughes, TRW, and IBM. It is a de facto standard, not because it is a good measure but because it is simple to understand, data collection is easy and accurate, it is used by "other" companies, and its substitute is not found easily.

One of the factors determining the level of productivity achieved is the complexity of the software being developed. This is not the only factor and its measurement does not include directly many factors on which software productivity depends (e.g., service, reviews, and work breakdown structure). However, it is quite possible that it may be a better measure of software productivity than the lines of code per man-month metric. Comparing and evaluating three software complexity metrics to measure software productivity and lines of code per man-month are a major part of this paper. The three software complexity metrics that are widely studied and included for comparison purposes here are Halstead's effort,[7] McCabe's cyclomatic complexity,[8] and Albrecht's function point.[9]

In the next section, some of the important properties that any software productivity metric should possess are described. Next, the advantages one expects to gain from using productivity metrics are described. A goal of the software engineering community is to develop a standard software productivity metric that exhibits such properties and provides such advantages as well as others. The evaluation of the four metrics is based on the properties and advantages. I should make it clear that I am not judging the metrics with respect to their effectiveness and current applications. I am interested in describing what properties they will have and what advantages they will provide if they are used to measure software productivity.

PROPERTIES OF SOFTWARE PRODUCTIVITY METRICS

A software productivity metric should exhibit the following seven properties: (1) universal applicability, (2) independence from methodology, (3) ease of application, (4) cost effectiveness, (5) dependence on other software attributes, (6) usefulness, and (7) reliability.

Universal Applicability

A software productivity metric should be applicable to the full universe of software including commercial software, embedded software, software tools, operating systems, artificial intelligence applications including knowledge based data management systems, and diagnostic software. Such applicability is important because if software houses use totally different sets of metrics to measure software productivity, then there can never be a standard for such an important software attribute. In turn, lack of a standard may disallow the fundamental use of metrics to compare one product against another similar product.

Independence from Methodology

Measurements relating to software productivity may be performed on both relative and absolute scales. In fact, sometimes trend measures also can be very useful. However, a productivity measure should be independent of a specific software development methodology in the sense that the data input to the metric formula should be independent of the methodology. This means that a piece of software does not possess a higher productivity than another simply because it is developed using a "better" software development methodology. Certainly the methodology plays a very important role in the quality of the software developed. However, the relationship should be brought out by the dependence of productivity on other software attributes rather than on the methodology itself. It is conceivable that there may be a metric with a qualification that it applies only to a specific methodology.

Ease of Application

It is very difficult in the software engineering field to define a metric that will remain unchanged for a long time period. Technological improvements are made so rapidly that any metric based on today's knowledge must be modified depending on tomorrow's increased knowledge. However, changes can never be made appropriately if we do not understand a basic metric and its parameters. We cannot understand a metric fully if we do not have sufficient experience working with it and observing its dependence on its parameters. Thus, it becomes very important to use a metric as much as possible, and that demands that the metrics be very easy to use.

That means that data on which software productivity metrics depend should be comparatively easy to obtain; it would be best if the data were routinely reported.

Cost Effectiveness

An important goal of any corporation is to make as much profit as possible. Management might use measurements to achieve productivity improvements in the future which translate into increased profits. But for this assumption to be valid, it is imperative that the process of obtaining data to quantitatively measure and calculate software productivity should be cost effective. If the cost is more than its anticipated future savings, it is not going to be useful.

Dependence on Other Software Attributes

Software productivity depends on many software attributes such as quality, reliability, verifiability, and usability. Any software system that has achieved the required levels of quality, reliability, and verifiability should have a higher measure of software productivity than one which does not attain those levels. Thus, quality and reliability measures should be included in any metric for software productivity. This is another reason why defining software productivity is so difficult. How can we define a standard for software productivity metrics when we do not even know what is a standard for measuring software quality?

Usefulness

One of the properties of any software productivity metrics discussed earlier is universal applicability. We do not wish to have one metric for one type of software and another metric for a different kind of software. For a similar reason, any productivity metric should be useful to all kinds of software practitioners including management at all levels, software developers, users, buyers, quality assurance personnel and researchers. Without this common utility, it would be impossible for one group to use the results obtained by other groups or to learn from their experiences.

Reliability

Obviously any software productivity metric should be reliable, or "good." Many factors can be evaluated to indicate the reliability of a specific metric. Some of these factors are indicated in the following questions:

1. It is necessary to use the measure alone, or can it be used in conjunction with other measures?
2. Is the purpose of the metric to measure a productivity level or its trend or percent of achieved productivity as compared to some existing standard?
3. Are the data needed for the measure easy to obtain without hurting personal feelings and morale (i.e., what are the politics involved in collecting and using the measure)?
4. Are the data for this measure coming from a stable process? If not, the actual data are not very reliable; consequently, the metric will give the wrong results.
5. Are the measures controllable by the manager of the

entity being measured? Once again, if this is not the case the measure does not serve its purpose.

6. Does the metric take into account its impact on other parts of the organization?
7. What is the relation of the measure to the goals and questions established for productivity measurement?
8. Does the metric give accurate results when applied to historical data?
9. Does the metric give reliable results? That is, are the same results produced with each consecutive application of the metric?

ADVANTAGES OF MEASURING SOFTWARE PRODUCTIVITY

There are many advantages of measuring software productivity. At different levels in an organization, people realize these advantages in different ways. Some of the major advantages are discussed in the following sections.

Management-related Advantages

According to Munson and Yeh:[4]

Management actions and reactions to the increasingly pervasive impact of software development on corporate products and processes have considerable impact upon a corporation's ability to develop software, i.e., its productivity. Each level of management has a natural set of decisions to make which impact productivity.

When some measures of productivity become available to managers at all levels in a hierarchy, the decision making capability of management increases. Once the relationship of software to corporate products and processes is recognized, productivity measures become the basis for evaluating capitalization for software development, corporate strategy for acquiring additional technology, and performance of groups within the company and other organizations. The measures also recognize and identify the specialized skills required to improve productivity and thereby support the corporate goals.

Middle-level management can use productivity measures to explain to top-level management how the corporate goals can be achieved through software development. Measurements of productivity allow for tracking progress within budget and schedule. Sometimes measurements can be useful in imposing a methodology on developing a maintenance process.

Productivity measures allow software managers to accurately predict group performance. The group performance prediction will allow software managers to accurately predict cost and to schedule subsequent projects. Such information can be used by upper levels of management to decide on the life/death of individual projects or to evaluate the benefits of new tools, for example, keeping the corporate goals in mind. Appropriate measures can also be used by software managers to identify support requirements and to foster creativity, initiative, and innovation.

Motivation

The results of productivity measurements can serve to motivate personnel if such results are made available. One group may identify that its productivity was low compared to that of another group. Thus, productivity may become a prestige issue resulting in internal competition. Clearly, this outcome depends on the commitment of every individual to improve regardless of whether management uses such measures in any other aspects of productivity assessment.

Another advantage of making available results of productivity measurements is that it allows groups and individuals to concentrate on desired behaviors, events, and objects that serve the identified goals for which productivity assessments are being made. For example, if productivity was assessed for each phase of a software life cycle, groups working in the earlier phases of the life cycle would focus their attention on how their actions and decisions are going to affect the productivity of subsequent phases of the software life cycle. The productivity of the software in its entirety will definitely improve if such motivation exits.

Another motivational benefit, albeit a short-term one, is that psychologically the fact that productivity measurements are being made improves the performance of groups or individuals. This is called the Hawthorne effect.

An indirect advantage of motivational benefits induced by measuring productivity is that measuring productivity heightens the self-awareness and self-improvement needs among groups or individuals in an organization. In turn, the need to closely control personnel is reduced.

Understanding Software Attributes

As indicated in the Introduction, the field of software metrics is in its infancy. We need to employ measurements for as many software attributes as possible. The software attribute measurements for one depend on another. Thus, when more measurements are made our understanding of not just one but many related software attributes is improved. This certainly is true for measuring software productivity because productivity is clearly dependent on software reliability, quality, validity, and other such attributes. Wrestling with fundamental issues in measurement may open new areas of investigation and cause us to reorganize our thinking about existing ideas.

Software Evaluation

Currently, almost all software evaluation techniques are qualitative in nature. One gets an idea of how good a software system is through comments from colleagues or sometimes from the users. Availability of software productivity metrics will assist programmers in comparing their product with other products developed in the same environment or with similar products developed by other organizations. Managers will be able to evaluate software produced in different types of programming environments that use different programming languages and methodologies. In time, it will be possible for project developers to identify which methodologies work best in a given environment, what tools are needed to improve software productivity, and how their product compares with some industry standard.

Software Buyers

A measure for software productivity is a boon to software buyers. They can use this measure to evaluate the available software that solves their problems and buy the software that is most productive or that has the highest productivity per unit of cost. For software manufacturers, this measure becomes a goal, and a competitive level to attain the highest productivity is established among many manufacturers of similar software systems.

Advantages to Researchers

The practice of measuring software productivity quantitatively has many advantages to researchers. This group of people is devoted to making computer science a true science, and to making software engineering what it claims to be—an engineering discipline. It is anticipated that when software productivity metrics become available, their continued usage will not only shed light on all software features on which productivity depends, but also will illuminate how to measure other attributes of software, where the pitfalls are, and where more knowledge is required. When they try to tackle many complex issues relating to productivity, researchers undoubtedly will open new frontiers of knowledge, new areas of investigation, and better understanding of existing software engineering principles.

Improved Economic Measures

The goals and questions established for software productivity measurement are directly related to the economic measures for a corporation. Thus, improved measurements and increased software productivity will directly help in improving economic measures which, after all, is the ultimate goal of any organization.

COMPARATIVE EVALUATION

In view of the desired properties of a software productivity metric and the expected advantages derived from its use, the following sections compare four metrics: (1) lines of code per man-month (LOC/MM), (2) Halstead's effort (HE), (3) McCabe's cyclomatic complexity (MCC), and (4) Albrecht's Function point (AFP).

Lines of Code Per Man-month

Lines of code per man-month (LOC/MM) is the most popular productivity metric in the industry. It is considered good because:

1. It is simple to understand.
2. It matches our intuition of programmers' programming problems.

3. Data collection is easy and reasonably accurate.
4. It is cost effective.
5. It is almost universally applicable.
6. It is used by many companies.

It is a poor productivity metric because:

1. It rewards reinvention rather than reuse.
2. It addresses only 10-20 percent of the products of software development; it does not take into account products such as documentation, services, reviews, and plans.
3. Its dependence on other software attributes such as quality and reliability is almost non-existent.
4. It does not help software evaluation or software buyers.
5. It has no relevance to improved economic measures for an industry.

Halstead's Effort

The Halstead's effort (HE) metric is a postcoding-phase metric, that is, its value is available when coding is done. Therefore, it cannot be applied in the design phase for any productivity measurements. This is also true of LOC/MM metric. Determining the values of Halstead's software science parameters is an easily automated process, thus this metric is very cost effective. HE is universally applicable for a variety of applications. However, there are problems with obtaining a value for the HE metric when the development language is a complex high order function-oriented language such as APL. HE is fairly independent of the development methodology in the sense that it is not possible to increase the productivity by following a particular methodology. Its dependence on other software attributes is minimal. Measuring the productivity using the HE metric in no way gives any measure of quality, reliability, or usability of the software.

The HE metric can be useful to management in evaluating and predicting group performance and identifying problem areas in the development process. It is not going to provide much help in understanding other important software attributes. Software buyers do not realize many advantages from HE but researchers have a good tool with which to work and experiment. It is difficult to identify its impact on the economic measures used in that environment.

McCabe's Cyclomatic Complexity

McCabe's cyclomatic complexity (MCC) is also a postcoding-phase metric but since it completely depends on the number of simple predicates in a program conceivably it also could be available after detailed design. Its advantages and disadvantages are similar to Halstead's effort. MCC is easily automated and therefore it is a very cost effective metric. Its dependence on programmer's idiosyncracies is less than that of LOC/MM and HE because the number of simple predicates used in the code depends on the algorithms and data structures used, and they are determined by the time the detailed design is complete. MCC's dependence on other software attributes is slightly more than that of the HE metric because, for example, the reliability of software decreases with increasing numbers of predicates in the program. In turn, the number of execution paths is increased.

The MCC metric is not very useful for software buyers and is only slightly more useful for software evaluation purposes. However, the metric is quite useful for researchers. Gaining an understanding of other software attributes through using this metric is more likely than with using the HE metric. Management can use MCC for evaluating group performance, predicting coding time a bit more accurately after detailed design, and for identifying difficult tasks in particular development processes.

Albrecht's Function Point

Albrecht's function point (AFP) metric depends on the number of inputs and outputs of a system, the number of master files used by a program and the number of inquiries made by a user. All of this information is available after the software requirements and functional specifications are written and thus it can be applied very early in the software life cycle. It is very straightforward and inexpensive to determine the value of this metric and the metric can be used easily. However, AFP is not as universally applicable as the other three metrics. Business applications, database applications, and the like are most suitable for the function point metric. The quality and reliability of a system used in business and database applications is directly dependent on the system's input-output characteristics and its file-handling capabilities. Thus, this metric will give a higher productivity value for those systems which are good quality, reliable systems than for others which are not. AFP is as independent of the development methodology used as it is dependent on the functional characteristics of a system.

For management at all levels, the function point metric is very useful. Management related advantages including schedule estimates are more accurately derived, difficult design and programming areas are easily identified, group performances can be evaluated, and expensive maintenance efforts can be estimated. The AFP metric can be used as a basis for competition and hence as a motivating factor for developers. Its study is likely to increase our understanding of other software

TABLE I—Evaluation of productivity metrics based on their properties

	P1*	P2	P3	P4	P5	P6
LOC/MM	1	3	1	1	5	4
HE	2	2	2	1	4	3
MCC	2	2	2	1	3	3
AFP	3	2	2	1	2	2

* P1 = Universal applicability; P2 = Independence from methodology; P3 = Ease of application; P4 = Cost effectiveness; P5 = Dependence on other software attributes; P6 = Usefulness
1 = Very good; 2 = Good; 3 = Average; 4 = Bad; 5 = Very bad

TABLE II—Evaluation of productivity metrics based on derived advantages

	A1*	A2	A3	A4	A5	A6
LOC/MM	4	4	5	4	5	4
HE	3	3	4	3	4	2
MCC	3	3	3	3	4	2
AFP	2	2	2	2	3	2

* A1 = Management related advantages; A2 = Motivation; A3 = Understanding of software attributes; A4 = Software evaluation; A5 = Advantages to software buyers; A6 = Advantages to researchers
1 = Very good; 2 = Good; 3 = Average; 4 = Bad; 5 = Very bad

attributes and help us evaluate similar software developed in different environments.

Summary of Evaluation

Table I summarizes the comparative evaluation of the four metrics with respect to the property attributes required of any productivity metric discussed in the section Properties of Software Productivity Metrics. Table II provides a summary evaluation with respect to the expected advantages of a productivity metric as discussed in the section Advantages of Measuring Productivity Software.

CONCLUSIONS

Based on the evaluation shown in Tables I and II, it appears that Albrecht's function point metric is the best of the four productivity metrics discussed in this paper. It is followed by Halstead's effort and McCabe's cyclomatic complexity metrics. Lines of code per man-month, the most popular among them, seems to be the worst productivity metric.

REFERENCES

1. Boehm, B.W. *Software Engineering Economics.* Englewood Cliffs, NJ: Prentice-Hall, 1981, p. 16.
2. Fairley, R.E. *Software Engineering Concepts.* New York: McGraw Hill, 1985.
3. Boehm, B.W., J.R. Brown, H. Kaspar, M. Lipon, G.J. Macleod, and M.J. Merritt. *Characteristics of Software Quality.* Amsterdam: North-Holland, 1978.
4. Munson, J.B., and R.T. Yeh. *Report by the IEEE Software Engineering Productivity Workshop.* San Diego, March 1981.
5. Navlakha, J.K. Software Productivity and Its Management, *AFIPS, Proceedings of the National Computer Conference* (Vol. 54), 1985, pp. 501–506.
6. IEEE Standard Glossary of Software Engineering Terminology, *IEEE Standard 729–1983.*
7. Halstead, M. *Elements of Software Science,* New York: Elsevier North-Holland, 1977.
8. McCabe, T.J. "A Complexity Measure." *IEEE Transactions on Software Engineering,* (Vol. SE-2), December 1976, pp. 308–320.
9. Albrecht A.J., and J.E. Gaffney, Jr. "Software Function, Source Lines of Code, and Development Effort Prediction: A Software Science Validation." *IEEE Transactions on Software Engineering,* (Vol. SE-9), November 1983, pp. 639–648.

Software Maintenance Management

David H. Longstreet

Abstract

Software maintenance should be a critical function within most large and small organizations. The reliability of software systems upon which these organizations depend is the main function of the managers of information systems (MIS). Despite its importance to the organization, software maintenance often has been ignored as a significant management concern.

Introduction

The goal of any MIS is simple; that is, to produce higher quality software at lower costs. Is it simple to achieve that goal? No, it's just simple to understand what the goal is and nearly impossible to achieve it. First, the MIS has a superior (who may not have a technical background) setting deadlines. Second, the MIS has a fixed budget (limited number of programmers, equipment, etc.) to work within. Therefore, the MIS has to produce a given number of lines of code (and maintain it) with a fixed number of programmers. This paper tries to present some concrete suggestions on how an MIS can solve some of the software problems within current constraints.

Software maintenance should be a critical function within most large and small organizations. The reliability of software systems upon which these organizations depend is the main function of the MIS. Despite its importance to the organization, software maintenance often has been ignored as a significant management concern.

This article explores many different variations on the theme of software maintenance management. It considers the implications and relationships of acceptance testing, software reuse, and software maintenance management. Futhermore, it describes some important attributes necessary for software maintenance personnel.

Software Maintenance

Software maintenance are formal activities to keep a software system operational. A software system contains much more than just code, it contains requirements, design, documentation, test data, and other elements of the software. It is currently estimated that software maintenance accounts for 60-80 percent of each software dollar.[1]

In short, software maintenance consists of the changes that occur to the originally accepted (baseline) product. These changes consist of correcting, inserting, deleting, extending, and enhancing the baseline software system.

Software Life Cycle

A computer software system's life cycle is defined as the period from its initial conception until it is no longer used. The life-cycle phases have been defined as initiation, requirements, design, programming, testing, operation, and conversion.

There is a set of products associated with each life-cycle phase. These products encompass requirements and design documentation, code, the database, users' manuals, test plans, procedures and results, operators' manuals, etc. All of these products make up the baseline product. Therefore, software maintenance is a set of activities that result in changes to the baseline product. These changes keep a software system operational and responsive to its users after it is accepted and placed into production.

Software maintenance involves many of the same activities associated with software devels pment. One way to describe activities of software mainteance is to identify them as successive iterations of each phase of the software life cycle. It should be conducted after every phase of the software life cycle.

After each phase of the cycle is completed, acceptance testing should be conducted. This will ensure that the previous life cycle phase (requirements, for example) meets its acceptance criteria to enable the project manager to determine whether to begin the next phase of the cycle (in this example, that would be design). Acceptance testing criteria should be established by the project manager to enable him to better control the project.

---

[1] Martin, J. and C. McClure, *Software Maintenance: The Problem and Its Solution*, Prentice-Hall, Inc., Old Tappan, N.J., 1983.

What Is the Relationship of Quality to Maintenance?

Software maintenance management deals with every aspect of the software life cycle. A software system that has been developed using software maintenance techniques can be characterized by such attributes as reliability, understandability, testability, modularity, and expandability, all of which make the software system of higher quality. The greater the number of quality attributes engineered into the software during development, the higher the degree of confidence in its maintainability. The cost of adding quality to existing software is significantly more expensive than building quality into software.

Categories of Software Maintenance

Maintenance activities are traditionally broken into three categories as shown in Table 1. They are perfective, adaptive, and corrective.

Adaptive: Adaptive maintenance includes all modifications made to meet the changing structure in which the software must operate. That is, data formats may change, hardware changes, and the operating software system changes. It accounts for 20 percent of all software maintenance conducted during the operation phase.

Corrective: Corrective mainteance are changes necessitated by actual errors. The main reasons for corrective maintenance are logic and design errors. These types of modifications account for 20 percent of all software maintenance conducted during the operation phase.

Perfective: Perfective mainteance are the changes and modifications that take place because of changing or expanding needs of the user. This accounts for 60 percent of all software maintenance during the operation phase.

Maintenance and Acceptance Testing in Each Phase of the Life Cycle

Acceptance testing is conducted to determine if the particular phase meets its established criteria, as determined by the project manager. Software maintenance are those activities that will modify baseline products created during the phase.

Requirements Phase

The primary objective of this phase is to provide the information necessary to accomplish a detailed plan. It is obvious that the user (the person who initiated the request) must be consulted. After all of the users' needs and requirements are understood, the following must be conducted:

- Workload estimation and refinement
- Project team staffing and organization
- Personnel requirements
- Facilities requirements
- System software requirements
- Any other requirements that need to be addressed

Table 1: Maintenance Activities Categories

Maintenance Activities in Each Category	
Category	Activity
Perfective	Making code easier to understand
	Improving documentation
	Adding a new capability
Adaptive	Modifying application for new version of operating system, compiler, or DB
Corrective	Quick fixes and fire-fighting

After all the requirements are understood, a written plan, which should include all of the user requirements as well as those listed above, should be prepared. This written plan should be included with the documentation.

Design phase: The objective of this phase is to create a map for the programmers to follow. During the design phase, the following steps should be conducted:

- Peer reviews
- A written narrative describing what the program should do and how it is going to do it.
- Any pseudo coding
- Design review

During the design review, acceptance testing should be conducted to ensure that the design meets all the criteria established during the requirements phase.

Programming phase: As in the case with the software system, the actual code should be developed with future needs in mind; that is, considerations of the needs of the maintainer. Techniques should be adopted that will allow the maintainer to easily understand, test, and modify the code. This can be accomplished by:

- Using a high level language (try not to use assembly)
- Use standard programming conventions
- Use standard compiler options
- Provide meaningful documentation and comments
- Use one standard language for your organization

During the programming phase of the life cycle, it is important to avoid "bad habits" that will contribute to software problems and will inhibit maintenance. There are generally key contributors to software problems. The following is a brief listing.

- Deeply nested DO loops
- Unneeded code that has not been removed
- Excessive use of IF statements
- Excessive use of global variables
- Excessive use of GOTO statements
- Excessive interaction between modules
- Redundant calls and modules
- Lack of top-down design
- Lack of or no documentation (within the code)

- Overly complex program structure and logic

What Is the Relationship between Software Testing and Software Maintenance?

Testing is conducted to find errors and omissions in the software and to ensure that the logic and structure of the program are appropriate. In short, testing provides assurance that software maintenance has been performed correctly.

Testing phase: During the testing phase of the life cycle, tests should be designed that are appropriate for the code. It is important to determine all of the known and unknown paths, and then to test them. Testing should be conducted of the upper and lower bounds (always test at zero), and several different types of testing should be employed. A few of the several types of testing methods are listed below.

- Black-box (input data with known and unknown results)
- Glass-box (testing with full knowledge of the code, and the results of black box testing)
- Code walk-through
- Standards audit

Operation Phase: The bulk of all software maintenance is performed in this phase. The major objective during the operation phase is a smooth operation of the software system. Sometimes there will be a need to modify the software system. Three types of software maintenance techniques that are applied are adaptive, corrective and perfective.

There is some argument as to what items need to be classified as maintenance. One paper suggests maintenance is any programming effort that requires at least 25 percent of a programmer's time to understand an existing system.[2] This definition is too broad. The best definition of software maintenance is all activities made to enhance, change, or modify an existing software system.

Management Problem

---

2   Bell, Florence, "Technology Transfer in the Maintenance Environment," *1984 AFIPS National Computer Conference Proceedings*, AFIPS Press, Reston, Va., Vol. 53, 1984, pp. 229-234.

Generally, the MIS lacks the necessary resources to effectively maintain existing software. Recognizing the problems associated with maintaining an existing system is an important start, but the MIS should make software maintenance one of the most important aspects of the software life cycle. The MIS should emphasize the importance of software maintenance throughout the life-cycle of the software and should stress the need to plan, develop, use, test, and maintain software with future needs in mind.

When software is written by several programmers, there may not be any individual who thoroughly understands the entire program. Also, the programmer who maintains the program may not have participated in the development process, which only excerbates the problem of keeping software operational. Too often the programmer assigned to maintenance is a novice. The position of maintenance should be the most important staff job.

Managing the Maintainer

Maintenance work is different: Once a problem has occurred, the software, which is often poorly written, designed and documented, is turned over to the maintainer. The maintainer has a poorly structured product to repair without the proper information to understand it. Therefore, the maintainer must perform some detective work based upon analytical skills and perseverance, and must be able to reconstruct the processing scenario at the time the problem occurred. After the problem has been isolated, the maintainer must then decide how to modify the code without affecting the remainder of the program. Sometimes this can be a nearly impossible task.

If software maintenance management were used in the development of the software system, the maintainer could review the documentation of each level of the software life cycle. Then, an understanding of where and why the error occurred could be made and recorded.

Key Attributes

Software maintenance should be a critical function in most organizations, therefore it is important that the staff be highly skilled and motivated. The key attributes to maintenance personnel are listed below.

- *Experienced*: must have good application skills.

- *Versatile*: must have knowledge of various hardware, operating systems, and languages.

- *Analytical*: must be able to find errors and understand how changing the code affects the entire program.

- *Adaptable*: must be able to work under poor conditions and strict time constraints.

- *Thorough*: modifications and changes must be thoroughly debugged and tested.

Management Solutions

The most important aspect of the management solution is keeping accurate data on the number and type of errors that occur and in what phase they were found or detected. First, by collecting this information, the MIS can give feedback to the programming teams. This will prevent programmers from making the same mistakes repeatedly. Even if most of the errors are found in the coding or in the design phase, the rework will have adverse affects on productivity. Therefore, the sooner defects are detected, the less rework and the greater the productivity.

Second, unless changes to a software system are recorded and documented, a software system will begin to degenerate with time. Eventually so many changes will occur that the current software will have varied dramatically from the original design and requirements (baseline). Futhermore, as time passes, the software will lack structure and errors will occur more frequently; therefore, confidence in the software will decline and reusing software will be worthless.

Record Performance

Record individual and project performance on a chart to allow everyone to see how well they are doing compared to everyone else, and how well this project is going compared to previous projects. Identify the results of the recording errors. Let everyone know how much time or money is being saved.

Software Reuse

The popular notion of software reuse focuses on the software source and object code. While source and object code can be reused, software consists of more than just code. Research has shown that greater benefits can be accrued through the use of the requirements, specifications, design, documentation, test data, and other elements of the software.

Can Software Reuse Improve Software Maintenance?

Software reuse should be at the heart of the software maintenance strategy because research has shown that the quality of software deteriorates when the only elements for the software that are reused are the source and object code. By effectively reusing the requirements, specifications, design, documentation, test data, and other elements on which the code is based, the quality of the software can be maintained or even enhanced during repeated modifications that occur after the software has been developed and placed into operational use.

Conclusion

The most important piece in the puzzle of controlling software costs is strong, effective, and disciplined management of the entire process. Greater discipline invoked in the software maintenance process results in higher quality software.

Suggested Reading

This article was not intended to be an in-depth paper on software maintenance but to make you think about software maintenance and quality assurance. You will either agree or disagree with my notations on software maintenance. Hopefully, it challenged you to think about your quality problems and provided a foundation for developing solutions to your unique software problems.

MANAGING SOFTWARE MAINTENANCE COST AND QUALITY

D. N. Card, D. V. Cotnoir, and C. E. Goorevich

Computer Sciences Corporation
4600 Powder Mill Road
Beltsville, MD 20705

ABSTRACT

This paper describes how measurement, estimation, and management interact to control software cost and quality in a large, long-lived maintenance project. Measures of effort expended and work performed from past releases assist managers in developing the accurate cost estimates necessary for effective planning. Tracking error reports allows managers to monitor quality trends and develop corrective actions when problems occur. The cost estimation and quality tracking procedures described support an established management structure based on a formal software development methodology (DSDM®).* It incorporates well-defined project control and product assurance functions that facilitate on-time delivery of reliable software.

I. INTRODUCTION

Maintenance of a software system intended for a long operational life poses special management problems. Agresti states that long-term maintenance must be managed explicitly to be effective.[1] Hamlet describes the alternative--unplanned and undocumented "emergency maintenance"--as being destructive to the software maintained.[2] This paper describes the initial results of steps taken to formalize and quantify management and planning on a large software maintenance project.

The system under maintenance--the Network Control Center (NCC) project at Goddard Space Flight Center (GSFC)--schedules resources for the Tracking and Data Relay Satellite (TDRS). It is a central node in the National Aeronautics and Space Administration (NASA) space network. NCC development began in June 1977. It became operational in October 1983 with the launch of the TDRS-A spacecraft and online support of several 'user satel-

---

*DSDM (Digital System Development Methodology) is a registered trademark of CSC.

lites. Since that time the NCC support contractor, Computer Sciences Corporation (CSC), has maintained the operational NCC system and prepared for major augmentation of the baseline system. Collection of software cost and quality data for management is incorporated into all software development and maintenance activities.

The results described in this paper show how feedback from that data affects the management and planning of maintenance activities. Data was collected from eight software releases delivered to GSFC in 1984, 1985, and 1986. Key points discussed in this paper include the NCC maintenance process (Section II); measurements taken and data used to develop models for cost estimation and quality tracking (Section III); and application of the models to improve planning and management for maintenance work (Section IV). The conclusions suggest further steps to improve measurement and management (Section V).

II. THE SOFTWARE MAINTENANCE PROCESS

The NCC maintenance process extends CSC's DSDM, which is used for new development projects throughout the corporation.[3] DSDM is a comprehensive life-cycle methodology. Its components include incremental development (builds and releases), structured analysis and design, structured programming, formal product assurance, and independent testing. DSDM's product assurance approach stresses design reviews, code inspections, and software engineering notebooks. Basic DSDM features are adapted to the NCC project via customized standards and procedures for both new development and maintenance activities.

Figure 1 presents the NCC maintenance life cycle. It includes three major stages: maintenance implementation, system test, and acceptance testing and operations. All maintenance activities are scheduled as part of a formal release, with two or three releases normally planned for each calendar year. System changes in a release may be either software fixes for problems reported by the system testing, acceptance testing, and operations groups, or new/changed requirements. Problem reports are classified into four priority levels that indicate the operational severity of the observed condition (one is highest, four is lowest). New/changed requirements are described in minispecifications. These "minispecs" drive changes to the baseline requirements and specification documents as well as the design.

Before work on a release is initiated, a release review meeting is held to select the minispecs and problem reports to be implemented in the release. Customers, developers, and users participate in the release review. The approved list of modifications is developed into a maintenance plan for implementation, integration, and testing.

The product assurance office (PAO) monitors all design, coding, unit testing, and integration work for adherence to development standards. New and revised software is reviewed and certified by the developers, then submitted to the PAO for final inspection. The PAO delivers the approved software to the configuration management (CM) group. The CM group integrates the delivered software into the baseline system and updates the system for independent system testing. When system testing is complete, CM prepares the release for delivery to the customer (GSFC). Acceptance testing is conducted by an independent contractor before the updated system is used to support regular network operations. In sum, maintenance of the NCC project is a lengthy, complex process in which cost and quality must be carefully managed to ensure success.

III. ESTIMATING COST AND QUALITY

Accurate estimation is a prerequisite for effective planning and management of maintenance activity. Because so many factors influence software cost and quality, it is difficult to transport measures from different environments. Demarco suggests that the best results

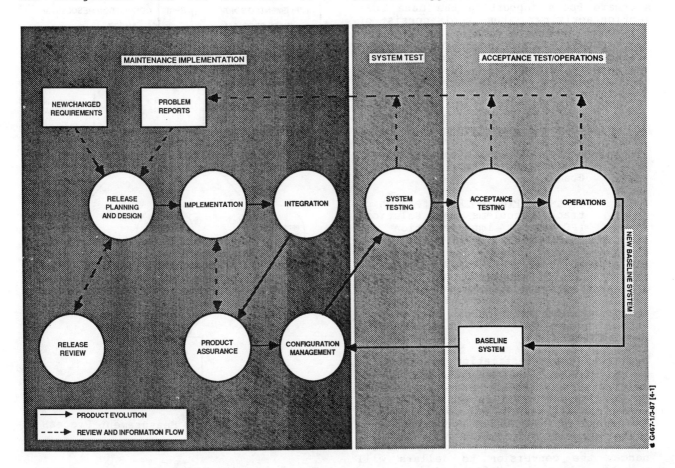

Figure 1. Overview of NCC Maintenance Life Cycle

are obtained when local historical data is incorporated into the estimation process.[4] This section describes the measurement, estimation, and reporting mechanisms employed to support NCC maintenance management. Although this approach is transportable, the specific numerical results may not be.

Maintenance Measurement

The NCC project began an extensive program of cost and quality data collection and analysis in 1984 as part of a larger productivity and quality improvement effort. Effort, errors, and lines of code measures were captured for eight consecutive releases. Table 1 defines the specific measures collected and analyzed for NCC. This set of data items closely parallels the metrics recommended by Schaefer.[5] Figure 2 shows where in the life cycle these data types are obtained. Effort, and therefore productivity, currently is measured only in the maintenance and system testing phases, although in the future the process may be extended to acceptance and operations. Figure 2 also identifies software tools supporting the data collection activity. These tools consist of

- **Performance Measurement System**, which tracks work performed and resources expended using an earned-value scheme on a personal computer (PC)

- **Source Analyzer Program**, which counts source code features like statements, decisions, etc. (the Software Engineering Laboratory Program[6] rehosted to the mainframe)

- **Software Problem Reporter**, which tracks problems and solutions (PC-based implementation in progress).

The use of tools facilitates timely and accurate data collection and reporting. Results are incorporated in a productivity and quality report for each release.

Cost Estimation

Typically, cost estimation proceeds in three steps: (1) count units of work to be performed, (2) estimate corresponding effort in staff-days (or hours), and (3) convert effort to dollar cost. To avoid introducing issues such as inflation and overhead that might distract from this discussion of software maintenance, the conversion to dollars will not be addressed. Unfortunately, estimation for maintenance has not been studied as extensively as estimation for

new development. For example, Boehm's large volume treats this topic in about 25 pages.[7] Consequently, CSC used its own data to develop an NCC cost model from basic principles rather than relying on existing models.

Table 1. Definition of Measures

NAME	CODE	DEFINITION
SOURCE LINE OF CODE	SLOC	PROGRAM SOURCE LINE; 80-COLUMN CARD IMAGE
DELIVERED SOURCE INSTRUCTION	DSI	NONBLANK, NONCOMMENT PROGRAM SOURCE LINE
EXECUTABLE STATEMENT	EXST	TRANSFORMATION/TRANSFER; NOT NECESSARILY A LINE
SYSTEM IMPLEMENTATION DAY	SID	ANY UNIT OF 8 HOURS CHARGED TO A RELEASE
NEW UNIT	NU	SUBPROGRAM ADDED IN THIS RELEASE
SOFTWARE PROBLEM REPORT	SPR	A FORMALLY DOCUMENTED ERROR DESCRIPTION
IMPLEMENTED SOFTWARE PROBLEM	SPRF	CORRECTION RESOLVING AN SPR

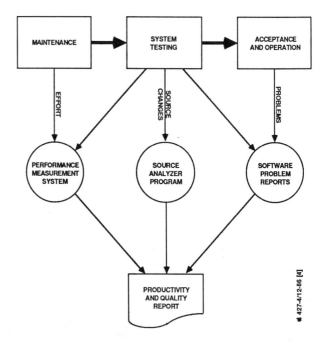

Figure 2. NCC Measurement Process

The first step was to identify an appropriate measure of the work performed. Arnold and Parker distinguished two major maintenance work types: fixes and enhancement/adaptations.[8] Both result in the production and/or modification of software. Therefore, CSC had to study and choose the methods and units of counting lines of code (e.g., SLOC, DSI, and EXST). Table 2 compares the composition of NCC source code with that of a typical new development project at CSC. The table indicates a higher percentage of comments for NCC. This may indicate a tendency for comments to accumulate during maintenance. On the other hand, the DSI-to-EXST ratio seemed comparable to new development. DSI was selected as the unit of work for cost estimation purposes in conformance to current trends.[7]

Table 2.   Composition of NCC SLOC

| SOFTWARE TYPE | PERCENT OF TOTAL SLOC | |
	TYPICAL NEW DEVELOPMENT	NCC SOFTWARE
COMMENTS, BLANKS, ETC.	50	67
SOURCE INSTR. LINES (DSI)	50	33
EXECUTABLE STATEMENTS (EXT)*	(25)	(14)

*A SUBSET OF DSI (NOT ADDITIVE).

806-1/5-87[8]

Unlike the final product of new development, the software output of maintenance includes deleted and changed lines. Basili and Freburger showed that modified lines cost about as much as new lines but did not discuss deleted lines.[9] Figure 3 shows the application of an exploratory data analysis technique[10] to determine the relative weighting of new/changed and deleted DSIs with respect to cost. The results indicate that the weights are about equal (0.5 each): it costs as much to delete a DSI as it does to add a new one.

Of course, all maintenance activity does not result in software production or modification. Significant amounts of effort must be expended to evaluate changes and update documents. Many problem reports can be closed without any software change. Consequently, productivity calculations based on line counts alone vary widely during maintenance. Figure 4 plots productivity (DSI/SID) versus relative "fix" activity (SPRF/DSI); it shows that fix-oriented releases demonstrate lower productivity. The figure indicates that in the absence of SPRFs, enhancement-only productivity for the NCC project would be about 70 percent of the organization's nominal

productivity for new development. At the other end of the trend line, fix-only productivity is about 25 percent of nominal productivity.

The next step was to develop a cost model relating work performed to effort expended. Using lines-of-code measures for estimating cost has the same drawback for maintenance as it does for new development: the lines cannot be counted until the work is finished. However, design identifies new units, an appropriate measure for the enhancement/adaptation component of maintenance. Furthermore, implementation of SPRFs, the fix component of maintenance, is assigned to releases by management.

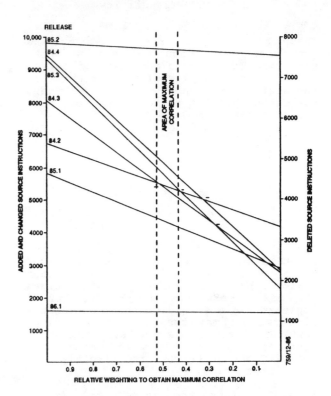

This procedure identifies the linear combination of new/changed and deleted DSIs and best reproduces the rank ordering of NCC releases, which are numbered sequentially within the year of delivery, in terms of total cost. An intersection indicates the relative order of two releases has been reversed by changing the weighting of the two components. The results suggest that the components should be about equally weighted. See Reference 10 for a full explanation of this procedure.

Figure 3.   Measuring NCC Workload

93

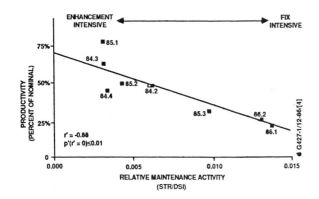

Figure 4. Effect of Maintenance on NCC Productivity

These two measures appear to provide a good characterization of the work to be performed in implementing any given release. The application of a multiple regression technique[11] to the NCC data for seven releases produced the following cost estimation model:

$$SID = 42 + 4.8 \ NU + 46.6 \ SPRF**$$

where

SID	=	system implementation days required
NU	=	new units to be implemented
SPRF	=	SPR fixes to be implemented

Note that the model includes a fixed cost of 42 SIDs for delivering any release. Furthermore, the model indicates that fixing a problem requires almost 10 times the effort of developing a new unit. Implementing a single enhancement/adaptation request may result in the development of several new units. Thus, the cost of the two types of maintenance activity cannot be compared directly with this information.

Figure 5 plots the actual and fitted values of cost for seven releases. It also shows the predicted value, based on the previous seven releases, and the actual value for an eighth release. Note that the predicted cost lies within 25 percent of the actual cost in SID. This model is recalibrated with the data from each new release; thus far it has proven to be relatively stable. Note that the last three releases cost less than indicated by the model. This suggests a productivity improvement trend.

Rone developed another approach to maintenance cost estimation based on the concept of a "critical skills level."[12]

**Correlation coefficient = 0.89, p < 0.01

He postulated a minimum staffing level for effective maintenance that exceeds the requirements for implementing error fixes alone. The critical skills level depends on the nature of the application being maintained. Thus, Rone's approach assumes a lower bound to maintenance cost. Staffing below that level could result in schedule and quality problems. This may be an important consideration in the near future of shrinking budgets.

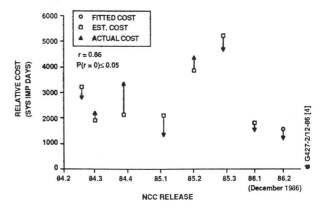

Figure 5. Estimation of NCC Cost

Problem Reporting

One basic feature of maintenance is problem reporting and tracking. The flow of problems determines the "fix" portion of the maintenance workload. It also indicates the quality of the software being maintained as well as the effectiveness of the maintenance effort. Arnold's and Parker's criteria for "adequate maintenance"[8] require substantially more detailed information than is available from the current NCC problem reporting system. However, NCC experience shows that maintenance adequacy can also be determined from less detailed data (see also Reference 5).

The NCC project records all problems reported during system testing, acceptance testing, and operations. Classifying problems into four categories of criticality facilitates orderly planning for their resolution. Levels 1, 2, and 3 are referred to as "serious errors." Level 4 problems include "cosmetic" changes and spelling mistakes. Figure 6 plots annual totals of all problems and serious errors. The descending trend line for serious errors indicates that the reliability or quality of the system tends to improve over time. The rate of problem discovery declines from year to year.

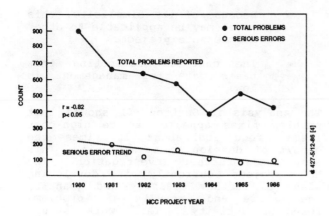

Figure 6. NCC Reliability History

IV. MANAGING SOFTWARE MAINTENANCE

The cost and quality models presented in the preceding section support the NCC project's view of software maintenance as an extension of new development. Thus, it can be managed in much the same way: software maintenance is planned, scheduled, budgeted, controlled, and measured using methodologies, tools, and philosophies similar to those used for new development. However, maintenance planning and execution differs from that for new development in several important respects.

Planning With the NCC Cost Model

The scope of maintenance release planning encompasses the entire life cycle of the release from definition to testing and delivery. The planning sequence consists of three steps: (1) definition of the items to be included in the release, (2) estimation of the resources required, and (3) development of detailed plans and schedules. The result of these three steps is a maintenance plan, which is much like a development plan in content and detail.

The content of a maintenance release responds to customer and operational priorities. Contents are finalized at a release review (see Figure 1). Attendees include representatives from the customer, user, systems engineering, software maintenance, system/database, product assurance, and independent test organizations. The agenda includes a detailed discussion of each item proposed for inclusion in the release: technical issues, preliminary estimates of resources required for implementation, and dependencies. The NCC cost model discussed in Section II facilitates preliminary resource estimation. The NCC reliability history noted in Section III supports decisions about the relative priority of problem fixes versus enhancement requirements.

Once the contents of the release are established, detailed estimates of the resources needed to complete the work are developed by experienced managers. The effort estimation model described in Section III provides an independent check on these estimates. Detailed schedules are developed iteratively to obtain the best fit in terms of multiple criteria:

- Mission (spacecraft) schedules

- Operational needs (severe functional impact)

- Availability of resources

- Schedules for other development (software, hardware, other facilities).

All development and maintenance personnel (including programmers, testers, and support staff) are fully integrated into the NCC project organization. If necessary, the maintenance staff is supplemented by personnel from development groups, a decision that may affect development plans.

Execution of the Maintenance Plan

Ostensibly, maintenance implementation begins once planning is complete. However, maintenance is subject to constraints and risks similar to those affecting software development, which may prevent perfect execution of the plan. For example, requirements "creep" often occurs (although it manifests itself more as "drift" in the maintenance environment) as items are added and deleted from a release. Demarco provides a good explanation of these factors and strategies for dealing with them.[14] However, two other areas must be given special consideration during maintenance: integrating the changes into the existing system[13] and assembling and motivating maintenance teams.[14]

Software changes are integrated into the existing system by following product assurance and CM standards and procedures defined by DSDM and modified for NCC use. Maintaining documentation is an essential component of effective maintenance.[15] Updates to users' guides are handled in a formal manner: appropriate sections are updated by maintenance programmers and delivered as necessary with each release, using established document change notice procedures. To reinforce the notification process, user's guide changes are also cited in the release delivery letter, which is used by acceptance testing personnel to assess operational changes and any related training needs. A demonstration of the release that highlights any operational changes is also provided for test and operations users. Because acceptance and operations are performed by different organizations, strict adherence to standards and procedures is essential for an orderly transition to operations. To make this process smoother, a release leader is assigned to support this transition.

People implement the maintenance process. As Glass points out, the role of maintenance programmer has "diverse and unique requirements" but is often regarded as less desirable than that of developer.[15] This can result in personnel motivation problems if not addressed properly.[14] Because the NCC project organization includes both new development and maintenance activities, programmer assignments can be varied without losing special skills and experience. This has enabled the NCC project to attain a very low personnel turnover rate. However, the consequences of this organization for cost and quality are not yet fully understood because of the difficulty inherent in comparing different organizations and environments.

V. CONCLUSIONS

The data collection and analysis effort described in this paper has made a significant contribution to improving NCC manageability as well as increasing our understanding of the maintenance process. Furthermore, practical experience as well as the results of the data analysis results presented in this paper have led to some specific conclusions about managing large software maintenance projects:

- Effective maintenance depends on following a rigorous methodology

- Long-term maintenance requires formal planning and explicit management

- Personnel enthusiasm can be maintained by periodically providing alternative assignments

- It costs as much to delete a line of code as it does to write a new one

- A simple cost model and reliability history are valuable tools for planning

- A count of new units and problem fixes accurately predicts maintenance cost

- Because of its simplicity, this model may be applicable to other maintenance projects

- The cost of collecting this basic data for management is low.

The analysis in Section III showed that problem fixes appeared to be high-cost items, requiring about 10 times the effort of developing a new unit. This area needs further investigation. The NCC project currently is developing plans to further classify and quantify the nature and results of problem-response activity. This work should eventually lead to greater insight into the maintenance process and how it can be improved in terms of both cost and quality. As Schneidewind concludes, maintenance will be a major factor in the software industry for the forseeable future.[16] It is, therefore, an important topic for further research.

ACKNOWLEDGMENTS

The authors would like to recognize the significant contributions made to this work by J. Dodd (CSC) and by P. Ondrus and A. Maione (NASA/GSFC).

REFERENCES

1. W. W. Agresti, "Managing Program Maintenance," Journal of Systems Management, February 1982, pp 34-37

2. R. Hamlet, "Program Maintenance: A Modest Theory," Proceedings: Fifteenth Hawaii Conference on System Sciences, January 1982

3. S. Steppel, T. L. Clark, et al., Digital System Development Methodology, Computer Sciences Corporation, March 1984

4. T. Demarco, Controlling Software Projects. New York: Yourdon Press, Inc., 1982

5. H. Schaefer, "Metrics for Optimal Maintenance Management," Proceedings: IEEE Conference on Software Maintenance, November 1985

6. W. J. Decker and W. A. Taylor, FORTRAN Static Source Code Analyzer User's Guide. Greenbelt, Maryland: NASA/Software Engineering Laboratory, July 1986

7. B. W. Boehm, Software Engineering Economics. Englewood Cliffs, N.J.: Prentice-Hall, 1981

8. R. S. Arnold and D. A. Parker, "The Dimensions of Healthy Maintenance," <u>Proceedings: IEEE Sixth International Conference on Software Engineering</u>, March 1982

9. V. R. Basili and K. Freburger, "Programming Measurement and Estimation in the Software Engineering Laboratory," <u>Journal of Systems and Software</u>, April 1981

10. P. F. Velleman and D. C. Hoaglin, <u>Applications, Basics, and Computing of Exploratory Data Analysis</u>. New York: Duxbury Press, 1981

11. O. J. Dunn and V. A. Clark, <u>Applied Statistics: Analysis of Variance and Regression</u>. New York: John Wiley & Sons, Inc., 1974

12. K. Y. Rone, "Maintenance Estimation Methodology," <u>Proceedings: NASA/ GSFC Seventh Annual Software Engineering Workshop</u>, December 1982

13. M. A. Branch, M. C. Jackson, and M. D. Laviolette, "Software Maintenance Management," <u>Proceedings: IEEE Conference on Software Maintenance</u>, November 1985

14. J. D. Couger and R. A. Zawacki, <u>Motivating and Managing Computer Personnel</u>. New York: John Wiley & Sons, Inc., 1980

15. R. L. Glass and R. A. Noiseux, <u>Software Maintenance Guidebook</u>. Englewood Cliffs, N. J.: Prentice-Hall, 1981

16. N. F. Schneidewind, "The State of Software Maintenance," <u>IEEE Transactions on Software Engineering</u>, March 1987, pp 303-310

MANAGING APPLICATION PROGRAM MAINTENANCE EXPENDITURES

TOR GUIMARAES *Weatherhead School of Management
Case Western Reserve University*

*Tor Guimaraes is Director of
the postgraduate MIS
Certificate Program at Case
Western Reserve University.
His latest research reports
include management of
systems development
alternatives and the
development of guidelines for
the establishment of
information centers.*

Author's Present Address:
Tor Guimaraes, Managerial
Studies, Weatherhead School
of Management, Case
Western Reserve University,
311 Wickenden, Cleveland,
Ohio 44106

INTRODUCTION

Traditionally, literature regarding application software has consistently advocated the investment of greater resources during the program development stage to improve the maintainability of those programs [5,6,8,10,13,16,18,26,28]. The underlying assumption of this argument is that the application program will have a long life with maintenance costs comprising a large share of the total costs (development plus maintenance) for the program.

Application program maintenance expenditures represent a considerable portion of the total application program expenditures (Table I). The estimated percentage figure varies 40%–75% of the total application program costs. While research by different authors shows wide variance due to sampling error, different research methodologies, and measurement problems, the economic importance of maintenance activities has been strongly corroborated regardless of the approach used to study it.

For this study, *development costs* are defined as costs incurred to make an application program operational. *Maintenance costs*, on the other hand, are incurred after the program is officially turned over to operations, to correct any errors in the program, to expand its functionality to users, and/or to tune up its execution. When the separation of maintenance versus development expenditures was not clearly expressed through different unit budgets, MIS directors were asked to estimate costs.

Beyond recognizing the economic importance of software maintenance, literature dealing with this subject often proposes ways to deal with the problem. Two of the more representative efforts are presented by Braddock [8] who addresses the organizational, administrative, and technical areas; and Boehm [25] who covers detailed technical suggestions on how to reduce program maintenance costs. Similar contributions have been surveyed by other authors [3,16,20,22,23,26,27].

Despite the apparently sound prescriptions available in the literature, the problem of high application program maintenance costs has persisted over the years and remains a major concern to MIS practitioners.

*ABSTRACT: Program maintenance
represents a major portion of the
total expenditures on application
programs. Despite the attention this
subject has received in the MIS
literature, new guidelines to action
in this area remain of great interest
to practitioners. A large number of
variables thought to be
determinants of application
program maintenance expenditure
have been studied through the
inspection of application portfolios
and personal interviews with top
computer executives and systems
development personnel. Based on
the results, recommendations are
made on how to reduce application
program maintenance
expenditures.*

"Managing Application Program Maintenance Expenditures" by T.
Guimaraes from *Communications of the ACM*, Volume 26,
Number 10, October 1983, pages 739-746. Copyright ©1983,
Association for Computing Machinery, Inc., reprinted with
permission.

TABLE I. Estimations of Percentage of Total Costs Represented by Maintenance Costs

Maintenance Cost (percentage)	Study Estimation
40	[17 and 18]
40–60	[6, 7, 8, 10, 11, 16, 19, 26]
67	[28]
70	[6]
75	[1, 12]

* The great variance in the estimates of maintenance cost percentage is due partially to the type of software being studied (business, military), sampling error, and measurement problems.

MOTIVATION FOR RESEARCH AND METHODOLOGY

Important questions in the area of application program maintenance remain unanswered. Two major objectives of this study are to address several of these unanswered questions and to corroborate (or not) findings by previous studies on application program maintenance. For that purpose, the following steps have been followed:

1. A list of potential determinants of application program maintenance expenditures was identified by an extensive survey of the literature. This list was modified to reflect the personal opinion of several academics and practitioners known for their knowledge in the area. An adaptation of the Delphi technique was used to integrate and converge the experts' opinions.

2. A pilot study, involving four organizations, was used to refine the variables (Table II shows the final set of variables considered) and to identify any operational problems. As a result, the use of mailed questionnaires was dropped in spite of convenience and ability to reach a large number of organizations quickly: The pilot study clearly indicated the necessity of using personal interviews because of the great variance in electronic data processing (EDP) terminology.

3. A general survey encompassed two major research procedures to: 1) determine management of application programs (Data collection was done through personal interviews with the MIS managers and immediate subordinates within each organization. Originally, 69 organizations were approached; but for a variety of reasons, 26 did not participate in the study), and 2) to analyze for a more detailed, company-specific program of maintenance (Data collection was accomplished through the inspection of application programs, available program documentation and through personal interviews with program developers, users, and maintenance personnel).

Due to the amount of time necessary to research each company, the number of case studies was limited to five. Within each organization a minimum random sample of 30 application programs was selected.

The organizations participating in the study were selected on a convenience basis and had to satisfy the following characteristics:

1. An MIS department of any budget size utilizing a service bureau for no more than 50% of the company's MIS-related activities.

2. Not a service bureau or consulting organization providing services in the MIS area.

3. Not an educational institution.

4. A central processing unit classified as at least a minicomputer. Organizations using only microcomputers and/or other automatic data processing equipment without at least one minicomputer were excluded.

5. Computer equipment operational for at least three years. (All organizations in the sample had computer equipment operational for at least six years.)

A detailed discussion of the variables studied and of the research methodology is documented by Guimaraes [15].

COMPANY SAMPLE DEMOGRAPHICS

The following dimensions characterize the companies surveyed.

Sample Description Through Selected Company Attributes

A list of important descriptors is shown in Table III which contains (1) the arithmetic mean, (2) the median, (3) standard deviation, and (4) range for 10 company attributes. For the last three attributes, which are categorical, the percentage of companies in the sample presently using the items and the percentage of companies planning to use the items in the very near future, i.e., within one year, replace the sample median and standard deviation.

Sample Distribution by Industry Classification

As recognized by McLaughlin [21], companies in different industries differ in their EDP operations. For this study, organizations were classified according to their Standard Industrial Classification (SIC) code. All classifications except Food Processing, are general industrial classifications. Due to its predominance in the Twin Cities area, Food Processing has been separated out from Manufacturing.

TABLE II. List of Variables Studied

Company attributes:	Industry-type and company sales or revenue
MIS Department Attributes:	Department budget, system development budget, maintenance budget, use of project team separate maintenance group, other related department subunits, specific program development standards, number of program development standards, documents used for maintenance, self-contained query language use, system development charge-back, system maintenance charge-back, languages available at the installation, language transitions at the installation, total number of application programs, hardware/operating system conversions, other technical changes, DBMS utilization, MIS manager estimation of average program life length, application package expenditures, environment sophistication, environment transition.
Program General Attributes:	DSS versus EDP user process, DMBS or shared files or self-contained files, user or staff written, batch or online, new system or redevelopment, time spent on documentation, type of documents, maintenance personnel estimate of documentation effectiveness, life length.
Program Physical Attributes:	Number of lines of code, development cost, development time, maintenance average yearly cost, source language used.
Program User(s) Attributes:	Number of users served, number of organization functions served, number of business functions served, rank.

TABLE III. Sample Description Through Selected Attributes

Organization Attribute	Mean	Median	Standard Deviation	Range
(1) Gross Revenue or Budget	$550M	$220M	$750M	$2.98B
(2) EDP Shop Budget in absolute terms and as % of (1)	$5.2M 1.2%	$2.8M 1.0%	$7.3M 1.9%	$34.8M 3.3%
(3) Yearly Expenditures for Systems Development in absolute terms and as % of (2)	$845K 19%	$335K 19%	$1M 10%	$4.5M 42%
(4) Year Expenditures for System Maintenance in absolute terms and as % of (2)	$584K 13%	$240K 11%	$970K 8%	$5.8M 31%
(5) Yearly Expenditures for Application Software Packages in absolute terms and as % of (3)	$50K 1.3%	$30K 1%	$85K 1.5%	$500K 31%
(6) Number of Programs	2.2K	1.3K	2.3K	9.8K
(7) Number of Development Standards	4	4	—	10
(8) Using Chargeback For System Development	35% (additional 10% within next year)			
(9) Using DBMS	58% (additional 29% within next year)			
(10) Using Query Language	67% (additional 7% within next year)			

K = Thousand; M = Million; B = Billion.
Sample size = 43.

Five industry classifications plus a government class are used. A sample frequency distribution in absolute and relative terms is presented (Table IV).

Equipment Usage

Several of the 43 organizations taking part in this research adopted a multivendor approach to equipment configuration. Table V suggests that most organizations (91%) have at least some IBM equipment, e.g., minicomputer or larger. Other equipment patterns indicate that: (1) The IBM share of the market seems to be higher (91%) than expected (about 60%). (2) While having a smaller share of the market, Burroughs and Amdahl seem to be doing well in terms of percentage increases. (3) Univac seems to be poorly represented in the sample, in terms of both quantity and quality. (Note that Table V does not indicate how many machines from a particular vendor are in operation at the company. However, in most cases, the organization had one machine from a particular vendor.)

EDP Budget as Percentage of Gross Income

McLaughlin [21] conducted a study which involved a sample of 112 companies in the United States and Canada (88 companies were excluded from his study because they were service bureaus or were users of a service bureau, or because the companies were going through major changes.) illustrating a distribution of data processing budgets as a percentage of gross revenue by industry classification. While the categories used were somewhat unique, a comparison against a similar frequency distribution is presented in Table VI.

TABLE IV. Frequency Distributions by Industry Type

Class	Sample	
Financial	7	(16.3%)
Merchandising	8	(18.6%)
Transportation and Utilities	6	(14.0%)
Food Processing	6	(14.0%)
Manufacturing	14	(32.6%)
Government	2	(4.7%)
	43	(100.0%)

The exhibit contains EDP budgets as a percentage of gross sales, or budget, for government organizations. The sample size used to derive the percentage figure is also shown (within parenthesis). Because the two studies use some categories which do not overlap, some cells of the exhibit are empty.

FINDINGS ON PROGRAM MAINTENANCE EXPENDITURES

Findings on program maintenance expenditures are derived from two sources: (1) the data collected on all 43 organizations (general survey), and/or (2) the data collected on the five case-study companies.

Findings from the General Survey

Several descriptive measures regarding maintenance expenditures as a percentage of total expenditures are presented (Table VII).

The arithmetic mean of 41% (Table VII–A) for maintenance expense percentage is lower than most studies estimated (see Table I). However, unlike the other studies, application program maintenance does not include enhancements to the programs in this case. A detailed discussion of different types of maintenance activity is done elsewhere [15]. If the expenditures on program maintenance includes application program enhancements (as in the studies listed in Table I), the arithmetic mean is 53%. This corroborates the already impressive evidence that, on the average, maintenance expenditures indeed represent a sizable proportion of total expenditures on application programs.

Most organizations in the sample (81%) have no more than half the total programming expenditures associated with maintenance (see Table VII–A); yet, some extreme cases do exist. Companies undergoing massive application program portfolio conversions may temporarily stop all maintenance activities and concentrate on the development of new application programs or the reprogramming of existing programs. The other extreme also exists—available resources do not meet what is required (in the opinion of MIS management) to maintain operational application programs and to concurrently develop new application programs. Under these conditions, one of the organizations studied declared a moratorium on new program development. Whichever extreme exists,

TABLE V. Sample Percentages Regarding Specific Vendor Equipment Usage

Vendor	Using	Dropping Within Two Years	Adopting Within Two Years
IBM	91	7	12
UNIVAC	5	2	0
CDC	9	2	5
HONEYWELL	12	9	2
AMDAHL	5	0	5
BURROUGHS	9	0	7
OTHER	12	7	0

Percentages rounded to nearest whole number.
Sample Size = 43.

both usually represent emergency situations for EDP/MIS managers.

In the case shown in Table VII–A where a minimum of 0% of EDP budget was used for application program maintenance, and available resources were used solely for the development of new programs, the manager involved was completely surprised by his company being bought out by another. The event forced the conversion of the whole application program portfolio to a incompatible machine. The program maintenance expenditures necessary because of the conversion, coupled with a backlog of desirable application program enhancements, made massive reprogramming the chosen alternative. Because the pressures of time and limited resources, all available resources were dedicated to the reprogramming effort.

Two situations in which maintenance activities totally absorbed available resources are indicated:

1. One organization was in the process of installing a large number of purchased application software packages over time. All development of new application programs was suspended, at least temporarily, while maintenance activities on existing programs continued. However, this seems to be a rather unusual situation in practice.

2. In order to properly satisfy user needs another organization lacked MIS resources. Under these circumstances, perhaps as a tool to attract the attention of top management to his predicament, the EDP manager decided that no new application programs would be developed; available resources would be used to maintain the application programs already in operation. Although this also seems to be an extreme case,

TABLE VI. EDP Budgets as a Percentage of Gross Revenue by Industry Type

Class	McLaughlin Study	This Study
Manufacturing	0.93 (24)	1.2 (14)
Food Processing	—	0.5 (6)
Retail Trade	0.90 (6)	1.0 (8)*
Wholesale Trade	3.1 (6)	
Transportation and Utilities	—	1.1 (6)
Financial	2.6 (6)**	1.7 (7)**
Education	2.7 (13)	
Medical and Health Care	3.7 (4)	—
City/County Government	1.2 (9)	1.8 (1)***

Sample sizes are given within parentheses.
* Retail and Wholesale companies classified under Merchandising.
** All small banks.
*** One government organization was excluded from computation because it was an unusual case.

many EDP managers, given the reality of limited resources, view the maintenance of the existing application programs as a higher priority than the development of new programs. While recognizing the importance of developing new application programs, most MIS managers feel that a sufficient amount of resources must be dedicated to maintaining present commitments (application programs) to users before new commitments are made by developing new application programs.

Findings from Case Studies

The five case-study companies are, on the average, representative of the forty-three organizations sampled (see Table VII–B). Within each of the five companies, the randomly selected application programs again indicate a wide variance in total maintenance expenditures as a proportion of total program expenditures (development plus maintenance) for individual programs. Much of the variance can be partially explained by several variables (see Table VIII).

1. *Program age.* Total application program maintenance expenditures obviously tend to increase with program age. Program age is directly related to increases in the average maintenance expenditures over the years the program has been in operation. Program changes over time tend to complicate the logical flows of the program and to render program documentation obsolete, thus increasing maintenance expenditures. (Program age is measured in months.)

2. *Program size.* While the data presented in Table VIII does not indicate a relationship between program size and maintenance expenditures, anecdotal evidence suggests that size and complexity have a great impact on maintenance expenditures. Program size has been measured as total lines of code, excluding comment code.

3. *Program redevelopment.* Despite the small number of observations in this category [17], within the five case-study companies, programs which represent redevelopment (replacements) of other programs apparently require less maintenance expenditures. The statistical evidence is even stronger ($t = 3.61$, $p = 0.01$) if one considers average maintenance per line of code.

4. *Program usage.* Online programs require greater maintenance expenditure than their batch-mode counterparts.

5. *Database Management Systems Interface.* Application programs using a host language, database management systems (DMS) tend to have lower maintenance expenditures than programs not using a DMS. Further analysis (see Table IX) indicates that programs with DMS interface tend to have lower average maintenance expenditures in proportion to development costs, and lower maintenance expenditures per line of code. Also, these programs tend to be larger and more expensive (in terms of total costs but not per line of code) than their DMS-independent counterparts. The impact of host language DMS on development and maintenance costs of application programs is being researched further by the author.

6. *Program documentation.* Maintenance programmers responsible for specific programs were asked to rate the usefulness of the available program documentation to the task of program maintenance (5 = "clearly yes," 1 = "definitely not"). A significant inverse relationship exists between the rating for a program and its average yearly program maintenance expenditures. The same is true if one considers average maintenance per line of code.

7. *Programming language.* Whether the application program is written in assembly language or on a higher level,

TABLE VII. Application Program Maintenance Expenditures as Percentage of Total Expenditures. (Total Expenditures = Development Expenditures Plus Maintenance Expenditures)

A) Aggregate Measures for the 43 Organizations*			
PERCENTAGE	PERCENTILE		MEAN = 41%
			MEDIAN = 40%
29	26th		MINIMUM = 00%
38	49th		MAXIMUM = 100%
50	81st		STD. DEV. = 22%

B) Case Studies Measures Based on Each Company's Programs**					
	A (n = 34)	B (n = 32)	C (n = 37)	D (n = 37)	E (n = 40)
Mean	26%	43%	59%	33%	31%
Median	22%	27%	16%	19%	07%
Minimum	00%	00%	00%	00%	00%
Maximum	77%	84%	72%	81%	87%
Average Age of Programs (months)	37.8	49.3	61.9	37.3	58.5

* The top computer executives (and/or immediate subordinates) in each company estimated the proportion and MIS budget used for application software development and maintenance.
** Application programs were randomly selected within each mini case study company.

procedural language also affects the level of maintenance expenditures for the program. Anecdotal evidence gathered while interviewing maintenance programmers agrees with this finding.

OTHER FINDINGS AND RECOMMENDATIONS FOR REDUCING APPLICATION PROGRAM MAINTENANCE EXPENDITURES
Based on the results of this study, the following recommendations are made to better manage application program maintenance expenditures.
Utilize Database Management Systems (DMS)
The costs/benefits of using a DMS is a controversial subject. Companies with longer DMS experience (5 years or more)

tend to evaluate them more favorably ($\bar{X}$ = 4.2, σ_x = 0.60, n = 11) than organizations which are relatively inexperienced ($\bar{X}$ = 3.0, σ_x = 1.1, n = 14), along a scale where 5 = "greatly cost beneficial," 3 = "costs and benefits about even," 1 = "not cost beneficial." The t test in this case shows t = 3.17, df = 23, p = 0.01.

It is apparent that the learning process regarding DMS utilization has been fairly expensive and has occurred by trial-and-error in most organizations. Experienced organizations have made a strong commitment of resources to the DMS approach. The DMS training of system development personnel receives strong emphasis in these organizations.

The data on application programs from 4 of the 5 case studies (Company A had just begun using a DMS) strongly

TABLE VIII. Explaining Variance in Program Maintenance Expenditures Based on the Case Studies

Independent Variable	Company					
	A (n = 34)	B (n = 32)	C (n = 37)	D (n = 37)	E (n = 40)	Pooled (n = 180)
Program Age*	N.S.	0.44	0.32	0.23	N.S.	0.11
		0.01	0.03	0.09		0.06
Program Size*	0.43	N.S.	N.S.	N.S.	N.S.	N.S.
	0.01					
Program Redeveloped	1.88	N.S.	3.49	N.S.	2.72	1.87
	5.83		34.52		37.94	178.00
	0.10		0.01		0.01	0.03
Program Usage	N.S.	2.62	2.72	1.85	2.36	5.55
		15.62	16.61	3.5	22.84	82.96
		0.01	0.01	0.04	0.02	0.00
Program Type	N.S.	2.24	N.S.	N.S.	2.26	N.S.
		29.98			32.99	
		0.03			0.02	
DBMS Interface	N.D.	3.22	1.40	5.03	1.89	3.26
		29.61	34.50	32.18	35.26	127.66
		0.01	0.09	0.00	0.04	0.00
Program Documentation*	−0.29	−0.25	−0.51	N.S.	−0.28	−0.29
	0.05	0.09	0.01		0.04	0.00
Programming Language	N.D.	0.21	0.32	N.D.	0.26	0.31
		0.04	−0.02		0.03	0.00

All values are rounded up to two decimals.
Dependent Variable: Average yearly program maintenance expenditures (to date and since cutover to operations) as a proportion of total program development expenditures.
* These three variables were treated as continuous; the table shows the Pearson correlation coefficient and significance level. For the other variables, t tests results are shown in the format: t value, degrees of freedom, one-tail probability.
N.S. = not significant (.10 probability); N.D. = no data available.

TABLE IX. DBMS Interface Programs: Further Analysis

	Company B (n = 32)	Company C (n = 37)	Company D (n = 37)	Company E (n = 40)	Pooled (n = 146)
Average yearly maintenance expenditures of development costs (%)	3.22,29.61,0.01	1.40,34.50,0.09	5.03,32.18,0.00	1.89,35.26,0.04	3.26,127.66,0.00
Average yearly maintenance expenditure of lines of code (%)	1.48,30.00,0.08	N.S.	1.50,35.00,0.07	4.28,30.41,0.00	4.03,90.39,0.00
Lines of code excluding comment code	N.S.	−2.22,12.35,0.03	−3.36,35.00,0.00	N.S.	−3.94,38.42,0.00
Total program development cost	N.S.	N.S.	−3.15,35.00,0.00	N.S.	−1.84,47.16,0.04
Development cost per line of code	N.S.	N.S.	N.S.	2.19,32.46,0.02	2.33,141.65,0.01

N.S. = not significant (0.10 probability).
The table contains results from t tests, the report format: t value, degrees of freedom, one-tail probability.

indicate that application program maintenance expenditures are lower for programs using a DMS (see Tables VIII and IX). The benefit of this is much lower in the two case-study companies (C and E) with a shorter history of DMS utilization. The data from the 43 companies did not show a significant relationship between host language DMS availability and the ratio of maintenance budget to development budget.

Many MIS managers surveyed expressed dissatisfaction with DMS usage. The more commonly given reasons are the shortage of personnel with knowledge about DMS, the cost, and the difficulty of training. In many instances, the source of dissatisfaction can be traced to a lack of knowledge on how to select a DMS [2, 9]. Evidence from the five case studies, as a whole, suggests that DMS utilization has the benefit of reducing application program maintenance expenditures. However, before reaping this benefit, organizations must invest time and resources to properly plan and implement database technology.

Do Not Use Assembly Languages
Results from this study (Table VIII), indicate that application programs written in assembly language require higher maintenance expenditures than their higher level language (e.g., Cobol, RPG, Fortran, PL1) counterparts. Also, data from the 43 companies show (Pearson's correlation coefficient of 0.37, p = 0.01) a direct relationship between the percentage of application programs written in assembly language and the company's total program maintenance expenditures. Since execution efficiency has been cited as the primary reason for the use of assembly language, this researcher endorses the recommendation that it may be cost beneficial to develop the program in a high-level language and reprogram in assembly language those parts of the program which execute more frequently. Results from this study also indicate that advice in this area may be somewhat delinquent since a fast migration to a high-level language (i.e., Cobol) seems to be presently under way. The primary motivator for this migration is the extremely high maintenance costs associated with assembly language programs.

Use Application Software Packages
Data from the 43 companies show a direct relationship (Pearson correlation coefficient of 0.35, p = 0.01) between the use (average yearly expenditures over the past 5 years) of application software packages and company program maintenance expenditures as a proportion of total program expenditures (development plus maintenance). The reason for this apparent contradiction is that the sample is dominated by small- to middle-sized organizations which are relatively maintenance-bound and are using application software packages to quickly reduce the backlog of user requests for new applications.

The utilization of commercially available application software packages is thought to be beneficial in at least three ways:

1. Their purchase prices are considered much lower than the expenditures necessary to develop them in-house. This is primarily due to the developer's amortization of development costs over a relatively large number of prospective buyers.
2. An important reason for purchasing commercially available packages is that, in general, the developer's level of expertise in the area is usually greater than what most organizations will have.
3. Commercially available packages tend to be more generalizable than in-house developed programs, thus accommodating user requirement differences to a greater extent. Greater flexibility in satisfying changing user requirements is translated directly into lower maintenance expenditures.

The MIS managers of the organizations surveyed are fully aware of the economic advantages of packaged application software. Most managers, however, also expressed dissatisfaction with the amount of tailoring necessary to suit their particular needs. Some severe cases of underestimation of tailoring expenditures were described and caution is recommended in this area.

While 70% of the organizations in the sample spend less than 10% of the new application program budget on application software packages, 33% of the organizations are planning to increase their expenditures in this area. No apparent relationship seems to exist between the organizations' current and planned levels of expenditures on packaged application software.

Use Self-Contained Query Language Facility (SCQL)
The data from the 43 companies indicate an inverse relationship (t = 1.91, 0.04 significance level), between the availability of a self-contained query language (SCQL) and the ratio of maintenance budget to development budget. More informal evidence gathered through the interviews leaves no doubt about the potential usefulness and the increasing importance of SCQL. In growing numbers, users expect their MIS departments to satisfy ad hoc user requests for information and support relatively unstructured user processes. These types of user requirements usually lead to short-lived or unstable application programs. Because these application programs are relatively expensive to develop and maintain, the use of a SCQL to satisfy ad hoc requests and unstructured user processes will lead to lower application program maintenance expenditures.

Twenty-eight of the organizations (67%) visited have been using SCQLs for over three years to satisfy ad hoc user requests. In the other organizations, the MIS department either rejects such user requests or attempts to satisfy them with

103

hastily developed application programs. In the organizations rejecting *ad hoc* user requests, user frustration is likely to be higher than in the organizations using SCQL or developing "quick and dirty" application programs. The top computer executives in the 28 organizations with SCQLs unanimously expressed the opinion that SCQL utilization has been cost beneficial for supporting *ad hoc* user requests and represents a good user relations tool. Further advantages and limitations of SCQLs are surveyed by the author [15].

Provide Direct User Access to Equipment

In this study, equipment represents hardware/software systems which users are willing and able to interact with. Software items include "canned" programs such as statistical packages, simulation packages, etc. Self-contained query languages also represent an important software item. Hardware items, besides a central processing unit (CPU), refer to various types of online terminals used for input–output. Depending on user requirements, special peripheral devices such as graph plotters, color graphical terminals, etc., are important items. User friendliness and system transparency are important attributes of the equipment being used.

The primary objective is to permit users to have direct contact with the equipment in satisfying their requests for information. Based on anecdotal evidence from six companies which widely use this direct user access approach, three advantages seem to have been derived.

1. Part of the expenditures associated with the computerization of related user processes has been incurred by the user departments or by the organization as a whole. In two cases, the organization has provided the MIS department with extra funds to set up a small group (two or three people) to satisfy user requests. In the other four organizations, user departments have intermediaries to use the system.

2. If application programs had been developed to satisfy some of the user requests presently being serviced through the "user direct-access facility," some relatively expensive, short-lived programs would have been developed. Furthermore, application program maintenance expenditures would have been higher. In both cases, the MIS department would have had to bear the increased costs involved, unless a charge-back mechanism had been established.

3. In all, six companies using the "user direct-access approach," the MIS personnel interviewed stated that the approach has contributed to better relations between the MIS department and the user departments involved.

While only six organizations are using this approach to satisfy user requests for information, their top computer executives all reported great satisfaction with the results. Because MIS equipment transparency and user friendliness are likely to increase in the future, in addition to the three advantages enumerated above, it is apparent that increasingly large numbers of organizations will adopt the "user-direct access to equipment" approach in the near future.

Preplan Equipment Changes

Equipment in this case includes CPU, operating systems, system software packages interfacing with application programs, programming languages, peripheral devices, etc.

The survey of the 43 organizations indicates that many companies have incurred massive application program maintenance expenditures (or program discontinuations) because of unplanned equipment changes. Unfortunately, the process of planning equipment changes is so complex that generalized

prescriptions cannot be made. One must develop plans based on individual case analysis.

Implementing the plan in many cases will require a great deal of persuasion and understanding of the political forces within an organization. In some cases, MIS managers have chosen MIS equipment based on the political pressure from top managers. For example, in one case, a major computer equipment vendor was selected by top managers because it was thought to be financially more stable than its competitors. The selection completely ignored the technical, economic, and operational advantages of the equipment from an alternate vendor which had been selected by the EDP manager with a great deal of care.

One must also account for industry practices and the operational idiosyncrasies of individual companies. For example, some MIS managers changed from a more transparent database management system (DMS) to one which requires considerably more knowledge by the user about the logical and physical structure of the database. The reason for the conversion was related to the organization being an insurance company. Many (most?) insurance companies have the particular DMS being converted with the conversion undertaken for the sake of industry compatibility.

Have Effective Application Program Documentation

Results from this study indicate that program documentation plays an important role in facilitating the program maintenance process and in reducing maintenance expenditures (see Table VIII). Maintenance programmers seem to appreciate the following documents in descending order of preference (Table X):

1. English narrative describing what the program(s) and program modules are supposed to do.

2. A system flowchart showing the programs, files, etc., involved in the system; particularly useful when the system is large and complex.

3. Input–output layout forms.

One unexpected finding from this study is that program flowcharts seem to be totally ignored by maintenance programmers. As an aid to program development, some programmers apparently prefer program flowcharts if the logic flow is relatively complex. However, practitioners should not enforce the use of programming flowcharts at the development stage with the expectation of reducing maintenance expenditures.

TABLE X. Application Program Documentation

Documentation Method	Percentage of Programs with (n = 180)	Average Maintenance Programmer Rating*
Program Listing	100	5.0
Comment Code	72	4.8
Narrative Description	69	5.0
Input–Output Layout Forms	63	4.3
Decision Tables	38	4.4
Program Flowcharts	37	1.8
Systems Flowcharts	29	4.5
Structured Programming	17	4.8
Warnier Diagrams	11	4.3
Pseudocode	8	1.9
HIPO	5	3.9

* The maintenance programmer for each program rated the specific documentation method available as to its usefulness for the maintenance task (5 = Clearly yes; 1 = Definitely not).

SUMMARY

The economic importance of program maintenance is widely recognized in the MIS literature. Several studies have proposed guidelines to reduce these expenditures. Nevertheless, MIS practitioners are far from satisfied with the current state of affairs.

This study has identified a list of probable determinants through personal interviews with experts in the area of software management. A pilot study was used to refine the list of variables and to foresee operational difficulties in the study.

A final survey involving 43 organizations and five detailed case studies were conducted. The data collection process was accomplished by inspecting the companies application program portfolios, program documentation and through personal interviews with top computer executives and systems development personnel.

Seven important management controllable determinants of application program maintenance expenditures have been identified and practical recommendations are made on how to reduce the level of such expenditures.

REFERENCES

1. AC, Program maintenance: User's view. *Data Process.*, Sept.–Oct. 1973.
2. Berg, J., Ed. Database directions: The next steps. *NBS* Special Publication 451, Sept. 1976.
3. Braddock, F. How to stretch your software lifecycle. *ICP Interface*, Spring 1980.
4. Boehm, B. W. Software and its impact: A quantitative assessment. *Datamation* (May 1973).
5. Boehm, B. W. Software engineering. *IEEE Trans. Comput.* (Dec. 1976).
6. Brantley, C. L. and Osajima, Y. R. Continuing development of centrally developed and maintained software systems, IEEE Computer Society Conference Proceedings (Spring, 1975).
7. Brooks, F. P., Jr. *The Mythical Man–Month*, Addison-Wesley, Reading, Massachusetts, 1975.
8. Canning, R. G. That maintenance "iceberg" *EDP Anal.* (Oct. 1972).
9. Codasyl. Selection and acquisition of DBMS: A report of the CODASYL systems committee. (March 1976)
10. Daly, E. B. Management of software development. IEEE Trans. Softw. Eng. Forthcoming.
11. Ditri, A. E., Shaw, J. C., and Atkins, W. *Managing the EDP function*, McGraw-Hill, New York, 1971.
12. Elshoff, J. L. An analysis of some commercial PL/1 programs, IEEE Trans. Softw. Eng. SE-2, 2 (June 1976).
13. Fewer, A. R. and Fowlkes, E. B. Relating computer program maintainability to software measures. Proceedings of the 1979 National Computer Conference, June 1979.
14. Guimaraes, N. Survey and classification of implementation studies. Management Information Systems Research Center, University of Minnesota, unpublished paper, 1978.
15. Guimaraes, N. An analysis of application program life patterns, Ph.D. Thesis, University of Minnesota, 1981.
16. Gunderman, R. E. A glimpse into program maintenance. *Datamation* (June 1973).
17. J. Hoskyns and Co. Implications of using modular programming, Guide No. 1, Hoskyns System Research, London, 1973.
18. Khan, Z. How to tackle the systems maintenance dilemma. Canadian Data System, March 1975.
19. Lientz, B. P., Swanson, E. B., and Tompkins, G. E. Characteristics of application software maintenance. *Comm. ACM*, 21, 6 (June, 1978).
20. Lientz, B. P., Swanson, E. B. Problems in application software maintenance, *Comm. ACM 24*, 11 (November 1981), 763–769.
21. McLaughlin, R. A. 1975 DP Budgets. *Datamation* (March 1975).
22. McGreggor, Bob. Program maintenance. *Data Process.* (May–June 1973).
23. Mooney, J. W. Organized program maintenance. *Datamation* Feb. 1975.
24. Olson, M. H. An investigation of organizational contingencies associated with structure of the information systems function. Ph.D. Thesis, University of Minnesota, 1978.
25. Punter, M. Programming for maintenance, *Data Process.* (Sept.–Oct. 1975).
26. Riggs, R. Computer system maintenance, *Datamation* (November 1969).
27. Snyders, J. Taking the drudgery out of documentation, *Comput. Decis.* (July 1979).
28. Zelkowitz, M. V. Perspectives on software engineering. *Comput. Surv.* 10, 2 (June 1978).

CR Categories and Subject Descriptors: J.1 [**Computer Applications**]: Administrative Data Processing; D.2.9 [**Software Engineering**]: Management

Additional Key Words and Phrases: application program maintenance, managing application program maintenance expenditures

Received 3/82; revised 10/82; accepted 1/83

After the Purchase: Software Maintenance and Outside Support

by David Bellin

Introduction

As small computer systems are becoming increasingly popular it is timely to address the smaller computer users' specific needs for ongoing maintenance, enhancement, and support. Fortunately, it has been some 15 years since the minicomputer emerged as a force in the business community, giving us a variety of experiences upon which to draw in suggesting areas of concern and caution for microcomputer purchase and operation.

The importance of the continuing maintenance of computer equipment has been adequately emphasized in the past. It is generally agreed that only the most foolhardy or naive manager would neglect to purchase ongoing hardware service contracts. Chips fail, CRTs break, and fuses blow.

Unfortunately, this attitude has not generally applied to the programs that embody the functions that a computer is purchased to execute. Only after the fact do we become aware that new reports may be needed, that additional fields would be helpful on the CRT diplay, that the data storage requirements are higher than we thought they would be, and that an additional terminal is needed.

Of course, the purchaser is not the only person who may have overlooked the need for ongoing *software* maintenance. The salesman may be eager to sell a system, make his commission, and move on to the next customer. The hardware manufacturer may choose not to emphasize ongoing needs, as performance in this area might reflect poorly in comparison with the claims of a competitor. As a result, the user may be under the impression that all that has to be done is to start the machine on day one and then leave the computer to run itself forever!

Of course this is not true. There are a number of areas that may result in added cost and the need for expert advice after the computer is installed. These include:

- training;
- software maintenance;
- communication with other computers;
- program enhancement and modification; and
- system expansion for increased data usage and/or storage.

After examining each, we will review the considerations for employing outside experts to maintain software equipment.

Training

Training includes instruction of both the staff operating the computer system and the casual or part-time user as well. Proper documentation in the form of manuals on operating procedures, system narratives and system use is essential for adequate

David Bellin is an Assistant Professor in the Department of Computer Science at the William Paterson College of New Jersey.

training. If such documentation does not exist, it may be helpful to employ the services of a professional to produce the manuals. Other than creating the manuals themselves, which in most cases are provided with the computer system, third parties are generally of little aid in training at a small computer installation. People already familiar with the computer are the best instructors for new users.

Software Maintenance

An overlooked, yet crucial, post-installation concern is the software itself. The user must ensure its ongoing maintenance: it must be copied ("backed-up"), restored in event of disaster, modified (euphemistically always called "enhanced"), and continually examined for security and growth constraints.

The user of a small computer should make an intelligent decision regarding the installation of new revisions of operating systems and language software. There is a tradeoff between maintaining compatibility with other computer users and possible incompatibility with application programs. For example, when revision Two of the popular CP/M operating system was announced, many older programs written for version One were not compatible. Disk structures changed. However, in the intervening years, version Two almost totally eclipsed version One. A computer site running version One in 1983 will have difficulty finding trained programmers to modify their programs.

The small–computer user must ensure that operations can survive disasters such as the destruction of the master disk drive. A nerve–wracking but certain test is actually to pull the plug in the middle of data entry and determine whether the back-up procedures are sufficient to completely restore the system to its previous state. Such an approach is not recommended, but it does point up a frequently overlooked but common problem area. When disaster strikes and an outside expert is called in to fix the system, the consultant often finds users who, while certain they are making daily backups, are actually following by rote instructions which were incorrect in the first place! The situation will, of course, only come to light on the day *after* the disk drive fails.

Modifications to applications software are frequently required. Columns must be added to the president's report. The office manager thinks of a new approach that would save hours of hand calculations. The computer system contains a great deal of information not previously available in one place and, over time, people think of new ways of using and displaying this information.

Who will make these modifications? Is the source code (the original "changeable" program) on the premises or even available? Is there enough expertise in-house to make the changes or not?

Finally, familiarity breeds use. The longer a computer has been installed, the more people in the organization feel comfortable with it and know how to use it. Also, an operation may be growing; more orders may be entered each month than a year ago. And new programs use up more disk space for data storage. How much room is left? Do you know, and how do you find out before there is *no* room to put in your next orders? All these areas of software maintenance must be addressed.

Communications

It is becoming increasingly common and economical to use a micro-based system to access large external data bases. There are a number of data base services of interest to the library and academic communities (not to mention stock market and news services). Justifiably, many micro users are investigating adding the capability to access these data bases and to store information from them locally, allowing a more leisurely perusal of the data. While very straightforward in principle, data communications and retrieval services are not standardized—nor is the software that allows micros to "talk to" and retrieve information from these services. This is yet another application in which it may well be worth the investment to pay an outsider to investigate and recommend, or to install completely, the hardware and software needed to access these services.

Program Enhancement and Modification

Usually after installing a small computer, new uses are found for the equipment. For example, managerial information needs are subject to change. Or the computer itself will suggest benefits that may accrue by capturing additional data previously overlooked. It may be that additional information is required in that book inventory report which is printed weekly. Or a teacher discovers how useful a spread sheet program could be to a school.

All this suggests that continued programming will have to be done after installing the computer. Often no outside help is needed to continue programming the computer. Most schools and libraries, for example, have access to the periodicals and people needed to review available software packages. Advanced students, when applied with systematic direction, have proved to be very capable in programming new modules or making small changes to existing programs. In the opinion of the author the services of an outside consultant are often not needed. Care must be taken, however, to ensure that adequate backups and complete written documentation of programming changes are kept.

System Expansion

Often, additional hardware is desirable. Another terminal would be useful. It may be found that more information should be kept online and readily available than was originally intended. These changes may involve installing terminal driver boards or a simple cable and an additional disk drive. Changes may also have to be made to the software, such as modifying applications programs or revising the operating system. The choice of incompatible terminals or disk drives can be very confusing and may involve large expenditures. Outside help in reviewing and selecting hardware—if not in the final purchase and installation of it—is necessary. In this area expert advice can save many headaches and much needless expense.

Reviewing Outside Expertise

There are many factors to be considered when choosing an outside expert, not least of which is determining *why* you need help. Always clearly explain why you are seeking assistance. Calling someone in and turning the job over with the comment "I think we need some help—your job is to tell me where," is vague and increases the chances of failure. This type of unpreparedness leaves too much room for an unscrupulous or inexperienced consultant to maneuver. Your organization must define its specific areas of concern and the topics for the assignment before potential consultants are interviewed.

In an initial interview, maintain the attitude that the consultant is not there on a "sales call." The consultant is selling expertise. You must be able to communicate freely, trusting in the individual's knowledge and confidentiality. Not only should you be interviewing the consultant, exploring strengths and weaknesses, but you also should find that the consultant is interviewing you. Distrust the 'expert' who answers all your questions and asks you none. Consultants must establish in their own minds that you have real needs that can be met by their expertise.

You must also establish the credibility of the consultant. Although it is relatively simple to amass a list of consultants and their phone numbers, it is wise to call a reference and explore what the consultant has done for another organization. There is nothing inherently wrong with the one-person consultancy, but you should expect honesty. One person posing as a representative of a 60-person operation is suspicious. If the firm has an office, *visit it,* unannounced, and verify that it is more than an answering service. Ask your banker for a Dun & Bradstreet check on the firm to establish its longevity and financial strength. Of course, in some cases, you will not be interested in an ongoing relationship, so longevity may not be important. The cost of outside expertise varies anywhere from $15 per hour for a moonlighter, up to the $75 an hour that most computer manufacturers charge for software consulting time. Some consultants may also quote a fixed-fee basis per job. In all cases, the definition of the duties, the actual results expected—and a timetable—should be drawn up in a *written* agreement for all to sign.

Summary

Micro purchasers should be aware of the needs they will have for ongoing software support and the occasional use of outside services for this support. With some preparatory work and judicious use of available in-house expertise, outside costs can be clearly defined and held to a minimum. Some understanding of these areas will contribute to more productive and increased use of the computer.

Two perceptions of software maintenance performed by an on-site contractor

by BERNARD NARROW

NASA Goddard Space Flight Center
Greenbelt, Maryland

and

JOHN KELLY

Lockheed, EMSCO
Greenbelt, Maryland

ABSTRACT

Software maintenance is a difficult task under the best of circumstances. Having work performed by an on-site contractor adds an additional layer of complexity to the customer's task. This type of relationship places greater emphasis on formal work procedures and detailed reports of the work in progress. It also promotes the use of performance norms for evaluating contractor performance. These factors are all on the positive side. However, such a relationship also calls for a special awareness of contractor ploys calculated to increase their performance evaluation.

From the contractor's point of view, being on-site imposes a more disciplined environment and places special importance on the manner and means of dealing with the customer. Another special feature is that the contractor receives formal feedback from the users, through periodic performance evaluations, indicating how well the software maintenance group measures up to expectations.

This paper describes the lessons learned by one customer and one on-site contractor.

THE CUSTOMER'S VIEW

On-site contracting is likely to become more pervasive due to its emphasis in the federal government[1] (à la the Office of Management and Budget Circular A-76) as well as in state governments and municipalities. An account is given here of how a large data processing facility with extensive experience in contracting out software maintenance has learned to cope.

Our data processing installation is a large, multisystem government facility, comprised of a mix of manufacturers and types. Included are on-line systems, database systems, batch systems and intercomputer systems. Types of hardware include IBM (370, 4341), UNIVAC (1100, Varian), SEL (32), and Honeywell (Sigma). Altogether, there are 20 stand-alone systems that require software maintenance support. A large measure of the applications run on these systems deal with scientific data; however the operational mode is akin to a large, multistep production process. Other applications relate to production control, cost accounting, inventory control, and database maintenance.

Centralized vs. Decentralized Support

Initially, our technical control over the work performed by the contractor was split along application and functional lines. This led to several independently run units, both on our side and on the contractor's side. However, we exercised overall technical stewardship over the contractor's activities for evaluating performance.

This arrangement, while providing us with a close working relationship and a strong grasp of the technical details, naturally led to parochial viewpoints on both sides. If a key systems person in one area resigned, contractor personnel could not easily call upon another area for temporary assistance because of reluctance by the latter to dilute their level of support. Support problems, resulting from poor management, inexperienced or inadequate numbers of personnel, and the like, tended to be prolonged and not pursued aggressively.

In early 1982, we reorganized to centralize all software maintenance within a single unit. The contractor's organization also was reconstituted on a centralized basis. A number of benefits—some obvious and some not so obvious—were achieved, including

1. uniform reporting of maintenance activities
2. uniform and tighter configuration control
3. more effective communications channels
4. improved response in correcting or resolving problems
5. separation and independence of programming and testing groups

6. improved documentation (due to configuration control oversight)
7. more effective control within the program library
8. more effective establishment of priorities and better allocation of resources
9. more consistent manner evaluation of contractor performance and determination of award fees
10. more availability of the information to build a centralized database for deriving work performance metrics

Establishing an Effective Working Relationship

Because software maintenance cannot easily or readily be translated into a set of well-defined products, the connection between customer and contractor needs special emphasis. This is a critical factor in determining the quality and cost effectiveness of the support provided by the contractor. The key elements characterizing the customer–contractor relationship can be labeled as the three Cs: credibility, coverage, and clout. Credibility hinges largely on the competence of customer personnel. The level of competence should be such as to convince the contractor personnel that the customer is fully aware of work factors—do's and don'ts—and that expectations of the contractor's performance are reasonable. Customers need to be candid in their dealings with contractors and to view them as co-workers rather than as subordinates or in a potentially adversarial position. Unfortunately, this can easily lead to a "chummy" relationship, which can be harmful. Customer personnel should not forget that, basically, this is a business relationship that calls for critical assessment of the contractor's performance. In particular, customer personnel need to distinguish between legitimate extenuating circumstances and groundless excuses. Otherwise, the contractor will not make a concerted effort to correct deficiencies.

Coverage, as used here, refers to the organizational or functional level at which the customer–contractor connection takes place, as well as the depth of reporting detail. Good starting points are the systems and methods for selecting and controlling the jobs to be performed. These come under the general heading of configuration control. In our case, a formal system was agreed upon that would govern the submission, review, disposition, and reporting of change requests. These include system and application software errors, deficiencies, enhancements, and new system releases. Also included are special tasks that compete for the programming group's resources.

At least weekly status meetings should be held and should include contractor line managers (the heads of system software, applications software, and testing), along with the customer technical monitors. Coverage is really a corollary of credibility in that it is meant to ensure that the technical discussions are substantive and are more likely to flush out causes, rather than treat symptoms.

Clout is a two-edged sword. It can be and should be used both to reward the contractor for better-than-expected performance and to penalize for below-expected performance. One way to accomplish this is by way of a cost-plus-award-fee contract, with the award ranging from 0% to 10% of the cost. Expected performance results in a fee in the 4% to 6% range, thereby leaving ample allowance for award level variations based either on positive or negative factors. Another important consideration is the level of management—both sides— that is involved in or is made aware of the fee determination. On the customer side, this should mean the top person in charge of the data processing facility; on the contractor's side, it should mean at least one level above the on-site manager, depending on whether software maintenance represents part or all of the contract. If the latter, the involvement should be at least two levels above the contract manager.

What You Need to Know

What do customers need to know about the contractor's activities in order to monitor and evaluate the contractor's performance effectively? In our case, we have stipulated that reporting should be at the functional (or third) level with system and project reporting being the higher levels.

For our purposes functional reporting was broken down as follows: validation and assessment of the effects of a proposed change (prior to approval by the configuration control board); programming (analysis, coding, and unit testing); acceptance testing; and implementation. This breakdown is predicated on the objective of closely monitoring the work in progress so as to be conversant with current problems and to assess effectively whether proper and timely actions are being taken to resolve them.

Some might argue that on a routine basis it is only necessary to monitor the contractor's activities at either the system or project levels and thereby reduce the cost of monitoring. It is further argued that either periodic or unannounced audits can be made to determine the contractor's performance at the functional level. The problem with this argument is, assuming that substantive deficiencies are uncovered by an audit, the customer monitors are not in a position to assess independently whether the contractor is taking the proper corrective measures—and doing so in a timely manner. Waiting until the next audit takes place to make such a determination is not an effective way to deal with such problems.

It should not be inferred that effective monitoring calls for an item-by-item review. One suggestion is to have an asterisk placed in the margin of a report to highlight those items for which actual hours exceeded estimated hours or for which a data change was made since the last report period. This directs the monitor's attention to the items that require close observation and that should be accompanied by a written explanation. A complementary tactic is to specify the ten most important items in a separate report, which is distributed to a higher level of management than is the full detailed report.

Specifying the detailed items to be reported on is only half the battle. The reports must be reviewed carefully for accuracy, completeness, and currency. Contractor personnel are prone to adopt a casual attitude toward reporting if they are not held closely and consistently accountable for the report contents. Figures 1 and 2 are sample formats of monthly summary reports by system, showing, respectively, the change in status of all work in progress and the actual hours expended by type of job.

Games Contractors Play

Wherever there are performance-type contracts, there is an inclination to "shade" the reporting of activities and events in a way that is advantageous to the contractor. Although shading can, in reality, be a euphemism for fraudulent practices, it is more likely to manifest itself in more subtle and less odious forms. Also, on-site contractors are less likely to engage in these practices than off-site contractors, because of the more personal relationship in the former case.

Noted here are both known and suspected tactics that contractors have used. These tactics represent an overall compilation drawn from a number of different contractors.

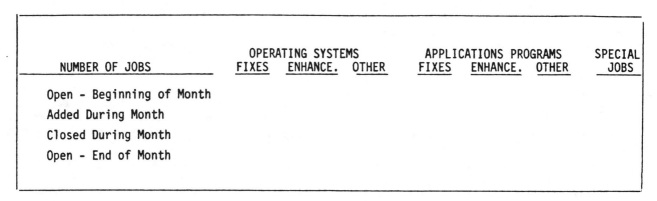

Figure 1—Monthly change in work status

| TOTAL HOURS EXPENDED FOR | OPERATING SYSTEMS | | | APPLICATIONS PROGRAMS | | | SPECIAL |
	FIXES	ENHANCE.	OTHER	FIXES	ENHANCE.	OTHER	JOBS
Analysis							
Code and Unit Test							
Implementation							
FOR CLOSED JOBS							
Analysis Hours - Est.							
Act.							
Code & UT Hours - Est.							
Act.							
Implementation Hours-Est.							
Act.							
Total Hours - Est.							
Act.							

Figure 2—Manhours expended during month

Creative bookkeeping

To prevent actual hours from exceeding estimated hours on a given job, time is charged to "miscellaneous." A variation of creative bookkeeping is where the contractor in the process of trying to correct an error takes a shortcut, e.g., bypassing testing, in order to stay on schedule. Should this in turn cause additional errors, these are reported as new errors and are disposed of expeditiously. This, of course, leads to "favorable" measured performance.

Technical obfuscation

When analysis or diagnosis of a persistent problem does not turn up anything definite, or when an embarrassing event occurs, the contractor might try to talk his way around it. Jargon and vague but technically imposing reasons might be offered to convince customer monitors that the problem is not due to any fault of the contractor.

All in the family

Here, contractors try to be particularly responsive to the customer monitor's pet projects. This is coupled with ego-boosting tactics, which together are an attempt to foster the impression that "we are all family" and we ought to be protective of the other party's interests. A variation of this game is to seek the company monitor's advice and suggestions about how to handle a given problem. This tends to compromise the company monitor's objectivity in assessing the contractor's performance.

End-around play

Should the customer monitors prove rather astute in dealing with the contractor's games, or if the customer monitors are frequently critical of the contractor's performance, a play can be made to a higher level of management. An attempt is made first to establish a close liaison with higher management and then to convince them that the monitors are biased and unreasonable.

Old standbys

Briefly noted here are the more familiar excuses and tactics used by software personnel.

1. overly generous padding of estimates to perform jobs

2. blame it on the vendor's documentation
3. blame it on the operating system
4. blame it on the hardware
5. blame it on the person no longer employed by the contractor

Performance Measurement

Under an incentive-type contract, it is necessary to face the issue of performance measurement squarely. First to be addressed is the formulation of which elements and factors are to be evaluated and measured. The candidate elements are those from which one can derive the desired factors. Examples of such factors include management, productivity, responsiveness, timeliness, communication, planning, and initiative. Factors such as management, communication, and planning are highly subjective in nature and are evaluated in an indirect or on an event basis. Others, such as productivity, responsiveness, and timeliness, are adaptable to objective measurement, and these are the ones discussed herein.

Before qualifying a set of metrics for performance evaluation, it is necessary to define and establish a database. In our case, pertinent information is collected from all jobs including application software changes, operating systems maintenance, and special software tasks. Information about these jobs is collected from the individual programmers, and entered into a database. Weekly reports compiled from this information are carefully reviewed both by the contractor supervisors and the monitors to assure complete reporting and overall accountability. A list of the metrics that we observe is shown in Table I.

Each of the metrics in the table can be further categorized by computer system, language, type (i.e., systems or application software), and so forth. Such breakdowns enable comparisons to be made within the given category; e.g., how does the average time per fix for system A compare with that for system B?

After a sufficient amount of time has elapsed to compile a substantial database and to analyze and interpret the derived metrics, the final step can begin. This is to establish the norms for each of the selected metrics. Here again, contractor personnel should participate in this determination in order to arrive at a set of norms that is deemed to be fair and reasonable to both parties.

Such objective performance measures can be weighed and coupled with the subjective factors referred to earlier so as to arrive at the contractor's overall technical performance assessment.

THE CONTRACTOR'S VIEW

Interfacing with Customer Personnel

The role of the software professional within a company that performs facility management services is somewhat different from that of a programmer nestled comfortably in a corporate structured arena. Being on-site readily exposes a casual or

TABLE I—Performance Metrics

Metric	Derivation
Average time to make a fix or enhancement	Total hours for analysis, coding, unit testing divided by total number of fixes and enhancements
Average elapsed time to make a fix or enhancement	No. of days from start to implementation divided by total number of fixes and enhancements
Actual vs. estimated time per fix or enhancement	Total actual hours divided by total estimated hours for fixes and enhancements
Elapsed time of highest priority fixes vs. others	Average elapsed time to make highest priority fixes divided by average of elapsed time to make all other fixes
Trend analysis of reported software failures	Comparison of distributions of failure occurrences for different systems
Correlation of number of fixes with size of program	Dependent variable is the number of fixes for each program; independent variable is the size of each program
Standard deviation of estimates of large vs. small programs	Standard error of actual vs. estimated hours for each fix, grouped by program size
Ratio of analysis time per fix to coding and unit testing	Total hours for analysis of all fixes divided by total hours for coding and unit testing

sloppily managed working group and calls for an awareness or presence that should be calculated to command the respect of the customer. Sloppy personal demeanor, unoccupied desks, persons reading newspapers, and so on, are perceived by the customer as indicators that the contractor is unreliable, unprofessional, or underworked. In effect, the contractor has two "bosses"—the on-site customer as well as company management. This presents a unique dilemma—how to please both factions and maintain proper professional perspective (and sanity) in successfully fulfilling job requirements.

Acquiring the confidence of customer-monitoring personnel is an important goal that must be achieved quickly if successful performance ratings are to be attained. The ability to grasp the technical jargon and the complexities of the customer's subject matter makes customer communication a natural extension of the monitor's working environment.

When special requirements are addressed, the contractor should obtain customer concurrence on how the workload should be adjusted to satisfy all affected users. Too often, additional task requirements are accepted by the contractor without informing the customer of current manpower constraints and the effects of new tasks on current completion schedules. The contractor must not be afraid to oppose additional customer requests and should be prepared to convey to customer management that in reality there is no free lunch. When possible, suitable alternatives should be recommended.

Effective communication of task performance appraisals is an area that requires special contractor attention. The customer needs appropriate status information to provide a sufficient base for pointing out shortcomings, giving plaudits for tasks well done, and recommending an appropriate award fee. Formats for contractually required reports should be determined mutually, at the beginning of the contract, and should be reviewed periodically for possible alteration to respond to changing customer management reporting requirements. In addition to these reports, regularly scheduled status meetings between software management and key customer-management–technical-monitoring personnel should be established. These meetings, which are by design less formal and in the nature of committee sessions, are multipurpose. They not only provide a forum for presenting firsthand status information, but also are an excellent opportunity for discussing customer priorities and perceived deficiencies prior to their being written into the customer's evaluation report. Another helpful measure is to provide a self evaluation—representing the software management's view of task performance—to the customer for consideration in determining periodic award fees.

How Work is Divided and Allocated

As noted in the first part of this paper, we are a centralized software organization, responsible for maintaining more than 50 software systems functioning on more than 20 mainframes, and for all developmental work. Major functions are separated into applications programming, systems programming, and software acceptance testing. By definition, applications programmers are responsible for maintaining the production software (primarily FORTRAN coding, with some assembly language) and the systems programmers are the caretakers of all operating system software. Systems analysts, however, provide the necessary expertise for assuring the validity of both new and modified software through the development and execution of detailed acceptance test plans.

Because of the size of this organization—approximately 85 software professionals—the numerous specially developed computer systems, and the frequency of software changes attributable to data-related and user requirement variances, it is difficult to impose conventional software management techniques. An internal task-tracking system has been developed to monitor several hundred tasks ranging from discrepancy reports (something doesn't look right) to change requests (modifications to accommodate specific problems or requirements). Included within this range are customer-initiated tasks (often new requirements) and tasks generated internally by software management (usually related to normal maintenance activities, such as evaluating release tapes for existing operating systems). Due to the high volume of tasks, complexities of interorganizational interface, and management

requirements for up-to-date status reporting, a full-time administrator is employed to maintain and coordinate all transactions and report generation attributed to this tracking system.

Assignment of programmers to support each system can often be a difficult process. Software management must be prepared to evaluate the overall complexity of the system, be familiar with the intricacies of various program components, and be knowledgeable about the stability or volatility of the software. These variables are then matched against individual programmer experience profiles to determine the most appropriate manpower allocation.

Acquiring and Retaining Technical Personnel

Our typical maintenance programmer has almost five years of college training and more than six years of technical experience. Turnover, however, is surprisingly low in our case, because of an unusual phenomenon known as incumbency. Many of our software professionals have selected this area because of the nature of the work—it is highly scientific and very interesting; the physical plant is conveniently located and easily accessible; there is no charge for parking; etc. Even though the contract is bound by a prenegotiated amount of time, the technically oriented employee has little fear of losing a position due to contract expiration. Obviously, even under a new contractor, the job must continue to be performed. Who else, other than those currently doing the job, could satisfy customer requirements with no untoward effect on daily operations? Of course, if there is a new contract awarded, management must be sensitive to the apprehension programmers are likely to exhibit during the recompetion and, if necessary, the changeover periods.

Programmers, like many other skilled professionals, consider themselves creative and take special pride in developing "eternal" systems. There exists, then, an innate stigma attached to the label of "maintenance programmer." This is a difficult but not insurmountable hurdle for software management to overcome. One of the ways to maintain good personnel morale is by offering diversification in mainframes, operating systems, and programming languages. For example, in our case the opportunity to use FORTRAN, assembly language, or PL/I may be found on IBM (370/145 and 4341) using VS1, VM, or MVS; IBM (Series-1) using EDX; UNIVAC (1100/82) using EXEC-8 38R2; SEL (32/77 and 32/75) using RTM and MPX-32; VARIAN 77 using VORTEX; SIGMA 5/9 using BPM and CP-V; and various other special purpose image-processing systems.

Although the term maintenance is used to describe the main functions, many tasks require such extensive systems analysis prior to making appropriate changes that the programmer receives as much challenge and satisfaction as if the program was actually being developed. Another factor is training. In order to keep the staff abreast with state-of-the-art developments, management encourages formal vendor-supplied training classes. Specific analytical and systems-oriented techniques and skills are addressed in these courses. Attendance at user and general conferences is also an added incentive provided to the programming professional for acquiring and dispensing information.

Dealing with Newly Developed Software

Almost all software maintenance groups encounter the problem of assuming responsibility for new software developed by another organization. In our case, this problem is compounded by the fact that the new programs are developed by another contractor. To deal effectively with this situation requires getting involved well before the software is delivered. Plans and interface definitions should be mutually agreed upon and include acceptance testing, documentation, and formal sessions for acquainting the maintenance personnel with the inner workings of each program.

The development of the acceptance test plan requires extensive communication between the maintenance and the development groups. Program design walk-throughs are highly recommended for this purpose, as well as for familiarizing the maintenance personnel with the software. This should be done prior to the turn-over of the program since afterwards development personnel are reassigned to other tasks and often are not easily accessible.

As on-site contractors, we need to be particularly concerned with the way information concerning our dealings with development personnel is presented to the customer. Group interaction problems, such as competing for computer time, should if possible be transparent to the customer. When these problems need to be brought to the customer's attention, it is best to avoid a finger-pointing session. Such sensitivity and awareness contribute measurably to harmonious relations with the customer.

CONCLUSION

Overall, the use of on-site contractors can be a viable and effective means for accomplishing software maintenance in a large data processing facility. To achieve these ends, however, calls for a proper appreciation by both the customer monitors and the contractor management personnel of the factors and considerations described herein.

REFERENCE

1. Office of Management and Budget Circular A-76. This circular has been incorporated into the Federal Acquisition Regulation as Subpart 7.3, effective April 1, 1984.

SOFTWARE CONFIGURATION MANAGEMENT
AN UPDATE

R. L. Van Tilburg

HUGHES AIRCRAFT COMPANY

ABSTRACT

This paper presents an overview of significant changes that are occurring in the discipline of Configuration Management (CM), particularly with respect to the evolution of Software Configuration Management (SCM). It describes the current perception of SCM in terms of a model of the software engineering process and then presents the thesis that SCM is evolving from a "management" discipline to include the "technical" disciplines of design and implementation. The development of software programming environments with automated tooling is the driving force in this evolution.

1. INTRODUCTION

The Software Configuration Management (SCM) discipline has been with us a long time - it is one of the better understood software engineering disciplines. For those of us that have been involved in the management of software projects, the configuration management activities involved are very familiar. Freezing of specifications, labeling documents and reels of tape, reviewing and approving changes to documents or programs, running a change control board, and maintaining records of the history of changes are a part of normal day-to-day work. Others of us who are technically active in the generation of code know that configuration management means keeping track of changes and identifying different versions of a program so that one knows just what is being loaded into the computer.

However, despite this understanding of the need for SCM by the software community, there are still differences in perception of the SCM process between the technical software community and the older, more formalized configuration management (CM) community. Many times they use the same terms but mean different things. This mis-communication is typically found in systems development wherein the software is embedded in a concurrently developing hardware system. Some of the symptoms of the mis-communication can be found in observations being made by general industry management. Examples are:

1. Software is out of control look at the number of changes that are being made!

2. Making a change means an error has been made. Why can't the programmer do it right the first time?

3. All changes have to be reviewed and accounted for.

The attitudes of the technical software community, on the other hand, reflect different concerns. Examples are:

1. The program (module) is still in the development process. It is not ready to be put under configuration control.

2. Needs just a little more work to clean it up.

3. Why shouldn't I make this change? This is my program.

In this meeting of two different points of view the CM professional, with the disciplines based on hardware experience, and the software engineer, with experience based on engineering of highly complex functional logic, are evolving a better CM discipline in the generation of practices and disciplines appropriate to software development. The CM disciplines that have evolved over the years in the hardware world reflect the lessons of experience in control of manufacturing. The experience of the software engineer reflect the understanding of the use of a new technology which requires an extension of the more traditional CM concepts to the engineering process.

EH0302-0/90/0000/0117$01.00©1985 IEEE

This paper examines the emerging SCM discipline using a model of the Software Engineering Life Cycle [1] to analyze the significant differences in the disciplines of SCM and CM. The model highlights the use of SCM disciplines in the management of change in the iterative engineering process of design and packaging of functional logic in a software product. The paper uses this model to define the differences between macro CM disciplines needed for support of project management and the micro CM disciplines needed for support of the technical engineering process. The full import of the distinction is still not fully realized but the distinctions between the two levels of CM do clarify many of current issues in SCM. Hopefully, the concept will help extend the technology of SCM to the general CM community.

2. THE SOFTWARE ENGINEERING PROCESS MODEL

The model used to examine the SCM process is based on a generic model of the engineering process [2]. The model recognizes three separate, yet interdependent kinds of activities that are necessary for the development of complex (software) systems. They are separate in that they have different goals, techniques and applicable standards; interdependent in that each alone is not sufficient for the production of professional quality software, either as a part of a system or as a stand alone product for the general marketplace.

The three part model, as illustrated in Figure 1, shows the technical activities of generating software as a pyramid, with a distinction made between the design-type activities and the packaging-type activities. The pyramid representation is chosen to 1) indicate something of the hierarchical relationship of design to packaging; and,

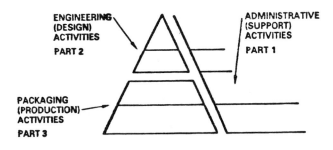

Figure 1. Model of the Engineering Process

2) convey an impression of the expanding detail of information generated in the process of software engineering. The administration activities supporting the management of the project are represented as a modified waterfall chart to indicate the sequential nature of the administrative activities.

The design-type activities may be thought of as being a two-part process. They begin with the analysis of a problem, determining the nature of the problem to be solved and setting of the boundaries of the solution. These activities are most often summarized in a requirements specification. The second part of the engineering activities is the development of a solution to the needs stated in the requirements specification. The natural relationship of this process is an iteration of requirements and design as the two complementary activities evolve to a design that can be implemented. The objective of the design activities is to produce a design that solves the problem defined by the requirements.

The packaging activities translate the design into product that can be executed. They begin with the design (top-level) and progress through detail design of individual units. The packaging activity then shifts to the integration of units into a package acceptable for general use. As in the design part of the engineering activities, the packaging process is characterized by a high degree of iteration between detail design and integration (which also includes the testing activities). The objective of the packaging activities is to produce a product that meets design specified by engineering.

The distinctive characteristic of administrative activities is that they are oriented to a calendar time-line. Events are grouped by phases and activities are coordinated by transitions between phases at scheduled milestones. The objective of administrative activities is to meet schedule and cost goals set for the project.

3. THE SCM MODEL

The more traditional CM supports the interfaces between the technical activities and the administrative activities. It is primarily concerned with the activities centering on the formal baselines that mark the transitions between the phases as seen by the administrative cycle. CM supports the identification of specifications and documentation and administers the changes made to these representations of the design. It also supports the administration of changes made to the product baseline that is released for general use. In this sense, traditional CM activities are the same for hardware and software in that they maintain an accounting and verification (audit) of the big picture or support the "macro" level CM for a project.

SCM carries the discipline of change management further into the engineering process by supporting the detail change coordination practiced in the iteration of conceptual changes that accompany the process of developing requirements specifications and top-level designs in the engineering activities and the iteration of detail design to executable code in the implementation of units into a usable product package. Both of these levels of change management are internal to the technical activities and focus on the details of technical change. In a sense they are concerned with the "micro" CM of software engineering.

Another area where SCM differs from CM practiced on hardware is in the administration of the interface between the engineering and packaging activities. In hardware engineering, the engineering organizations normally complete the detailed design activity and release a representation of the detailed design (in the traditional format of a drawing) to a fabrication, either in a model shop or to production, for implementation in a physical product. In software engineering, there is no equivalent transition in the engineering process. The organizations currently supporting design and packaging do not have significant differences in methodology and supporting environments. Indeed, there is a fundamental difference in the nature of the software product and hardware product. Software products represent a logical process for handling data. This process can be described in abstract terms or represented symbolically, just as a design for hardware can be represented in abstract terms. The significant difference is that the process used to generate the final form of the software package is highly automated and does not require additional knowledge of physical characteristics of materials or production problems associated with replication of parts and assemblies. There is no major change in technology of production associated with development of software products as there is for hardware products. The release of a top-level design from engineering to packaging activities does not impose a major transformation as in hardware release of a drawing to manufacturing. Micro CM management is not an issue at this interface and SCM systems can more

easily be developed to handle all of the change control and status reporting functions.

4. GENERAL OBSERVATIONS

4.1 CM Organization vs CM Function

The CM disciplines do provide the general framework for SCM but focus heavily on the macro CM activities and release function to the exclusion of the micro CM support necessary to the technical activities within engineering and packaging. This raises a very practical problem: who has the responsibility for SCM, the entrenched CM organization versed in the formal hardware change control disciplines or the software engineering activity versed in the technology of management of change? The problem becomes more evident in discussions where representatives of the CM disciplines define the SCM function in terms of what a CM organization does versus how the functions are performed by the different activities involved in the software development.

The SCM community can provide a pioneering action by supporting the reconciliation of these different points of view. Most published standards for SCM focus on the macro CM functions with some recognition to the micro CM needs, such as use of programming libraries and CM tools [3].

4.2 Entrenched Attitudes

There is a lot of reluctance on the part of the software technical community to use of CM discipline because of the wide spread idea that once a unit or program is put under configuration management it can no longer be changed. This idea is correct when the CM discipline provided for a project has the practices and change procedures for hardware engineering applied to the software engineering process. SCM requires appropriate use of software technology for change coordination within an engineering phase (the micro CM activity).

An equally difficult attitude to handle is the one often exhibited by the entrenched CM organizations that all changes must be handled by the centralized CM organization. This negates the development of effective CM tools that are needed in an interactive engineering environment. SCM again has an opportunity to pioneer advances in general engineering disciplines by providing the appropriate micro CM tools for management of change in engineering.

Successful SCM organizations are those with an attitude of providing a service to the technical engineering process while supporting the administration of the change processes. Essentially this may be a clerical type function but one that is essential where the level of automation is low. Less successful SCM organizations are those that look on the SCM activity as a "control" activity with the iron fist of bureaucratic inflexibility. This concept of control may be comfortable for project management but isolates the iteration of design and implementation activity from the benefits of good CM.

4.3 CM for Highly Complex Engineering

A major opportunity for general improvement of digital engineering technology lies with the extension of SCM type practices to the design of hardware, especially digital hardware. An example can be found in the VLSI engineering environment. Here, the complexity of the engineering process is at the level where management of the day-to-day design activity requires the same discipline that is evolving for the management of change in software engineering. The same issues of reusability of design, modification and management of design libraries, certification of units of design, and maintaining identities of different versions of a design during the evolution is needed.

The basic issue appears to be that whenever we undertake the engineering of a very complex process, whether it be a VLSI chip or a large software program, the engineering process involves large numbers of iterations of designs, of iteration of various levels of design and iteration of the interactions of many different units at each level of the design evolution. This complexity makes the management of change, the micro CM, a critical discipline for engineering. The change control disciplines that are appropriate for CM in hardware fabrication and production, while necessary, are not sufficient for the needs of the future engineering disciplines.

4.4 The Data Management Problem

The need for SCM technology for management of change is even more critical when one considers the current speculations on the paperless factory wherein all engineering will be controlled by computer aided engineering systems (CAES), computer aided design (CAD, and computer aided manufacturing (CAM) systems integrated by means of a common engineering data base. One can reasonably question whether we have the data management technology to support such an integration.

4.5 Levels of Change Management

One of the pertinent observations that can be drawn from examination of the software engineering process model is that the nature of change needed to support the iterations of design activity in the technical process is different from that needed in management of the overall process in the administrative side of the model. The problem is that the two aspects of SCM are often merged in the planning and practice on a project, making for confusion in in the decision making process. Often the people making macro change control decisions try to make micro change decisions which they are not qualified to make. The ground rules for distinguishing between macro level of change control and the micro level of change management need to be explicitly recognized.

4.6 The Micro Change Process

The use of micro CM change management in engineering produces a large amount of change paper as compared to the change paper circulating in macro CM change control. This gives the impression that software is out of control whereas in reality the software engineering activity has management visibility at a level far deeper into the engineering process than ever exercised for the hardware engineering process. Naturally, there are many times more changes at the micro level in the iteration of design as there is at the macro level. Unfortunately, top management sees only the statistics for hardware at the macro level and all of the statistics for software at both the micro and macro level.

Iterative changes made during the software engineering process are misidentified as errors by reliability analysts who then try to apply hardware reliability models to the failure data accumulated in SCM status reports. This leads to broad generalizations (MTBF and MTR predictions) and some questionable modeling of reliability figures [4] on the part of statistical analysts.

There needs to be a better understanding of the difference between changes made in the micro change process and in the macro change process as well as an appreciation for the fundamental nature of software products as compared to hardware products.

4.7 Reusable Software

For most of its history, software engineering has been focusing on the tailoring of a system to specific problems. The thrust of top-down design approach and emphasis on requirements development illustrate this preoccupation. Only recently has the hardware capacity (time and memory) been available where the need for the tight coupling of software design to system/ hardware requirements been relaxed. embedded software. SCM has not been constrained by the parts identification requirements that has characterized hardware CM and has been able to use simpler forms of identification of components of a configuration item. The VDD is an example of the simplicity in in component identification.

The emphasis on reusable software brought on by need for generation of larger amounts of code and the application of the technology of generic packages and abstract data types as in Ada[1] leads to consideration of parts identification and maintenance of different aspects of SCM identification. The problems will not be so much related to use of the parts since replication in software is a trivial activity but the source of design will become critical as issues of copyright, proprietary data rights and security become more important.

5. SUMMARY

The discipline of software configuration management cannot be thought of as being the same as the configuration management discipline applied to hardware. SCM is extending the scope of configuration management to the iterative design process of engineering. In the process of this extension, it is developing the practices and tools needed to support the detailed engineering process (the micro CM discipline). The macro CM discipline supporting the project administrative management, which is basically similar to the old hardware CM discipline, is still used.

The driving force for the evolution of the SCM in the micro CM discipline is the complexity of the software design process. This complexity is also characteristic of the hardware engineering design process as used in design of VLSI applications. An even more critical need for micro CM disciplines is in the development of integrated CAES/CAD/CAM engineering systems. In this sense, SCM is generating the technology needed to support a general systems engineering technology.

There are many open issues in the application of micro CM to the software engineering process. Many, such as status reporting, use of corrective action statistics, and application of hardware reliability models have to do with the difference in the basic nature of software and hardware products. As our understanding of the basic nature of these differences increases, we will better be able to provide CM support to the engineering processes, be they software engineering, hardware engineering, or systems engineering.

REFERENCES

[1] "Notes on Software Cycle" - R. L. Van Tilburg, Third Software Engineering Standards Applications Workshop, Oct 2-4 1984, IEEE Catalog # 84CH2071-9.

[2] "Guidebook to System Development" - Timothy L. Ramey, Hughes Aircraft Co, ICAM project 1701, Systems Engineering Methodologies.

[3] "IEEE Standard Software Configuration Management Plan" IEEE Std 828-1983 and "IEEE Guide to Configuration Management Plans" IEEE Project 1042

[4] "Software Defect Removal" - Robert H. Dunn, McGraw-Hill 1984

---

1. Ada is a registered trademark of the Department of Defense.

SOFTWARE CONFIGURATION MANAGEMENT TOOLS
CHANGE MANAGEMENT VS. CHANGE CONTROL

Bert Moquin

Texas Instruments, Inc.

Abstract

The business management aspects of change management and control issues should include such variables as contract and/or user requirements, procedural and organization controls, cost, and visibility of the software being developed. Change management focuses on the WHATs to be accomplished while change control focuses on the HOWs. The relationships between change management and change control can be used to focus in on the approach to developing automated Software Configuration Management (SCM) tools. Establishing and balancing priorities between these two areas and their relationships is a method for defining a long term strategy of tool development which provides effective control for minimum cost and resources.

Introduction

This discussion is centered on two major components of Software Configuration Management (SCM), Change Management and Change Control. The relationship of these two areas leads to a discussion of automated tools which may be developed to control change by the Software Configuration Management group during the software development life cycle. While consideration can be given to other selected variables pertinent to change management and control such as standards and procedures, the main thrust is to present a brief discussion of possible SCM tools. In other words, using automated tools to accomplish the WHATs of Change Management in order to provide management with comprehensive control, visibility, and traceability of all system change.

To begin on a common footing, the major terms used throughout this discussion require some definition. While the majority of these definitions are brief and general they are sufficiently broad to meet the needs of this discussion.

Software Configuration Management (SCM) is the discipline of identifying the configuration of a system at distinct points in its life cycle in order to control changes to the configuration and to maintain its validity, integrity, and traceability.

Change Management includes those plans, reviews, standards, and procedures that deals with the issue of "WHAT" to change. Proper management of change requires written, widely understood, enforceable change control standards or procedures.

Change Control involves applying those management disciplines such as procedures, standards, and methods to ensure that changes to systems are properly identified, recorded, analyzed, documented, and implemented in a timely and correct manner. Change Control is mainly concerned with the methods and means of "HOW" changes are actually incorporated into and reflected a system as it evolves.

Software Evolution is defined generally in the following phases:

DEFINITION	analysis, planning, and preliminary design.
DESIGN	planning, design, detailed design, integration test preparation, and system test preparation.
IMPLEMENTATION	detailed design, coding-testing-documentation, integration test preparation, system test preparation, and acceptance test preparation.
SYSTEM TEST	system test, acceptance test preparation, and customer/user training.
ACCEPTANCE	demonstration and customer/user training.

Software Configuration Control is the process through which various components of a software system are made visible throughout its life cycle. Various standards, procedures, methodologies, and organizational elements are used during this life cycle to accomplish this control. Some of the methods used to highlight and control the system and changes to it are defined in the following three paragraphs.

Software Configuration Identification includes the means by which the software system structure and its parts are designated, uniquely identified, and recorded.

Software Configuration Status Accounting is the means by which the results of applying control, identification, and auditing methods are collected, recorded, and reported.

Software Configuration Auditing consists of verifying that the software system configuration is what it was designed to be, and ensuring that the configuration meets the requirements by performing reviews, tests, and other checks to determine if the system is acceptable.

With this foundation established, let's look at change from a business management viewpoint.

Change Management

Change management appears to have two facets relevant to this discussion. The first is how it is applied, and the second is what its primary motivating factor is. Depending upon the force of the requirements for any given development effort, the application of change management covers the compliance spectrum from ad hoc, informal, undocumented, unplanned, nebulous, and sometimes contradictory to complete, in-full-accordance-with approaches. Other management techniques applied with varying degrees of success include, Configuration Control/Change Boards (CCBs), procedures, methodologies, standards, plans, reviews, mirrors, magic, and other black arts. Use of many of the above approaches have evolved as a result of disasters in attempting to apply the low end of the compliance spectrum's methods to a development effort. At this point, cost and visibility become the motivators.

In order to meet change management requirements during system development, cost and visibility must be balanced. In fact, this aspect of change management may be called the cost of visibility. Cost of visibility is based on those actions, plans, procedures, standards, and organizations generated or constituted which are required to ensure minimum compliance to requirements. More directly, how much does it cost to manage and control change at a given level of visibility. The higher the complexity of the system the finer the detail of visibility required, and the higher the cost of change management becomes. And, as change management directly drives change control, change control also becomes more costly.

Now that we have discussed the main areas of change, let's address the question of, "WHAT are some of the specifics of change to be considered?". Certainly the range of WHATs to be defined is a function of the requirements of the software system being developed. Some of the WHATs that may be considered are as follows:

WHAT is the complexity of the system?
* Small effort, software component only?
* Medium effort, software and hardware components?
* Large effort, software, hardware, and interface components?
* Any effort and complexity in the range cited above?

WHAT changes in the software environment are important?
* Are all changes to be managed?
* What baselines are to be used?
* What level of change is to be tracked?

WHAT is the cost of change visibility requirements?,
* Are changes to be recognized on the highest level only (system)?, lower levels (program, module)?, lowest level (line of code)?
* What's the cost to make each of these level visible?

WHAT level of control and guidance is necessary?
* What procedures are needed or desired?
* What reviews?
* What walkthroughs?
* What methodologies?
* What standards are necessary?

WHAT change reports are needed or desired and on WHAT basis are they required?
* Who is to receive what change reports?
* How are they distributed?
* What format?
* How often are they distributed?
* What's their content?

WHAT phases of the life cycle must be controlled?,
* All changes after release to the user/customer?
* All changes during the development, and following phases?
* All changes to all phases?

WHAT baselines are necessary?
* Is just the a delivery baseline sufficient?
* Is software and hardware to be baselined separately?
* Is a developmental configuration required?

WHAT system(s) to record and status changes, manual or automated, are to be used?,
* Will the change control be just a clerical function?
* Will the record and status of changes be kept in a computer system? Wordprocessor system?, manual?
* If an automated system is to be used, which one(s)?

WHAT internal and external organizational requirements must be addressed?.
* Software Quality Assurance?
* Hardware Engineering?
* Drawing Control?
* Subcontractors?
* Data Management?
* Software Engineering?

These are but a few of the myriad of WHATs to be considered and resolved in managing evolutionary program development. Many, if not all, of the above WHATs are listed as minimum areas to be addressed and resolved in various plans. Whether military or commercial guidelines are used, these areas are addressed by several documents including: Software Development Plans, Software Quality Assurance Plans, and Configuration Management Plans.

A few WHYs may be in order at this point to put the WHATs in perspective. A never ending list of WHYs jumps to mind not only from logical and experience considerations but also from military requirements and standards. Some of these WHYs include:

* profitability
* reproducibility
* maintainability
* reliability
* reuseability

Change Control

Given the four functions of software configuration management, identification, control, status accounting, and audit and reviews, the control function appears to map directly to change management while the remaining three functions map to change control. Although this dividing line may be possibly moved to include identification as a management control function, for the sake of this discussion let's leave it as formerly stated. This division, therefore, vests the major control of change into those methods and tools that are used to satisfy the requirements of identification, status accounting, and auditing and reviews. Let's take a look of some of these methods and tools currently used to perform change control.

Change Tools

This section addresses the types of software tools currently available to accomplish change control.

At the onset, we can classify tools used to control change into three general categories. The first category contains procedures, standards, and documentation which may be individually applied to accomplish some control function. Tools in this area include:

* Software Development Plans,
* Problem reporting procedures,
* Military standards, and
* Release procedures.

The second category of control tools includes those tools which are applied in an organizational context. While procedures and standards underlie this approach, and may well include some or all of the tools suggested in category one above, this category is identified by it multilateral application of control. This category may not only contains the various internal disciplines such as Configuration Management, Quality Assurance, Integration and Testing, and Project Management, but also such external groups as customer organizational elements, and contractor and subcontractor organizations. These organizational control groups may use any or all of the tools below:

* Configuration Change Control Boards,
* Software Requirements/Specification Reviews,
* Preliminary Design Reviews,
* Critical Design Reviews,
* Physical Configuration Audits,
* Functional Configuration Audits, and
* Internal/External Design and Code Walk-throughs.

The last category, although it may not fit neatly as a separate category, contains those tools (manual and automated) which may support the technical and administrative aspects of change management and control over the evolution of the entire software product. The systems cited here are generically titled, but in many cases represent real systems currently in use. Although these units are listed as systems, they should be viewed as functional units that at some point in time would be integrated into a unified approach to change control. Some tools and their configuration management areas of applicability are:

* CONTROL
   Requirements Traceability Systems.
   Specification Support Systems
   PERT/CPM Scheduling Systems
   Cost Modeling, and Estimating/Determination
    Systems

* IDENTIFICATION
   Version Control Systems
   Code Management Systems
   Module Management Systems
   Library Management Systems
   Generation Support Systems

* STATUS ACCOUNTING
   Computer Program Change Notice Systems
   Engineering Change Tracking Systems
   Trouble/Enhancement Reporting Systems.
   Software Release Systems
   Parts List/Components List Generating
    Systems

* AUDITS AND REVIEWS
    Baseline Management Systems.

* MISCELLANEOUS
    Report Generation Systems
    Library Control Systems
    Archival Systems
    Roll Back/Recovery Systems

In the three areas of tools discussed above, category three, Automated Software Evolution Tools, appears to be the least defined, the least standardized, the least understood, the least available, and the least applied. At the same time, it appears to be the most needed, the most wanted, and the most cost effective. Most, if not all, SCM organizations have recognized this situation for a long time and have experienced varying degrees of success in resolving this dilemma.

Conclusion

The conclusions to be reached from this discussion ARE CENTERED ON the visibility of required changes through change management, and the cost of the methods needed to make those changes visible via change controls. Both of these areas, change management and change control, also seem to have a common goal to meet minimum requirements with maximum visibility at optimum cost. Ideally, a viable approach by management to attain this goal to establish a long-term tools strategy that anticipates new requirements, technologies, and tools. This long term approach must be directed to incrementally increasing the capabilities of the SCM group to respond to changing environments and unforeseen or unanticipated requirements. Specifically, "what computers, operating systems, compilers, and languages will be supported?", "what level of detail and visibility have been generally required in the past?", "what other approaches may be appropriate?", and "how can such techniques as reuseable software be used to minimize reaction time to ad hoc requests for effective support?".

This is a brief discussion of two areas of SCM that can have a major impact on an organization's ability to manage and control change. Hopefully it will stimulate further study and discussion in the SCM community as we brace ourselves for the continuing software explosion.

EXPERIENCES OF DEVELOPING AND IMPLEMENTING A CONFIGURATION MANAGEMENT SYSTEM FOR A LARGE DEVELOPMENT SWITCHING SYSTEM

Edward J. Chauza

GTE Communication Systems
2500 West Utopia Road
Phoenix, AZ

ABSTRACT

This paper describes the process and history of developing and implementing a Configuration Management(CM) discipline for the GTD-5 EAX switching system. It describes development and implementation experiences with emphasis on CM as a management discipline rather than a collection of software tools.

The GTD-5 EAX CM process is an integral part of the development methodology and continually evolves to provide the designer with support and control functions without adding burden to creativity. The system comprises a set of software tools that are used in conjunction with a set of standardized administration policies and procedures.

Special aspects of this system are the abilities to provide version control which allows maintenance to be performed in parallel with new development, control of derived developments from a common base plus satisfaction of the standard requirements of identification, auditing, accounting and change control.

INTRODUCTION

The GTD-5 EAX system is an integrated family of stored program controlled digital processors whose purpose is to provide a wide range of applications for the telecommunications local and toll switching networks. Planning of the project was initiated in the mid 1970's with the specification/requirements phase beginning in the 1978 time frame. The system design is based on multiple distributed processors which can be categorized into five general types of processor loads.

The system at the commercial availability stage was composed of over 100,000 source lines of generic code with a manhour expenditure in excess of a million staff hours.(1) The source language of the target system was a GTE implementation of Pascal. System development is now at a stage undergoing the forth level of base software release. Also from the base system of software (which is referred to as the domestic system) there are two additional versions of software that have been derived from the base, those being a version incorporating Centrex features and a version designated for the European market.

The Configuration Management(CM) system was originally defined to support the development activities of hardware, software and documentation. Change processing was viewed from a system application standpoint rather than a specific subsystem perspective of hardware or software. The discipline of CM for hardware has been in existence such that practices and procedures have been substantially refined and are well understood for development, manufacturing and maintenance. Software, on the other hand, is a development area which is very new as yet and the methodologies, practices and procedures are still being refined as the project matures.

This paper will describe some of those experiences or "lessons learned" in establishing a CM system for a large scale development and provide some wisdom to those future development efforts such that some of the common pitfalls can be avoided. From these experiences, perhaps future developments will be more efficient, and will benefit from the knowledge of the mistakes of their predecessors.

This was a large system development with many unknowns or like going thru a maze with many corners, not knowing what was around each corner. As the general CM knowledge base is increased, there will be an awareness of potential problems and future development will be better equipped to develop CM systems dealing with those new situations.

BACKGROUND

The management of software libraries has become very refined at GTE Communication Systems R & D. Techniques were initially developed upon entering the market of stored program switching systems(SPSS) for telecommunications and have continually been refined to meet present day development and support requirements. Through the development, integration, and support of a series of SPSS commercial products (viz. No. 1 EAX, No. 2 EAX, No. 3 EAX, GTD-4600, & GTD-5 EAX) we have achieved the implementation of a management process which provides a central core of practices and procedures for all current software development and support.

These practices and procedures have been integrated into a Configuration Management (CM) cross discipline requiring the participation of many GTE Communication Systems organizations. This discipline insures that the end product does indeed fulfill all the specification requirements. What this means to a customer is that the product is delivered on schedule, properly documented, and functions as expected.

CM SYSTEM DESCRIPTION

CM is comprised of four major elements—identification, change control, status accounting, and auditing. These four elements are applied to three major areas of product development—software, hardware, and documentation. CM provides the mechanism for integrating these three product development areas into marketable packages. These are System Version Releases and Point Releases.

Rigorous nomenclature and identification schemes allow for each system component to be uniquely identified. Through a hierarchy of stocklists; component organization, interchangeability, and interface requirements can be readily determined.

The change control mechanism used provides an organized procedure for preparing, evaluating, authorizing, processing, and tracking design changes. An accounting mechanism provides records that show the chronological evolvement of a design as related to new features, enhancements, and maintenance changes. Configuration status accounting also provides the data source for determining the current state of design as well as data for determining base level design and derivations from it. The auditing functions serve two purposes, verification and validation.

The approach taken to auditing is to effectively perform it at the lowest level in the organization and at the earliest point in the development cycle that is feasible. The earlier problem areas are identified, the cheaper they are to fix.

SOFTWARE TOOLS

Our present CM environment consists of an integrated set of software tools(2) and administrative practices which support a formalized development methodology(3) that has evolved from

well over 3 million hours of real-time software experience. This methodology integrates the concepts of commonly accepted techniques in structured software design and programming with those of structured management techniques, formal design walk-through, code reading, build-up testing, and advanced documentation approaches that couple the documentation directly to the software.

The Software Management Support System (SMSS)(4) through an integrated set of interactive commands provide the CM organization with a convenient efficient set of tools to manage and control software development. The identification, storing, up-dating and retrieving of any file within SMSS is a controlled process whereby the who, when, where and why aspects of the transaction are recorded.

The SMSS in its original configuration functioned within a network utilizing both mini and maxi computers in different geographical locations. The user and master data bases are distributed such that all code and data associated with a particular class of software is co-located with the responsible designer to maximize response time and minimize network traffic. Complete flexibility exists to perform across machine transactions.

The multiple library control scheme provides the flexibility to:

- Accurately reproduce source code and text as it existed at specific reference points.

- Simultaneous support multiple variations of a unit module of software.

- Provide security levels as well as access privileges to read, write and execute attributes of a particular file.

- Provide audit trails of change history for all unit module piece parts.

Also integrated into the SMSS is a source patching support facility. This facility provides the capability to make a change to software components in a high-level language and then via an express processing mechanism generate a binary load module.(5)

The management and control of system software changes is handled using a Change Tracking System(CTS) and set of formalized administrative practices. The CTS is a collection of online interactive support programs coupled with a family of controlled access data bases within which all information pertinent to a problem and/or change are recorded. Integrated into the SMSS is the Load Generation System (LGS) which has the flexibility of using multiple IBM CPU'S to concurrently generate multi-processor system loads. The basic function is to build the load module for each processor community. This includes selecting the appropriate software piece parts from the SMSS master library and macro-processing them into a unit source module which is then compiled and the resulting listings and object code secured. The individual object modules are then link edited to provide a load module for an individual processor community. In each processor community there may be any one of the following combinations of software:

- Software that is common to other processor communities (The source and object code are the same).

- Software that is similar in function but has differences at the source or object code level.

- Software that is unique to only a single processor community.

The residency of each unit of software is controlled via the naming convention scheme as well as a unique load stocklist. The stocklist is an automated tool called the Masterlist(ML)(6) which maintains the reference issue level of each compilable unit as well as the piece-part components (multiple segments and data declarations) within the compilable unit. A model of this system is shown in Figure 1. Also shown in this figure is the interface to the Change Tracking System(CTS). This is used to authorize the update to any individual Masterlist component.

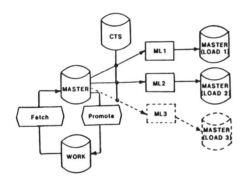

Figure 1 - Masterlist Control

Support Tools and Utilities

At the start of the GTD-5 EAX project, development tools and utilities were required to support designers doing the high-level system design. An approach was taken to develop an interim set of CM tools which would satisfy the initial designer requirements and those of CM. These were basically rapid prototypes using the "Shell" facility available in the UNIX operating system.

A design idea followed was to incorporate as much of the auditing capability into the tools as possible. Auditing at the software tool level was accomplished by having intelligence built into the tools such as checks to verify syntax, format, dates, values, authorization restrictions, etc. This level of auditing provides much control and enforces consistency of information with the additional benefit that it requires very little people resource to maintain after implementation.

The tools originally started out as standalone utilities. This has worked to to our advantage because it has provided a degree of flexibility to adapt to new requirements, change direction and satisfy the various pressures that can be exerted on a project from the development environment itself. Namely-- schedule milestones, reorganizations, new customer requirements, organizational dependencies, etc.

A situation that later became a problem as a result of building interim rapid prototype tools was that interim tools are generally designed to satisfy the immediate needs, support documentation is minimal and little concern is given to implementing a design that can be enhanced or easily maintained. The result being, you have a very good tool that meets the immediate requirements but requires a large amount of effort each time a change must be implemented. Also designers move to other responsibilities and the only tool knowledge that is available are some preliminary design notes.

Thus, the interim tools worked well enough but documentation and design was inadequate to support feature enhancement causing enhancements to be delayed. This delay has a net result of decreasing the efficiency of the design environment because known changes and enhancements cannot be made available as quickly as they could have been with a formalized tool design.

Designers also have a high affinity to customize tools to their personal needs and then look to a support organization to maintain the tool. The sooner a tool can be standardized for a development community, the less chance there is that multiple copies of the same tool(each copy customized to a particular designer need) must be supported.

CM within the Life Cycle

A model of the system life cycle presently used is shown in Figure 2. Also depicted is the early stage in the life cycle at which CM was started for the GTD-5 EAX project. This may not appear unusual and seem quite natural but in reality it requires management support with an understanding of the long term needs of a project. Beginning CM at a very early stage in a project is like buying life insurance when you are young. It is an extra expense and hard to justify when those same dollars could be expended on something else which would show an immediate return. To a degree it is a "Pay now or pay later" dilemma.

A concern with introducing "to much CM to early" into a project is that the additional overhead of control may reduce productivity by adding unnecessary designer frustration. The statement is made that design is one-percent inspiration and ninety-nine percent perspiration and what you want to avoid is drowning that one-percent of inspiration with unnecessary overhead.

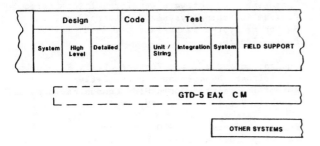

Figure 2 - GTD-5 EAX Development
Control Life Cycle

Decomposition of the system into manageable design units followed an existing methodology. The hierarchical structure is shown in Figure 3. Each element of this structure is identified with both a 48 character formal name and short mnemonic name(7). Controlled components of the design were secured at designated phases within the life cycle. The chart in Figure 4 depicts the major components and the point at which they are secured.

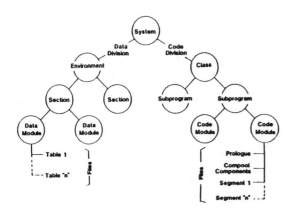

Figure 3 - Decomposition Hierarchy

Baseline scheduling

The CM organization was responsible for establishing freeze dates to support the project schedule. The majority of schedules were for developmental and baseline reference loads for the GTD-5 EAX prototypes.

Originally the software loads started out as a mass compilation of software source scheduled for the load. As the project progressed through the life cycle towards the first system release, the batch support computer resource requirements grew faster than the resource could be upgraded to handle the increased load. This resulted in extended load generation intervals, pre-empting lower priority development activities and creating significant organization frustration.

Figure 4 - Life Cycle Control

HIERARCHY	FILE DESCRIPTION	FILE NAME	SYSTEM DESIGN	HI-LEVEL DESIGN	DETAIL DESIGN	CODE
CLASS	PROLOGUE	_P	X			
SUBPROGRAM	PROLOGUE	_P	X			
MODULE	PROLOGUE	_P		X		
	SEGMENT PROLOGUES	_P			X	
	DATA PROLOGUES	MNEM_DP			X	
	FORMAL PROCEDURE DEFINITION	_FP			X	
	PARAMETER TYPE DEFINITION	_PT			X	
	COMPOOL COMPONENT	_C			X	
	DATA SECTION	MNEM_DD				X
	SEGMENT CODE	MNEM_S				X
ENVIRONMENT	PROLOGUE	_P	X			
SECTION	PROLOGUE	_P	X			
DATA MODULE	PROLOGUE	_P		X		
	DATA DEFINITION PROLOGUE	MNEM_P			X	
	MONITOR PROLOGUES	MNEM_S			X	
	PARAMETER TYPE DESCRIPTION	MNEM_PT			X	
	FORMAL PROCEDURE DEFINITION	_FP			X	
	COMPOOL COMPONENT	_C			X	
	DATA DEFINITIONS	MNEM_DD				X
	MONITOR CODE	MNEM_S				X
SYSTEM	PROLOGUE	_P	X			
	MACRO CODE	_M			X	
	MACRO DATA	_U			X	
ENCAP. DIR.	PRIMARY ECAPSULATION	_ED		X		
	SECONDARY ENCAPSULATION	MNEM_ED		X		
LINKER	PLACEMENT DIRECTIVES	_PD				X
USER GUIDE	USER GUIDE	MNEM_UG			X	

Currently, the process of incremental load generation is being used. Small reference miniloads (This is an edit of an existing load module of the changed modules.) are generated and loaded onto the previous reference load. Figure 5 depicts the relationship of miniloads to the original base load. A new base load (This is a total recompilation of all software source modules with a total re-link of the object modules.) is generated with the introduction of new feature software and at that time the changed source from the previous miniloads is recompiled and included in the load.

The advantages gained from this process is the reduced interval of testing and the reduced amount of batch support computer resource. It also tends to reduce the "last minute" promotion resource burden. (This is the situation where a designer must obtain a clean compile prior to promoting his software and the development support computer becomes overloaded with this point impulse of work.)

Another common problem area experienced was multiple definitions of software freezes plus conflicting deadline dates. During the early stages of the project, this problem wasn't as evident because the organization was still small enough such that dissemination of information could be easily accomplished by a single meeting with all involved parties. As the number of designers grows, so does the organizational structure, thus creating more levels and organizational interfaces thru which information must flow. The resultant solution was to have the CM organization maintain an online read only dataset with the current dates and definitions. Additionally, as critical dates were approached, the design community was notified at system logon time by an electronic broadcast.

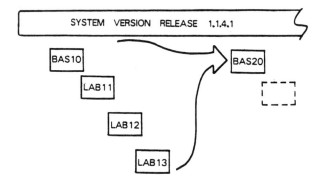

BAS10---FULL LOAD

LAB11---MINILOAD OF INCREMENTAL CHANGES
SEQUENTIALLY APPLIED TO PRIOR LOAD

Figure 5 - Product Load Baselines

CONCLUSION

Configuration Management as a discipline is treated more as an art rather than a science of systematized knowledge. Again, it is an insurance factor and the amount you accept is proportional to the risk you wish to take. The GTD-5 project has been very successful with manhour expenditures in the 4% to 8% range but has required about 50% of the development computer resources. CM is a tool available for managing development projects but management must gain confidence in using the data available for decision making. CM organizations also must create an awareness within the designer user community of the services that can be provided to aid the designer. Organizational structures without sound and stable support as a foundation can become very shaky, thus it is important that a sound CM plan be implemented early in the development cycle.

REFERENCES
----

1) Vanderlei, Kenneth W., and Wirth, Robert D., "GTD-5 EAX Development Language and Support Software System," International Switching System Symposium, September, 1981, Montreal, Quebec, Canada.

2) Begley, A., "The Software Development Environment for a Large Real-Time Project," Phoenix Conference on Computers and Communications, May 9-12, 1982, Phoenix, AZ.

3) Daly, Edmund B., and Mnichowicz, Donald A., "Management of Software Development for Stored Program Switching Systems," International Switching System Symposium, May 7-12, 1979, Paris, France.

4) Chauza, Edward J., and Fortune, Larry E., "GTD-5 EAX Software Management Support System," GTE Automatic Electric World-Wide Communications Journal, Vol.19, No.3, May, 1981.

5) Beaupree, Chris A., "GTD-5 EAX Source Patch Facility," GTE Automatic Electric World-Wide Communications Journal, Vol.19, No.3 May, 1981.

6) Styma, R. E., "Configuration Management for the Concurrent Development of Multiversion Shared Resource Projects," International Switching System Symposium, May 7-11, 1984, Florence, Italy.

7) Verbeek, Dennis H., "The Program Naming Convention for a GTD-5 EAX Project," GTE Automatic Electric World-Wide Communications Journal, Vol.18, No.5, September, 1980.

Part 3: Maintenance, Repair, and Testing

If you don't know what you program is supposed to do, you'd better not start writing it.

Inside every large program is a number of small programs trying to get out.

Tony Hoare, Computer Scientist

If you put tomfoolery into a computer, nothing comes out but tomfoolery. But this tomfoolery, having passed through a very expensive machine, is somehow ennobled, and no one dares to criticize it.

Pierre Gallois, *Science et Vie*, Paris

STANDARD SOFTWARE QUALITY METRICS

James Inglis

AT&T TECHNICAL JOURNAL

James Inglis is super-
visor of the Software
Quality group in the
Quality Assurance
Center of AT&T Bell
Laboratories, Holm-
del, New Jersey. The
group develops and
implements tech-
niques for measuring
and improving soft-
ware quality. He
received a B.A. from
Amherst College in
1967 and an M.S.
and a Ph.D. in statis-
tics from Stanford
University in 1968
and 1973. He joined
AT&T in 1978.

Standard measures of software quality have been set
up for AT&T Bell Laboratories. These metrics allow a
software project to be followed through its development, controlled introduction, and release to
customers. The metrics serve both project and corporate management needs. For project management,
they allow more effective management of development
effort, and they help to ensure a fast and effective solution to problems that arise at any stage. For corporate
management, they provide a vehicle for quantifying the
overall quality of software development, for setting
quality improvement objectives, and for tracking
results. In particular, the metrics provide quantitative
information on number of faults, normalized so that
corporate results can be summarized and projects of
differing size can be compared; the responsiveness of
support organizations in resolving problems; and the
impact of fixes on customers.

In 1983, AT&T Bell Laboratories established a standard set of
metrics, or measures, of software quality for reporting on all software
development projects within the company. These metrics were selected
for broad applicability across the wide range of software development
projects within Bell Laboratories and were based on data that were generally available. Since their introduction, the metrics have undergone
revision, but their general purpose remains the same.

Standardized Quality Metrics

The Quality Assurance Center assumed responsibility for generating a semiannual report on projects in terms of the standard
metrics. After two prototypes, a transitional pilot report appeared in

early 1984 and regular reports have appeared since then. The Software Quality Assurance Report (SQAR) provides information on the quality of AT&T generic software during system test, controlled introduction, and the postrelease period.

Quality Metrics in Use

The standard software quality metrics provide useful information to project and corporate management. The metrics permit the evaluation of trends and the quantifiable analysis of quality, starting with system test. The measurements quantify

- The number of faults in generic software, normalized by software size
- The responsiveness of development and customer support organizations in resolving customers' problems
- The impact of software field fixes on customers.

A description of each of these measurements follows.

Cumulative Fault Density

The cumulative fault density provides a cumulative measure of the known faults, normalized by total software size, contained in a release during its useful life cycle. Two metrics graph cumulative fault density: one shows faults found within the company, the other shows faults found by customers. This makes clear not just how many faults there are, but by whom they were discovered.

The Cumulative Fault Density—Faults Found Internally graph (Figure 1) depicts the faults found by the development organization (developers, testers, and customer support personnel), normalized by the total software size in the system test phase. The graph plots this metric cumulatively starting with system test.

The Cumulative Fault Density—Faults Found by Customers graph (Figure 2) depicts the faults found by customers in the normal operation of released software, normalized by the total size of the released software. Any fault that is identified as a result of a customer-initiated inquiry or complaint is counted as "found by a customer." The horizontal axis is in system-months after release, on a logarithmic scale. Using system-months reflects the differing numbers of customers different software products have and their differing exposure to opportunities for customers to find faults. The logarithmic scale keeps the graph from appearing distorted.

Serious Fault Status Distribution

The Serious Fault Status Distribution graph (Figure 3) reports the number of serious faults found and the status of those faults—open (uncorrected) or closed (corrected)—as of the graph date. This provides a "snapshot" of the current status of serious faults. It gives an indication of how fast the project staff moves on closing faults once they are discovered. This graph is plotted from the beginning of controlled introduction.

The Mean Time to Close and Mean Time Still Open for Serious Faults graph (Figure 4) provides a measure of the responsiveness of the development and customer support organizations by showing the average time that serious faults remain open. The Mean Time to Close curve reports the average time to close, using a three-month rolling average, for serious faults since the start of controlled introduction. The Mean Time Still Open value for each month is the mean length of time that the serious faults open at the end of the current month have been open. Thus, these two measures cover both recently closed faults and those that have remained open.

Field Fixes

The Field Fix Distribution (Figure 5) provides a measure of the impact of software field fixes on customers. A field fix may correct one or more faults and may be distributed in a variety of ways. This graph also shows the number of systems in service.

The Field Fix Applications graph (Figure 6) shows the number of applications of field fixes customers must install. This is basically the product of the two measures, field fixes and systems in service, in Figure 5.

Figure 1. Cumulative fault density—faults found internally.

Figure 2. Cumulative fault density—faults found by customers.

Figure 3. Serious fault status distribution.

Figure 4. Mean time to close and mean time still open for serious faults.

Figure 5. Field fix distribution.

Figure 6. Field fix applications.

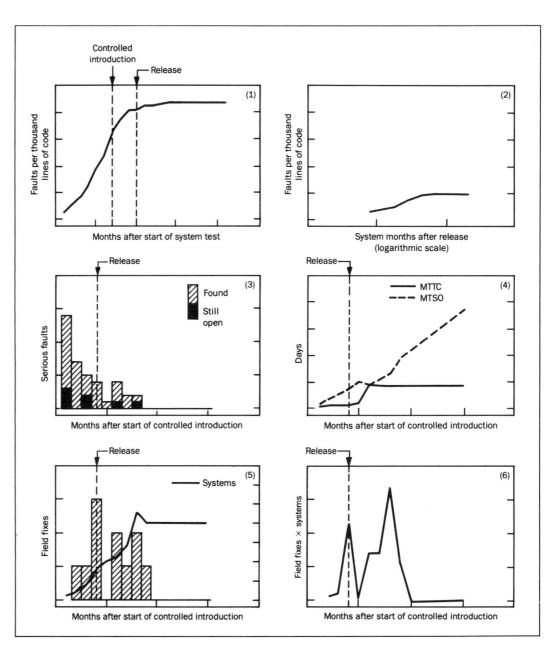

Metrics Summaries

Standard, broadly applicable metrics provide opportunities for several types of analysis. Two are of particular interest: summarization and comparison. Summarization yields a unified, overall view of software quality for the corporation. It shows where a group of projects are at a given time and where they are headed.

Comparison is equally useful, but must always be done with caution. Because software releases differ in many ways, simple comparisons based solely on the reported software quality metrics may not be appropriate. However, comparison of the metrics for a release with a previous version can indicate in a quantifiable, objective way what improvement (if any) has taken place. Comparison of the metrics for projects with different development methodologies, different development environments, or different management procedures can provide information on relative advantages and disadvantages.

The summary's purpose is to present an overview of selected values from the results for an individual software release. There are many ways to summarize the information in the six standard metrics graphs, Figures 1 to 6. Graphic summaries of three features are especially helpful:

- The variability of the measure of interest
- A reference measure of central tendency
- The variability in relevant time intervals.

These features lead to another series of graphs, with the vertical axis showing the measure of interest and the horizontal axis indicating time. Different projects have different time intervals for system test and controlled introduction. At any point in time, different software releases have been available and used by customers different amounts of time. Each summary graph presents certain key values from the individual software releases. Each graph also contains a line indicating the average value of the measure of interest. Each summary graph thus shows the the variability of the individual software release values about the averages and over time. Examples are the six summary graphs selected for the semiannual Software Quality Assurance Report:

- *Cumulative Fault Density at Release—Faults Found Internally*. The value of the cumulative fault density at the time of release for each participating software release is plotted in this summary graph (Figure 7). The horizontal axis shows the time interval from the start of system test until release for each participating release. The horizontal positions highlight the variation in testing time, which is important in evaluating the fault density values. The vertical position for a given project—the value at release—is a key point from the project managers' and the customers' viewpoints.
- *Cumulative Fault Density—Faults Found By Customers*. This summary graph shows the cumulative values of fault density for faults found by customers at the graph date, for all software releases (Figure 8). The horizontal axis indicates the time since a given project has been released.
- *Total Serious Faults Found*. This summary graph shows the total number of serious faults found between the start of controlled introduction and the report date (Figure 9). This summary graph does not permit general comparisons across all projects because projects of different sizes are likely to have different total numbers of faults. But it does give an indication of the overall variation in this measure.
- *Mean Time to Close Serious Faults*. Because this summary graph shows the mean time to make corrections for each project as of the graph date, comparisons are valid. This graph (Figure 10) makes it easy to see how quickly, on average, serious software problems are being solved.
- *Mean Time Still Open for Serious Faults*. Because this summary graph (Figure 11) shows the mean time that serious faults on a project remain uncorrected, as of the graph date, it too is good for comparisons.
- *Total Field Fixes*. This summary graph (Figure 12) shows the total number of field fixes, as of the graph date, for each software release in the time since its controlled introduction was begun. Releases can not be

Figure 7. Cumulative fault density at release—faults found internally.

Figure 8. Cumulative fault density—faults found by customers.

Figure 9. Total serious faults found.

Figure 10. Mean time to close serious faults.

Figure 11. Mean time still open for serious faults.

Figure 12. Total field fixes.

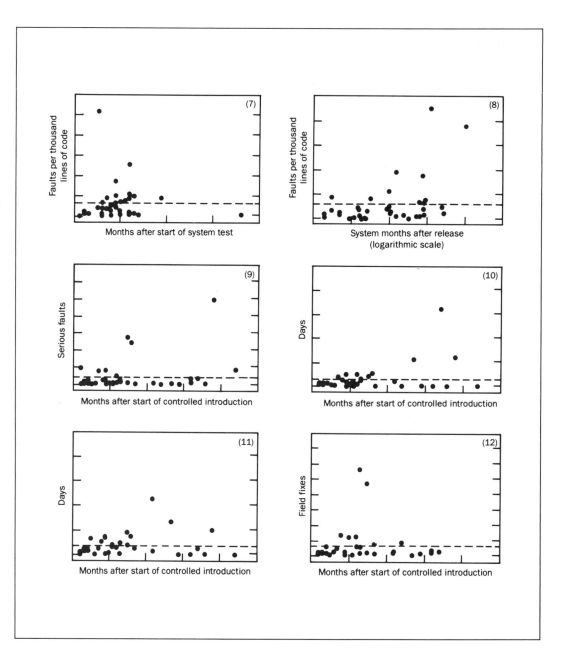

compared directly on this graph because they vary in size, but the overall status and variability are evident.

Conclusion

The standard software quality metrics have been in place for several years. A system for collecting the data, training the project personnel on how to provide the data, and reviewing data submitted for correctness has been set up to ensure reliable, accurate reports. Most recently, 42 projects provided data on 73 releases. This system of measuring software quality is an important part of Bell Laboratories' continuing efforts to improve the quality of the software it develops.

(Manuscript received November 19, 1985)

MARCH/APRIL 1986 • VOLUME 65 • ISSUE 2

ON VALIDATING SOFTWARE QUALITY METRICS

By

Gerald E. Murine, President

METRIQS, INCORPORATED, 390 Oak Avenue, Suite G
Carlsbad, California 92008

ABSTRACT

This paper presents the results of the application of Software Quality Metrics (SQM) by the author to three separate major military defense systems. The first system, a remotely piloted vehicle, consisted of a complex embedded computer network of twelve processors and fifteen functional software segments. The software included the modification of an existing operating system, flight software, mission support software, simulators and trainers, and diagnostic/maintenance software. The second defense system was a steerable missile built around a highly complex guidance and navigation system. The application included air, ground, and support software. The third system dealt with early detection of air/space vehicles and included a variety of communication, pattern recognition, and display software. All systems were written in different languages, and all had separate and independent Software Quality Assurance (SQA) activities performed. This paper reviews the results of one software development phase and a limited but identical set of quality factors.

INTRODUCTION

Software Quality Metrics (SQM) has been a subject of interest for over fifteen years. Since the early references by Hartwick and Rubey[1] in 1968 through the works of Boehm[2], McCall and Walters[3], and most recently, Murine[4], SQM has undergone a series of evolutionary changes as a by-product of intense reviews and investigations. SQM's basic premise of measuring an ordered set of deductively related software attributes over the life cycle to produce cost-effective "good" software is generally accepted as valid. Which particular attributes should be measured, their deductive associations and definitions, the means of extracting (and indeed calculating) the measurements, the meaning of establishing "cost-effectiveness", and finally the meaning of "good" or "quality" software itself are among the questions still felt to be unresolved by a few.

This paper will provide new data which it is hoped will help clarify, or verify, the SQM process. The data presented here is the result of the author's experience in applying SQM to three major U.S. defense software systems. While theoretical debate continues (and justifiably so), we will examine the lessons our experience in the "real world" has taught us. Although an advocate of SQM, the author does not pretend to have resolved all issues but has modified and adapted the SQM methodology to the realm of practicality.

The three programs discussed here do not constitute all the SQM applications the author has encountered. The three applications, however, were selected for their significance as major contributors to the development of a practicable SQM methodology. These examples span a period of five years and include the first major SQM measurement at the Requirements Definition Phase, an application uniquely tailored to the software quality characteristics as established by the software development team, and finally, an SQM application whose results were compared to those obtained by two other independent quality analysis techniques.

OVERVIEW

We will begin our examination of the selected examples by listing the basic assumptions and definitions used for all three programs. Then each system will be discussed in order by reviewing the environment and background in which the application was made, the software system itself, and finally some results obtained from one phase of SQM measurements will be given. The developmental phase selected for this paper is the Requirements Phase. This paper concludes with a summary of "lessons learned" and some projections for the role of SQM in future software development.

BASIC ASSUMPTIONS AND DEFINITIONS

Twelve (12) Software Quality Factors were used as the universal set for all three applications. The definitions first introduced by Boehm and later restated by McCall and Walters were preserved insofar as possible. The entire factor set is shown in Table 1. Each of the 23 criteria is defined as an attribute of the software.

```
+-----------------------------------------------+
|                  TABLE 1                      |
|         FACTOR TO CRITERIA ASSOCIATIONS       |
|-----------------------------------------------|
|        FACTOR            CRITERIA             |
|                                               |
|    1. CORRECTNESS      TRACEABILITY           |
|                        COMPLETENESS           |
|                        CONSISTENCY            |
|                                               |
|    2. RELIABILITY      CONSISTENCY            |
|                        ACCURACY               |
|                        SIMPLICITY             |
|                        ERROR TOLERANCE        |
|                                               |
|    3. TESTABILITY      MODULARITY             |
|                        SIMPLICITY             |
|                        SELF-DESCRIPTIVENESS   |
|                        INSTRUMENTATION        |
|                                               |
|    4. FLEXIBILITY      MODULARITY             |
|                        GENERALITY             |
|                        EXPANDABILITY          |
|                        SELF-DESCRIPTIVENESS   |
|                                               |
|    5. PORTABILITY      MODULARITY             |
|                        SELF-DESCRIPTIVENESS   |
|                        S/W SYSTEM INDEPENDENCE|
|                        H/W INDEPENDENCE       |
|                                               |
|    6. INTRAOPERABILITY MODULARITY             |
|                        DATA COMMONALITY       |
|                        COMMUNICATIONS COMMONALITY|
|                                               |
|    7. EFFICIENCY       EXECUTION EFFICENCY    |
|                        STORAGE EFFICIENCY     |
|                                               |
|    8. INTEGRITY        ACCESS CONTROL         |
|                        ACCESS AUDIT           |
|                                               |
|    9. USABILITY        TRAINING               |
|                        COMMUNICATIVENESS      |
|                        OPERABILITY            |
|                                               |
|   10. MAINTAINABILITY  CONSISTENCY            |
|                        SIMPLICITY             |
|                        CONCISENESS            |
|                        MODULARITY             |
|                        SELF-DESCRIPTIVENESS   |
|                                               |
|   11. REUSABILITY      GENERALITY             |
|                        MODULARITY             |
|                        S/W SYSTEM INDEPENDENCE|
|                        MACHINE INDEPENDENCE   |
|                        SELF-DESCRIPTIVENESS   |
|                                               |
|   12. INTEROPERABILITY MODULARITY             |
|                        COMMUNICATIONS COMMONALITY|
|                        DATA COMMONALITY       |
+-----------------------------------------------+
```

A few examples of factor definitions are:

o Correctness: The extent to which a program satisfies its specifications and fulfills the user's mission objectives.
o Reliability: The extent to which a program can be expected to perform its intended functions with required precision.
o Usability: The effort required to learn, operate, prepare input, and interpret output of a program.
o Maintainability: The effort required to locate and fix an error in an operational program.

As an example, the definitions of a few criteria are:

o Traceability: Those attributes of the software that provide a thread from the requirements to the implementation with respect to the specific development and operational environment.

o Completeness: Those attributes of the software that provide full implementation of the functions required.
o Consistency: Those attributes of the software that provide uniform design and implementation techniques and notation.
o Accuracy: Those attributes of the software that provide the required precision in calculations and outputs.

The actual elements selected are given by phase for each application. Currently, the universal set of elements number over 200 with their derivations ranging from "accepted good software practices" as established by the academic community through specific company Standards and Procedures, Military Specifications, Data-Item Descriptions, contractual requirements, or other constraints.

Nine separate scoring algorithms are available, however, in order to establish a basis for comparison, the results for this paper were translated into the two methods felt best suited to such applications. These scoring methods are:

o Direct Ratio Scoring where the score is basically the ratio of successes or compliances to events.

o Second-Order Averaging where the results obtained are independent of the individual population.

THREE SQM APPLICATIONS

U.S. ARMY RPV SYSTEM (1979)

The U.S. Army issued a contract to develop a sophisticated RPV system in the late 1970's. Six software quality factors were specified in this contract for a software quality incentive award. Measurements made at the Requirement Analysis phase using the SQM methodology are also presented. All inspections and evaluations were done in real-time in an engineering developmental mode by an independent organization.

The system developed was a Remotely Piloted Vehicle (RPV) with software and firmware operating in a fully distributed fashion. The RPV system was designed to perform target acquisition, designation, aerial reconnaissance, and artillery adjustment missions by carrying a mission payload over enemy territory aboard a small unmanned Air Vehicle (AV). The RPV system is comprised of an Air Vehicle/Ground Control Station (AV-GCS), Remote Ground Terminal (RGT), Launch Equipment, Recovery Equipment, Support Equipment operated by military personnel, and associated Training Devices.

The software/firmware (developed under Military Standards 490 and 483) was distributed over fifteen functional areas (Computer Program Configuration Items, or CPCI's). There were twelve processors in the system--nine microprocessors, two microcomputers, and one minicomputer.

In the RPV application, the factors given in their order of importance were: Correctness, Reliability, Testability, Flexibility, Maintainability, and Intraoperability.

The RPV application has produced a vast amount of data for the first real-time SQM measurement. The SQM methodology was applied to six critical CPCI's and complete Requirements Analysis was performed on two versions of the system. Table 2 summarizes some numerical results obtained for the Requirement Analysis phase of the RPV system.

and approved. This software application was developed under MIL-STD-1679. The SQM approach to measuring the quality of the software was: first, to identify the software goals, then, to select the appropriate metrics from various sources. The goals were extracted from the SDP, as inferred by the software development team. Since MIL-STD-1679

TABLE 2
RPV REQUIREMENTS ANALYSIS MEASUREMENTS BY SOFTWARE CLASS

Software Class	Total # inspections	Total # Conformities	Total # Non-conformities	FACTOR SCORES											
				Correctness		Reliability		Maintainability		Flexibility		Intraoperability		Testability	
				+	Σ	+	Σ	+	Σ	+	Σ	+	Σ	+	Σ
Airborne Software	4174	3250	924	1444	2020	796	999	566	685	148	160	45	46	251	264
Applications Software	3035	2707	328	1968	2247	277	307	281	300	9	9	160	160	12	12
Display Firmware	787	675	112	448	497	106	148	57	70	16	24	24	24	24	24
Systems Software	3407	3092	315	1720	1916	637	703	653	698	19	23	36	40	27	27
TOTALS	11403	9724	1679	5580	6680	1816	2157	1557	1753	192	216	265	270	314	327
% Conformance	85			84		84		89		89		98		96	

The number of requirements analysis elements measured for each factor were Correctness (8), Reliability (10), Maintainability (5), Testability (2), Flexibility (2), and Intraoperability (2). The number of elements measured per criteria were traceability (1), completeness (5), consistency (2), accuracy (2), error tolerance (5), simplicity (1), expandability (1), self-descriptiveness (1), communications commonality (1), data commonality (1), and conciseness (1). The number of software discrepancy reports per class of software were Systems Software (131), Display Firmware (42), Airborne Software (158), and Application Software (52). Table 3 provides a summary of the RPV SQM analysis.

TABLE 3
RPV REQUIREMENTS ANALYSIS SUMMARY

CPCI Name	No. Requirements RAD*	**	No. Inspections	No. Functions	No. Data Sources
Airborne Software	56	814	4174	113	308
Applications Software	29	140	3035	4	919
Display Firmware	33	343	787	8	45
Systems Software	154	434	3407	9	706

* RAD: Requirements Allocation Document (Requirements by CPCI)
** B-5 Functional Design Document

U.S. AIR FORCE STEERABLE-MISSILE-PROGRAM (1982)

At the time the SQM analysis was initiated on this particular Steerable Missile Program (SMP), a software development plan (SDP) had been developed

had been contractually imposed and identified as the vehicle for the software quality assessment, this document became the basis for the measurement guidelines. The metrics were selected to be responsive to the contractual quality requirements and the project's predefined scope. In addition, the reporting of SQM measurements was made adaptable to the existing SQA reporting system.

A total of 217 requirements which related to the 12 quality factors were extracted from the software development plan. A frequency of occurrence of these requirements, as they related to the software quality factors (explicitly or implicitly), was established whereby the three factors occurring most frequently were selected as the trial set of objectives.

The SDP document analysis provided sufficient data for the software QA and development team to establish an unbiased ordering of the software quality factors by group. The first group, considered to be of the highest priority, contained the factors of Correctness, Testability, and Intraoperability. From this group, a list of criteria was defined which, themselves, were measures of the three factors. These criteria were: traceability, completeness, consistency, simplicity, modularity, instrumentation, self-descriptiveness, communications commonality, and data commonality.

A final step in this systematic approach to identifying software goals and providing for their measurement was to establish a series of SQM elements for assessing their accomplishments. Since MIL-STD-1679 is not directly software quality metric oriented, it was necessary to identify the individual requirements, separate them into categories, and group the metric-related requirements by criteria. It was believed this major undertaking would complete the deductive association of contractual requirements to software quality metrics and to software quality goals.

A total of 416 requirements were extracted from the relevant sections of MIL-STD-1679 and divided into four categories. The distribution of the metric requirements by category was as follows: General Requirements, 93 (22%), General Checklist, 82 (20%), Test Items, 74 (18%), and Software Quality Metric Elements, 167 (40%).

The nine criteria, directly related to the three selected factors, contained 97 of the MIL-STD SQM elements. Some criteria were found to be without direct reference in the MIL-STD. Additional SQM elements were needed. From the Murine Metric Set (MMS), 87 additional SQM elements were identified to support the defined criteria as follows: traceability, 6, completeness, 42, consistency, 26, simplicity, 31, modularity, 15, instrumentation, 1, self-descriptiveness, 50, communications commonality, 5, and data commonality, 8. These SQM elements had been used previously on similar projects and were selected in part on this account. A final set of SQM elements was generated from the various Data Item Description (DID) documents.

The three quality factors measured were Correctness, Testability, and Intraoperability. Two program design specifications were examined—an initial version (Version I) and a refined version (Version II). SQM discrepancies from Version I were available to the software developers for use in producing Version II.

Even though the factors and criteria remained the same in the two measurements, additional SQM elements were added for Version II and some were modified or eliminated. Eliminations were a result of either complete compliance in an independent measurable partition of the software or SQM elements not relevant to the revised document. Modifications to SQM elements were made primarily to accomodate some specific language peculiarities. Additions were a result of a better understanding of the system.

The results of the measurements for the three criteria of Correctness were: traceability, from 91.1% (337/370) to 86.9% (377/434), completeness, from 66.9% (214/320) to 86.6% (427/493), and consistency, from 86.5% (199/230) to 97.2% (205/211).

Using the Second-Order Averaging (SOA) technique of scoring (all criteria are given equal weight), Correctness increased from 0.761 in Version I to 0.902 in Version II. The number of events measured and the number of correct responses were: total events measured from 92 to 1138, correct events measured from 750 to 1009, and direct ratio average score for this software segment from 0.815 to 0.887.

Some other results of Version II criteria measurements are:

- Simplicity   110/115 = (0.957)
- Modularity   94/120 = (0.783)
- Self-Descriptiveness   46/76 = (0.605)
- Communication Commonality   40/85 = (0.471)

These produced factor SOA scores of 0.782 for Testability and 0.627 for Intraoperability.

Generally, factor scores less than 0.900 were considered insufficient to permit the release of a design to begin code. Again, using the SOA scoring algorithms, a quality score for this software segment in terms of the selected factors, criteria, and elements was found to be 0.770.

U.S. AIR FORCE EARLY WARNING SYSTEM (1983)

The results of the SQM analysis on a major Air Force Early Warning System Functional Design Specification are presented here. A total of 1857 inspections were made and recorded using 22 elements and four criteria. There were 1341 compliances with 98 of the non-compliances rated as Priority I errors (errors which could cause the mission to fail). The over-all Direct-Ratio score for the four criteria is 0.722. The highest SOA criteria score was 0.890 for consistency and the lowest SOA criteria score was 0.253 for communications commonality.

Communication commonality element scores included: element metrics CC1 (0.769), CC2 (0.000), CC3 (0.087), and CC4 (0.154) with a SOA score for communications commonality of 0.253.

Data commonality scores included: element metrics DC1 (0.615), DC2 (0.917), and DC3 (0.610) with an SOA score for data commonality of 0.714.

Consistency scores included: element metrics CS1 (0.792), CS2 (0.768), CS3 (1.000), and CS4 (1.000) with an SOA score for Consistency of 0.890.

Completeness scores included: CP1 (0.786), CP2 (0.857), CP3 (0.969), CP4 (1.000), CP5 (0.800), CP6 (0.000), CP7 (0.000), CP8 (1.000), and CP9 (1.000) with an SOA score for completeness of 0.712.

Two separate independent Quality Assurance analysis (Quality Analysis One [QA1] and Quality Analysis Two [QA2]) were made in addition to the SQM Review. Their results are included here.

The ratio of the total SQM comments to was computed from the following totals: Total SQM Comments (513), Total QA1 Comments (73), Total QA2 Comments (348). The ratios are thus: SQM/QA1 7.027 and SQM/QA2 (1.474).

The distribution of SQM comments to recorded QA1 and QA2 comments was computed from the following totals: Total QA1 Comments (73) with SQM Comments contained in QA1 Comments (42) and Total QA2 Comments (348) with SQM Comments contained in QA2 Comments (233). The ratios are thus: SQM/QA1 (0.575) and SQM/QA2 (0.669).

The QA1 and QA2 distribution of SQM comments in relationship to the total SQM comments was computed from the following data: Total SQM Comments (SQM Total) (513) with SQM Comments contained in QA1 Comments (SQM/QA1) (42) and SQM Comments contained in QA2 Comments (SQM/QA2) (233). The ratios are thereby computed as: SQM/QA1:SQM Total (0.082) and SQM/QA2:SQM Total (0.454).

Finally, when viewing the intersection of SQM comments with QA1 and QA2 comments (alone and again as a single universal set), the following observations are made:

rapidly emerging embedded computer architecture presented new impacts of existing element selections. Duplication of effort between Software Quality Assurance (SQA) and SQM had not been considered and hence the cost of quality measurements approached very high levels (33% of the software development cost). No separation of product vs. process quality measurements had been made. Reports exhibiting the SQM results approached, and sometimes exceeded, the size and magnitude of the software specifications themselves.

SQM vs. PAIR	COMPARISON
QA1, QA2	SQM comments common to QA1 and QA2 comments . . . . 25 % SQM comments common to QA1 and QA2 comments 4.87%
QA1, $\overline{QA2}$	SQM comments contained QA1 comments but not QA2 comments . . . . 17 % SQM comments contained QA1 comments but not QA2 comments 3.31%
$\overline{QA1}$, QA2	SQM comments contained in QA2 comments but not QA1 comments . . . . .208 % SQM comments contained in QA2 comments but not QA1 comments 40.55%
$\overline{QA1}$, $\overline{QA2}$	SQM comments not contained in QA1 or QA2 comments .263 % SQM comments not contained in QA1 or QA2 comments 51.27%

Table 4
SQM, QA1, and QA2 COMPARISONS

There is some set of assumptions necessary to provide a transformation between the three Quality Assurance Measurement processes. This is caused in part by the finer resolution of the SQM approach in examination when compared to the other methods. Also, this finer resolution of SQM inspection is itself often transformed into a more general grouping of data per discrepancy. To some extent, we may be "comparing apples and oranges".

Specifically, 37% of the QA1 comments, 32% of the QA2 comments, and 51% of the SQM comments produced independent results. On the other hand, 34% of the QA1 comments, 7% of the QA2 comments and 5% of the SQM comments were common to all. Considering that only 3.82% of all 655 comments were common, a strong case could be made for the necessity of more than one approach.

Finally, given the radial integrals of 22.65 for SQM, 18.65 for QA2 comments, and 8.54 for QA1, it is apparent that SQM and the QA2 tend to enclose a larger environment and hence, produce the possibility of greater error detection. Further investigation is necessary here; particularly after the 115 QA2 comments and 33 QA1 comments not related to the SQM elements selected have been analyzed.

LESSONS LEARNED

The first application in 1979 reinforced the generally accepted view that SQM had promise but lacked validation in "real world" environments. Little information was available which enabled us to trade off the impacts of schedule and cost against theoretical performance. Furthermore, the

Major improvements in both the methodology and the technique were established on the second example presented here. Duplication of SQA and SQM efforts was virtually eliminated by the careful integration of SQA and SQM into a single SQAM approach. A single individual or team was assigned responsibility for SQAM analysis of specific major functional software components or Computer Program Configuration Items. Improvements in SQM recording, scoring, and reporting methods were devised. An SQAM notebook consisting of SQM element, criteria, and factor scores and data together with SQA process data checklists reduced both the need for separation and the duplication of effort and cost. The reduction in cost alone was over 50% (from 33% to 16%). The involvement of software engineering in the factor selection process produced a cooperative working environment whereby software quality became synonymous with software development. New elements emerged which reflected both state-of-the-art software architecture (federated systems, firmware impacts, etc.) and the influences of an on-going R & D environment.

The third example illustrated in this paper not only added to the improvement of a practical SQM approach but also was the first attempt to independently access the merits of the approach itself. By relating all SQM measures to individual requirements, we were able to quickly relate deficiencies to primary sources. Reporting scores at the element and criteria level rather than at the factor and CPCI level reduces hierarchical assumptions and provides adequate visibility for status accounting. Second-Order Averaging for all criteria (except traceability) seems to be as useful for the class of application measured as does the more elaborate forms of measuring. The extraction of elements from contractual requirements (e.g., Military Standards) provides a useful means of customer acceptance. The importance of focusing on specific targets (criteria) produces a much greater chance of detecting error as opposed to traditional SQA or customer review approaches. Furthermore, SQM analysis more closely associates with the type of error discovered by government review than in-house SQA error.

WHAT NOW?

Although it is now both practicable and feasible to perform SQM on developing software systems, refinements should continue. Fundamentally, a true basis for an SQM kernal is missing. The Non-orthogonality of factors substantiates this premise. Furthermore, changes in both software (firmware) and hardware as well as system architecture require a reassessment of the role of such criteria as Modularity and Complexity (Simplicity) and such factors as Correctness and Testability. Automated tools, specifically designed with SQM as a system basis should be developed. Reliability measures during design for a predictive assessment should be reexamined and, in particular, the role of error tolerance and accuracy as criteria should be reviewed.

It is the author's opinion that a serious SQM analysis performed in conjunction with software development does produce significant results and value with existing technology. It is imperative that, in order to maximize the benefits of an SQM application, the measurements must begin as early as possible--at the Requirements Definition Phase. It is also imperative that problems discovered be systematically resolved and that the status of all discrepancies be placed under independent control. Furthermore, the reporting of SQM measurements should have the same emphasis in review meetings as software engineering. It is only when we view the "goodness" of a system to include characteristics other than correctness that we will have evolved beyond a short-sighted contribution to quality software.

REFERENCES

[1] R. Hartwick and R. Rubey, Quantitative Measurement of Program Quality, Proceedings 23rd ACM National Conference, pp. 671-677, October 1968.

[2] B. W. Boehm, Quantitative Evaluation of Software Quality, Proceedings 2nd International Conference on Software Engineering, pp. 592-605, October 1976.

[3] G.F. Walters and J.A. McCall, Factors in Software Quality, RADC TR-77-369, 1977.

[4] G. E. Murine, Improving Management Visibility Through the Use of Software Quality Metrics, Proceedings from IEEE Computer Society's Seventh International Computer Software & Application Conference, 1983.

Edgar H. Sibley
Panel Editor

An analysis of the distributions and relationships derived from the change data collected during development of a medium-scale software project produces some surprising insights into the factors influencing software development. Among these are the tradeoffs between modifying an existing module as opposed to creating a new one, and the relationship between module size and error proneness.

SOFTWARE ERRORS AND COMPLEXITY: AN EMPIRICAL INVESTIGATION

"Software Errors and Complexity: An Empirical Investigation" by
V.R. Basili and B.T. Perricone from *Communications of the ACM*,
Volume 27, Number 1, January 1984, pages 42-52. Copyright
©1985, Association for Computing Machinery, Inc., reprinted
with permission.

VICTOR R. BASILI and BARRY T. PERRICONE

1. INTRODUCTION

The identification of the various factors that have an effect on software development is of prime concern to software engineers. The specific focus of this paper is to analyze the relationships between the frequency and distribution of errors during software development, the maintenance of the developed software, and a variety of environmental factors. These factors include the complexity of the software, the developer's experience with the application, and the reuse of existing design and code. Such relationships can provide an insight into the characteristics of computer software and the effects that an environment can have on the software product. Such relationships can also improve the *reliability* and *quality* with respect to computer software. In an effort to acquire knowledge of these basic relationships, change data for a medium-scale software project were analyzed. (Change data include any documentation that reports an alteration made to the software for a particular reason.)

The overall objectives of this paper are threefold: first, to report the results of the analyses; second, to review the results in the context of those reported by other researchers [2, 3, 5, 6]; third, to draw some conclusions based on the first two objectives. The analyses presented in this paper encompass various types of dis-

tributions based on the collected change data. The most important are the error distributions observed within the software project.

1.1 Description of the Environment

The software analyzed in this paper is from a large set of projects being studied in the Software Engineering Laboratory (SEL). This particular project is a general-purpose program for satellite planning studies. These planning studies include mission maneuver planning, mission lifetime, mission launch, and mission control. The overall size of the software project was approximately 90,000 lines of code. The majority of the software project was coded in Fortran for execution on an IBM 360.

Although the system outlined here uses many algorithms similar to those of the original SEL projects, it still represents a new application for the development group.

The requirements for the system kept growing and changing, much more so than for the typical ground-support software. Owing to the commonality of algorithms from existing systems, the developers reused the design and code for many algorithms needed in the new system. Hence a large number of reused (modified) modules became part of the new system.

An approximation of the software's life cycle is displayed in Figure 1. This figure only illustrates the ap-

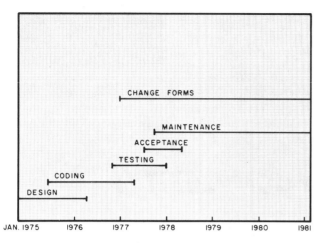

FIGURE 1. **Life Cycle of Analyzed Software**

proximate duration in time of the various phases of the software's life cycle. The information relating the amount of manpower involved with each of the phases was not specific enough to yield meaningful results, so it was not included.

1.2 Terms
This section defines the terms used in this paper. Please note that many of these terms often denote different concepts in the general literature.

Module: A module is defined as a named subfunction, subroutine, or the main program of the software system. Only segments that contained executable code written in Fortran were used for the analyses. Change data from the segments that constituted the data blocks, assembly segments, common segments, or utility routines were not included. However, a general overview of the data available on these segments is presented in Section 4.

There are two types of modules referred to in this paper. The first type is denoted as *modified*. These are modules that were developed for previous software projects and then modified to meet the requirements of the new project. The second type is referred to as *new*. These are modules that were developed specifically for the software project under analysis.

The entire software project contained 517 code segments, comprised of 36 assembly segments, 370 Fortran segments, and 111 segments that were either common modules, block data, or utility routines. Three hundred seventy out of 517 code segments (72 percent of the total modules) met the adopted module definition and constituted the majority of the software project. Of the modules found to contain errors, 49 percent were categorized as modified and 51 percent as new modules.

Number of Source and Executable Lines: The number of source lines within a module refers to the number of lines of executable code and comment lines contained within it. The number of executable lines within a

module refers to the number of executable statements; comment lines are not included.

Some of the relationships presented in this paper are based on a grouping of modules by module size in increments of 50 lines. This means that a module containing 50 lines of code or less was placed in the module size of 50, modules between 51 and 100 lines of code into the module size of 100, and so on. The number of modules contained in each module size category is given in Table I for all modules and for modules that contained errors (i.e., a subset of all modules) with respect to source and executable lines of code.

Error: An error is something detected within the executable code that caused the module in which it occurred to perform incorrectly (i.e., contrary to its expected function).

Errors were quantified from two viewpoints, depending upon the goals of the error analysis. The first quantification was based on a textual rather than a conceptual viewpoint. This type of error quantification is best illustrated by an example. If a "*" is incorrectly used in place of a "+," then all occurrences of the "*" will be considered an error, even if the "*"s appear on the same line of code or within multiple modules. The total number of errors detected in the 370 software modules was 215 contained within a total of 96 modules. This implies that 26 percent of the modules analyzed contained errors.

The second type of quantification measured the effect of an error across modules. Textual errors associated with the same conceptual problem were combined to yield one conceptual error. If a procedure was called with the same incorrect parameter list in multiple modules, this would constitute multiple textual errors but only one conceptual error. This is done only for the errors reported in Table II. There are a total of 155 conceptual errors. All other studies in this paper are based upon the first type of error quantification.

Statistical Terms and Methods: All linear regressions of the data presented in this paper employ the least

TABLE I. Module Size Categories

Number of Lines	All Modules		Modules with Errors	
	Source	Executable	Source	Executable
0–50	53	258	3	49
51–100	107	70	16	25
101–150	80	26	20	13
151–200	56	13	19	7
201–250	34	1	12	1
251–300	14	1	9	0
301–350	7	1	4	1
351–400	9	0	7	0
>400	10	0	6	0
Total	370	370	96	96

squares principle as a criterion of goodness. (That is, "choose as the 'best-fitting' line the one that minimizes the sum of squares of the deviations of the observed values of y from those predicted." [7])

Pearson's product moment coefficient of correlation was used as an index of the strength of the linear relationship, regardless of the respective scales of measurement for y and x. This index is denoted by the symbol r. The measure for the amount of variability in y accounted for by linear regression on x is denoted as $r2$.

All of the equations and explanations for these statistics can be found in [7]. It should be noted that other types of curve fits were conducted on the data. The results of these fits will be mentioned later in the paper.

2. BASIC DATA

The change data were collected over a period of 33 months (August 1977–May 1980). These dates correspond in time to the software phases of coding, testing, acceptance, and maintenance (Figure 1). The data collected for the analyses are not complete since changes were still being made to the analyzed software. However, enough data were viewed in order to make the conclusions drawn from the data significant.

The change data were entered on detailed report sheets, which were completed by the programmer responsible for implementing the change. A sample of the change report form is given in the Appendix. In general, the form required that several short questions be answered by the programmer implementing the change. These queries documented the cause of a change in addition to other characteristics and effects attributed to the change. The majority of this information was found useful in the analyses. The key information used from the form was:

- The data of the change or error discovery.
- The description of the change or error.
- The number of components changed.
- The type of change or error.
- The effort needed to correct the error.

It should be mentioned that the particular change report form shown in the Appendix is the most current form but was not uniformly used over the entire period of this study. In actuality there were three different versions of the change report form; each form required slightly different information. Therefore, for the data that were not present on one form but that could be inferred, the inferred value was used. An example of such an inference is that of determining the *error type*. Since the error description was given on all of the forms, the error type could be inferred with a reasonable degree of reliability. Data not incorporated into a particular data set used for an analysis were data for which inference was deemed unreliable. Therefore, the reader should be alert to the cardinality of the data set

used as a basis for some of the relationships presented in this paper. A total of 231 change report forms were examined for the purpose of this paper.

The quality of the change and error data was checked in the following manner. First, the supervisor of the project looked over the change report forms and verified them (denoted by his or her signature and the date). Second, when the data were reduced for analysis, they were closely examined for contradictions. It should be noted that interviews with the individuals who filled out the change forms were not conducted. This was the major difference between this work and other error studies performed by the SEL, where interviews were held with the programmers to help clarify questionable data. [2]

The review of the change data yielded an interesting result. The errors due to previous correction attempts were shown to be three times as common after the form review process was performed, that is, before the review process they accounted for 2 percent of the errors and after the review process they accounted for 6 percent of the errors. These recording errors are probably attributed to the fact that the corrector of an error did not know the error was due to a previous fix because the fix occurred several months earlier or was made by a different programmer.

3. RELATIONSHIPS DERIVED FROM DATA

This section presents and discusses the relationships derived from the change data.

3.1 Change Distribution by Type

Changes to the software can be categorized as error

TABLE II. Number of Modules Affected by an Error (data set: 211 textual errors; 174 conceptual errors)

Number of Errors	Number of Modules Affected
155 (89%)	1
9	2
3	3
6	4
1	5

TABLE III. Number of Errors per Module (data set: 215 errors)

Number of Modules	New	Modified	Number of Errors per Module
36	17	19	1
26	13	13	2
16	10	6	3
13	7	6	4
4	1**	3*	5
1	1**		7

TABLE IV. Effort to Correct Errors in the Three Most Error-Prone Modified Modules

	Number of Errors (15 total)	Average Effort to Correct (hrs)
Misunderstood or incorrect specifications	8	24.0
Incorrect design or implementation of a module component	5	16.0
Clerical error	2	4.5

TABLE V. Effort to Correct Errors in the Two Most Error-Prone New Modules

	Number of Errors (12 total)	Average Effort to Correct (hrs)
Misunderstood or incorrect requirements	8	32
Incorrect design or implementation of a module component	3	0.5
Clerical error	1	0.5

corrections or modifications (specification changes, planned enhancements, and clarity and optimization improvements). For this project, error corrections accounted for 62 percent of the changes and modifications accounted for 38 percent. In studies of other SEL projects, error corrections accounted for 40–64 percent of the changes.

3.2 Error Distribution by Modules
Table II shows the number of modules that had to be changed because of an error. (Note that these errors are counted as conceptual errors.) It was found that 89 percent of the errors could be corrected by changing only one module. This is a good argument for the modularity of the software. It also shows that there is not a large amount of interdependence among the modules with respect to an error.

Table III shows the number of errors found per module. The type of module is shown in addition to the total number of modules found to contain errors.

The largest number of errors found were 7 (located in a single new module) and 5 (located in 3 different modified modules and 1 new module). The remainder of the errors were distributed almost equally between the two types of modules.

The effort associated with correcting an error is specified on the form as (1) 1 hour or less, (2) 1 hour to 1 day, (3) 1 day to 3 days, or (4) more than 3 days. These categories were chosen because it is too difficult to collect effort data to a finer granularity. To estimate the effort for any particular error correction, an average time was used for each category; that is, assuming an 8-hour day, an error correction in category (1) was assumed to take 0.5 hour, in category (2) 4.5 hours, in

category (3) 16 hours, and in category (4) 32 hours.

The types of errors found in the three most error-prone modified modules (* in Table III) and the effort needed to correct them is shown in Table IV. If any type contained error corrections from more than one error correction category, the associated effort for them was averaged. The fact that the majority of the errors detected in a module is between one and three shows that the total number of errors that occurred per module is, on the average, very small.

The twelve errors contained in the two most error-prone new modules (** in Table III) are shown in Table V along with the effort needed to correct them.

3.3 Error Distribution by Type
Figure 2 shows the distribution of errors by type. It can be seen that 48 percent of the errors was attributed to incorrect or misinterpreted functional specifications or requirements.

The error classification used throughout the Software Engineering Laboratory is given below. The person identifying the error indicates the class for each error.

A: Requirements incorrect or misinterpreted.
B: Functional specification incorrect or misinterpreted.
C: Design error involving several components.
   1. Mistaken assumption about value or structure of data.
   2. Mistake in control logic or computation of an expression.
D: Error in design or implementation of single component.
   1. Mistaken assumption about value or structure of data.
   2. Mistake in control logic or computation of an expression.
E: Misunderstanding of external environment.
F: Error in the use of programming language/compiler.
G: Clerical error.
H: Error due to previous miscorrection of an error.

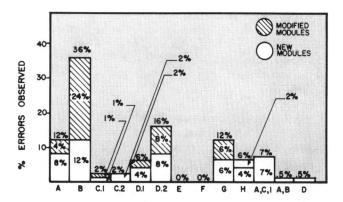

FIGURE 2. Sources of Errors

The distribution of these errors by source is plotted in Figure 2 with the appropriate subdistribution of new and modified errors displayed. This distribution shows that the majority of errors were the result of functional specification (incorrect or misinterpreted). Within this category, the majority of the errors (24 percent) involved modified modules. This is most likely due to the fact that the reused modules were taken from another system with a different application. Thus, even though the basic algorithms were the same, the specification was not well-enough defined or appropriately defined for the modules to be used under slightly different circumstances.

The distribution in Figure 2 should be compared to the distribution of another system developed by the same organization, shown in Figure 3(a) [3]. For a basis of comparison, the categories in Figure 2 are mapped into a classification scheme [Figure 3(b)] equivalent to

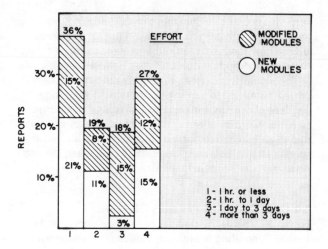

FIGURE 4. Effort Graph

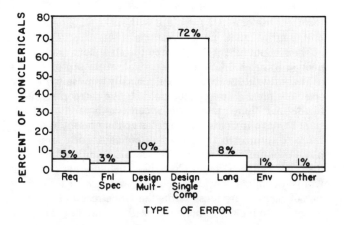

FIGURE 3(a). Sources of Errors on Other Nonclerical SEL Projects.

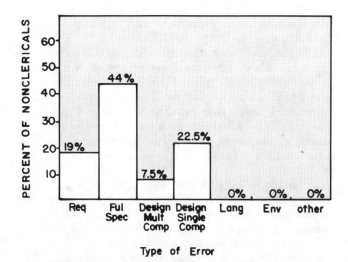

FIGURE 3(b). Sources of Nonclerical Errors on this Project

those for Figure 3(a) (eliminating the categories of G and H within Figure 2). Figure 3 represents a typical ground-support software system and was rather typical of the error distributions for these systems. It is different from the distribution for the system we are discussing in that the majority of the errors were involved in the design of a single component. The reason for the difference is that in ground-support systems, the design is well understood and the developers have had a reasonable amount of experience with the application. Any reused design or code comes from a similar system and the requirements tend to be more stable. An analysis of the two distributions makes the differences in the development environments clear in a quantitative way.

The percent of requirements and specification errors is consistent with Endres' work [7]. Endres found that 46 percent of the errors he viewed involved the misunderstanding of the functional specifications of a module. Our results are similar even though Endres' analysis was based on data derived from a different software project and programming environment. The software project used in Endres' analysis contained considerably more lines of code per module, was written in assembly code, and was within the problem area of operating systems. However, both of the software systems Endres analyzed did contain new and modified modules. In this study, of the errors due to the misunderstanding of a module's specifications or requirements (48 percent), 20 percent involved new modules while 28 percent involved modified modules.

Although the existence of modified modules can shrink the cost of coding, the amount of effort needed to correct errors in modified modules might outweigh the savings. The effort graph (Figure 4) supports this view: 50 percent of the total effort required for error correction occurred in modified modules; errors requiring one day to more than three days to correct accounted for 45 percent of the total effort with 27 per-

cent of this effort attributable to modified modules
within these greater effort classes. Thus, errors occurring in new modules required less effort to correct than
those in modified modules.

The similarity between Endres' results and those reported here tend to support the statement that, independent of the environment and possibly the module
size, the majority of errors detected within software are
due to an inadequate form or misinterpretation of the
specifications. This seems especially true when the software contains modified modules.

3.4 Overall Number of Errors Observed
Figure 5 displays the number of errors observed in both
new and modified modules. It can be seen that errors
occurring in modified modules are detected earlier and
at a slightly higher rate than those in new modules.
One hypothesis for this is that the majority of the errors
observed in modified modules are due to the misinterpretation of the functional specifications. Errors of this
type would certainly be more obvious since they are
more blatant than those of other types and, therefore,
would be detected both earlier and more readily. (See
next section.)

3.5 Abstract Error Types
The authors adopted an abstract classification of errors
that classified errors into one of five categories with
respect to a module: (1) initialization, (2) control structure, (3) interface, (4) data, and (5) computation. This
was done in order to see if there existed recurring
classes of errors in all modules, independent of size.
These error classes are only roughly defined. It should
be noted that even though the authors were consistent
with the categorization for this project, another error
analyst may have interpreted the categories differently.

Failure to initialize or reinitialize a data structure
properly upon a module's entry/exit is considered an
initialization error. Errors that cause an "incorrect path"
in a module to be taken are considered *control errors*.
Such a control error might be a conditional statement
causing control to be passed to an incorrect path. *Interface errors* are those that were associated with structures existing outside the module's local environment
but which the module used. For example, the incorrect
declaration of a COMMON segment or an incorrect
subroutine call is an interface error. An error in the
declaration of the COMMON segment is considered an
interface error and not an initialization error since the
COMMON segment has been used by the module but is
not part of its local environment. *Data errors* are those
errors that are a result of the incorrect use of a data
structure. Examples of data errors are the use of incorrect subscripts for an array, the use of the wrong variable in an equation, or the inclusion of an incorrect
declaration of a variable local to the module. *Computation errors* are those that cause a computation to erro-

neously evaluate a variable's value. These errors could
be equations that are incorrect not by virtue of the
incorrect use of a data structure within the statement
but by miscalculations. An example of this error might
be the statement $A = B + 1$ when the statement really
needed was $A = B/C + 1$.

These five abstract categories basically represent all
activities present in any module. The five categories are
further partitioned into errors of commission and omission. Errors of *commission* are those errors present as a
result of an incorrect executable statement. For example, a commissioned computational error would be $A =
B * C$ where the '$*$' should have been '$+$'. In other
words, the operator was present but was incorrect. Errors of *omission* are those errors that are a result of
forgetting to include some entity within a module. For
example, a computational omission error might be $A =
B$ when the statement should have read $A = B + C$. A
parameter required for a subroutine call but not included in the actual call is an example of an interface
omission error. In both of the above examples some
aspect needed for the correct execution of a module has
been forgotten.

The results of this abstract classification scheme are
given in Table VI. Since there were approximately an
equal amount of new (49) and modified (47) modules
viewed in the analysis, the results do not need to be
normalized. Some errors and thereby modules were
counted more than once, since it was not possible to
associate some errors with a single abstract error type
based on the error description given on the change report form.

According to Table VI, interfaces appear to be the
major problem, regardless of the module type. Control
is more of a problem in new modules than in modified
modules. This is probably because the algorithms in the
old modules had more test and debug time. On the
other hand, initialization and data are more of a problem in modified modules. These facts, coupled with the
small number of errors of omission in the modified

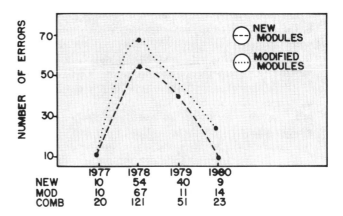

FIGURE 5. Number of Errors Occurring in Modules

TABLE VI. Abstract Classification of Errors

	Commission		Omission		Total	
	New	Modified	New	Modified	New	Modified
Initialization	2	9	5	9	7	18 – 25 (11%)
Control	12	2	16	6	28	8 – 36 (16%)
Interface	23	31	27	6	50	37 – 87 (39%)
Data	10	17	1	3	11	20 – 31 (14%)
Computation	16	21	3	3	19	24 – 43 (19%)
	28%	36%	23%	12%	115	107
	64%		35%			

modules, might imply that the basic algorithms for the modified modules were correct but needed some adjustment with respect to data values and initialization for the application of that algorithm to the new environment.

3.6 Module Size and Error Occurrence
Scatter plots for executable lines per module versus the number of errors found in the module were graphed. It was difficult to see any trend within these plots, so the number of errors/1000 executable lines within a module size was calculated (Table VII). The number of errors was normalized over 1000 executable lines of code in order to determine if the number of detected errors within a module was dependent on module size. All modules within the software were included, even those with no detected errors. If the number of errors/1000 executable lines was found to be constant over module size, this would show independence. An unexpected trend was observed: Table VII implies that there is a

higher error rate in smaller sized modules. Since only the executable lines of code were considered, the larger modules were not COMMON data files. Also the larger modules will be shown to be more complex than smaller modules in the next section. Then how could this type of result occur?

The most plausible explanation seems to be that the large number of interface errors spread equally across all modules is causing a larger number of errors per 1000 executable statements for smaller modules. Some tentative explanations for this behavior are that: the majority of the modules examined were small (Table I), causing a biased result; larger modules were coded with more care than smaller modules because of their size; and errors in smaller modules were more apparent. There may still be numerous undetected errors present within the larger modules since all the "paths" within the larger modules may not have been fully exercised.

3.7 Module Complexity
Cyclomatic complexity [8] (number of decisions + 1) was correlated with module size. This was done in order to determine whether or not larger modules were less dense or complex than smaller modules containing errors. Scatter plots for executable statements per module versus the cyclomatic complexity were graphed. Since it was difficult to see any trend in the plots, modules were grouped according to size. The complexity points were obtained by calculating an average complexity measure for each module size class. For example, all the modules that had 50 executable lines of code or less had an average complexity of 6.0. Table VIII gives the average cyclomatic complexity for all modules in each of the size categories. The complexity relationships for executable lines of code in a module are shown in Figure 6. As can be seen from Table VIII, the larger modules were more complex than smaller modules.

Table IX gives the number of errors/1000 executable statements and the average cyclomatic complexity only for those modules containing errors. When these data are compared with Table VIII, one can see that the

TABLE VII. Errors/1000 Executable Lines (Includes all modules)

Module Size	Errors/1000 Lines
50	16.0
100	12.6
150	12.4
200	7.6
>200	6.4

TABLE VIII. Average Cyclomatic Complexity for all Modules

Module Size	Average Cyclomatic Complexity
50	6.0
100	17.9
150	28.1
200	52.7
>200	60.0

average complexity of the error-prone modules was no greater than the average complexity of the full set of modules.

4. DATA NOT EXPLICITLY INCLUDED IN ANALYSES

The 147 modules not included in this study (i.e., assembly segments, common segments, utility routines) contained six errors. These six errors were detected within three different segments. One error occurred in a modified assembly module because of a misunderstanding or incorrect statement of the functional specifications for the module. The effort needed to correct this error was minimal (1 hour or less).

The other five errors occurred in two separate new data segments with the major cause of the errors also being related to their specifications. The effort needed to correct these errors was on the average from 1 hour to 1 day (1 day representing 8 hours).

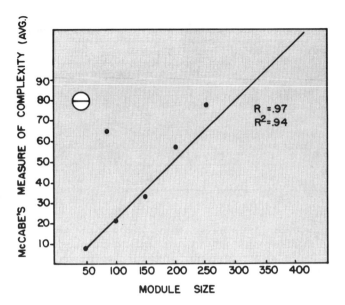

FIGURE 6. Complexity versus Module Size

5. CONCLUSIONS

The data contained in this paper help explain and characterize the software developed. It is clear from the data that this was a new application for the developers, with changing requirements.

Modified and new modules were shown to behave similarly except for the types of errors prevalent in each and the amount of effort required to correct an error. Both had a high percentage of interface errors. However, new modules had an equal number of errors of omission and commission and a higher percentage of control errors. Modified modules had a high percentage of errors of commission and a small percentage of errors of omission with a higher percentage of data and initialization errors. Another difference was that modified modules appeared to be more susceptible to errors due to the misunderstanding of the specifications. Misunderstanding of a module's specifications or requirements constituted the majority of detected errors. This duplicates Endres' earlier result, which implies that more work needs to be done on the form and content of the specifications and requirements in order for them to be used more effectively across applications.

There are some disadvantages to modifying an exist-

ing module for use instead of creating a new module. Modifying an existing module to meet a similar but different set of specifications reduces the development costs of that module. However, the disadvantage is that there are hidden costs. Errors contained in modified modules were found to require more effort to correct than those in new modules, although the two classes contained approximately the same number of errors. The majority of these errors were because of incorrect or misinterpreted specifications for a module. Therefore, there is a trade-off between minimizing development time and time spent to align a module to new specifications. However, if better specifications could be developed, it might reduce the more expensive errors contained within modified modules. In this case, the use of "old" modules could be more beneficial in terms of cost and effort since the hidden costs would have been reduced.

One surprising result was that module size did not account for error proneness. In fact, it was quite the contrary—the larger the module, the less error prone it was. This was true even though the larger modules were more complex. Additionally, the error-prone modules were no more complex across size grouping than the error-free modules. This result implies we are not yet ready to put artificial limits on module size and complexity.

In general, error analysis provides useful information. For this project, it shows that the developers were involved in a new application with changing requirements. It provides insight into the different ways of handling new and modified modules. It shows areas of potential problems with a new application. It ultimately allows us to identify the various factors that influence software development.

TABLE IX.   Complexity and Error Rate for Errored Modules

Module Size	Average Cyclomatic Complexity	Errors/1000 Executable Lines
50	6.2	65.0
100	19.6	33.3
150	27.5	24.6
200	56.7	13.4
>200	77.5	9.7

APPENDIX—Change Report Form

PROJECT NAME _____ CURRENT DATE_____

SECTION A - IDENTIFICATION

REASON: Why was the change made?_____
_____

DESCRIPTION: What change was made?_____
_____

EFFECT: What components (or documents) are changed? (Include version)_____ –
_____

EFFORT: What additional components (or documents) were examined in determining what change was needed?_____
_____

	(Month	Day	Year)
Need for change determined on			
Change started on			

What was the effort in person time required to understand and implement the change?

_____1 hour or less,   _____1 hour to 1 day,   _____1 day to 3 days,   _____more than 3 days

SECTION B - TYPE OF CHANGE (How is this change best characterized?)

☐ Error correction

☐ Planned enhancement

☐ Implementation of requirements change

☐ Improvement of clarity, maintainability, or documentation

☐ Improvement of user services

☐ Insertion/deletion of debug code

☐ Optimization of time/space/accuracy

☐ Adaptation to environment change

☐ Other (Explain in E)

Was more than one component affected by the change?   Yes_____ No_____

FOR ERROR CORRECTIONS ONLY

SECTION C - TYPE OF ERROR (How is this error best characterized?)

☐ Requirements incorrect or misinterpreted

☐ Functional specifications incorrect or misinterpreted

☐ Design error, involving several components

☐ Error in the design or implementation of a single component

☐ Misunderstanding of external environment, except language

☐ Error in use of programming language/compiler

☐ Clerical error

☐ Other (Explain in E)

FOR DESIGN OR IMPLEMENTATION ERRORS ONLY

If the error was in design or implementation:

The error was a mistaken assumption about the value or structure of data _____

The error was a mistake in control logic or computation of an expression_____

580-2 (6/78)

APPENDIX—Change Report Form

FOR ERROR CORRECTIONS ONLY

SECTION D – VALIDATION AND REPAIR

What activities were used to validate the program, detect the error, and find its cause?

	Activities Used for Program Validation	Activities Successful in Detecting Error Symptoms	Activities Tried to Find Cause	Activities Successful in Finding Cause
Pre-acceptance test runs				
Acceptance testing				
Post-acceptance use				
Inspection of output				
Code reading by programmer				
Code reading by other person				
Talks with other programmers				
Special debug code				
System error messages				
Project specific error messages				
Reading documentation				
Trace				
Dump				
Cross-reference/attribute list				
Proof technique				
Other (Explain in E)				

What was the time used to isolate the cause?

_____one hour or less, _____ one hour to one day, _____more than one day, _____never found

If never found, was a workaround used?_____ Yes _____ No (Explain in E)

Was this error related to a previous change?

_____Yes (Change Report #/Date_____) _____No _____Can't tell

When did the error enter the system?

_____requirements _____functional specs _____design _____coding and test _____other _____can't tell

SECTION E – ADDITIONAL INFORMATION

Please give any information that may be helpful in categorizing the error or change, and understanding its cause and its ramifications.

Name:_____ Authorized:_____ Date:_____

580-2 (6/78)

The results of this study are by no means conclusive. They pose more questions than they answer; they suggest that software development must be better understood. More data must be collected on different projects.

Acknowledgments. The authors would like to thank F. McGarry, NASA Goddard Space Flight Center, for his cooperation in supplying the information needed for this study and his helpful suggestions on earlier drafts of this paper.

REFERENCES
1. Basili, V., and Freburger, K. Programming measurement and estimation in the Software Engineering Laboratory. *The Journal of Systems and Software* 2, 1 (Mar. 1981), 47–57.
2. Basili, V., and Weiss, D. A methodology for collecting valid software engineering data. University of Maryland Tech. Rep. TR-1235, Dec. 1982.
3. Basili, V., and Weiss, D. Evaluating software development by analysis of changes: The data from the Software Engineering Laboratory. University of Maryland Tech. Rep. TR-1236, Dec. 1982.
4. Belady, L. A., and Lehman, M. M. A model of large program development. *IBM Systems Journal* 15, 3 (1976), 225–251.
5. Endres, A. An analysis of errors and their causes in system programs. In *Proceedings of the International Conference on Software Engineering.* (April 1975), pp. 327–336.
6. McCabe, T. J. A complexity measure. *IEEE Transactions on Software Engineering SE-2*, 4 (Dec. 1976), 308–320.
7. Mendenhall, W., and Ramey, M. *Statistics for Psychology.* Duxbury Press, North Scituate, Mass., 1973, pp. 280–315.
8. Schneidewind, N. F. An experiment in software error data collection and analysis. *IEEE Transactions on Software Engineering SE-5*, 3 (May 1979), 276–286.
9. Weiss, D. M. Evaluating software development by error analysis: The data from the architecture research facility. *The Journal of Systems and Software 1*, 1 (Mar. 1979), 57–70.

CR Categories and Subject Descriptors: D.2.8 [**Software Engineering**]: Metrics
General Terms: Experimentation, Measurement, Reliability
Additional Key Words and Phrases: error analysis, complexity metrics

Received 10/82; revised 6/83; accepted 7/83

The research for this study was supported in part by the National Aeronautics and Space Administration grant NSG-5123 to the University of Maryland.

Authors' Present Address:
V. R. Basili and B. T. Perricone, Dept. of Computer Science, University of Maryland, College Park, Maryland 20742

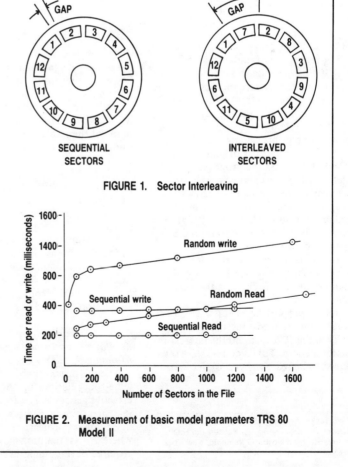

Corrigendum. In the Computing Practices article "Estimating File Access Time of Floppy Disks" by M. A. Pechura and J. D. Schoeffler [October 1983, pp. 754–763], Figures 1 and 2 appeared without their respective legends. The corrected figures appear below.

FIGURE 1. Sector Interleaving

FIGURE 2. Measurement of basic model parameters TRS 80 Model II

QUALITYTIME

Reprinted from *IEEE Software*, Volume 4, Number 9, September 1987, pages 84. Copyright ©1987 by The Institute of Electrical and Electronics Engineers, Inc. All rights reserved.

Editor: Vincent Shen
MCC
3500 W. Balcones Center Dr.
Austin, TX 78759
Compmail+: v.shen
CSnet. shen@mcc.com

A little quality time

Vincent Shen,
QualityTime Editor

The goals for all software-engineering research are improvements in productivity and quality.* Proposals for new tools, methods, and environments all include claims along these lines. But what is productivity? What is quality? What are the factors that influence them, and to what degree? Our field is apparently not yet mature enough to provide answers to these important questions. Software engineering does not yet have the precise and reliable measurements that other traditional engineering disciplines take for granted.

IEEE Software has introduced this department to discuss current productivity and quality issues. The purpose is to promote a dialogue between researchers and practitioners. The software-engineering community must be aware of the needs for productivity and quality measurements and the dangers of not knowing the inherent risks.

For readers not familiar with this area, let me provide some historical background. Software metrics were not of much interest in the 1960s when software cost was only a small part of the total cost of computer systems. The size of a computer program was determined simply by the number of punched cards it took to contain the program. This metric (which was almost a weight measure for people who had to carry the programs) is basically equivalent to today's lines-of-code metric. Programmer productivity can be measured by the number of lines written (or debugged) during a month's time. Program quality can be measured by the number of bugs found in a thousand lines of code.

As the proportion of software cost to total computing cost increased drastically in the 1970s, so did the interest in better metrics. Token counts were introduced to increase the precision of size

measures for programs written in the period's higher-level languages that permitted free-format coding.

Programming models were introduced that contained various assumptions about *complexity* — the time to produce, to understand, or to debug computer programs is a mathematical function of the counts of various tokens. Unfortunately, a series of empirical studies conducted in the late 1970s failed to offer concrete evidence that any of these complexity measures was significantly better than the classic lines-of-code measure.

Metrics researchers in the 1980s are generally less optimistic than their colleagues in the 1970s. Even though the pressure to find better metrics is greater because of the greater cost of software, fewer people today are trying to formulate combinations of complex-

ity metrics so that they relate to some definition of productivity and quality.

Instead, they set very narrow goals and show whether these goals are reached using focused metrics. For example, producing higher quality software is a general goal. One corresponding narrow goal would be to test the software thoroughly. An appropriate metric might be some measure of test coverage. The measurement results can be an effective guide for the testing process.

Although metrics research is not a panacea for weaknesses in software development, its evolution has produced many benefits for the industry. The accompanying report gives examples of such benefits. The specific numbers came from the experiences of many practitioners, but they may vary in your organization.

---

*See, for example, *Encyclopedia of Computer Science and Engineering*, A. Ralston and E.D. Reilly, eds. (Van Nostrand Reinhold, New York, 1983).

Industrial software metrics top 10 list

Barry Boehm, TRW, Inc.

I am always fascinated by top 10 lists. So, when Vincent Shen asked me to write a piece for this department, I decided to present my candidate top 10 list of software metric relationships, in terms of their value in industrial situations. Here they are, in rough priority order:

1. *Finding and fixing a software problem after delivery is 100 times more expensive than finding and fixing it during the requirements and early design phases.*

This insight has been a major driver in focusing industrial software practice on thorough requirements analysis and design, on early verification and validation, and on up-front prototyping and simulation to avoid costly downstream fixes.

2. *You can compress a software development schedule up to 25 percent of nominal, but no more.*

There is a remarkably consistent cube-root relationship for the most effective schedule T_{dev} for a single-increment, industrial-grade software development project: $T_{dev} = 2.5 \times MM^{1/3}$ where T_{dev} is in months and MM is the required development in man-months.

Equally remarkable is the fact that virtually no industrial-grade projects have been able to compress this schedule more than 25 percent. Thus, if your project is estimated to require $512MM$, your best schedule is $2.5 \times 512^{1/3}$, or 20, months. If your boss or customer wants the product in 15 months, you will barely make it if you add some extra resources and plan well. If he wants it in 12 months, you should gracefully but firmly suggest reducing the scope or doing an incremental development.

3. *For every dollar you spend on software development you will spend two dollars on software maintenance.*

A lot of industry and government organizations created major maintenance embarrassments before they realized this and instituted thorough software life-cycle planning. This insight has also stimulated a healthy emphasis on developing high-quality software products to reduce maintenance costs.

4. *Software development and maintenance costs are primarily a function of the number of source instructions in the product.*

This was the major stimulus for

migrating from assembly languages to higher order languages. It is now a major stimulus for developing and using very high-level languages and fourth-generation languages to reduce software costs.

5. *Variations between people account for the biggest differences in software productivity.*

Studies of large projects have shown that 90th-percentile teams of software people typically outproduce 15th-percentile teams by factors of four to five. Studies of individual programmers have shown productivity ranges of up to 26:1. The moral: Do everything you can to get the best people working on *your* project.

6. *The overall ratio of computer software to hardware costs has gone from 15:85 in 1955 to 85:15 in 1985, and it is still growing.*

This relationship has done more than anything else to focus management attention and resources on improving the software process.

7. *Only about 15 percent of software product-development effort is devoted to programming.*

In the early days, there was a 40-20-40 rule: 40 percent of the development effort for analysis and design, 20 percent for programming, and 40 percent for integration and test. Now, the best project practices achieve a 60-15-25 distribution. Overall, this relationship has been very effective in getting industrial practice to treat software product development as more than just programming.

8. *Software systems and software products each typically cost three times as much per instruction to fully develop as does an individual software program. Software-system products cost nine times as much.*

A software system contains many software modules written by different people. A software-system product is such a system that is released for external use. The discovery of this cost-tripling relationship has saved many people from unrealistically extrapolating their personal programming productivity experience into unachievable budgets and schedules for software-system products.

9. *Walkthroughs catch 60 percent of the errors.*

The structured walkthrough (software inspection) has been the most cost-effective technique to date for eliminating software errors. It also has significant side benefits in team building and in ensuring backup knowledge if a designer or programmer leaves the project.

I had a hard time picking number 10. I ended up with a composite choice:

10. *Many software phenomena follow a Pareto distribution: 80 percent of the contribution comes from 20 percent of the contributors.*

Knowing this can help a project focus on the 20 percent of the subset that provides 80 percent of the leverage for improvement. Some examples:
- 20 percent of the modules contribute 80 percent of the cost,
- 20 percent of the modules contribute 80 percent of the errors (not necessarily the same ones),
- 20 percent of the errors consume 80 percent of the cost to fix,
- 20 percent of the modules consume 80 percent of the execution time, and
- 20 percent of the tools experience 80 percent of the tool usage.

I think it has been a strong credit to the software metrics field that it has been able to determine and corroborate these and many other useful software metric relationships. And there are many useful new ones coming along. I look forward to reading about them in this department.

The Use of Software Risk Assessment
In Testing and Maintenance

Susan A. Sherer

College of Business and Economics
Lehigh University
Bethlehem, PA 18015

Eric K. Clemons

Department of Decision Sciences
Wharton School
University of Pennsylvania
Philadelphia, PA 19104

ABSTRACT

This paper demonstrates how to measure and use software risk assessment to test and maintain software systems. The expected loss from failure because of faults in individual software modules is measured, then this assessment of module risk is used to make critical decisions about the allocation of resources throughout the software life cycle.

INTRODUCTION

Software testing and maintenance consumes a substantial proportion of the software life cycle. It has been estimated that testing accounts for as much as one-half of the development effort (Yourdon and Constantine 79, Zelkowitz 78). Thereafter, programmers spend 50 percent, and in some case 80 percent, of their time in ongoing maintenance (Parikh 82). The trend toward increasing computerization is expected to exacerbate the need for improved productivity in testing and maintenance as new code is added to inventory faster than the old code is discarded (Boehm 81). Jones has proposed that the pattern of development within a large multinational corporation will require and increase in programming staff of fifteen percent per year just to meet the growing need for maintenance (Jones 86). Continued development of computer applications at an ever increasing rate will require better utilization of programming resources, particularly in the time consuming and costly tasks of testing and maintenance.

Systems are tested to uncover faults (i.e., defects) in their components (i.e., the individual modules composing the system). Since faults in different modules may cause failures with different consequences, the criticality or significance of faults in each software module varies. This fact can be used to guide software development, testing, and maintenance. Effective utilization of programming resources can be attained by allocating these resources proportionally, based on the potential impact of failure.

Neither traditional reliability measurement techniques nor traditional development and testing methodologies consider the fact that the implications of software failures differ (Sherer and Clemons 87). Software reliability measurement techniques have been adapted from hardware reliability, where a failure typically has a single consequence. Software reliability has been defined in terms of either the number of residual errors in a program or as the mean time between failures. These definitions assume that the consequences of all errors or failures are the same. However, since different software failures have different expected consequences, these reliability measurement techniques are inappropriate for measuring the true economic risk associated with failure.

Traditional development, testing, and maintenance methods do not consider expected consequences of errors. Tradeoffs concerning allocations of test resources are made through consideration of code complexity (white-box testing) or functional use (black-box testing). These methods are of limited use in allocating available resources to the portions of the system with the greatest risk (Sherer 88b, Sherer and Clemons 87). An assessment of the risk of software failure in various portions of a system could serve as a theoretical basis to guide software development efforts.

We present an overview of a methodology for assessing software risk. Software risk is defined as the expected loss because of failure during a given time period. It is measured by the frequency or likelihood of loss (events resulting in loss per unit time) times the magnitude of loss or the level of exposure caused by loss (consequences of events).[1] Measurement of risk begins with an assessment of external exposure (i.e., the magnitude of loss caused by invalid actions). The external exposure is mapped onto the system to determine the magnitude of loss caused by failures caused by faults in individual modules. Assessment of the likelihood of failure for each module is based upon characteristics of the code and its use, as well as upon results obtained through test efforts.

We describe how risk assessment can be used to guide software development. In particular, its application to the allocation of software test and maintenance resources will be discussed. We illustrate our approach with an application of the risk assessment methodology to a system used by a commercial bank.

Methodology for the Assessment of Software Risk

To develop a measure of software risk that may be used to guide testing and maintenance, we need to perform several functions:

1. External exposure identification: What actions by the user can result in losses and what are the consequences of these actions?

2. Structural exposure analysis: What system failures can cause these actions? What is the potential magnitude of loss caused by failures caused by faults in each module?

3. Software failure likelihood estimation: What is the a priori estimate of the likelihood of failure caused by faults in each untested module? What is the resulting estimate of risk? How do we use test results to update failure assessments?

Here, we present an overview of methodology that can be used for each of these functions. Details of the analysis can be found in (Sherer 88b).

External Exposure Identification

External exposure identification is the first step in the measurement of software risk. We begin with an analysis of the environment in which the software will operate. The objectives of external exposure assessment are:

1. to determine what actions in the environment external to the software can contribute to loss

2. to assess the significance of the loss.

To accomplish these objectives, we use a procedure involving the following steps:

1. definition of environmental hazards

2. identification of accident sequences

3. failure modes analysis

4. consequence analysis

---

[1] This is analogous to the work of Henley and Kumamoto (81).

Definition of Hazards

We begin by investigating the environment(s) in which the software is to operate. A thorough understanding of the environmental context is necessary to identify the major consequences resulting in loss. It is also essential to the satisfactory design of a software system. This understanding is obtained through discussions with users rather than with software developers. Software developers tend to emphasize what the software is supposed to do. We want the external picture: how the software will be used, what can go wrong, and what can happen when it does. We consider financial hazards as well as the potential for physical hazards such as fire, explosion, airplane crash, military loss, or incorrect patient treatment.

When defining hazards, we consider how the organization plans to use the system and the actions and decisions that will be made while using the system outputs. We also consider how this usage might change, a critical factor since many failures can be attributed to environmental changes or to new uses of the system.

Identification of Accident Sequences

After identifying the environmental hazards, the investigation proceeds to consider how these hazards can occur. Consideration is given to all events that can precipitate these hazards as well as actions that can alter the course of an accident. Event trees are graphical aids that lay out the sequence of events linked by conditional probabilities. They are useful in displaying the accident scenarios.

Basic questions in the identification of events that can lead to hazards are:

1. What operator actions can cause disaster by violating norms of behavior?
2. What hardware failures can result in loss?
3. What environmental circumstances can cause situations that may lead to these hazards?
4. What functions can alter the effect of these occurrences?

If this procedure is used before the system is developed, it may help determine what the design criteria of the software system should be. We can also use this technique to discover errors of omission in an existing design.

Failure Modes Analysis

The analysis proceeds with an identification of the failure modes of the external events identified in the accident sequences. These include the relationships among environmental conditions, human actions, hardware states, and erroneous information and control procedures that can contribute to these external events. Our ultimate objective is to determine where software failure can affect the accident scenario.

Failure modes of the external top events are revealed by working backwards, considering relationships among all conditions leading to each event. Fault trees are useful to provide graphical aids, directing the analysis and pointing out important aspects of the failure of interest (Henley and Kumamoto 81). The process of developing fault trees forces us to consider the events and relationships involved. It allows us to obtain a logical identity between the top event and a set of basic events (Pate-Cornell 84).

Consequence Analysis

To assess the consequence of the hazards, the environmental conditions that affect the loss associated with each consequence are identified. Because there is virtually an unlimited number of such factors, the information is consolidated by utilizing expected values for each condition. The potential exposure is computed by weighting the loss estimated for each accident scenario by the likelihood of the accident scenario conditional upon software failure.

If the software will be located in different, readily distinguishable environments, it may be appropriate to consider a separate analysis for each. In addition, it may be useful in some cases to categorize certain environmental conditions into several groups, especially when the value of a variable varies widely depending upon the value of a preceding event. The degree of classification is a function of our ability to estimate losses. In either case, the decision is application dependent.

Structural Exposure Analysis

Structural exposure analysis is performed to discover how and where software faults could contribute to loss identified in external exposure assessment. The objective is to assign an exposure level caused by faults in individual modules, based upon the module's capacity to cause failures considered in the external exposure assessment.

To accomplish our objective, we must:

1. identify software failure modes
2. determine module fault potential
3. analyze module use
4. compute module exposure

Software Failure Modes

External exposure assessment indicates where erroneous information can contribute to loss. Next, it is necessary to investigate how the software may fail, resulting in this erroneous information. We determine a set of software failure modes that can be assigned to each accident scenario by considering what software functions could produce the erroneous information.

Module Fault Potential

The structure of the software system is now analyzed to determine the location of potential faults related to each software failure mode. We propose "gray-box" analysis of the system, defined as analysis of the structure of the software system: the modules and how they are used. Consideration is given to the relationship between the module's function and the system's potential for loss.

The size and interrelationships of most software systems make it infeasible to consider analysis of all software branches and conditions (white-box analysis). On the other hand, functional analysis of the software system (black-box analysis) does not give us sufficient information about the potential location of faults. However, if we concentrate on the code at the module level, we feel it is feasible to consider module function and relate it to potential loss.

For each module, we wish to determine whether it performs any functions related to a software failure mode. Software system failure is manifested by invalid system output or lack of anticipated output. Any modules involved in producing the output could be the source of the failure, so we begin by identifying modules involved in the production of the output related to each failure mode.

How can we identify modules related to a particular failure mode? The process is similar to that used when debugging software to uncover the potential location of the fault leading to a failure. Critical data are identified and the specifications are used to identify program modules that use or update these data. We use reverse engineering, working backward to determine what input gives us these data, then we work forward to identify all programs involved in transforming these data. We identify significant reports, again using reverse engineering to determine all programs involved with the production of these reports. Key input transactions identified are traced forward to find out how and where this information is updated. We then look at each module individually to see if it might be related to the processing of any data related to the critical data identified.

Distribution of Use

We have determined which modules are involved in the processing of data related to each software failure mode. However, invalid processing may not always result in loss, it depends upon the way in which the module is being used. Thus, we need to relate module use to the external risk assessment. We partition the system input space functionally, estimating the probability that the system will be used in different ways. The external risk assessment is mapped onto the system input space by considering what function the system is performing when each failure mode could occur. We then estimate the probability distribution by describing how we expect to use modules by partitioning the software system into sets of modules invoked for each system use.

Module Exposure

The exposure of a module is estimated by summing its expected loss for all accident scenarios to which it may be related. The module is related to a scenario if it is involved in the processing of any invalid data produced by the system in the course of the accident. Its expected loss is equal to the consequence of the accident scenario weighted by the probability that the module is used in such a way that it may possibly result in this loss.

Software Failure Likelihood

Software failure likelihood is predicted first from characteristics of the code and of the development process. As testing proceeds, information about the testing process is used to update our initial estimate of failure likelihood. A Bayesian estimation approach is used to update prior predictions with test results.

Prior Prediction of Failure Likelihood and Risk

The likelihood of software failure depends upon:

1. the number of faults or errors in a program and
2. the probability that a fault or program defect will be encountered in operation and cause a failure.

Most research has concentrated on studying the relationship between characteristics of the code, such as size and complexity, and the number of faults found (Musa et al. 87, Feuer and Fowlkes 79, Gremillion 84, Shen et al. 85, Basili and Perricone 84, Card et al. 86, Basili and Phillips 82). In addition, it is expected that characteristics of the development process also affect the number of faults (Basili and Hutchens 83, Takahashi and Kamayacki 85, Youngs 81). However, it has been difficult to develop and relate objective measures of these characteristics to the error frequency. Most researchers have used the size of the program as the key factor in predicting the number of faults in a program because research relating the number of faults to program complexity has been inconclusive. We use historical information on similar size modules developed by the same organization to estimate the parameters of prior probability distributions describing the mean number of faults in a module. We do feel that better methods of predicting errors based upon characteristics of the development process would improve the operational performance of our methodology. In particular, information on historical performance of individual programmers, if collected and recorded properly, might improve the ability to predict errors.

The probability that a fault produces a failure depends upon the number of ways in which the module can be used and the frequency of each use. We assume that each fault in a module is independent and has the same likelihood of causing a failure (per fault hazard rate). It would be extremely difficult to attempt to determine what portions of a module have the greatest potential for producing failures and, in all likelihood, this would yield only marginally superior results. Researchers have reasoned from similar, known programs to estimate a fault exposure ratio, or fraction of time that a fault will result in failure when the program is executed (Musa et al. 87). We use similar modules to estimate the parameters of a prior distribution of the probability that a fault will cause a failure when that module is used.

In operation, certain modules are used more often than others, resulting in unequal hazard rates for faults in different modules. If the fault in a module is located on a main branch of the code or in a portion of code well traversed, it should have a higher probability of causing a failure than if it is located in a section of code rarely traversed. We use our analysis of the operational use of a module, describing how often we expect to use the module, to estimate the module's failure probability.

The risk for each module is equal to the probability of each type of failure times the cost of that failure. Because we do not know the probability of each type of failure, we estimate risk for each module as the product of the expected exposure level times the aggregate failure likelihood for that module. The expected exposure level depends upon the expected use of the system during operation. Failure likelihood depends upon the number of faults and the probability that faults will produce failures.

Differences between test and operational environments mean that the testing process will generally give us little information to update our assessments of exposure. However, examination of failure and debugging information will yield new knowledge about the number of faults in a module and the probability that a fault will produce a failure when that module is used.

We update our prior distributions with a likelihood function derived from a software reliability model. In particular, we use a finite failures software reliability model of Poisson type and exponential class[2] (Musa et al. 87). Bayesian analysis is used to develop a posterior joint distribution of our two parameters, the number of faults in a module and the probability that a fault will produce a failure when that module is used. Estimators of these parameters are derived from the posterior marginal distributions. These estimators are then used to update the probability of failure developed for this software reliability model.

Software Development and Maintenance Using Software Risk Assessment

Our methodology for estimation of software risk provides a theoretical basis for project management decisions during all phases of the software development process. External exposure identification should be accomplished prior to systems design. It has been reported that over 60 percent of errors discovered during software development testing arise during the requirements or design phases (Lipow 79). "Omissions are particularly pernicious and difficult to discover" (Adrion et al. 82) and have been reported to be the most persistent and expensive types of errors (Glass 81). By focusing on actions in the environment that can cause loss, the external exposure analysis may reveal design requirements that may not have initially been considered. This should reduce errors of omission in the requirements phase.

The structural exposure analysis is a very useful project management tool in the design and programming stages of development. Because prior theory has suggested that program size affects error density, it is suggested that alternative designs be considered when high exposure modules are expected to be very large. As more information becomes available concerning other factors affecting error density, managers may consider design changes to reduce the number of errors in modules with high exposure. Decisions concerning the selection of programmers and programming tools may be based in part on the exposure of a module.

Software risk assessment is especially useful as a project management tool during all phases of the critical testing process. During each test phase, management must decide how to allocate limited resources such as personnel and test time. In the module test phase, the test manager is faced with decisions such as what modules to test, what test data are necessary, and how to allocate personnel. Software risk assessment can aid in these decisions. By identifying the risk of failure in each module, management can allocate test personnel time most effectively to modules that not only have the greatest likelihood of failure, but that have the potential to cause failures with the greatest consequence.[3] During integration, the test manager must decide how to combine and test modules. In some cases, this is based upon the availability of test tools. Software risk assessment may help identify which combinations of modules have the greatest risk, thus aiding in the integration decision.

During function and systems testing, management typically decides how to allocate test efforts to various equivalence test classes (sets of similar input states) that are developed from the external specifications (function testing) and from the user requirements (systems testing). During these tests, inputs are often chosen at random from the operational distribution, the probability distribution of inputs in operation. Software risk assessment can be used to estimate the risk associated with a particular equivalence class from the expected risk of failure in the modules invoked when input from that class is tested. Equivalence classes with greater potential risk can then be tested more thoroughly than those with less risk.

---

[2] This model assumes that a finite number of failures will be experienced in infinite time. The type (Poisson) is the form of the distribution of the number of failures in time and the class (exponential) is the functional form of the failure intensity.

[3] This has been done previously but without adequate treatment of economic significance (Kubat and Koch 83).

As testing proceeds, management must finally decide when to release the software. Because the risk assessment measures expected loss caused by failure, a cost-benefit analysis can be developed comparing this expected loss with the cost to continue testing and the benefits of releasing the software.[4] The impact of fault correction and tolerance techniques that may be used in one module to either correct for errors in another module or to minimize the significance of errors in another module needs to be considered when deciding to release a software system.

As the software is used, the module risk assessments can be updated with failure information to aid in decisions concerning the time and location of software maintenance. Continued failure of a high exposure module will indicate need for software maintenance. Fix-and-improve reviews[5] have been suggested, particularly for modules that have large maintenance costs (Freedman and Weinberg 82). Software risk assessment can be used to identify modules that not only have high maintenance costs, but that have a high cost of failure as well. These modules would then profit most from preventive maintenance. As the number and scope of software systems grow, maintenance resources will need to be better utilized. Managers will need methods of allocating limited resources. The relative risk of failure of each module could be used to accomplish this task.[6]

An Application of Software Risk Assessment

We have applied the methodology outlined here to a software system used by a commercial lender. We describe the system, some results of the application of the risk assessment methodology, and our suggested use of the risk assessment to guide the testing and maintenance of this system.

We analyzed software that creates and maintains all information describing commercial loans offered by a savings and loan association. The software, written in Cobol, consists of more than 200 online, batch, and report program modules, ranging in size from 14 to more than 11,000 executable lines of code.

External exposure identification yielded a set of twelve major hazards including such occurrences as failure to produce customer invoices, invalid interest accruals on loans, and invalid access to financial information. Consequences of each hazard were estimated by using expected environmental conditions. Even and fault trees, constructed for each of the hazards, were used to identify software failure modes. The methodology we outlined for structural exposure analysis was used to compute the exposure of each module in the system. Exposure assessments for several of the modules are shown in Table 1. For example, faults in the payoff inquiry module typically affect customer service. The expected consequence of customer dissatisfaction, one of the hazards identified, was estimated to be $3,000.[7] The payoff inquiry module is used only when the system is used to inquire about the status of customer payments. The estimated probability of this system use is .0069, based upon an estimate of the number of monthly transactions of this type. Thus, the exposure assessment is $20.7/month.

To estimate software failure likelihood prior to test, logs of problem reports for programs by the developers of this commercial loan system were analyzed. Failure data from these modules were used to develop the prior probability distributions of the mean number of faults in modules of various sizes and the probability that a fault in an online or batch module would cause a failure when that module was used.

---

[4] Again, this has been attempted previously, but without treatment of the economic significance of various failures (Koch and Kubat 83).

[5] These are maintenance reviews that attempt to leave the code better than it was originally, not only fixing the code but "cultivating" it as well (Freedman and Weinberg 82).

[6] This has also been attempted previously without adequate treatment of the economic significance of failure (Adams 84).

[7] The consequence of customer dissatisfaction was estimated at approximately .01 percent of the anticipated average monthly billings of the bank. This is an estimate of potential lost business because of dissatisfaction with handling of current loan accounts.

Table 1:
Risk Assessments of Several Modules in a Commercial Loan System

Module Description	Exposure ($/mo) Prior to Test and Use	No. Failures After 8 Months of Operation		No. Failures	
		Expected Risk	Estimated Risk	Expected	Estimated
Online Interface	1800	0.015	27	0.012	22
Borrower Number Assignment	8	0.000	0	0.000	0
Payoff Inquiry	21	0.000	0	0.001	0
Turndown Reference Inquiry	7	0.000	0	0.000	0
Financial Posting	1879	0.616	1157	0.747	1404
Billing Print	2573	0.021	54	0.158	406
Report Extract	1804	0.433	781	0.236	406
Cash Flow Extract	50	0.208	10	0.337	17
Validation and Update	1804	0.004	7	0.075	135
Create Billing Extract	2573	0.921	2370	0.485	1248

Problem reports generated at the bank were then used to indicate failures and location of fixes during the execution of the system. Operational logs were analyzed to evaluate the bank's execution time of a module at the time of failure.

It is interesting to note that only three of the modules, representing two percent of all modules analyzed, demonstrated substantial risk prior to test and use at the bank. Approximately 89 percent of the modules had negligible estimated risk (less than one dollar per month) and 98 percent of the modules had an estimated risk less than $100 per month (Sherer 88a). This demonstrates that random testing may not be a cost-effective approach to testing.

Our methodology for estimation of software risk gives us the ability to combine information about the software and its use into an assessment of the criticality of a module as it is being developed and used. Traditional software reliability estimates do not give us the ability to include information about the exposure of a module, a very significant contributor to the criticality of a module. For example, consideration of failure probability in this system would indicate that the cash-flow extract module has a higher failure probability than the module that prints bills (see Table 1). However, the exposure of the latter module is significantly greater. The inclusion of this information makes the risk assessment a very useful measure of the criticality of a module.

As we applied our methodology to this system, we noted that alternative designs for some of the high-exposure modules could have been considered had the exposure analysis been accomplished prior to programming. For example, the financial posting module has one of the highest exposures. It is also the longest module (over 11,000 executable lines of code) with a high failure probability. Knowledge of this information could have been used prior to design and development to suggest alternative designs for the functions of this module.

As the system was tested, knowledge of the relative risk of each module would have indicated that much more significant testing efforts should be allocated to the three modules whose risk was substantially greater than any of the other modules. The modules creating the billing extract file, financial posting, and extracting report data had significantly higher risks than any of the other modules prior to test by the bank (see Table 1). Many of the online inquiry modules had a very small risk of failure. Testing effort could have been allocated accordingly.

Reevaluation of the estimated risk periodically throughout the life cycle of the system would indicate where maintenance effort would be warrranted. Table 1 shows the updated risk of some modules in this system after almost eight months of operation at the bank. This risk of failure in several modules had increased significantly as the system was used. The number of failures found during this time period resulting from faults in two modules, the one that prints bills and the one that validates and updates some of the data files, was in excess of what was expected for this time period. The risk of failure in these modules increased, suggesting that these modules be carefully reviewed. They are modules for which preventive maintenance, such as fix-and-improve reviews might be indicated.

The wide variation in software risk among modules of this system indicates that uniform or random testing and maintenance may not be cost-effective methods. Decisions concerning resource allocations can be made more effectively using an assessment of risk that is updated as new information about the system becomes available.

Conclusions

Once we can assess the variation in software risk between different portions of a system, we can more effectively test and maintain our systems. We have shown how we can measure and use software risk to guide software development, testing, and maintenance.

Future work in software failure likelihood prediction will improve the operational performance of our work. Additional research regarding factors in the development process that affect the error density would enable us to make important development decisions in relation to our exposure assessments.

References

Adams, E.N., "Optimizing Preventive Service of Software Products," *IBM Journal Reasearch and Development*, Vol. 28, No. 1, January 1984, pp. 2-14.

Adrion, W.R., M.A. Branstad, and J. Cherniavsky, "Validation, Verification and Testing of Computer Software," *Computing Surveys*, Vol. 14, No. 2, June 1982, pp. 159-192.

Basili, V.R. and T.Y. Phillips, "Evaluating and Comparing Software Metrics in the Software Engineering Laboratory," *NASA Collected Software Engineering Papers: Vol. 1*, July 1982, pp. 4-18-36.

Basili, V.R. and B.T. Perricone, "Software Errors and Complexity: An Empirical Investigation," *Communications of the ACM*, Vol. 27, No. 1, Jan. 1984, pp. 42-52.

Boehm, B., *Software Engineering Economics*, Prentice-Hall, Inc., Old Tappan, N.J., 1981.

Card, D.N., V.B. Church, and W.W. Agresti, "An Empirical Study of Software Design Practice," *IEEE Transactions on Software Engineering*, Vol. SE-12, No. 2, Feb. 1986, pp. 264-271

Feuer, A.R. and E.B. Fowlkes, "Some Results from an Empirical Study of Computer Software," *Fourth International Conference on Software Engineering*, Munich, Germany, September 17-19, 1979, pp. 351-355.

Freedman, D. and G. Weinberg, *Guide to Walkthroughs, Inspections and Technical Reviews*, Winthrop Publishers, Cambridge, Mass., 1982.

Glass, R.L., "Persistent Software Errors," *IEEE Transactions on Software Engineering*, Vol. SE-7, No. 2, March 1981, pp. 162-168.

Gremillon, L.L., "Determinants of Program Repair Maintenance Requirements," *Communications of the ACM*, Vol. 27, No. 8, Aug. 1984, pp. 826-832.

Henley, E. and H. Kumamoto, *Reliability Engineering and Risk Assessment*, Prentice-Hall, Inc., Old Tappan, N.J., 1981.

Jones, C., *Programming Productivity*, McGraw-Hill, New York, 1986.

Koch, H.S. and P. Kubat, "Optimal Release Time of Computer Software," *IEEE Transactions on Software Engineering*, Vol. SE-9, No. 3, May 83, pp. 323-327.

Kubat, P. and H.S. Koch, "Managing Test-Procedures to Achieve Reliable Software," *IEEE Transactions on Reliability*, Vol. R-32, No. 3, August 1983, pp. 299-303.

Lipow, M., "On Software Reliability," *IEEE Transactions on Reliability*, Vol. R-28, No. 3, August 1979, pp. 178-180.

Musa, J.D., A. Iannino, and K. Okumoto, *Software Reliability: Measurement, Prediction, Application*, McGraw Hill, New York, 1987.

Parikh, G., *Techniques of Program and System Maintenance*, Winthrop Publishers, Inc., Cambridge, Mass., 1982.

Pate-Cornell, M.E., "Fault Trees vs. Event Trees in Reliability Analysis," *Risk Analysis*, Vol. 4, No. 3, 1984, pp. 177-186.

Shen, V.Y., T. Yu, S. Thiebaut, and L. Paulsen, "Identifying Error-Prone Software--An Emperical Study," *IEEE Transactions on Software Engineering*, Vol. SE-11, No. 4, April 1985, pp. 317-323.

Sherer, S.A., "Analysis of Bank's Commercial Loan System," unpublished, 1988a.

Sherer, S.A., "Methodology for the Assessment of Software Risk," Ph.D. dissertation, Wharton School, University of Pennsylvania, 1988b.

Sherer, S.A. and E.K. Clemons, "Software Risk Assessment," *AFIPS Conference Proceedings*, AFIPS Press, Reston, Va., Vol. 56, 1987, pp. 701-707.

Takahashi, M. and Y. Kamayachi, "An Empirical Study of a Model for Program Error Prediction," *Proceedings Eighth International Conference on Software Engineering*, London, 1985, pp. 330-336.

Youngs, E., "Human Errors in Programming," *International Journal of Man-Machine Studies*, 1974, Vol. 6, pp. 361-376.

Yourdon, E. and L. Constantine, *Structured Design: Fundamentals of a Discipline of Computer Program and Systems Design*, Prentice Hall, Inc., Old Tappan, N.J., 1979.

*Management of
Computing*

*Gordon B. Davis
Editor*

Determinants of Program Repair Maintenance Requirements

"Determinants of Program Repair Maintenance Requirements" by L.L. Gremillion from *Communications of the ACM*, Volume 27, Number 8, August 1984, pages 826-832. Copyright ©1984, Association for Computing Machinery, Inc., reprinted with permission.

LEE L. GREMILLION

ABSTRACT: *Considerable resources are devoted to the maintenance of programs including that required to correct errors not discovered until after the programs are delivered to the user. A number of factors are believed to affect the occurrence of these errors, e.g., the complexity of the programs, the intensity with which programs are used, and the programming style. Several hundred programs making up a manufacturing support system are analyzed to study the relationships between the number of delivered errors and measures of the programs' size and complexity (particularly as measured by software science metrics), frequency of use, and age. Not surprisingly, program size is found to be the best predictor of repair maintenance requirements. Repair maintenance is more highly correlated with the number of lines of source code in the program than it is to software science metrics, which is surprising in light of previously reported results. Actual error rate is found to be much higher than that which would be predicted from program characteristics.*

1. INTRODUCTION

Whenever a piece of software is released for production, management information systems (MIS) executives make a commitment to devote resources in the future to the maintenance of that software. Some of this maintenance is unavoidable and its occurrence unpredictable since it is due to changes in user requirements or the computing environment. Unless the software is trivially simple, it will also undergo maintenance to

correct errors present but undetected at the time of release. Predicting the number of such errors, and therefore, the extent of the requirement for corrective or repair maintenance, would provide management with valuable planning information.

A number of theories exist relating program characteristics to the expected occurrence of errors in the programs. This study examines those theories and hypothesized relationships between program characteristics and repair maintenance rates using data on 346 programs in a system used by a large electronics manufacturing firm. Results show that the occurrence of errors are in fact strongly related to measures of size and complexity of the programs and less strongly to the intensity with which the programs are used. Surprisingly, the actual number of errors reported against the program is larger than that predicted by software science measures. For these programs, size (numbers of lines of code) is found to be the best predictor of the number of errors remaining in a program after prerelease testing.

2. REPAIR MAINTENANCE AND FACTORS BELIEVED TO AFFECT IT

2.1 The Repair Maintenance Issue

Maintenance refers to changes made to operational programs in order to keep the programs operational and responsive to user needs. Maintenance activities can be broken down into several categories (e.g., [25, 27]) one of which is corrective or repair maintenance. This essentially refers to fixing errors or "bugs," discovered after the program has been made operational. Other types of maintenance involve adapting programs to meet changing user needs or a changing computing environment.

Maintenance activities can account for a significant fraction of the cost and effort expended on a program during its life cycle. Lientz et al. [16] surveyed a number of studies which estimated that fraction to range between 40 and 75 percent. Less information is available specifying which part of that is repair maintenance. Lientz and Swanson [15] found it to be about 20 percent in one study of 487 data processing (DP) organizations, whereas Vessey and Weber [27] found it to be "a minor problem" without making a specific resource-expenditure estimate. Popular wisdom, as reflected in MIS textbooks [4] and MIS management publications [6] holds that the cost is significant enough to be a real management concern.

2.2 Program Complexity

Most research on factors affecting program repair maintenance has focused on the relationship between the number of bugs and some measure or measures of the "complexity" of the program. This complexity has been defined in a number of ways, most often utilizing the software science metrics developed by Halstead [14]. The basic idea is that the more complex the program or module, the more likely it is that the programmer made logic errors *and* failed to detect the errors before the module was released.

2.2.1 *Program Size.*   A number of empirical studies-have been reported using different complexity measures and with varying results. A common approach involves some measure of program size as an indicator of complexity. Lientz and Swanson [15] found that larger systems (as measured by numbers of source language statements) seemed to require more maintenance effort including debugging, as perceived by their respondents. Bell and Sullivan [2] examined a number of published algorithms and found a strong relationship between an algorithm's length and the occurrence of errors. Thayer [26], in a study of 249 modules, reported that the larger modules did experience a greater number of bugs, but he did not report correlation coefficients. Bowen [3] examined the correlations between errors and program length for 75 modules in three projects for the Department of Defense, and found correlation coefficients ranging from 0.51 to 0.91. (He found similar correlations when using McCabe's measure of cyclomatic complexity [18] as a predictor variable.) Vessey and Weber used categorical complexity measures, "simple," "moderately complex," and "complex," derived from the number of procedure-division statements and subjective evaluations as a predictor variable for 447 commercial programs in three organizations. They found only a weak relationship between this variable and the rate of repair maintenance for one organization's programs.

2.2.2 *Software Science Program Complexity Measures.*

A complexity measure which has had some empirical support is Halstead's E—the measure of mental effort required to create a program. E is derived from two other measures of a program—*difficulty* and *volume*. A program's difficulty is a function of the number of operators used in the program and the number of times variables are manipulated within the program. As pointed out by Christensen et al. [7], it appears to be a measure of both the "ease of writing" and "ease of reading" of the program. Volume is a function of the total usage of operators and operands and the number of unique operators and operands appearing in the program. It is a measure of the number of bits required to specify the program. E is the product of these two measures: As the size (volume) and/or difficulty of an algorithm increases, so should the effort required to code it into a program. (For a more complete explanation of these and other software science metrics, see [14].)

Some very impressive results have been obtained using these measures. Funami and Halstead [12] calculated the value of E for nine modules reported by Akiyama [1] and found a 0.98 correlation between the E measurement and the reported number of errors. Fitzsimmons and Love [11] calculated E measures for 140 programs in three large General Electric software development projects, and found correlations ranging from 0.75 to 0.81 between E and the number of documented errors for the programs.

Fitzsimmons and Love [11] pointed out that a likely problem in comparing their results with those of Halstead and his colleagues was a difference in the way the dependent variable was defined. For them, "delivered bugs" meant those discovered *after* the initial round of testing. The arguments made by Halstead [14] for the relationship between E and the number of bugs refers to all bugs initially coded into the program and the correlations reported by Funami and Halstead [12] were derived on that basis. Managers interested in future repair maintenance rates will be concerned with the bugs remaining in a program after all pre-release testing and debugging has been done. One issue that is addressed in this study is the strength of the correlation between E and only those bugs which remain after formal debugging is complete.

Ottenstein et al. [21] further argued that the number of bugs coded into a program was a function of two factors: the number of mental discriminations required to code the program (E) and the average amount of work (i.e., number of mental discriminations) a programmer can do without making an error. They claim that this function can be approximated by

$$B = E^{2/3}/3000$$

where B is the predicted number of bugs in a module. They found that the predictive power of this model was supported by Akiyama's data [1] and by Bell and Sullivan's suggested maximum module size [2].

2.3 Intensity of Program Use

A second factor which might affect the occurrence of repair maintenance is the intensity with which a program is used. Musa [20] and Littlewood [17], for example, suggested that the more "stress" a program undergoes, that is, the more it is executed, the shorter the expected time to failure, the sooner a bug will be discovered and have to be fixed. Gilb [13], likewise, pointed out that one should measure program reliability not in terms of absolute number of bugs but in terms of the number of transactions with failures as a fraction of the total number of transactions. The idea here is that the more a program is exercised, the more likely it is that the logic path with the hidden bug will be taken, sooner rather than later. Thus, all other things being equal, a program which is run more frequently would be expected to have a higher incidence of repair maintenance than one which is run less frequently. Vessey and Weber [27] cite this logic in using repair maintenance rate (the number of repairs carried out divided by the number of production runs) for a program as their dependent variable.

2.4 Program Age

A related but slightly different issue is that of program age. Vessey and Weber [27] reflected the common belief that the rate of discovery of bugs declines as the program grows older—fewer and fewer untried logic paths remain. On the other hand, it is only with the passage of time that some of these logic paths will be tried, when certain unusual circumstances arise. For example, there is the (possibly apocryphal) story related by Moore [19] about the early days of the SABRE system which crashed when a reservation was attempted in which the names totaled 244 characters ending with an "n." This bug was not discovered until one day when an agent attempted to book a flight for the Boston Bruins hockey team. Because only unusual circumstances will activate some logic paths, one would expect to find a correlation between program age and the incidence of repair maintenance, beyond that attributable to frequency of production runs. The older a program is, the more likely it is that those rarely encountered bugs have, in fact, been encountered.

2.5 Programming Style

There is popular support for the notion that certain programming practices, specifically modular programming and structured programming, tend to reduce the number of delivered bugs in a program [5]. (Sheil [22], however, shows that support for this notion in the research literature is very weak indeed.) The basic idea is that the factoring, in the case of modular programming or formal structuring, in the case of structured programming, of the program makes it easier to understand and to debug more completely before release. These effects may be interpreted as resulting from a reduction in program complexity due to the use of the techniques. Christensen et al. [7] pointed out that the use of structured programming techniques should be

captured in the Halstead difficulty measure which, in turn, affects the effort measure E. Breaking a program into modules reduces the number of unique operators used, which therefore reduces both difficulty and volume, reducing E. Thus, a larger, that is, nonmodularized or unstructured implementation of a given algorithm would be expected to require more mental discriminations (higher E measurement) than the same algorithm implemented using these programming techniques.

2.6 Programmer Competence

A final factor which might be expected to affect the number of delivered bugs is the competence of the programmer who wrote the program. Published findings on this question are sparse and conflicting. Endres [10] found evidence that programmer quality was an important determinant in the number of bugs in a release of an IBM operating system. Vessey and Weber, on the other hand, were unable to find any relationship between programmer quality and repair maintenance in their study [27]. Unfortunately, the data used in this study was captured for other purposes, and does not include information on the competence or experience of the programmers involved. This issue, therefore, will not be addressed, except to recognize it as a possible confounding variable.

2.7 Hypotheses

Several hypotheses can be identified which this study will test. These are:

H1: The more complex a program is, in terms of size (lines of code or volume), difficulty or Halstead E, the greater the number of errors the program will contain when released.

H2: The more intensively a program is used, the more errors will be discovered in it.

H3: The older a program is, in terms of time since release, the more errors will have been discovered in it.

Each of these can be stated in the form of a null hypothesis; that is, there is no statistically significant relationship between number of delivered bugs in a program and any of the other factors mentioned. An additional prediction to be tested, although it is not in hypothesis form, is that the actual number of delivered bugs discovered in the programs will be related to but less than the number derived from the formula by Ottenstein et al. [21].

3. RESEARCH METHODOLOGY

To test these hypotheses, an analysis was performed on the 346 programs making up a manufacturing support system (manufacturing database maintenance and requirements planning) used by a large electronics equipment manufacturer. This system was developed and maintained by a central programming group which developed and maintained other systems as well. It is currently installed in 28 locations worldwide (all in-

TABLE I. Complexity Measurements and Repair Requests for Programs Included in the Analysis*

Measurement	Mean	SD	Minimum	Maximum
Halstead Volume (Kbits)	45.5	52.7	0.4	290.1
Halstead Difficulty	70.2	67.4	3.0	1,129
Halstead E (000)	4,769	8,521	1.6	81,965
Lines of Code (excluding comments)	1,173	1,168	51	6,572

* $n = 346$

house). All software maintenance done, for whatever reason, is performed by the central programming group. For repair maintenance, the user who discovers an error submits a formal request to this group for correction of the error.

The programs themselves are written in PL/I and vary in length from 51 to 6,572 source statements. All were written in a highly structured style according to the organization's programming standards. Halstead metrics were computed for each of these programs by means of a program which took as input the PL/I source code. It counted the number of unique operators and operands and the number of total occurrences of operators and operands along with the total lines of code for each program. Further, Halstead metrics were computed from these counts according to the procedures described in [14]. Table I summarizes this information.

The Halstead measurements were taken at one point in time, and, therefore, do not reflect changes in a program's complexity due to adaptive or perfective maintenance. The few programs which were so substantially rewritten as to significantly change their complexity measures were from the analysis. Changes in complexity over time for the remaining programs should have been small, and should not have biased the results.

User records were examined to determine the frequency of use of each program. Table II shows the categorizations which were made and the distribution of

TABLE II. Distribution of Programs by Frequency of Use

Level	Description	N	%
0	Used rarely (monthly or less)	113	32.7
1	Used at least monthly but not daily	99	28.6
2	Usually used once per day	84	24.3
3	Used several times per day	28	8.1
4	Used many times per day	22	6.4
	Total	346	100.0

TABLE III. Distribution of Programs by Age
(Number of Years since Initial Release)

Age	N	%
Less than one year	7	2.0
At least one year but less than two	4	1.2
At least two years but less than three	9	2.6
At least three years but less than four	1	0.3
At least four years but less than five	325	93.9
Total	346	100

programs by category. Although it would have been more desirable to use a continuous measure of frequency of use (e.g., number of times the program was run per month), this was not possible. The different system users kept their usage records in different formats and at differing levels of detail, so that only categorizations as shown in Table II could be made accurately.

Age of the programs was obtained from records showing the date of initial release. Table III shows the distribution of programs by age. One shortcoming in this data becomes apparent from an examination of Table III—the lack of variation in program age. This reflects the fact that most of the programs were initially released as a group when the system as a whole was released. This severely limits the extent to which the effects of program age on repair maintenance ($H3$) can be tested.

The dependent variable is the total number of repair requests made for each program over its life. (One repair request represents one bug to be fixed.) This was obtained from records maintained by the programming group. For the 346 programs included in the study, the number of requests per program ranged from zero to a high of 268 with an average of 16.8 per program, and a standard deviation of 31.7.

4. ANALYSIS
4.1 Correlations Among Variables
The first step in the analysis of the data is to look at the paired (zero-order) correlations among variables as shown in Table IV. Several points should be noted in this data. The correlation between volume and difficulty is significant, but not perfect, suggesting that these measure related, but different, aspects of the program. The number of lines of code is more highly correlated with volume than with difficulty, lending support to the notion that a longer program is not necessarily a more difficult one. Age is not very highly correlated with anything, including the number of repairs. The apparently significant negative correlation between age and difficulty is probably spurious due to the limited variability in age. Frequency of use is significantly correlated with the number of repairs, as anticipated, but is also significantly correlated with volume, difficulty, E, and lines of code. These latter correlations are unexpected, and may indicate some coincidental patterns in the programs, for example, that the biggest and most difficult programs happen to be run fairly frequently.

The data lends support to $H1$, that the number of delivered errors increases as program complexity in-

TABLE IV. Paired (Zero-Order) Correlations among Variables**

	Vol	Diff	E	Loc	Age	Freq
DIFF	0.44*					
E	0.85*	0.79*				
LOC	0.97*	0.47*	0.82*			
AGE	0.05	−0.18*	−0.07	0.04		
FREQ	0.19*	0.20*	0.21*	0.22*	0.05	
REPAIRS	0.72*	0.25*	0.57*	0.74*	0.08	0.27*

* $p < 0.001$ ** $n = 346$

creases. The number of repairs is significantly correlated with E, although at a lower level than would be expected from previously reported findings. There is also a significant, but somewhat weak correlation between difficulty and number of repairs. Most striking, however, is the correlation between the measures of size of the program—volume and lines of code—and the number of repairs. It would appear that for these programs, lines of code would be the best measure of complexity to use for predicting repair requests.

4.2 Regression Model
Regression analysis lets us look at the combined effects of these variables. To do this, a series of regression analyses were run, in which the dependent variable was number of repairs. All the possible combinations of difficulty, volume, lines of code, E, program age, and frequency of use were used as independent variables. Table V shows the "best" regression model that could be built from the data predicting repair requests as a function of the independent variables mentioned above. This model is best in the sense that substituting any other measure of program complexity for number of lines of code reduced the overall R^2. Also, if any other complexity measure was added to the equation along with number of lines of code, the model's explanatory power was not significantly enhanced. Program age was not a significant variable in any formulation. The variability in the two measures used accounted for 56 per-

TABLE V. Results of Least-Squares Regression (Dependent Variable = Number of Repair Requests)

Variable	Beta	t Statistic
Constant term	−9.85	−5.2*
Number of lines of code	0.0194	19.5*
Frequency of use	3.12	3.2*

$R^2 = 0.56$ $F = 218.5$ (Significance of $F < 0.001$)
* Significance of $t < 0.001$

TABLE VI. Results of Least-Squares Regression (Dependent Variable = Number of Repair Requests per 1,000 Lines of Code)

Variable	Beta	t Statistic
Constant term	4.46	3.9*
Number of lines of code	0.0017	2.84**
Frequency of use	3.87	6.5*

$R^2 = 0.15$ $F = 30.7$ (Significance of $F < 0.001$)
* Significance of $t < 0.001$ ** Significance of $t < 0.01$

cent of the variability in the number of repair requests. Although both independent variables were significant at the 0.001 level, most of the explanatory power of the model lies in the lines of code measure. As was shown in the correlation matrix, there was statistical support for H2, that the number of errors discovered increases with increasing intensity of program use, but operationally, this relationship was weak.

Beta in Table VI was the coefficient in the regression equation for each variable. It was the amount the dependent variable changes for each unit change in the independent variable. Since frequency of use was an ordinal variable, its actual coefficient value was less meaningful than is the coefficient for lines of code, which was a ratio-level variable [23].

4.3 Program-Error Characteristics
The number of bugs in these programs, as reflected by the number of repair requests, was significantly greater than that predicted by Ottenstein et al. [21]. Actual repair requests showed a total of 5,822 bugs (an average of 16.8 per program) while the predicted number was 2,613 (an average of 7.6 per program). These results were particularly surprising in light of our expectation that the actual number of discovered bugs should be, if anything, *less* than the predicted number due to some having been caught in pre-release testing. Instead, it appears that the larger the program (number of lines of code), the greater the error in the prediction. The correlation coefficient between number of lines of code and the difference between actual and predicted number of bugs was 0.58, which was significant at the 0.001 level.

Four possible explanations for this discrepancy come to mind. The first is that the formula proposed by Ottenstein et al. is incorrect for programs such as the ones studied here. Size of the programs may be a factor—there are some very large programs in this set, and it is for these large programs that the discrepancy is greatest. It may be that programs become more error prone as they increase in complexity at a rate even faster than that predicted.

A second possibility is that we are seeing the effects of uncontrolled intervening variables. Ottenstein et al. point out that the relationship they postulate may be confounded by factors such as programmer experience, method of programming, and amount of machine time available for testing. Since programmer characteristics and test time are not measured in this study, their effect is impossible to determine.

TABLE VII. Frequency of Repair Requests

Number of Repair Requests	Frequency	%
0	59	17.1
1– 5	127	36.7
6–10	32	9.2
11–20	42	12.1
21–30	30	8.7
31–40	15	4.3
41–50	9	2.6
51–100	26	7.5
101–200	3	0.9
201–300	3	0.9
Totals	346	100.0

Third, it may be that some of the repairs were to fix bugs introduced by previous maintenance efforts. In particular, one would expect some bugs to be introduced by adaptive maintenance which added code to a program. Since extensively rewritten programs were excluded from the data set, however, it seems unlikely that this would account for such a large discrepancy between predicted and actual bugs.

Finally, there is the possibility that some of the "repair requests" were actually requests for adaptive maintenance (i.e., changes to the program's function, not fixes). As Swanson [24] points out, MIS organizations tend to resist requests for repair maintenance less than they do requests for adaptive maintenance, leading users to try to disguise their requests for changes as requests to fix bugs. While there is no evidence that this has occurred with the programs included in this study, it is a possibility that must be recognized. Clearly, this is an area which merits further study.

We can look at the distribution of frequency of repair requests as shown in Table VII. While a number of programs (59) have had no repair maintenance at all, most have had some repairs, and almost half have had more than five repair requests. For the 346 programs as a group, there were almost 6,000 repairs requested over a 4½-year period. These findings are in sharp contrast to those reported by Vessey and Weber [27]. One possible explanation for this discrepancy would be that Vessey and Weber studied systems with much shorter programs. This is supported by the fact that they classify programs with more than 600 source statements as "complex," while the average length of programs included in this study was 1,168 lines of code.

5. CONCLUSIONS

In drawing conclusions from this data, one must remember that it represents only one particular situation, utilizing one programming language and style, and it would be improper to generalize beyond this situation. Still, it is instructive to look at the results obtained from particular cases in light of predictions which have been made concerning factors affecting the occurrence of delivered bugs. Only through the examination of empirical evidence can the theories be tested and refined.

The most surprising result was the large number of bugs discovered in the programs relative to the number of bugs which would be predicted by the formula developed by Ottenstein et al. Unfortunately, measures of possible intervening variables which may account for this difference—programmer characteristics and the extent of adaptive maintenance performed on the programs—were not available in the data used. Given the strong correlations reported by Ottenstein et al. in support of their model, and the potential usefulness of that model, the need for further investigation is clearly indicated.

The data analyzed above agree with the widely held view that the number of delivered bugs in a program is strongly related to the complexity of that program. Surprisingly, however, the best measure of this complexity appears to be simple count of the lines of code in the program, rather than such measures as Halstead's E, which have been used successfully in previously reported research. The correlation between E and number of repair requests, while significant, is lower than that reported in previous studies. The number of mental discriminations a programmer makes in creating a program (measured as E) may be an important determinant of the number of bugs initially coded into the program. It appears, however, that the size of the program (as measured by lines of code or volume) is more important in determining the number of those errors which are found during debugging, and, therefore, the number of remaining bugs which are delivered to the user. These findings appear to vindicate those who advocate limiting program module size in order to help reduce delivered bugs (see [2, 21]).

Frequency of use of the programs studied does not seem to be as important a predictor of repair maintenance as the literature suggests. While the correlation between frequency of use and number of repair requests is statistically significant, the amount of variation explained is small, only about 6 percent. Perhaps the fact that most of the programs were over four years old influenced this. After four years, one might hypothesize, all the programs would have been run so many times that any effect of frequency of use would be lost. This badly skewed distribution of program age also made it possible to test the hypothesis that the occurrence of repairs increases with program age.

The need is clearly indicated for further research to refine our understanding of what factors relate to delivered bugs and, therefore, to repair maintenance. Almost one half of the variability in occurrence of repair maintenance among the programs included in this study remains unexplained—despite the fact that program size, complexity, intensity of use, and age were included as predictor variables, and programming style was common across all modules. As mentioned above, other factors not included as predictor variables or controlled for in the experimental design may be at work. This is a disadvantage of using existing data captured for purposes other than the one under study—important constructs may simply not have been measured.

This problem is best addressed by studies in which constructs and the way in which they will be measured are determined before or during the time the programs are actually written. In addition, where certain factors do not vary within a particular study (e.g., programming style did not differ in this study), multiple comparative studies are required to see the effect of that factor. The justification for such studies is clear—the more we know about the factors affecting the occurrence of bugs in delivered programs, the better we should be able to predict, and ultimately, control those bugs.

REFERENCES

1. Akiyama, F. An example of software system debugging. *Proceedings of the IFIPS Congress*, 1971, 353–359.
2. Bell, D.E., and Sullivan, J.E. Further investigations into the complexity of software. *MITRE Technical Report MTR 2874*, vol. II, Bedford, Maine, 1974.
3. Bowen, J.B. Are current approaches sufficient for measuring software quality? *Proc. Softw. Quality Assurance Workshop*, 3, 5, 148–155.
4. Burch, J.G., Strater, F.R., and Grudnitski, G. *Information Systems: Theory and Practice*. New York: John Wiley and Sons, Inc., 1983.
5. Canning, R.G. Modular COBOL programming. *EDP Anal. 10*, 7 (July 1972), 1–14.
6. Canning, R.G. That maintenance "iceberg." *EDP Anal. 10*, 10 (Oct. 1972), 1–14.
7. Christensen, K., Fitsos, G.P., and Smith, C.P. A perspective on software science. *IBM Syst. J. 20*, 4 (1981), 372–387.
8. Curtis, B., Sheppard, S.B., Milliman, P., Borst, M.A., and Love, T. Measuring the psychological complexity of software maintenance tasks with the Halstead and McCabe metrics. *IEEE Trans. Softw. Eng.* SE-5, 2 (Mar. 1979), 96–104.
9. Elshoff, J.L. Measuring commercial PL/I programs using Halstead's criteria. *SIGPLAN Not.* (May 1976), 38–46.
10. Endres, A. An analysis of errors and their causes in systems programs. *IEEE Trans. Softw. Eng.* SE-1, 2 (June 1975), 140–149.
11. Fitzsimmons, A. and Love, T. A review and evaluation of software science. *Comput. Surv. 10*, 1 (Mar. 1978), 3–18.
12. Funami, Y., and Halstead, M.H. A software physics analysis of Akiyama's debugging data. *CSD-TR-144*, Purdue University, Lafayette, Ind., May 1975.
13. Gilb, T. *Software Metrics*. Winthrop Publishers, Cambridge, Mass., 1977.
14. Halstead, M.H. *Elements of Software Science*. Elsevier North-Holland, Inc., New York, 1977.
15. Lientz, B.P., and Swanson, E.B. *Software Maintenance Management*. Addison-Wesley Publ. Co., Inc., Reading, Mass., 1980.
16. Lientz, B.P., Swanson, E.B., and Tompkins, G.E. Characteristics of application software maintenance. *Commun. ACM, 21*, 6 (July 1978), 466–471.
17. Littlewood, B. How to measure software reliability and how not to. *Proc. Third International Conf. Softw. Eng.*, Apr. 1978, 37–55.
18. McCabe, T.J. A complexity measure. *IEEE Trans. Soft. Eng.* SE-2, 4 (Dec. 1976), 308–320.
19. Moore, T.E. *The Traveling Man*. Doubleday & Co., Inc., Garden City, N.Y., 1972.
20. Musa, J.D. The use of software reliability measures in project management. *Proceedings*: COMPSAC '78, 493–498.
21. Ottenstein, L.M., Schneider, V.B., and Halstead, M.H. Predicting the number of bugs expected in a program module. *CSD-TR-205*, Purdue University, Lafayette, Ind., Oct. 1976.
22. Sheil, B.A. The psychological study of programming. *ACM Comput. Surv. 13*, 1 (Mar. 1981), 101–120.
23. Stevens, S.S. On the theory of scales of measurement. *Science 103* (1946), 677–680.
24. Swanson, E.B. On the user-requisite variety of computer application software. *IEEE Trans. Reliab.* R-28, 3 (Aug. 1979), 221–226.
25. Swanson, E.B. The dimension of maintenance. *Proc. Second International Con. Softw. Eng.*, Oct. 1976, 492–497.
26. Thayer, T.A., et al., Software reliability study. *RADC-TR-76-2238*, Rome Air Development Center, Grifiss Air Force Base, N.Y., Aug. 1976.
27. Vessey, I., and Weber, R. Some factors affecting program repair maintenance. *Commun. ACM 26*, 2 (Feb. 1983), 128–134.

CR Categories and Subject Descriptors: D.2.7 [**Software Engineering**]: Distributions and Maintenance—*corrections*; D.2.8 [**Software Engineering**]: Metrics—*software science*; K.6.m [**Management of Computing and Information Sciences**]: Miscellaneous
General Terms: Management
Additional Key Words and Phrases: program maintenance, repair maintenance, program complexity, software science

Received 6/83; revised 12/83; accepted 1/84

Author's Present Address: Lee L. Gremillion, School of Management, 704 Commonwealth Avenue, Boston University, Boston, MA 02215.

Maintenance as a function of design

by JAMES R. McKEE

International Monetary Fund
Washington, D.C.

ABSTRACT

Changing one's point of view on the maintenance function can lead to a better understanding of the relationship between maintenance and other aspects of software products. This can lead to an improved allocation of effort when building software products.

INTRODUCTION

The maintenance requirements of software products are generally given insufficient consideration by software product designers because they miscalculate the importance of the maintenance function as a cost component in the life of a software product. One aspect of the problem may be attributable to an inappropriate point of view. The life cycle model most commonly used to portray software development misrepresents the activity it is intended to explain and gives insufficient emphasis to maintenance.

Corrections to these problems may lead to more optimal solutions in the process of software development. This is likely because the trade-off between maintainability and other components of a software product will become more properly balanced. Correspondingly, the analysis and design documents associated with software products will include items of greater value to the maintenance function.

POINTS OF VIEW

When practitioners first started trying to bring some order to the process of software development, they developed the concept of a "life cycle" for new software. The cycle generally began with problem recognition or goals. It then stepped through analysis, design, coding, installation, testing, and operation. The last step of the cycle was maintenance. The problems with this model are numerous. As Zvegintzov has pointed out, this model does not accurately describe a system's life. Moreover, the model is generally portrayed as a linear concept, not as a cycle.[1] In reality the life cycle model mixes a linear concept with a cyclical concept. It ties the concept of the process by which good operational product is generated to the operation of a system that uses the product.

Perhaps the most egregious error in the traditional life cycle model is the mishandling of the concept of maintenance. Maintenance is generally shown as a single step at the end of the cycle; in fact, it is better portrayed as second- (or 3rd-, 4th-, . . . , nth-) round development. The life cycle then becomes develop, operate, develop, operate, develop, and so forth. The model now looks more like a cycle, but has become less useful. This is because the relationship between product building and operations is not so tightly coupled. Much as an airframe manufacturer typically does not operate an airline (and vice versa), the operations of most software products are separated from their manufacture. As an aside, one can make the argument that the failure to isolate software development from operations is a fundamental error that results in a product of extremely poor quality.

There is one other effect of the wide acceptance of the life cycle model with which we must deal. When maintenance (dealing with old products) is included at the end of the cycle, then it is presumed that the beginning sections of the cycle are to be applied to new products. This leads not only to a rather wrong-headed view of how the efforts of the analyst–programmer are distributed, but also fosters the impression that structured techniques are best applied only to new projects. As shown in Figure 1, if we are to divide analyst–programmer activity between existing and new applications, at least two thirds of the activity will be attributable to existing applications.[2,3]

Although the analysis to prove the point has not been developed here, it is perfectly clear that the application of structured techniques is equally valid for all analyst–programmer activity. It then follows that the greatest absolute benefit will occur when the analyst–programmer is engaged in maintenance. While this conclusion has been recognized, the process by which we obtained it here has not.

COSTS AND ALLOCATION OF EFFORT

In software development, the validity of a project should be determined by traditional cost–benefit analysis.[4] This approach uses a model in which costs are seen to be rising and benefits falling as the scope of a project expands. The discus-

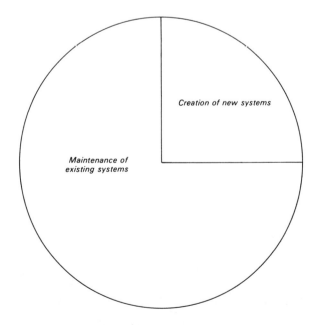

Figure 1—What analyst-programmers do

sion here will be limited to the cost side of the model with the operating assumption that minimization of the total cost of a software product over its entire useful life is a reasonable objective function for the software engineer. This assumption is held to be valid whether the product is an addition, correction, or modification to an already existing product, or a completely new product.

For our discussion the total cost to be minimized consists of three fundamental components: maintenance cost, operating cost, and original development cost. This schema includes all costs of fixing problems or errors, all enhancements, and all changes required by alterations in the operating environment of a product—that is, the costs of any and all changes to a product after it is first delivered—within the definition of maintenance. Operating costs include hardware costs, consumables, and any labor and management costs associated directly with the running of the product. Development costs include all the original analysis, design, coding, and testing costs of a new product. The behavior of these cost components is of considerable interest to the software engineer, as they should be a major determinant of the structure of his product.

The historical trends of these cost components are worthy of review. Operations costs per unit of work are declining largely because the hardware component of these costs is rapidly declining—this overwhelms other operations cost components. However, as the cost of a unit of work has declined, the demand for additional units has expanded in greater proportion. Thus, the overall trend of this expenditure is up, not down. (This behavior can be explained by a concept well known to economists, that of elastic demand. The demand for computer hardware has been highly price elastic throughout the history of the industry and is expected to remain so for the foreseeable future.) Development costs and maintenance costs are both labor intensive and thus are increasing. Maintenance costs may also be increasing because the useful life of software products is increasing. Certainly, our realization of the enormity of maintenance costs is increasing.

The distribution of costs between these major components is likely to vary widely depending on the nature of the work, the maturity of the system, and the work style of the organization. Figure 2 shows the implied distribution between maintenance activity, hardware operations activity, and all other activity within fifteen federal installations surveyed by the General Accounting Office (GAO).[3] The other category includes personnel costs attributable to operations, administrative support, and management, as well as new-product development. The figure is interesting because it demonstrates the great importance of the maintenance function as well as the continuing importance of hardware cost.

The point of this aspect of our discussion is that while hardware costs have traditionally been given, and should continue to be given, great attention, the next most important cost component is software maintenance. Original development costs, which receive tremendous attention in the structured-analysis literature, are a distant third in the actual cost of most systems.

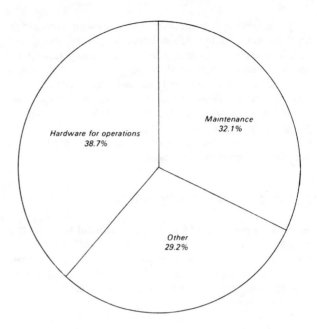

Figure 2—Implied distribution of costs in GAO study

TRADE-OFFS

In all development projects there are many trade-offs. For our purposes, the trade-off between maintenance and other cost components is of interest.

The strong relationship between a well-structured development process and the maintainability of a system is well recognized in the software-engineering literature. In almost every treatise on structured analysis or structured design, long arguments are made about the efficacy of these structured techniques. The arguments always include testimony to the fact that structured development produces systems that have fewer errors, are much easier to understand, and thus much easier to maintain. However, they tend to view maintainability as a fallout of good structured techniques. A better point of view would be to view maintainability as a quantifiable characteristic of software. Maintainability could then be included more usefully in the objective function for a product, and more or less of this quality could be included in the delivered product as a result of design decisions.

Using this view, one can trade additional product development effort for reduced maintenance costs. The technical optimum is when the last added-development costs are just covered by the reduced-maintenance costs, the assumption being that any further development efforts generate insufficient benefits. On a practical basis very few people have hard numbers to cover this issue. Nevertheless, it is probably safe to assert that in most cases the trade-off between development and maintenance costs can be pushed much further in terms of increased development costs. It is also most likely to be the case that this development effort should be pushed beyond the amount of maintainability that falls out of good structured techniques. This additional maintainability is designed in the product.

The same optimality presumptions apply with respect to the trade-off between maintenance and operations costs. However, one should take great care in making any assumptions about operations costs. In all probability the sum of all operations costs for a product over its useful life is not declining. Nevertheless, operations costs have always been given considerable attention, while maintenance costs have not. Thus, on this latter basis alone one could presume that some trade-off in favor of increased operations costs and lowered maintenance costs would be reasonable.

PLANNING FOR MAINTENANCE

As Reutter points out (see Figure 3), most of the activity in maintenance is directed toward product capabilities or characteristics not included in the original product design.[5] Moreover, most of the remaining maintenance activity is directed toward changes in the environment in which the software product operates. Only a small portion of maintenance is directed toward correction of errors. While this may not reflect the experience with all software, it probably does represent what one should expect from fairly well-designed and well-written software products. In high-quality software the error rate may approach zero; this should be an attainable objective. On the other hand, we expect the environment to be changing. We also expect demands for enhancement. Moreover, we expect both of these to occur on a regular basis. What needs to be done is to develop software that is very amenable to these expected changes.

Many areas of expectation for change are identified at the analysis and design stages of product development. In these stages decisions are made that determine the scope of the project. Characteristics to be included in the product are then given the detailed attention necessary to complete the development process and characteristics to be excluded are frequently forgotten. While it is true that many specification documents have a brief statement about avenues of possible extension for the product—and a few even have sentences scattered throughout about points of expandability—these statements are usually treated as asides to the process of building the specified product.

There is another side to the coin of features not included in a product design. This has to do with features or technical solutions that were rejected as being in some way unsuitable for the product. These include all those dead ends encountered during the anaysis and design stages. Also to be considered are those features that once looked so promising, only to be found fundamentally inconsistent with the accepted development of the product. The information and knowledge associated with these considered but rejected features are almost never found in any specification document.

A major set of additions to the specification document is necessary to capture the analysis of features excluded from a product. These additions may be of some value to the builders of the currently specified product, but their objective is specifically to aid the maintenance analyst–programmer. In a sense, these additions will be a resource library that the maintenance

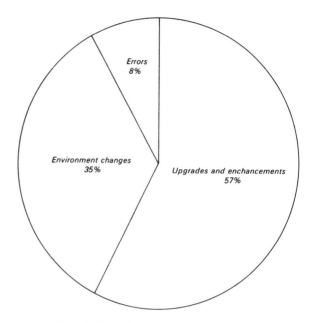

Figure 3—Reutter's distribution of maintenance costs

programmer can explore to see if his problem has already been addressed. It will also serve another important purpose. It will stand as the justification for the design decisions in the current product that are related to potential extensions of the product. Finally, these additions will be spread throughout the specification and design documents. They will serve as a continuing reminder to all those involved in the development process to include maintenance-related issues in every decision process.

Case Study—The Economic Information System

The Economic Information System (EIS) is a large (15 gigabyte) database system for the time series data describing the economies of all countries in the world. The system is currently under development at the International Monetary Fund and is scheduled to begin operation in June 1985. The EIS serves well to illustrate some of the points that have been made in this paper. It is a moderately large software project (budget in excess of $3.5 million) that in some aspects is a conversion of a current system and in other aspects a major extension of that system. Thus, it is typical of most of the software projects found in the commercial world. Both components of the project fall within the realm of maintenance.

The current database system consists of a set of ISAM files and home-grown database programs resident on a Burroughs mainframe. In addition, a large set of operations programs have been developed to generate a number of major publications that are run from the database. Most of the code for both the database and the operations are in COBOL. All of the operations code and a subset of the original database code (152,000 lines) will be converted directly to the IBM environment. This will be the batch production part of the new system. An on-line access and update system is also being constructed as an addition to the previous system.

The original charge to the development team was to move the current system to an IBM environment with the on-line extensions, use a commercially available database management system (DBMS), and be up in 18 months. In the initial justification for the project it was stated that "productivity aids would become available in the form of programming tools and software packages which will significantly reduce staff resources required for future systems development and ongoing systems maintenance."[6] Thus, the continuing cost of maintaining systems was given primary focus prior to project initiation.

The first major decision in this project was the choice of DBMS. The question was formed around the type of DBMS (hierarchical, network, inverted file, and relational) as much as the particular vendor. Hierarchical- and relational-type DBMSs were dropped early in the decision process, the former because of its inflexibility to change and large up-front design requirements, and the latter because of known performance problems and the absence of any product with performance experience in large database applications. In the evaluation of the remaining two types of DBMSs, three critical areas—DBMS data structures, database implementation and maintenance, and user access and manipulation capabilities—were identified. Critical requirements were developed within each of these areas. Candidate systems were then evaluated against these requirements.

This DBMS choice provides an excellent example of trade-off. Because of the mix between batch and on-line activity in this application, neither the network- nor the inverted-file-type of DBMS was found to have an advantage with respect to hardware resources. However, with respect to implementation and maintenance, the inverted-file-type DBMS had an overwhelming advantage. The database design process is much simpler in an inverted-file database. Moreover, inverted-file structures are much more amenable to extension and change than network structures. This became the basis of our choice.

Another example of the maintenance concept entering into a major decision in this project arose in the database design process. In the batch operations process on the current system large data records (10 Kbyte) are read into a buffer. The applications then use a central utility to obtain the sections of the records that they need. This works well in the current batch system; however, the approach is completely inappropriate for on-line update and inquiry activities. The on-line requirements of the project have led to the development of much smaller records in the target database. The question is then whether to build up the large buffer the entire batch stream expects, or to make some major changes in the data-gathering procedures of the batch application code. From the design and development effort point of view, building the buffer would be the best choice. From an operations point of view, building the buffer would be more expensive. However, overnight batch costs are 10% of daytime costs in our environment and there is a succession of use of various parts of the large buffer in our current operations. Thus, the operations costs are not an overriding issue. What is clear is that the large

buffer structure is not likely to be suitable for the extensions of this application that will be forthcoming after it is put in place. Moreover, the structure that is chosen now will be cast, if not in steel, at least in bronze for some years to come.

It was decided to change the data presentation procedures. This decision will raise development costs for the project. The decision will also have a negative effect on our ability to produce a product on a timely basis. However, the ability to enhance the product after its initial delivery will be significantly increased.

CONCLUSION

There is still substantial room for improvement in our understanding of the process by which software products are constructed. A more carefully constructed life cycle model will improve this understanding. In addition, a clear analysis of the cost trade-off between maintenance and other cost components of a software product is likely to lead to a better resource allocation. However, these suggestions are limited to creating the setting in which improved maintainability may be developed. The many techniques that may be employed for improving maintainability have not been explored. This remains the task of future explorers in this field of endeavor. The growing cost of software maintenance suggests such efforts be given high priority.

ACKNOWLEDGMENTS

I would like to thank my colleagues, Soon Choi, Thomas L. Williams, Kathleen X. Nelick, and S. Stuart Morrison, and my wife, Mary Jane McKee, for the many suggestions and improvements they have provided in the production of this paper, and the Graphics Section of the IMF, for providing the charts. The errors and omissions remain my own.

The ideas and opinions expressed herein are solely those of the author and are not necessarily representative of, or endorsed by, the International Monetary Fund.

REFERENCES

1. Belady, L. A. "Software Complexity." In *Tutorial on Models and Metrics for Software Management and Engineering*. Los Alamitos, Calif.: IEEE, 1980.
2. Belady, L. A., and Lehman, M. M. "A Model of Large Program Development." *IBM Systems Journal*, 15 (1976), pp. 225–252.
3. Boehm, B. W. *Software Engineering*. Redondo Beach, Calif.: TRW, 1976.
4. Boehm, B. W., Lipow, M., and White, B. B. *Software Quality Assurance: An Acquisition Guidebook*. Redondo Beach, Calif.: TRW, 1977.
5. Chapin, Ned. "Productivity in Software Maintenance." *AFIPS, Proceedings of the National Computer Conference* (Vol. 50), 1981, pp. 349–352.
6. IMF. *IMF Economic Information System Planning Document*. Internal (mimeographed) document, International Monetary Fund, Washington, D.C.

SUGGESTED READINGS

1. DeMarco, T. *Structured Analysis and System Specification*. Englewood Cliffs, N.J.: Prentice-Hall, 1979.

2. Elshoff, J. L., and M. Marcotly. "Improving Computer Program Readability to Aid Modification." *Communications of the ACM,* 21 (1982), pp. 512–521.

3. Harrison, W., K. Magel, R. Kluczny, and A. DeKrock, "Applying Software Complexity Matrice to Program Maintenance." *Computer,* 15 (1982), pp. 65–79.

4. Hester, S. D., D. L. Parnas, and D. F. Utter. "Using Documentation as a Software Design Medium." *The Bell System Technical Journal,* 60 (1981), pp. 1941–1977.

5. Linger, R. C., H. D. Mills, and B. I. Witt. *Structured Programming: Theory and Practice.* Reading, Mass.: Addison-Wesley, 1979.

6. Myers, G. J. *Software Reliability: Principles and Practices.* New York: John Wiley & Sons, 1976.

7. Page-Jones, M. *The Practical Guide to Structured Systems Design.* New York: Yourdon Press, 1980.

8. Reutter, J. III. "Maintenance is a Management Problem and a Programmer's Opportunity." *AFIPS, Proceedings of the National Computer Conference* (Vol. 50), 1981, pp. 343–347.

9. Schwartz, B. "Eight Myths About Software Maintenance." *Datamation,* 28, (1982), pp. 124–128.

10. U.S. General Accounting Office. *Federal Agencies' Maintenance of Computer Programs: Expensive and Undermanaged.* Report AFMD-81-25, February 26, 1981.

11. Yau, S. S., and J. S. Collopello. "Some Stability Measures for Software Maintenance," *IEEE Transactions on Software Engineering,* SE-6, (1980), pp. 545–552.

12. Yourdon, E. *Techniques of Program Structure and Design.* Englewood Cliffs, N.J.: Prentice-Hall, 1975.

13. Zvegintzov, N. "What life? What cycle?" *AFIPS, Proceedings of the National Computer Conference* (Vol. 51), 1982, pp. 561–568.

Software manufacturing techniques and maintenance

by PAUL BASSETT

Netron Incorporated
Toronto, Ontario, Canada

ABSTRACT

"As ye sow, so shall ye reap."

A good solution to the reusable code problem turns out also to provide a solid technical basis from which to understand and deal with the production, quality, and maintenance issues of the software industry. To this end, a software manufacturing methodology has been developed called Computer-Aided Programming. CAP is based on a functional programming concept called a frame. Frames were originally developed as a means of resolving the maintenance problems associated with reusable code.

The introduction explains the necessary background ideas about frames and the types of maintenance that they address. Section two presents the design principles for software that uses frames as subassemblies for program assembly purposes. The components of an existing CAP system are described in section three, and section four discusses the use of CAP as a manufacturing technique. Statistics from a case study are presented to indicate that: (1) production-quality commercial software can be manufactured at rates exceeding 2000 lines of debugged COBOL per man-day (including systems design time), and (2) less than 10% of this code needs to be hand-written or maintained.

INTRODUCTION: THE MAINTENANCE PROBLEM

Software has had a precocious, turbulent childhood, as is typical of newly emerging disciplines. In spite of many important advances, software still remains a hand-made commodity designed in an ad hoc manner with few standards; a product that is almost always late, poorly documented, and difficult to maintain.

Maintenance, more than any other factor, holds the software industry captive, strangling productivity and tying up vital programming resources. The half-life of a typical program is approximately 14 months. The maintenance statistic now approaches 70% and is still climbing.

The central thesis of this paper is that a substantial portion of the maintenance effort stems from the reusable code problem. A good solution to this problem turns out also to provide a solid technical basis to understand and deal with both the production and quality of software and the maintenance issues currently besieging the software industry.

The Reusable Code Problem

In the software industry's current cottage industry style, it is common practice to build new programs by cutting and splicing pieces of old programs together. This approach demonstrates that there is great deal of potentially reusable code available, and that it is worth the effort to adapt it rather than starting from scratch. Reference 16 shows that unfortunately

1. The programmer does not have any systematic way of isolating just what portions of programs are relevant
2. The customization process is time consuming, tedious, and prone to error
3. Once the process is finished, both old and new programs must be maintained as if each were completely unique, despite the considerable common functionality. Maintenance effort should be proportional to the novelty in the system, not the number of source statements.[4]

External Subroutines

It is still widely believed that external subroutines form a satisfactory repository of reusable code. Separately compiled and linked subroutines are obviously useful, but they are limited because there is no graceful or systematic means of effecting local customization of an external subroutine to fit each calling program's particular context of use, or of effecting global evolution of a subroutine when it must change to benefit all future callers of that subroutine without victimizing current callers.

The subtle and often frustrating side effects introduced when common components undergo maintenance directly contributes to the severity of the maintenance problem.

The root cause is that a subroutine is a representation for a single function that is not adaptable at source-program (function) construction or maintenance time. It may have considerable run-time flexibility, but at the time of actually molding the subroutine into the program that must use it, an external subroutine (by its very nature) has no flexibility at all.

Code Generators

Code generators have been around for years (e.g., RPG). Although they offer a potential to drastically simplify the maintenance of large portions of a program, their potential goes unrealized.[2,10]

The simplest kind of code generators are those that generate "raw" source code. The problem with such generators is that they are basically "one-shot" tools. Because each generator is expert at only a part of the overall problem,[3,17] programmers must supplement and modify the generated source code to suit their own needs. Having adapted the code, they have no means of reusing the generator without destroying all of their manual modifications. This forces the programmer to support the life-cycle maintenance of the program at the more difficult and error-prone level of generated source code, rather than the succinct, declarative level of the original input to the generator.

To be more useful, a code generator must allow some follow-on mechanism that can adapt the generated source code automatically, thus allowing reuse of the generator without the loss of the customizations.

More sophisticated code generators typically supply "user exits" for handling this problem. These provide linkage to separately compiled, external suroutines that usually can be written in a variety of general purpose languages. The trouble is that this is always an additive technique; there is no way to change or remove generated functionality. Also, predefined interfaces often omit information that is essential in the customization (the "black box" effect). In addition, all non-procedural parts of the generated code, such as data declarations, are simply unavailable for refinement. A proper solution requires generators to provide for automatic customization of generated code (not just run-time communication with generated modules).

The Frame Methodology

A frame methodology,[13,14] has been developed to address the reusable code problem from the perspective both of programmers and of code generators.[3] A frame is a machine-processable representation of an abstract data type,[9] with "abstract" meaning functional.[1,3] Because the data operators are functionals, not functions, frames can accommodate both local customization into an individual program and global evolution to benefit all future embedding programs. Frames are implemented as files containing a mixture of source code (e.g., COBOL) and preprocessor macro commands, but are quite unlike the proposals of Backus[1] or Evans.[8] This mixture is called frame text.

There are just four macro commands whose essential role is to automate the cutting and splicing of programs:

1. COPY-INSERT allows a frame hierarchy to be copied into a program (by naming the frame at the root of the hierarchy), and causes customizing frame text to be INSERTed anywhere into that hierarchy.
2. BREAK-DEFAULT defines a named "breakpoint." Breakpoints mark arbitrary places in a frame where custom frame text can be INSERTed to supplement or replace DEFAULT frame functionality.
3. REPLACE systematically substitutes a specific code string for a generic one (throughout a frame hierarchy). For example, field names and picture clause elements are generic if they tend to vary from program to program.
4. SELECT incorporates into a program one text module from a set of modules in the frame. SELECTs are like CASE statements (with arbitrary nesting), which operate at text construction time. An important use of SELECT is to automate version control (global evolution).

Frames are written both by analysts and by generators. Having code generators produce frames solves the problem of destroying subsequent refinements by automating the cutting and splicing of the customizing frame text into the generated frame text.

All customizing frame text for one program is localized for maintenance purposes into a SPECIFICATION, or SPC, frame. Typically, the size of this file will be less than 10% of the generated source code. An SPC governs the entire process of building the compilable source program from its frame components. As will be seen, a methodology incorporating frames at its heart offers a potential for

1. Fill-in-the-blank program specifications (rapid prototyping)
2. Automation of the process of reusing previously built, high-quality software (both human- and machine-written)
3. Automatic customization in context
4. Maintenance of only what is unique in a program
5. Evolution of reusable components without obsolescence (elimination of unnecessary retrofits)
6. Painless enforcement of good programming techniques (standards)

THE DESIGN OF SOFTWARE MANUFACTURING TOOLS

In order to realize the potential of frames, especially with regard to maintenance, a software development environment has been created, called Computer Aided Programming. CAP is fundamentally a manufacturing paradigm, in which standard frames are the standard subassemblies, various frame generation steps are the processing operations on basic components (raw materials) to produce fabricated parts, and the CAP processor operating on the SPC frame is the process of final assembly with any custom options.

The Role of Languages

Our industry continues to proliferate languages unabated, and this is both necessary and desirable.[17] The creation of each language is motivated by a desire to reduce the effort of solving, in computer executable form, some class of problems. But does this mean we can eliminate the programming?

In Reference 5 the following definitions were developed: Problem solving is fundamentally a process of finding or composing a suitable function (1) whose domain is the problem's input information, (2) whose range is the goal of the problem (i.e., the desired output), and (3) whose function is consistent with other problem constraints.

Playing chess is an example of problem solving. The domain of a chess function is the set of legal board positions. The range is the set of legal moves associated with each position. The constraints include the time available to select a move, the need to find a "good" legal move, any memory of what moves were "good" in past games and so on.

Programming is a form of problem solving by function composition, in which one must deal with either the order of composition, or the interfacing of component functions, or both. At one extreme, selecting from a menu is an effective way for nonprogrammers to solve their problems. At the other extreme, selecting assembly language instructions will solve an interesting problem only with a great deal of programming effort.

By distinguishing problem solving from programming, it becomes possible, with respect to a given class of problems, to group language expressions into three levels: underspecified, optimally specified, and overspecified.

Optimal specification languages

A language is said to optimally specify a function space (and hence an associated problem class) if and only if:[5]

1. The language is isomorphic to the function space; that is, each distinct function is denoted by only one distinct expression, and only the functions in the space are expressible.
2. The degrees of freedom (constraints) are independent, optimally specified subspaces (of constants, variables, or functions).

3. The language's well-formed expressions are the "most compact" with respect to all languages satisfying (1) and (2).

In practice, this definition is weakened. Part (1) is approximated by first designing the language to be virtually one-to-one, then assuming the function space (implied by the language's semantics) to be what was "really meant" by the solutions of the original, unformalized problem class. Part (2) is approximated first by striving for as much independence as possible, then by applying as many context-sensitive error tests as are practical to any remaining dependent degrees of freedom. Finally, Part (3) is ignored as long as the language users are happy.

It turns out that such "weak optimal-specification" languages are a realistic approach to problem solving without programming. Functions usually can be defined simply by grouping the names of some subfunctions under a new function name, without regard to the order in which these subfunctions are performed and without regard to how these subfunctions must communicate with each other. Their compilers are called code generators because each generator plays the role of a programmer, converting a declarative, optimal specification into procedural, overspecified code, which itself must be compiled. Examples of this type of language as used in CAP are described in this paper. As has been noted, CAP design principles require the generated code to be in the form of frames.

It should be clear that the properties of optimal languages permit maintenance efforts to be minimized, provided that the resulting programs can be produced automatically.

Underspecification

An underspecification language is like an optimal-specification one except that the relationship of well-formed expressions in the language to the possible solution functions is one-to-many. There may be many degrees of freedom that play secondary roles in the structure of the overall function space. There may be several functions, each expressible in a different language, which must be combined, but whose degrees of freedom intersect or are interdependent. In these situations, an underspecification language can be used to quickly "broad brush" the major functional features of the solution. The code generator then employs heuristics to specify one solution function at the optimal level that is reasonable and consistent with any overlapping degrees of freedom.

Thus, the underspecified level is the prototyping level, feeding the optimal level where the life-cycle maintenance efforts are performed. Again, the key requirement is that the software manufacturing tools automate the flow of specifications between levels.

Overspecification language

In an overspecification language, the relationship of well-formed expressions to functions is many-to-one, and properties (2) and (3) of an optimal language do not hold even weakly. Overspecification languages are ubiquitous. For example, every computer's binary or assembly language lacks the syntax to express directly the right degrees of freedom for most of the problem classes to which the machine is applied. So programming, which is often done by a compiler, is inevitable at this final stage of problem solving.

To date, virtually all software maintenance has been performed at the overspecified level (for reasons discussed earlier). This is a significant factor in increasing the maintenance effort required. Provided that the software environment is one where a homomorphic map from the optimal to the overspecified levels exists, an order-of-magnitude reduction in life-cycle maintenance effort can be expected based simply on the reduction of code to be maintained.

To sum up the role of languages, whenever a useful function space can be defined by an optimal specification language, programming can be relegated to the computer. To further enhance problem-solving leverage, multiple underspecification, front-end editor–generator pairs can be built that create optimal specifications. These expressions are processed in turn by editor–generator pairs and create programs at the overspecified level, but maintain them at the optimal level. Any special-purpose, custom functionality is kept in the SPC frame, which directs the CAP processor in its final assembly tasks of building or rebuilding the complete source program, then compiling and linking it into executable form.

The Role of Frames

Frames are used to formalize the common intermediate stage in the program construction process, prior to the frames being combined and customized into a single program (function). There are two reasons for having this stage. First, recognizing the open-ended nature of problem solving, an extensible library of standard frames and templates, together with generated frames, can support custom programming for any problem. Second, the ability to mechanize the assembly of a program, given the diversity of its components, depends on bringing them to a common notation.

Standard frames

As problems are discovered to be related, a standard frame can be *evolved* to span the implicit function space. Each frame represents a functional, whose domain defines (using the COPY and REPLACE commands) the degrees of freedom appropriate to the class of related problems, and whose range (all possible instantiations of the frame text) is the corresponding function space. By fixing those degrees of freedom in various ways, various problems in the class can be solved without programming.

This is not to say that programming has been eliminated. Usually real problems refuse to confine themselves to neat, predefined classes. Accordingly, a frame's breakpoints and SELECT clauses constitute open-ended degrees of freedom, where solutions can be arbitrarily extended, if necessary.[5]

Standard frames are used whenever the function space is too limited in scope or usage to warrant a new optimal specification language. This approach to problem solving is implemented by using templates. A template is an uncustomized SPC frame, and usually spans a hierarchy of frames. It collects in one linear list (a file) all degrees of freedom appropriate for a useful class of problems. The replacement strings, subfunction selection choices, and insertion points for the frames in the hierarchy constitute a fill-in-the-blank method of customizing the program. Thus, templates and frames together permit problems to be solved in a manner that progressively reduces traditional programming to a minimum, given the open-ended nature of real problems.

To the degree that system design expertise can be stored inside the system, the SPC frame can itself be created by designer tools working at the underspecified level.

Generated frames

Certain function spaces have degrees of freedom too dynamic to be represented by fixed, standard frames. Well-known examples are screen and keyboard interfaces and report definitions. For these cases, optimal languages can be developed in association with frame-writing generators.

By generating frames instead of raw source code, open-ended (programming) degrees of freedom become available. Such degrees of freedom are required in the overall problem class, but should be suppressed in the various optimal specification languages. Further customizing can be specified via an SPC without the hand editing or restrictive user exits associated with conventional generators. Basically what has happened is that the editing that would otherwise be necessary to properly customize the generated code has been mechanized. In so doing, we gain both an assembly line style of constructing programs and an ability to maintain the program using its optimally defined pieces (rather than its overspecified code).

Anatomy of a CAPtool

Figure 1 depicts the flow of specifications from the underspecified or designer level, through the optimally specified or customizer level, down to the overspecified or source and object levels. Life-cycle maintenance is performed with the customizer (special purpose) editors. Please note that where

Specific screen & report specifications
Fill-in-the-blank report & screen customizers
Fill-in-the blank designer
Specific Needs
Generate Custom Frames
Splice Compile Link
Custom Executable Program
Specific frame specifications
Fill-in-the-blank SPC frame customizer
Model
Solution
Frames

Figure 1—CAP flow specifications

reference is made to screen and report specifications, these are examples of optimal-specification languages with respect to the problems of commercial data processing. A CAP tool may use either, both, or neither of these languages, as well as other notations, if the problems warrant.

AN ACTUAL CAP SYSTEM

At Netron Inc., a CAP system has been developed for use on WANG VS computer systems applied to commercial data processing using COBOL. The following reflects current functionality and some soon to be released tools.

Underspecified Level Tools

1. CAPinput—for building interactive file maintenance and data entry programs
2. CAPoutput—for building report programs based on general data selection criteria
3. CAPfile—for building general file-to-file transforms and interfaces

These three tools are each structured as shown in Figure 1. Specification of a complete program requires that an analyst answer a small number of questions (most of which have defaults).

Optimal-Specification-Level Tools

1. CAPscreen—for designing and maintaining interactive screen and keyboard functionality
2. CAPreport–for designing and maintaining report functionality
3. CAPframes—a library of standard frames

The (weakly) optimal notations are used by designer tools and by analysts, either in conjunction with underspecified-level tools or independently.

A complete description of these languages is beyond the scope of this paper.[5] Very briefly, independence of degrees of freedom is typified by having screen (report) layout facilities completely independent of the attributes of each screen (report) variable. On the other hand, some degrees of freedom are not completely independent. For example, if a variable on a screen is declared as having run-time error checks, and is declared as not being assigned to an internal variable after the operator enters it at run-time, then these two degrees of freedom are in conflict (and the conflict must be resolved).

The tools themselves generate frames from the optimal specification. These frames in turn make extensive use of the hierarchy of available CAP frames. Because the frames are written using general-purpose (but overspecified) COBOL, the programmer has exact control over the "fine tuning" his particular application may need in order to convert a functional into the required function.

The CAPframes are the heart of the CAP system. Each frame implements a useful function space whose patterns have been recognized by their appearance in several programs. The frames are organized into a taxonomy that guides the problem solver to the relevant functionality.

DISCUSSION OF TOOL USAGE

Types of Users

The consistent application of the under–optimal–over design principle offers access potential to the industry's three major user groups: end-users, analysts, and programmers. In CAP's current implementation, it is an analyst-oriented software manufacturing system. The focus has been to provide tools that aid in the manufacture of larger, more complex systems.

CAP could be designed for nonprogrammers, but few are inclined to cope with the open-ended applications to building and maintenance that are CAP's main strengths. Most people like driving cars and some even enjoy fixing or rebuilding them. But who wants to design and manufacture them?

Because CAP is a manufacturing paradigm, most of the benefits stemming from the organization of a conventional manufacturing enterprise become available to data processing shops. In particular, the frame-engineering department is quite analogous to a conventional engineering department. A useful division of labor is created. Those responsible for designing and maintaining the organization's inventory of standard software components (frames) can work independently from those charged with getting the application software products out the door. The benefit of having centralized standards control is obvious.

Rapid Prototyping

While not part of maintenance as such, rapid prototyping is a very desirable feature of any software development system. Moreover, it is important to ensure that rapid prototypes do not lead to maintenance nightmares.

Conventional wisdom, stemming from the software disasters of the sixties and early seventies, has firmly entrenched the hedging policies of preparing exhaustive feasibility studies, formal requirements definitions, structured walkthroughs, and the like. Often, the time and costs to plan a system are greater than the costs of building it. In turn, the specifications are usually out of date by the time they are finally approved, and the end-users still don't really know what they are getting, or if what they get is what they need. Another danger is that it is so easy to specify features that turn out to be much more difficult to implement than they are worth to the user. In short, the institutionalized policies of large data processing groups are no small contributor to the enormous applications backlog.

Conventional wisdom can now be made wiser.[6,7,11,12,15] CAP tools can write formal specifications that are understood both by people and by computers, and then convert the specifications to equivalent programs. We can now adopt the attitude of "what you see is what you get," and even let small prototypes constitute part of the design specification.

End-users can "kick its tires" and iteratively guide the specifications. The implementation team can provide specific, detailed arguments as to why certain features should or should not be in the system, and can more accurately estimate the cost of a system's implementation based on deviations from the organization's current frame inventory.

Productivity and Quality

Using a tool such as CAPinput typically requires that the user spend a few minutes at the underspecified level. Without further customization, an executable program is available shortly thereafter. The following is the summary from a detailed case study that analyzes the actual use of CAP.

Case study: The manufacture of the Canadiana requisition system

Canadiana Garden Products Inc., is a subsidiary of NOMA Industries Ltd. In March 1983 Canadiana employed Netron Inc., to create a computerized system to replace Canadiana's manual requisition system. The system was created using CAP and is run on a WANG VS computer using interactive terminals. The system allows requisitions to be created, maintained, displayed, searched, authorized, ordered, recorded, and reported upon.

After the first week, enough of the system had been prototyped that the client recognized serious design problems. The system was subsequently redesigned and put into production by the end of the third week.

Sixteen programs were written using CAP tools to create and control the interaction of the 22 screens and three reports through which the requisition system is operated. CAP tools enabled the author to create the requisition system by writing less than 10% of the total COBOL lines needed.

One method of judging the effect on maintenance with and without CAP tools is to compare the total number of lines of submitted source code in the entire requisition system with the number of hand-written lines. Purely comment lines were discarded.

The results show a more than 10:1 reduction in lines of COBOL to be maintained. Of the 34,000 lines of submitted code contained in the 16 programs of the requisition system, only 3,000 lines were written by hand.

The following table shows, for each of the 16 programs forming the requisition system, the number of lines hand written in the SPC frame, in the generated frames, in standard frames, and in the total submitted to the COBOL compiler.

Quality

Of course, the issue here is not merely to show that there is much less code to maintain. Further analysis of the manufactured programs show that they are more consistent with respect to user-interface and structured program style, more reliable, more functionally complete, and no less efficient than conventional, hand-written programs.

TABLE I—Number of code liens

Program Name	Main CAPTool	Total Source	SPC Frame	Generated Frames	Standard Frames
PREQ1	CAPinput	2979	56	1731	1192
PREQ2	CAPinput	2130	71	1264	795
PREQ3	CAPinput	2318	78	1013	1227
PREQ4	CAPinput	1721	62	869	790
PREQ5	CAPinput	3440	421	1904	1115
PREQ6	CAPinput	2776	157	1766	853
PREQ7	CAPinput	1510	40	673	797
PREQ8	CAPinput	3018	206	1806	1006
PREQ9	CAPinput	3238	281	1910	1047
PREQA	CAPinput	3659	436	2223	1000
PREQI	CAPinput	3399	436	1916	1047
PREQF	Frame Lib.	274	187	0	87
PREQG	Frame Lib.	223	136	0	87
PREQR	CAPreport	954	140	198	616
PREQS	CAPreport	1086	226	216	644
PREQT	CAPreport	1152	179	290	683

The reason is that the standard frames and frame generators are highly seasoned components in the course of whose evolution many improvements and optimizations have been made. The cumulative effects are capital assets (no pun intended) that yield a return on investment in every incorporating program. Programs hand-written from scratch have no chance to acquire the quality and thoroughness that is the hallmark of a good frame.[15]

Life-cycle Support

As previously indicated, by storing all source code customizations in one spot, factored away from both standard and generated frames, typical program maintenance is collapsed from 50–60 pages of source listing to two or three pages. By having the code generators emit frame code that can be customized automatically, the declarative specifications also support the life cycle maintenance of the programs in a very convenient manner.

Frame maintenance

As with software, frames change through time. Standard frames tend to be relatively stable since they rapidly become seasoned through frequent reuse. But because they are functionals, they are able to absorb arbitrary amounts of change (including complete rewrites) without risking any previously written program. It is easy to arrange that the range (function space) of a new version of a functional be a superset of the previous version's range simply by providing a version control parameter governing a SELECT clause.

This still allows the improved functional to recreate all old functional versions. An old program's SPC, unaware of subsequent changes, references the frame hierarchy with its old version symbol (if any), and gets exactly the same code it has always gotten, even though new programs may get something quite different (the template always contains the latest version symbol).

This does not mean that frames and libraries become more cluttered than in conventional shops. Conventionally, complete copies are kept of all versions (using distinct names), even though only small changes might have been made. Frames keep an automatic audit trail of the version *differences,* with only occasional rewrites done to eliminate clutter. The obsolete (but still active) versions are placed in a separate library, again to eliminate clutter. Internal version references automate the retrieval of the correct version. Thus, a single external name is common to all versions and less space overall is actually required.

CONCLUSION

It is important to realize that programs are models: deliberate approximations to an elusive and ever-changing external reality. Models are useful because they exploit a simplified representation. We know that Newtonian physics is wrong, yet we never use Einstinian physics when programming everyday calculations. A payroll system has an extremely skimpy model of the human beings on file, but it is quite appropriate for the intended purpose.

From this perspective, development and maintenance are two sides of the same coin. Converging a software model to a useful approximation is called development. But the model also must be updated periodically in light of changing circumstances, and this is called maintenance. The payroll system must quickly incorporate each change to the income tax laws to the extent that its model of those laws becomes invalid.

The recent development of a software manufacturing paradigm has set the stage for changing our cottage industry into a mature technology. By unifying the techniques for program construction and maintenance, each productivity gain can simultaneously benefit both.

REFERENCES

1. Backus, J. "Can Programming Be Liberated from the von Neumann Style? A Functional Style and its Algebra of Programs." *Communications of the ACM,* 21, 8 (1978), 196–206.

2. Balzer, R. "An alternative approach to software automation." *In P. Wegner (ed.), Research Directions in Software Technology.* Cambridge, Mass.: MIT Press, 1979, pp. 851–856.

3. Bassett, P. B., and J. Giblon. "Computer Aided Programming (Part I)." In *Proceedings of IEEE Conference on Software Tools and Techniques.* (Soft Fair), Washington D.C., July 1983.

4. Bassett, P. B., and S. Rankine. "The Maintenance Challenge." *Computerworld In Depth,* May 16, 1983.

5. Bassett, P. B. *"Design Principles for Software Manufacturing Tools."* Presented at Symposium on Application and Assessment of Automated Tools for Software Development, Nov. 1–3, 1983, San Francisco, IEEE, (unpublished).

6. Bianchi, M. H., and J. R. Mashey. "Rapid Prototyping on UNIX. In *Proceedings of the Software Engineering Symposium: Rapid Prototyping.* (IEEE) Columbia, April 19–21, 1982.

7. Blattner, M., and R. Frobose. "Prototyping and the Life Cycle of Software." In *Proceedings of the Software Engineering Symposium: Rapid Prototyping.* (IEEE) Columbia, April 19–21, 1982.

8. Evans, M. "Software Engineering for the Cobol Environment." *Communications of the ACM,* 25, 12 (1982), pp. 874–882.

9. Goguen, J. A., J. W. Thatcher, and E. G. Wagner. "An Initial Algebra Approach to the Specification, Correctness and Implementation of Abstract Data Types." In R. Yeh (ed.), *Current Trends In Programming Methodology.* Vol. 4, Englewood Cliffs, N.J.: Prentice-Hall, 1979, pp. 80–149.

10. Hammer, M., and G. Rugh. "Automating the Software Development Process." In P. Wegner (ed.), *Research Directions in Software Technology.* Cambridge, Mass.: MIT Press, 1979, pp. 767–790.

11. Houghton, R. C., Jr. "Rapid Prototyping Tools: What Can We Learn from the MIS World?" In *Proceedings of the Software Engineering Symposium: Rapid Prototyping,* (IEEE) Columbia, Md. April 19–21, 1982.

12. Mason, R.E.A., and T. T. Carey, "Prototyping Interactive Information Systems." *Communications of the ACM,* 26, 5 p. 347.

13. Minsky, M. "A Framework for Representing Knowledge." In P. Winston (ed.), *The Psychology of Computer Vision.* New York: McGraw-Hill, 1975, pp. 211–277.

14. Rich, J. "Inspection Methods in Programming." Ph.D. Thesis MIT Technical Report AI-TR-604, June 1981

15. Taylor, T., and T. A. Standish. "Initial Thoughts on Rapid Prototyping Techniques." In *Proceedings of the Software Engineering Symposium: Rapid Prototyping,* (IEEE) Columbia, Md., April 19–21, 1982.

16. Wasserman, A. I., and S. Gutz, "The Future of Programming." *Communications of the ACM,* 25, 3 (1982), 196–206.

17. Wulf, W.A. "Some Thoughts on the Next Generation of Programming Languages." *In Perspectives on Computer Science.* New York: Academic Press, 1977, pp. 217–234.

SOFTWARE MAINTENANCE AND MODIFIABILITY

David Frost

Honeywell Information Systems, PO Box 8000, Phoenix, AZ 85066

ABSTRACT

Maintenance is an activity. Maintainability is a
set of properties that affect the cost and quality
of maintenance. When applied to hardware the two
terms have fairly standard meanings. However,
when applied to software, there is no common,
widespread agreement on what they mean. Nevertheless, most generally agree that modification is
the central activity of software maintenance, no
matter how defined. This paper describes the most
frequently used meanings for the terms software
maintenance and maintainability. It then discusses properties of software that contribute to
cheaper, more reliable modification. It recommends
methods to improve modifiability, offering references to other papers for those who wish to dig
deeper.

INTRODUCTION AND DEFINITIONS

The concepts underlying software maintenance
evolved from hardware maintenance. However, an
essential difference exists between hardware and
software maintenance [1]:

o For hardware the basic assumption is that the
  design is correct, and that operational errors
  result from physical causes ("faults"). Faults
  that require maintenance result from such things
  as physical wear, abuse, and manufacturing errors. (Other faults that result from transient
  causes are dealt with by recovery methods.) In
  any event, hardware maintenance consists of either keeping or returning hardware to a state in
  which it performs to specification.

o For software the analogous basic assumption is
  that an error during operation results from a
  program bug rather than from the program wearing
  out. An operational error occurs only when the
  environment reaches a state in which the bug
  manifests itself. Until that time it is latent.
  Software does not wear out.

Because of the analogy to hardware maintenance,
these program bugs are frequently called faults.
(They do indeed cause errors.) I will call them
bugs in this paper. The term is an ancient one by
computer science standards, and is well understood.

The term "software maintenance" has come to have
two different meanings:

1) Activities relating to fault correction:

- the methods for making an error known to
    those responsible for correcting its cause
    (the bug)
- the diagnosis of that cause.
- designing changes to prevent the error from
    recurring.
- the installation and testing of changed code.

2) Modification of software to

- correct bugs.
- extend or change functionality.
- improve its characteristics (frequently perform-
    ance, but other characteristics as well).
- adapt to a changing support environment (hard-
    ware or software).

The first definition is used mostly by system
programmers. Its focus is on correcting errors.
The second definition varies somewhat in the
literature, but is nearly standard [2,3,4,5]. Its
focus is on modifying already existing software
without changing its primary function [6]. It is
one most often recognized by application programmers and theorists. (A pleasant surprise. Theorists are usually attuned more to system programmers than to application programmers.)

For either definition the term "maintainability"
is used to indicate some (vague) measure of the
difficulty and cost of maintenance, however defined. And no matter which definition is of interest, the central issue is that changes must be
made to existing software. (This contrasts with
the usual preoccupation of software engineering
with the production of new software.)

Following are the steps relating to successful
change:
- A trigger for change: either an error or a
      new requirement
- Problem diagnosis, or specification of the
      changed requirement, depending on the
      trigger
- Modification and change control
- Installation and configuration control
- Test

Although problem diagnosis, requirements specification, installation, change control and test

are part of the software maintenance cycle, they are not the major subject of this paper. We will concentrate on the central issue, modification. [However, see reference 7.]

MODIFICATION

Modification is a central activity of software maintenance, by any definition. Ease of modification depends on the ease with which software is understood (clarity). Clarity, in turn, is dependent upon certain properties of the software and its documentation [3]. These properties include

- o modular decomposition
- o data characteristics
- o coding quality
- o documentation quality
- o language used
- o standardized methods

We will next discuss each of these properties in turn.

MODULAR DECOMPOSITION

A connection between two modules exists when one must know of the other's existence and properties in order to perform its own service [8]. That is, its programmer must know something about another module's functions and side effects. Connectivity is defined as the probability that a change in one module will require a change in another. It is an attribute of module pairs [9]. It is measurable from historical data for pairs of existing modules.

Connectivity is the single most important factor for ease and safety of modification; other factors have major effect only if they tend to lessen or increase connectivity [9,10]. The reason: Changes ripple through a set of connected modules and the "ripple effect" increases rapidly as connectivity increases [9].

Coupling is another measure of the existence and quality of connections. One cannot measure coupling numerically. Instead one analyses the ways by which modules are connected. And the ways modules are connected has a strong effect on connectivity, the primary factor in modifiability. The concepts of coupling are much used in the popular methods referred to as Structured Design [11,12]. As with connectivity, the references (as well as experience) are convincing that selection of coupling methods has a significant effect on ease of change. Although not verifiable, considerable Computerworld-level anecdotal evidence supports this as well. And I have found no anecdotal evidence to the contrary.

It has been shown that connectivity of large operating systems (and by analogy any large software system) increases with time unless improvements are explicitly undertaken [13]. This is true for smaller programs as well. The increase occurs because changes are inevitably optimized for solving the problem at hand. That is, the temptation

to kludge in extra connections is irresistible, and (unfortunately) nearly always cost effective in the short term.

Another important conceptual basis for ease of change is generality. Although not frequently written about, some principles exist for guiding the production of generally usable software modules [14,15]. They lead to

- o modules that are more easily modified, and to
- o modules more likely to be reused.

Cohesion is another frequently used measure of modifiability. Like coupling, it comes from the principles of Structured Design [11,12]. It is based on an analysis of how well a module succeeds in doing one function (as defined at a single level of abstraction) without producing confusing side effects and without having irrelevant functions packaged together within it.

Abstract data type [16] and information hiding [9,10] are related, very important methods for arriving at easily modified software - more important than the methods already described. Unfortunately, they are not as easy to understand or apply, and their use is not widespread.

Abstract data type and information hiding help the designer to separate the externally visible characteristics of a module from its internal characteristics. All characteristics of the module which must be made known to connected modules (and only those characteristics) are abstracted to a carefully-chosen view with a high probability of remaining constant in spite of internal changes to the implementation. Side effects are not allowed. The techniques apply especially well to a module which features operations on a data structure (e.g., an array, a stack, or a file). A set of service calls (e.g., entry points) define the various operations permitted on the data. The goal is that users of the existing interface will not have to change if either additional features are added (like a new stack operation) or the method for implementing the service changes.

The concepts of abstract data type and information hiding are embodied in many programming langauges, mostly of the research variety (that is, not widely used outside the university environment). Their genesis was in SIMULA [17], whose concept of classes contained the germ from which the others evolved. Ada, the programming language being promoted by the Department of Defense for command and control applications, is the most famous, and is most likely to be widely used. The concepts have also been extended to a type of design methodology (frequently called the constructive approach) which features rigorous top-down design and proofs of correctness [18].

When used in systems for which performance is an important criterion, the principles of information hiding and abstract data type cannot always be applied without compromise. Nevertheless, they should be used except when compromises are truly necessary, and even then should be perverted as little as possible. That is, the compromises should retain as much good structure as possible and also continue to hide any information that can be hidden without serious loss of performance.

Two other techniques, available only in some execution environments, are based on the concepts of communicating sequential processes [19] and controlled access to domains [20]. The principles of communicating sequential processes permit communication between modules only by sending messages between the modules. Thus only true values can be exchanged; references cannot be made by exchanging addresses to mutually available memory. This makes side effects quite difficult to produce. The use of domains permits (but does not necessarily guarantee) the design of highly secure interfaces with no ability to communicate via side effects.

In summary, the goal in modular decomposition is low connectivity. The lower the connectivity the less a change ripples throughout a system. And rippling of changes is the main reason for high cost and poor reliability when making software modifications.

DATA CHARACTERISTICS

The decisions one makes about data have a profound effect on the maintainability of a software system. This is true from very large systems to quite small programs.

There are two basic issues: (1) the relationship of variables to each other, and (2) the value sets and operations that can be used with variables (data type).

The former is the problem tackled by database theoreticians (and practitioners). Convincing arguments exist that a well-organized database, one with well-ordered relationships, can remain remarkably stable and permit change much more easily than one without these characteristics. [See reference 21, chapter 6.] On a smaller scale, even the decision as to how variables are categorized (logically or physically) into records can make a large difference in the clarity of the meaning and purpose of data, making change much easier and safer.

Categorizing variables consists of grouping them, then naming the groups so that stronger and weaker relationships are made clear. (Naming the groups is important. It is hard to reason about things that don't have names.) This categorization uses precisely the mechanism used for designating levels in COBOL records or PL/I structures. However, doing a good job consists of more than just using the mechanism. It consists of giving considerable thought to the categories before finally recording them.

Documenting the set of permitted values for variables (unless trivially obvious) is always useful to maintainers . Documenting the operations permitted on them is theoretically correct. (This is because value set and permitted operations togeth-

er define the data type for a variable.) However, in most cases the operations are defined by the language used. Defining them again just clutters the mind. Those highly desirable cases where the program actually polices the operations are in the realm of abstract data type, previously discussed.

Historically speaking, documentation has typically been centered around procedure, explaining the flow of a program. This is true both for design documentation and in listings. But for ease of understanding and for ease and safety of change, the most important documentation is that which describes the meaning and purpose of data. It is my experience that if I understand data I can easily deduce the procedure. But understanding the procedures does not lead to quick understanding of the data.

CODING QUALITY

Coding quality also affects ease of modification.

Large modules should be internally partitioned following the principles outlined in the previous section. Once partitioned, other principles apply to the coding of those partitions. These principles have to do with the programmer's success in writing and maintaining modules as sensibly-structured programs.

The principles of structured programming [22] and the difficulties in maintaining unstructured programs [23] are well known. Nevertheless, the use of a technique as simple as structured programming is far from universally applied. The problem in maintaining structured programs is that, when modification is required, quick, "easy" modifications are likely to be applied instead of the (usually more extensive) modifications required to maintain the program in a structured state. (Incidentally, one mustn't forget that modification starts much sooner in the life cycle than ordinarily assumed. It begins immediately at the completion of the first draft of a program.)

Some studies [24,25] and a lot of anecdotal evidence have shown that the use of structured programming decreases the bug rate of programs. Of interest is a study [26] that shows one need not be slavish to the pure principles of structured programming to reap benefits, and that sensible deviations can result in better programs than using the technique in its purest form.

DOCUMENTATION QUALITY

If user manuals are unclear or inaccurate, both the user and maintainer have a hard time deciding what is or is not an error. Although this view is not verified by studies, I believe that unclear user manuals correlate highly with bugs of all kinds, not just discrepancies between the program and the user manual. This is because programmers cannot clearly express the external characteristics of their programs aren't very good at expressing the internal characteristics (the program itself) either. An unclear user interface can also make it extremely hard to add functionality in a simple way: even if the underlying structure of the user interface is simple and regular and could be extended easily, poor documentation can mask that fact.

As discussed earlier, information about programs should be well segregated as to internal vs. external information. Therefore the information in design specifications should come in the same two flavors: external and internal. They should be kept well segregated so that modifications are less likely to blur the difference as the program ages. Actually, a nearly universal problem is that design specifications are not kept accurate as their programs change. As a result, most programmers depend on program listings. Program listings are nearly always the most used source of information. Therefore, comments in listings are correspondingly the most important documentation available to maintainers.

A survey of psychological studies on comments in listings [27] shows that too few experiments have been made to permit firm conclusions. Nevertheless there is an indication that, for all but very small programs, high-level comments are more helpful than low-level. Based on experience, many people agree.

The quality of comments in most programs I have seen is inadequate in comprehensiveness, style, and (in some cases) accuracy. Rather than the desirable high-level comments, the standard is line-by-line commentary to help follow the flow. And almost all comments, high- or low-level, are in the procedure, while it is the commentary on data that can be the most important.

A high-level language is commonly believed to produce self-documenting programs, reuiring few comments. This is not true. Every functional region of a program should have as commentary a brief description of its external characteristics so that maintainers are less likely to inadvertently change them, thereby affecting other regions dependent on them. Of even more importance are semantic descriptions of data: descriptions of their meaning and purpose. Data declarations are not enough. Indeed, I believe, as stated previously, that commenting carefully on the meaning and purpose of data is of the utmost importance. Functional documentation of program partitions takes second place. And the usual line by line commentary mimicking the flow (so common in assembly language programming) places a poor third.

For large or complex systems, information on functions and data may be at so many levels of abstraction that it just can't be organized sensibly in the listing. In this case, the maintenance of accurate, clear design specifications is crucial if the program is to remain well-structured as it ages. However, I am pessimistic; my experience shows that the maintenance of design specifications is almost universally ignored. One thing that does not help is to insist on including in design specifications detailed information that is best maintained in the listing. Having the same

information in two different places is just asking for trouble. Instead, design specifications should have information on the higher-level abstractions only.

LANGUAGE USED

For systems of any complexity, the choice of language used is less important than the previously discussed system attributes that lead to ease of modification: modular decomposition, data, coding quality, and documentation quality [28]. Certainly if a higher-level language is available, it should be used. Although I believe that problem-oriented languages apply best to the problems to which they are oriented [29], attempts to show that one general-purpose high-level language is better than another for general-purpose programming have failed [27].

STANDARDIZED METHODS

Proliferation of ways of doing things makes change much slower and more error-prone. People making changes must spend time trying to understand different styles, while a standard method would have made intent obvious.

Proliferation comes in two forms:

o Doing similar things in non-standard ways.

o Failure to identify common functions that could be provided as single modules, with functions that provide services to all. The result is more software than required, hence higher cost for writing and maintaining the extra software.

The provision of libraries of common functions is usually written about in the future tense [30] and is difficult to implement [31]. Some of the problems are

o Identification of common needs usually occurs after the fact; the functions have already proliferated.

o Common functions frequently do not precisely meet the needs of new users and/or are difficult to modify without causing changes to previous users. This is especially true with modules that produce side effects, i.e., those which do not meet criteria for obtaining generality (see above).

Additional problems exist when trying to gather programs from programmers whose main job is other than producing programs for the library:

o Even if identified in time, the usual way of obtaining a generalized function is to ask the group with the most pressing need for that function to provide it, but to do it in a general way. Schedule pressures and the primacy of their own needs frequently result in failure to assure generality.

o Schedules are frequently out of synchronization. A group that needs a common function is scheduled ahead of the group that would most logically provide it.

o The programs are likely to be inadequately documented. There are several reasons. Many programmers' writing skills are such that they may be unable to write from a novice user's point of view. Personal motivation may be lacking because the programmer knows the program well and doesn't need the documentation himself. Schedule pressures also may contribute. In any event, people are afraid to use programs for which they can't get detailed, accurate information on services provided, interfaces and side effects.

o Ad hoc programs placed in libraries are likely to be less reliable than products designed for general, widespread use, not having been tested or used in many ways.

Yet another problem is the difficulty of publicizing library contents in such a way that programmers can know what is available and whether it applies to their problems. Doing a good job requires knowledge of the technologies of human factors and information retrieval. Just setting up a library is not enough. It must be marketed to its users.

In general, successful libraries are likely to be made up of simple single-function programs (e.g., mathematical routines). Large, multi-function programs with complex interfaces are far less likely to be used.

METRICS

Maintenance metrics (which measure how well maintenance is actually done) have not been the subject of much research. Metrics identified as maintainability metrics are generally in the form of complexity metrics [32,33,34]. These are nearly all applied to single programs, although a small amount of research is being done in metrics for connectivity in systems [35]. There is as yet only conflicting evidence as to the validity of most metrics [2,32,33,36,37,38,39 and many others]. However, most are intuitively appealing, even though there validity is still doubtful.

Software maintainability attributes such as cohesion and coupling (see above) have no truly objective metrics at present. They can be measured only subjectively by examination of the design and code (although they are sometimes given numeric values, thus appear to be more objective). The primary usefulness of these subjective measurements is as criteria to be applied in peer reviews, with which considerable successful experience has been reported [40].

The industry needs better understanding of the definition and application of metrics for maintenance and maintainability. However, except in the field of complexity metrics and the somewhat-related field of test metrics, little research is apparently occurring.

SUMMARY AND CONCLUSIONS

Software maintenance has come to mean (especially among those doing research) changing software for any reason whatsoever. Others (especially system programmers) think of maintenance as primarily the detection and correction of program faults (coding bugs and design errors). In either case the central activity is modification. Thus modifiability has a great effect on the ease, safety, and promptness with which modifications can be made.

I believe that certain properties of software have the most effect on modifiability. These properties are modular decomposition, design decisions about data, coding quality, language used, and standardized methods. Except in the areas of measuring the complexity of code and in the use of high-level languages, little research has been done on the effectiveness of methods to improve these properties. Nevertheless, anecdotal evidence in many of the referenced papers gives encouragement that maintainability can be improved using techniques described in this paper.

REFERENCES

[1] Melvin B. Kline, "Software and Hardware R&M: What Are the Differences", Proceedings, 1980 Reliability and Maintainability Symposium.

[2] E. Burton. Swanson, "The Dimensions of Maintenance", Proceedings, 2nd International Conference on Software Engineering, October 1976.

[3] John B. Munson, "Software Maintainability: A Practical Concern for Life-Cycle Costs", Computer, vol 14 No 11, November 1981.

[4] LSRAD Task Force, "Towards More Usable Systems: The LSRAD Report", SHARE Inc., December 1979.

[5] R.S. Arnold and D.A. Parker, "The Dimensions of Healthy Maintenance", Proceedings, Sixth International Conference on Software Engineering, September 1982.

[6] B.W. Boehm, "Software Engineering", IEEE Transactions on Computers, Vol C25 No 12, December 1976.

[7] Martin Dickey, "A Taxonomy of Software RAS", Proceedings, Fourth Annual Phoenix Conference on Computers and Communications, March 1985.

[8] D.L. Parnas, "Information Distribution Aspects of Design Methodology", Information Prcessing 71, North Holland, 1972.

[9] Frederick M. Haney, "Module Connection Analysis - A Tool for Scheduling Software Debugging Activities", Proceedings, Fall Joint Computer Conference, 1972.

[10] D.L. Parnas, "On the Criteria To Be Used in Decomposing Systems into Modules", *Communications of the ACM*, Vol 15 No 12, December 1972.

[11] L.L. Constantine and E. Yourdon, *Structured Design*, Prentice-Hall, 1979.

[12] Glenford J. Myers, *Composite/Structured Design*, Van Nostrand Reinhold, 1978.

[13] L.A. Belady and M.M. Lehman, "The Characteristics of Large Systems", *Research Directions in Software Technology*, MIT Press, 1979.

[14] David L. Parnas, "Designing Software for Ease of Extension and Contraction", *IEEE Transactions on Software Engineering*, Vol SE-5 No 2, March 1979.

[15] David Frost, "Designing for Generality", *Datamation*, December 1974.

[16] Barbara Liskov and Stephen Zilles, "Programming with Abstract Data Types", *SIGPLAN Notices*, Vol 14 No 4, April 1974.

[17] Ole-Johan Dahl and Kristen Nygaard, "SIMULA - An ALGOL-Based Simulation Language", *Communications of the ACM*, Vol 9 No 9, September 1966.

[18] Donald L. Boyd and Antonio Pizzarello, "Introduction to the WELLMADE Design Methodology", *IEEE Transactions on Software Engineering*, Vol SE-4, No 4, July 1978.

[19] C.A.R. Hoare, "Communicating Sequential Processes", *Comunications of the ACM*, Vol 21 No 8, August 1978.

[20] G.A. Mann, "Software Design Implications of a Domain Architecture", *Proceedings, Third International Phoenix Conference on Computers and Communications*, March 1984.

[21] James Martin, *An Information Systems Manifesto*, Prentice-Hall, 1984.

[22] Harlan Mills, "How To Write Correct Programs and Know It", *Proceedings, International Conference on Reliable Software*, April 1975.

[23] Sylvia B. Sheppard et al, "Modern Coding Practices and Programmer Performance", *Computer*, Vol 12 No 12, December 1979.

[24] Barry Boehm et al, "Structured Programming, a Quantitative Assessment", *Computer*, Vol 8 No 6, June 1975.

[25] F.T. Baker, "System Quality Through Structured Programming", *Proceedings, Fall Joint Computer Conference, 1972*.

[26] Sylvia B.Sheppard et al, "Modern Coding Practices and Programmer Performance", *Computer*, Vol 12 No 12, December 1979.

[27] B.A. Sheil, "The Psychological Study of Programming", *Computing Surveys*, Vol 13 No 1, March 1981.

[28] Barry W. Boehm, "An Experiment in Small-Scale Application Software Engineering", *IEEE Transactions on Software Engineering*, Vol SE-7 No 5, September 1981.

[29] D.R. Frost, "Computer Languages for Process Control", *IEEE Transactions on Industrial Electronics and Control Instrumentation*, Vol IECI-16 No 3, December 1969.

[30] K.H. Kim, "A Look at Japan's Development of Software Engineering Technology", *Computer*, Vol 16 No 5, May 1983.

[31] John R. Rice "Remarks on Software Components and Packages in ADA", *ACM SIGSOFT Software Engineering Notes*, Vol 8 No 2, April 1983.

[32] W. Harrison et al, "Applying Software Complexity Metrics to Program Maintenance", *Computer*, Vol 15 No 9, September 1982.

[33] Murat M. Tanik, "A Comparison of Program Complexity Prediction Models", *ACM Software Engineering Notes*, Vol 5 No 4, October 1980.

[34] Paul A. Schaffer, "Comparison of Quality Metrics", *Software Engineering Notes*, Vol 6 No 3, July 1981.

[35] Sallie Henry and Dennis Kafura, "Software Structure Metrics Based on Information Flow", *IEEE Transactions on Software Engineering*, Vol SE-7 No 5, September 1981.

[36] C.T. Bailey, W.L. Dinger, "A Software Study Using Halstead Metrics", *Proceedings, 1981 ACM Workshop/Symposium on Measurement and Evaluation of Software Quality*, March 1981.

[37] Sallie Henry, Dennis Kafura, Kathy Harris, "On the Relationships among Three Software Metrics", ibid.

[38] K. Christensen et al, "A Perspective on Software Science", *IBM System Journal*, Vol 20 No 4, 1981.

[39] Bill Curtis et al, "Measuring the Psychological Complexity of Software Maintenance Tasks with the Halstead and McCabe Metrics", *IEEE Transactions on Software Engineering*, Vol SE-5 No 2, March 1979.

[40] Daniel P. Freeman and G.M. Weinberg, *Ethno-Technical Review Handbook*, EthnoTech, Inc., 1979.

System information database:
An automated maintenance aid

by LINDA BRICE
and JOHN CONNELL
Los Alamos National Laboratory
Los Alamos, New Mexico

ABSTRACT

Documenting application systems has long been considered a necessary evil. Necessary because documentation provides a map to present systems, serves as a maintenance aid, and is required by the auditors; evil because it is an activity generally dreaded by those who develop the systems. Since normal behavior regarding unpleasant chores is avoidance, application systems documentation is sometimes absent and often incomplete.

Documenting may be unpopular for a number of reasons, including psychological ones. One very obvious problem is that, except for a few automated tools at the program level, documentation is a manual process used in an automated environment. Automating the process is a way to reduce the laboriousness of the task.

This paper is a case study of how one data processing organization applied student labor and a relational database management system in a prototype to automate much of their applications systems documentation function. The capabilities, fringe benefits, and future enhancements of the tool are discussed.

INTRODUCTION

Why should maintenance aids be automated? In many installations system documentation is still a cumbersome manual process. There are automated data dictionaries and program documentors on the market, but few link to other aspects of an organization's functions, and most take several years to populate with data. Some organizations commit to five or ten years' worth of data gathering and data entry, unassured of the results. Others accept as a fact of life that manual documentation is not an effective maintenance aid, but continue to set up frameworks with strict requirements and standards.

This paper shows how a relational data base management system was used to develop an in-house automated documentation system for the Administrative Data Processing (ADP) Division of the Los Alamos National Laboratory. The database has been given the acronym SID, system information database. It contains much of the documentation pertaining to production application systems. This documentation has historically been maintained manually in Central File folders. At the time of this writing, SID has proven to be very effective for entering, updating, and retrieving documentation data rapidly and accurately.

WHY THE NEED TO DOCUMENT

Documentation is considered the "map" of present systems, and a valuable aid to maintenance programmers. Accurate documentation is also a reliable guide to relationships within and between systems. It provides a means for reducing the risk of introducing errors during maintenance work. If an error does occur, a visual picture of control flow is available to help locate the source of the error. In the normal course of events, clear documentation makes staff turnover less disruptive by providing a useful training aid. Finally, adequate documentation will satisfy auditors' requirements for information about how systems work.

Data processing professionals have long been admonished to document in certain standard ways. Most shops were led to believe, by the literature of the 1970s, that visual tables of contents (VTOCs), IBM's hierarchical input process output (HIPO), and flow charts, for example, were the best tools for documentation and were necessary. Now, we are told to produce data flow diagrams, structure charts, Chapin charts, data models, Jackson diagrams, and Warnier–Orr diagrams, as well as myriad forms supplied by structured methodologies.

Many installations simply have not sorted out which old tools to discard, which new ones to adopt, what to make retroactive, or whether or not all tools need to be applied at the system, task, and program level. Most organizations have viewed documentation as a program level activity, with recent emphasis on the data element level. There is much more than a program in the makeup of most application systems. They are also composed of operating system procedures, database interfaces, data files, and other elements. Documentation must not only be present, it must be flexible. Few DP organizations can bear the expense of throwing a system away and rewriting it from scratch. When "the intent is to modify functionality or capability or even performance, the trend is to add code, a front end, or a box ... 'Add on, not replace' is the trend in software."[1] Documentation must be enhanced easily, just like software. Martin and McClure state that "what is needed is succinct, high-quality documentation that is easily accessible and easily updatable. To be maintainable, programs and their associated documentation must be flexible and extensible."[2] To that statement we could add that all documentation pertaining to an applications system must fit the same description as that for a program.

BASIC ELEMENTS OF DOCUMENTATION GENERALLY NEEDED FOR EACH APPLICATION

Regardless of the tool used or the level at which it is applied, the basic elements of documentation needed for a typical business application include:

1. The basic purpose of the system
2. Identification of the customer
3. How the system runs (tasks, procedures, call files, jobs, operating system commands)
4. How execution begins and proceeds
5. Which groups of higher level languages or fourth-generation language instructions exist
6. How the groups of languages (or programs) are invoked
7. Which functions are performed
8. Which files exist
9. How is the data processed—and by which tasks or programs
10. What the output (input) looks like (files, screens, reports, etc)
11. Who is responsible for the system maintenance

Whatever the capacity of the hardware, the size of the application, the programming language employed, the number of staff members, or whether a database management system is used or not, these types of basic elements need to exist for maintainers and auditors of the system.

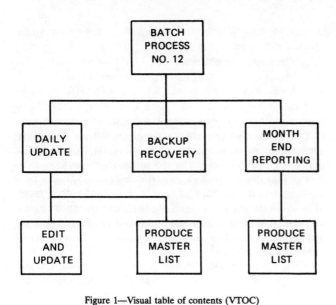

Figure 1—Visual table of contents (VTOC)

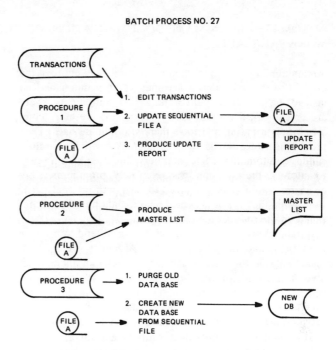

Figure 2—Hierarchial input process output (HIPO)

WHY DOCUMENTING IS SO UNPOPULAR

Documentation, useful if not absolutely necessary, is often the least favorite part of most DP professionals' duties. This is so because documentation is seldom scheduled as part of the job. When schedules slip, system implementation is a more important feature; there must be a system. The documentation portion of the schedule, often inadequately allotted at the start, is diminished because it is often performed after the fact and because it is usually a clumsy, manual system. Sometimes documentation begins when maintenance begins.[3]

Documentation in ADP was completely manual prior to the development of SID and included several elements: First was a visual table of contents (VTOC) describing the hierarchy of tasks. This is a manually drawn set of boxes within a strict format. The major functions of the system appear as text within the boxes of this system schematic (Figure 1). The VTOC was initiated during system design and maintained during the life of the system. It was normally produced after system implementation, to merely fulfill a documentation requirement, and often was not maintained because of the necessity to manually redraw and retype the chart.

The next item was a hierarchical input process output (HIPO) describing the flow of input and output with respect to the functions of a program or task. Special symbols to represent files, output listings, and direction of flow (arrows) were drawn by hand with the aid of a template, and a narrative was typed (Figure 2). HIPOs were intended to be design aids, but were usually produced post-implementation and then only because of standards requirements. Obviously, due to the nature of the format, changes of any consequence required redrawing of one or more pages, or a manual cut-and-paste procedure. Such inconvenience discouraged the maintenance of the charts to accurately reflect the state of the system as it changed character over time because of maintenance and enhancement.

Next were the indices of programs and files, which provided simple lists, usually alphabetized. Other information, such as what task invoked the listed program, or what files were referenced by the program was usually included (although some of the data existed in other forms in the HIPO). The frustration in manually maintaining such lists is that the data must be recorded at least twice (the I/O files are listed on the program index; the referencing programs are listed on the file index).

Also included was information about file and data elements. Data elements were typically described by a record layout form (Figure 3). The record layouts often were hand-drawn.

Finally, there were program listings, which were maintained in hard-copy form in folders arranged in an order meaningful to the organization (by section, by function, and so on). The listings were checked out to maintenance programmers in a library-type arrangement.

FILE NAME: A RECORD NAME: EMPLOYEE					
FIELD NAME:	EMPLOYEE NUMBER	EMPLOYEE NAME	DATE OF BIRTH	SEX	. . .
CHARACTERISTICS:	X(6)	X(14)	X(6)	9	. . .
RELATIVE POSITION:	1–6	7–20	21–26	27	. . .

Figure 3—Record layout

AUTOMATION CAN MAKE DOCUMENTATION MORE PALATABLE

Streamlining of documentation procedures may improve the product to the point that it becomes a true maintenance aid instead of a mere fulfillment of standards requirements. There are psychological reasons that programmers are more comfortable with automated tools than with manual ones. Data processing professionals, like the shoemaker with his barefoot children, automate the lives of others, but often have no time to automate their own business. Naturally, programmers become frustrated at being forced to deal with internal paper work when they are accustomed to automation in every other aspect of their work.

If manual processes are clumsy, they also tend to produce incomplete and inaccurate results. Although management makes rules in the form of standards, having an understandable incentive for profit, they reinforce the message to their staff that the most important part of a job is to get the system up and running. Of course, the message is well received by programmers, who often view documentation as a nuisance.

Automated documentation has all of the advantages of any other automated system, including interactive retrievals, simultaneous access by several parties, and easy aggregates. One particular advantage of automated documentation is the retrieval of information across systems. For example, manual documentation shows program and file relationships within a particular system, but if one wanted to list every program that reads File XXX because the format must change to increase the field length of a data item, then all manual documentation for systems suspected to relate to the file must be searched, or all machine-readable files across those systems must be searched to complete the list; an easy retrieval for a properly formatted system information database. Size considerations, an aid in estimation of the effort required for a job, are also available, e.g., the number of files within the number of systems that reference Purchase Order Number or one of its aliases. As Brown writes, "the most common error in documentation is to provide masses of detail . . . but little on overall organization . . . and on the relationship between parts."[4]

AUTOMATING DOCUMENTATION: A CASE STUDY

At Los Alamos National Laboratory, management and staff agreed that an automated documentation process should be attempted. A relational database system was already licensed in-house, had proved to be an excellent tool for other applications, and was chosen to inventory and manage parts of our documentation function. There existed, however, a resource problem. All available analysts, designers, and programmers were committed to other projects. Given the work load facing the entire division, there was little justification in hiring staff for the documentation project, which was considered overhead. It was not a development of an application desired by the customers who pay the bills. There also was a little skepticism on the part of management. There had been no official cost–benefit study performed for the project and management could not be certain it would be worth the effort to disturb the status quo to implement a new documentation system when the staff was in the throes of a great deal of new development.

By a fortunate circumstance, the ADP Division was host for the summer to four young men from the service academies.[*] The Service Academy Research Associates (SARAs) came to us from the Air Force and the Naval academies; three of them were in their senior year, one was a computer science major, and none had practical data processing experience. They were enthusiastic about learning a state-of-the-art tool, so it was decided to assign them the documentation project, even though they could not work as a true team since their four- to six-week tenures overlapped very little. Armed with a name, SID, and a database management tool, they produced a prototype that proved to be quite successful in convincing management and staff that the documentation procedures could indeed change for the better.

While the first SARA was en route to Los Alamos, a systems requirements definition was produced as a guide to the current manual system and what we wanted to accomplish with SID. Normally, a systems design document follows the requirements definition in the development of any new project. In this case, however, the detailed design was replaced with the prototype version of the system.

A pilot system was rapidly available for management to evaluate in terms of cost and benefit and for the staff to evaluate in terms of usability. The pilot project had small-scale actual data; data were entered for small but complete systems.

The system was refined by submitting the prototype version to selected members of the programming staff for critique. Tables were easily restructured to add and delete data elements or to modify attributes, without the loss or troublesome reloading of any of the real data. Additional live data were loaded from a hierarchical database on a separate computer via magnetic tape. Live data also were loaded from files that programmers had set up to keep track of various systems for which they were responsible. It was interesting to note that many programmers had already discovered that the manually maintained central files were inadequate for maintenance purposes and that several members of the staff had taken steps to record applications data in a more usable state.

A recent survey of programmer opinion indicated that the current ADP staff was 100% in favor of maintaining an automated system to map the state of present systems and the evolution of future systems. When a representative task force of the programming staff viewed demonstrations of the retrievals, they responded favorably.

Some of the automated retrievals that replaced manual documentation elements include the VTOC (Figure 4), HIPO (Figure 5), index of programs, index of files, index of tasks, and catalog of systems (Figure 6). The VTOC is somewhat different in format from the original. To allow for an unrestricted number of high level functions, the information is spread down the page instead of across. The informational

---

[*]Midshipman Christian N. Haugen, U.S. Naval Academy; Cadet Edwin O. Heierman, U.S. Air Force Academy; Midshipman Matthew J. McKelvey, U.S. Naval Academy; Midshipman Gard J. Clark, U.S. Naval Academy.

VISUAL TABLE OF CONTENTS
FOR SYSTEM 23
CAPITAL EQUIPMENT BUDGET SYSTEM
(CEBS)
PROCEDURE NO. 10

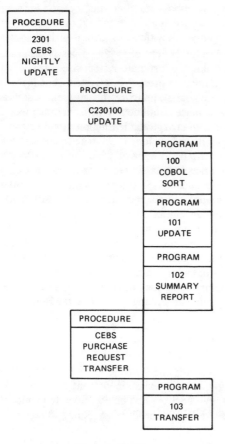

Figure 4—VTOC

HIERARCHICAL INPUT PROCESS OUTPUT
FOR SYSTEM 23
CAPITAL EQUIPMENT BUDGET SYSTEM
BATCH PROCESS NO. 27
PROCEDURE NO. 2301

INPUT FILES	PROGRAM	OUTPUT FILES
• TRANSACTIONS	230501	• FILEA
• FILE A	• EDIT TRANSACTIONS	• REPORT
	• UPDATE FILE A	
	• PRODUCE UPDATE REPORT	
• FILE A	230605	
	• PRODUCE MASTER LIST	• MASTER
• FILE A	230625	• NEW DB
• OLD DB	• PURGE OLD DB	.
	• CREATE NEW DB	.
.	.	.
.	.	
.	.	

Figure 5—HIPO

CATALOG OF SYSTEM,
TASK, PROGRAM, FILE

SYSTEM ID	TASK (PROCEDURE) ID	PROGRAM NAME	FILE(S) USED
23-CEBS	2301	230601 EDIT/UPDATE	FILE A REPORT
		230605 MASTER LIST	FILE A MASTER
		230625 NEW DB	FILEA OLD DB NEW DB
.	.	.	.
.	.	.	.
.	.	.	.

Figure 6—System catalog

elements are retained, however, and both hierarchical and sequencing attributes are preserved. A catalog of systems relates files to programs, programs to tasks, and tasks to systems. In the example in Figure 6, the capital equipment budget system (CEBS) is documented. CEBS is identified as system 23. Task 2301 is a procedure file that executes three programs—230601, 230605, and 230625. Each program is also identified by its generic name. Files appearing as I/O within the programs are documented in the rightmost column. Source data is input to the database using the input screen tools supplied by the database management system (Figure 7). Updates to documentation of the present system are accomplished using the same screens.

FRINGE BENEFITS

SID was devised with the intent of helping programmers to map present and future systems. However, once in place, it provided several other benefits. A matrix describing system identifiers and associated responsible programmers had been

maintained on word processing equipment. A similar matrix detailing application system, organizational section where the functional responsibility for that application resides, and programmers identified in order by level of responsibility (primary responsibility, back-up to primary responsibility, and secondary back-up responsibility) can now be made by a fairly simple merge of relations. The query language commands are collected into an executable procedure so that the matrix can be produced with one operating system level command. The

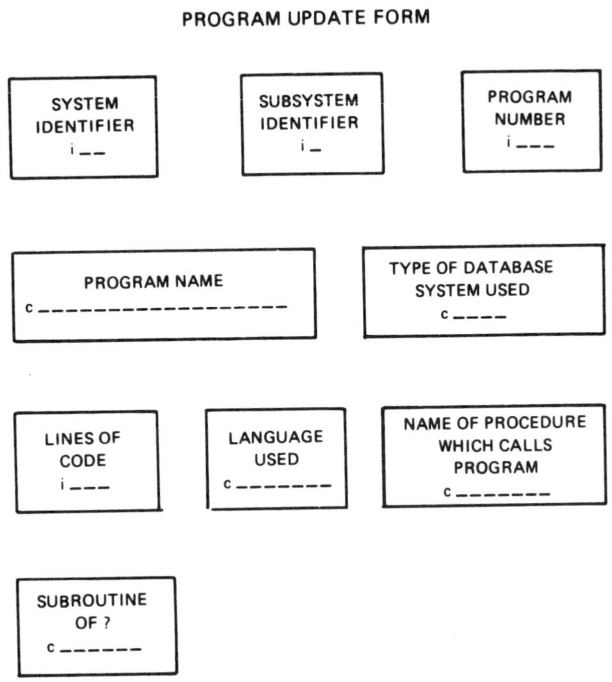

PROGRAM UPDATE FORM

SYSTEM IDENTIFIER
i __

SUBSYSTEM IDENTIFIER
i _

PROGRAM NUMBER
i ___

PROGRAM NAME
c _____

TYPE OF DATABASE SYSTEM USED
c ____

LINES OF CODE
i ___

LANGUAGE USED
c _____

NAME OF PROCEDURE WHICH CALLS PROGRAM
c _____

SUBROUTINE OF ?
c _____

Figure 7—SID data entry screen

member as well as by application system. It is sometimes useful for management to know—by employee—for which systems each employee maintains responsibility, and what constitutes the level of responsibility. Once system responsibility data are captured, it is a simple step to report organizational entity, telephone number, and location for members of staff, either as a complete organizational report or as retrievals for single individuals or groups of individuals.

Another fringe benefit of storing gross system data in one place is the ability to estimate system size. Many installations can list the modules present in a system, but few can report much about actual system size, because expansion and contraction take place continuously with modification. There is an occasional need to give at least approximate-figure answers to questions about how long it will take to convert completely to a new hardware vendor or what the estimate is for converting to a new language version or a different control language. These questions frequently are not just academic; entire installations can change hardware vendors, and it is not unusual for vendors of software to cease support of earlier versions. Approximate figures for lines of code per language, languages per system, programs per system, tasks (operating procedure level commands) per system, and other sums can provide the basis for estimating conversion effort, and therefore, monetary cost. Such queries can be processed easily by the count and sum features of most databases.

word processing files have been deleted and the clerical staff updates employee information as it relates to system responsibility directly on the database. Section leaders (first-line management to whom the responsible programmers report) likewise record responsibility changes directly on the database. Figure 8 is an example of the responsibility matrix. Of course, responsibility information can be retrieved by name of staff

FUTURE ENHANCEMENTS

While the primary intent of the database is to serve the programming staff who maintain present systems and develop new ones, the functions can be expanded to include the operations side of systems production. Run and recovery instruc-

RESPONSIBILITY TABLE

SYSTEM ID	SYSTEM NAME	ORGANIZATIONAL SECTION	PRIMARY	1st BACKUP	2nd BACKUP
12	PAYROLL	EMPLOYEE INFORMATION	HAWKINS	RICH	McCALISTER
20	COMMITMENTS	ACCOUNTING AND OPERATIONS	TOMLINSON	HUDGINS	ARMSTRONG
23	CAPITAL EQUIPMENT	BUDGET AND PLANNING	ROYBAL		HILL
70	GENERAL LEDGER	ACCOUNTING AND OPERATIONS	HUDGINS	OSBORN	
85	PROPERTY MANAGEMENT	MATERIALS	ARMSTRONG		

Figure 8—SID retrieval

tions, file access and permits, account restrictions, job setups, file retentions, expected outputs, and other operations data can be appended to system, task, program, file, or data element relations as appropriate. Operations information is a natural addition because operators and production controllers are also interested in employee system responsibilities and system functional descriptions, which have already been described in the database.

Information about system functions, responsibilities, and operations can form a useful link to controlling resources and measuring activities associated with a system. The level of activity against a system is a guide to future staffing in an organization. Activity in the form of customer requests for service (maintenance, enhancements) on a particular system can be married to the system information database to get a complete picture of current system activity levels. For example, it can be noted that system #98 is general ledger, that task #107 account update executes 12 programs and 7 files (from SID), that the task is executed approximately 30 times per month (from SID), that program #203 aborted seven times last month (from SID with operations data), and that program #203 had five service requests logged against it in the past six weeks (from the resource control or metrics database). Other data, such as the effort required to complete the requests for service on the program and history of the program, can be used in assessing staffing levels for the system as well as for considerations in the program's redesign.

CONCLUDING REMARKS

No database, even a modern relational database, is magic. The organization considering support of a SID must commit to some amount of overhead. As in the case of the automated systems we deliver to our customers, data must be entered, the database tool must be understood, and more likely than not, programs will have to be designed and maintained to perform sophisticated retrievals and to provide links from one database to another.

When SID was developed by ADP at Los Alamos, the prototype was brought up almost entirely by the SARAs, a real tribute to the ease of use of the relational database management system. Yet several programs were required, adding to the overhead of maintenance and documentation for those remaining after the student apprentices have left. Like all systems, data processing's management information systems must be staffed to watch for and prevent system degradation.

REFERENCES

1. Zvegintzov, N. "Nanotrends." *Datamation,* 29, (1983), pp. 105–116.
2. Martin, J., and C. McClure. *Software Maintenance: The Problem and Its Solutions.* Englewood Cliffs, N.J.: Prentice-Hall, 1983. p. 174.
3. Schneider, E. "Structured Software Maintenance." *AFIPS, Proceedings of the National Computer Conference* (Vol. 52), 1983, pp. 137–144.
4. Brown, P. J. "Why Does Software Die?" In G. Parikh and N. Zvegintzov (eds.), *Tutorial on Software Maintenance.* Silver Spring, Md.: IEEE Computer Society Press, 1983.
5. Parikh, G. "Structured Maintenance the Warnier/Orr Way." In G. Parikh and N. Zvegintzov (eds.), *Tutorial on Software Maintenance.* Silver Spring, Md.: IEEE Computer Society Press, 1983.
6. Yourdon, E., and L. L. Constantine. *Structured Design: Fundamentals of a Discipline of Computer Program and Systems Design* (2nd ed.). New York: Yourdon Press, 1978.
7. De Marco, T. *Structured Analysis and System Specification.* New York: Yourdon, 1978.
8. Chapin, N. "New Format for Flowcharts." *Software Practice and Experiences,* 4 (1974), pp. 341–357.
9. Rigo, J. T., and J. R. Rudikoff. "HIPO: Structured System Design Documentation." *Auerbach Information Management Series.* Philadelphia, Pa.: Auerbach Publishers, 1975.
10. Hunter, B. "Documentation—Management Problems and Solutions." *Auerbach Information Management Series.* Philadelphia, Pa.: Auerbach Publishers, 1977.
11. Page-Jones, M. *The Practical Guide to Structured Systems Design.* New York: Yourdon Press, 1980.
12. Yoder, C. M., and M. L. Schrag. "Nassi–Shneiderman Charts—An Alternative to Flowcharts for Design." *Software Engineering Notes of the ACM,* 5 (1978), pp. 79–86.
13. Nassi, I., and B. Shneiderman. "Flowchart Techniques for Structured Programming." *Sigplan Notices of the ACM,* 8 (1973), pp. 12–26.
14. Allen, F. W., M.E.S. Loomis, and M. V. Mannino. "The Integrated Dictionary/Directory System." *ACM Computing Surveys,* 14 (1982), pp. 245–286.
15. Center for Programming Science and Technology. "Functional Specifications for a Federal Information Processing Standard Data Dictionary System." National Bureau of Standards Publication 82-2619, Washington, D.C., 1983.

Redocumentation: Addressing the maintenance legacy

by GARY RICHARDSON and EARL D. HODIL
Texaco Inc.
Houston, Texas

ABSTRACT

Over the past decade or so there has been much attention paid to techniques and methodologies to produce high-quality systems. A concurrent development has been the emergence of software tools that aid in the production and maintenance of software systems; yet the maintenance environment continues to be littered with poorly written and poorly documented programs.

The focus of this paper is to outline a conceptual approach to the allocation of software maintenance resources and the role of automated tools in this process. It is contended that software maintenance tools cannot be simply purchased or built and then used indiscriminately. Rather, it takes an administrative activity to quantitatively decide which code units are best for resource allocation. Finally, to demonstrate the utility of this approach, a case study based on the author's experience is presented.

THE MAINTENANCE LEGACY

Over the past decade or so much attention has been paid to techniques and methodologies to produce high-quality, maintainable systems. Yet DP management still finds itself left with a swelling production library containing a hodgepodge of code that shows little resemblance to what we now define as good.

In the late seventies Dr. Gerry Tompkins of UCLA surveyed 120 DP organizations.[1] This survey found the mean age of installed systems to be nearly five years and the average size of these systems to be approximately 23,000 lines of source code. A review of the typical production library often reveals high levels of poorly written code with inadequate documentation, a statistic that is not surprising when one considers the time-consuming, laborious nature of manually producing high-quality code that is also well documented. This impetus has stimulated the recent proliferation of software maintenance tools.

The author believes that structured code, clear mechanical format, and other such forms of architectural definition are positive when produced at reasonable cost. Studies indicate somewhat conclusively that structured programming can lower maintenance costs. One point, however, is becoming increasingly clear. That is, methodologies and tools in and of themselves will not automatically correct all the errors of the past. Indeed, the new techniques can become costly and ineffectual if they are used randomly. Our challenge here is to describe a rational approach to correcting this maintenance legacy by proper allocation of resources, including a growing set of software tools designed to aid in this process.

PROBLEM DEFINITION

The road to reduced maintenance effort begins with the answers to two questions:

1. Which programs abend most frequently?
2. Which programs, though they may run perfectly, are so poorly written and/or documented that they cannot be easily changed?

The significance of these two questions is considerable when one considers that two of the essential activities associated with software maintenance are correcting program errors and implementing user-requested changes to software. Even though many firms have recognized the need to answer these questions, most large DP shops have found the quest arduous.

Surprisingly, many organizations find the first question difficult to answer. They can neither locate nor statistically quantify their production source code, much less begin to describe quantitatively which code units could be classified as good, average, or poor. This situation must be resolved before subsequent steps, outlined below, can be undertaken. The three administrative systems following can aid in this process.

Library Control

An automated control package to insure that all production source code is located in approved libraries and that production load modules contain only these source modules. Though there are many reasons for installing such a system, its purpose is to bind the execution errors associated with executing a load module to the source code responsible for them.

Operations Logging

A tracking system that traps all production jobs and records completion status (e.g., good completion, space abort, JCL error, bad completion code). This tool should provide execution information at least down to the load module level.

System Profile

A text-oriented system, summarizing basic system metrics such as

1. age,
2. language,
3. total lines of source code,
4. user evaluations of the current system,
5. future enhancement plans at the aggregate level.

By using these three techniques it is possible to identify the target code population accurately, then array the code units according to abort frequency.

Phase 2 of the problem definition activity begins once operational statistics are available regarding code performance. It is then necessary to divide code units into three broad categories:

1. Good Code—low abort frequency
2. Bad Code—high abort frequency
3. Marginal Code—borderline abort frequency

Here we are left with both a philosophical and a technological problem. Philosophically, we may believe that well-written code has a low abort history and vice versa. Alternatively, some believe that abort history is independent of code structure. It is observed that some systems require highly skilled operational support personnel and code modifications; are complex, owing to a lack of a coherent design architecture; yet are stable, judging by abort statistics. It is the authors' opinion that the subject of good versus bad code is multidimensional, involving both mechanical and operational factors. The maintenance function involves both aspects of operation and enhancement; therefore goodness of code must involve more than one view. A second philosophical issue surrounds the idea of documentation value. When one looks at the millennia of existing production code without supporting documentation, some doubt must exist about whether it is of value to be concerned about such things. In attempting to rationalize such behavior there is at least the obvious conclusion that the cost of documentation production outweighs its value. The authors believe that an automated approach to producing documentation improves both software accuracy and cost effectiveness.

Now for the technical problem: It is theoretically possible to quantify abort frequency and arbitrarily divide code units into good, marginal, and bad categories; however, we have already said that this is not enough. There are at least two other code grading technical issues that should be addressed. First, code complexity needs to be evaluated. McCabe[2] and others have defined quantitative measures of code complexity, although once again there is no broad agreement about when a code unit is too complex. Indeed, some productive code requires complexity; and in some cases it is rationally added to the code architecture for efficiency or other reasons. In any case, high-complexity index values could be warnings to review an existing code unit and decide whether it is feasible to simplify it in some way. A third aspect of the technical problem is the architecture of the code unit itself. This is manifested by unstructured or large modules. Within this realm one might attempt to review style, language, structure, size, and existing documentation of the unit in order to supply a qualitative grade. The final aspect of code review requires judgment about whether the code should be a candidate, based on strategic objectives. For example, if an old batch system is being replaced in less than one year with a new online system, then it makes sense not to give that code any extra support. Alternatively, an old system with no upgrade planned would be a candidate. This activity is designed with a view to future evaluation.

We have indicated that in order to effectively allocate maintenance resources it is necessary to quantify where current operational problems now exist through formalized abort history statistics. In addition to this we should provide some type of grading scheme at the code unit level to identify potential modules for which resources can be profitably allocated to repair. It is feasible to use automated tools to do much of the scanning work for items such as size (lines of code), complexity, adherence to code standards, and other related functions. After all the automated statistics are summarized it should be possible to select high-priority targets for closer manual examination. From this aggregation of data it is then necessary to select and rank code units to be given special consideration for rework. Some day this process can be highly automated; however, it currently will involve a high degree of subjective judgment.

THE PURIFICATION PROCESS

We have outlined an analytical process designed to identify systems and code units (i.e., programs) that are candidates for rework. The key question now is, "What do we do with the subset of problem code defined?" Figure 1 shows schematically the process described above. Note that two new items show up at the bottom of the figure, rewrite and redocumentation. Each of these deserves more discussion here. Rewrite represents code units in such shape that manual rearchitecture of the system is required to resolve the indicated problem. Typically this means that new functionality is required or that the basic database design approach is flawed. Obviously placement of code in this category should be done only as a last resort because of inherent cost and time to accomplish.

The second form of code repair is automated redocumentation, which is defined as the software-driven process of producing documentation for existing code directly from the syntax itself. Elshoff and Marcotty from General Motors have documented their company's approach to the use of similar automated techniques to improve code readability and modification.[3] We feel that these tools are most useful when used as an aid to the maintenance programmer who is trying to draw understanding from a block of unyielding (and usually undocumented) source code. These tools may be categorized as follows:

1. Dynamic analyzers
2. Static analyzers
3. Restructure/recoding tools

Dynamic analyzers have long been accepted as a part of the maintenance programmer's workbench. Debugging compilers and interpreters compose this group of tools. Usually, the dynamic analyzer is used in conjunction with test data during an interactive session. Features commonly associated with dynamic analyzers are (1) fast syntax checking, (2) one step

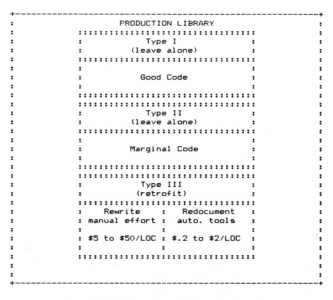

Figure 1—Decision schematic for production code

compile and run, (3) program path tracing, (4) execution suspension and restart, and (5) variable dump and modification.

The difficulty with this method of analysis is that it considers only the paths traveled by the selected test data. Dynamic analysis is, therefore, analysis by trial and error. It is best suited for the investigation of a particular test case or a limited set of test cases, not for gaining an all-path understanding of a program.

Static analyzers are more of a newcomer to the maintenance environment. To be sure, flowcharting programs have existed for some time. Yet the flowcharting program merely provides a rehashed version of program logic in graphic form. In the output of a typical static analyzer, we see the beginnings of an attempt to unravel program logic. Moreover, static analysis can provide useful information regarding program style and complexity.

Yet of all the tools now available to maintenance programming, the *restructuring/recoding tools* are surely the most exciting. They combine the intelligence of the static analyzer with the ability to generate code. Unstructured code (i.e., code with GOTO statements) is the input to this tool. The tool analyzes the unstructured code and produces a structured version. Collectively, this family of tools represents our central focus here.

THE ECONOMICS OF REDOCUMENTATION

We believe that automated redocumentation is the preferred alternative for code repair. For some justification of this let us first look at the resource economics involved in the code repair decisions.

Type I and II code (see Figure 1) represent the code library that is to be essentially left alone. For this segment of the library it is generally possible to allocate resources at the rate of one maintenance programmer per 40,000 to 70,000 lines of source code (independent of the language). This allows for a small amount of enhancement but generally provides for very little extra resources for more than daily operational requirements. Obviously, numerical guidelines such as this need to be validated locally before extensive reliance is placed on them. For the Type III subset, it is a truly complex job to specify an appropriate level of resource allocation. In many DP organizations, the aggregate resources dedicated to the maintenance function can range from almost 90% to as low as 30%. A proper number lies only in management's eyes and is closely tied to a general philosophy of maintenance. We are suggesting that at least 10% of the maintenance library has been neglected. Various studies, reported by Jones[4] at IBM and Hermann[5] at Shell Oil and others, document the development cost of systems at values ranging from $5 to $50 or more per line of code produced. Our experience, however, is that automated documentation can be produced at a cost of between 20¢ and $2.00 per line. This represents a cost ratio of 25:1! In stable database situations the redocumenation strategy is often viable and cost effective. A small allocation of resources can produce dramatic results for properly chosen code units. It is true that even more dramatic improvements can be made through the rewrite process. However, the allocation of resources is concomitantly much higher; and the benefit often occurs much later, after an extended development cycle.

Having now examined how to identify targets for profitable use of redocumentation tools and the economic rationale for using automated redocumentation, let us turn to a case study, drawn from the authors' own experience, to demonstrate the utility of this approach.

A CASE STUDY

Texaco Inc. is typical of many large DP operations and recently faced the problem of rising maintenance costs. There were a large number of diverse applications, each with its own maintenance staff and procedures. Also, like many DP organizations, Texaco had invested a considerable amount of money and staff time in learning to use new design technologies and tools. These efforts notwithstanding, many staff members felt that the level of effort expended on maintenance was still too high, primarily because of the large volume of old, poorly written code that had existed before the new methodologies were implemented.

To quantify the actual maintenance effort, functional applications were manually inventoried. This inventory confirmed the previously held suspicion that approximately half of the professional programming staff worked on maintenance. Because of the increasing backlog of new applications and enhancements to existing systems, and because of the omnipresent goal of holding costs to a minimum, this situation was deemed unacceptable. Early schemes to reduce this effort called for the mass redocumentation of all the production libraries via automated tools. Despite the relative cheapness of these tools, cost-benefit estimates precluded the use of this tactic. Hence it was decided that particular systems and subsystems would be targeted for rewrite or redocumentation.

First, manual methods were used to identify the relevant applications. Two points become apparent as this process was carried out: (1) manual code reviews were too time consuming, and (2) manual records of abends were difficult to organize.

It was decided to expand the use of automated tools to address these problems more effectively. In addition to the previously stated features, an automated library management system was required to improve control of source and load libraries across multiple sites. Having unsuccessfully searched the outside software market for an integrated tool that would meet these requirements, it was decided to create a custom library management system, LIBMAN. LIBMAN is a control system using the services of several existing software tools (SPF, VTAM, PANVALET, ACF2, etc.) to provide control over both the repair and enhancement of production programs. The operational logging system used for the actual identification of problem programs was the MVS Integrated Control System (MICS) from Morino Associates, Inc., which gathers information from diverse sources such as SMF and TSO/MON. This information was then collected on a SAS database from which reports on code unit performance were derived. Finally, profiles were created to assist in the process of describing current systems. Originally a manual effort, this system has now been converted into an online one, using DATAMANAGER as a repository.

After the administrative-level systems were in place and the code universe was well defined, it was possible to identify code that was structurally poor. This subset of the code population became the target code, which would be examined in more depth. Through the process outlined earlier, some of these code units were amenable to automated redocumentation. At this point several automated tools were applied to the selected programs. First, for the COBOL systems an outside product, SCAN/370 from Group Operations, Inc., was selected. SCAN/370 produces a report that traces all the logic paths of a given program. This program also provides a source listing containing imbedded path data, complete with identification of dead code.

Later a restructuring/recoding tool for COBOL source programs became available. This program, called SUPER-STRUCTURE (also by Group Operations, Inc.), creates a *scorecard* that identifies unacceptable program flaws such as (1) interparagraph GOTO statements, (2) run away paths, and (3) fall-through execution of paragraphs. Having created the scorecard and identified the paths of a program, SUPER-STRUCTURE rewrites the program paths using only structured constructs (sequence, iteration, and selection). The resultant source code contains essentially none of the flaws of the original source program.

Most of the company's developmental programming is produced in PL/I. Though the language itself contains elements that may encourage good programming style, a number of older systems were found to abend with regularity and were difficult to modify. A significant review was undertaken to find analyzers and documentors that fit a PL/I development environment. Unfortunately, no vendor-supplied tool was found that would be compatible with the current methodologies, so an in-house tool was developed. The tool, TEXJAX, conducts static analyses of program paths via code scanning and renders several forms of documentation:

1. Complexity measures
2. Jackson style structure charts
3. Module hierarchy charts
4. Annotated source code

The next documentation tool selected was a system redocumentation tool linked to JCL. This tool, DOCU/TEXT from Diversified Software Systems, Inc., was tested on a few selected applications; and it appeared that it could be used on all the JCL libraries. This was in marked contrast to the way the other tools were used, but in this case it seemed to be feasible. Our evaluation is that system-level tools of this type cause one of two events to occur. Either you modify the tool to fit the prevailing customs, or prevailing customs have to change. In this case, the traditional system documentation, manually produced, was so widely used that output from the purchased version of DOCU/TEXT required extensive modification to fit desired formats. Consequently, work is ongoing

to implement a JCL scanning process that will use DOCU/TEXT as a nucleus. Its output will be used to duplicate and replace the current manual run books used by the operations group.

All the tools and techniques outlined in this paper continue to evolve. As with most management-oriented concepts, it is difficult to quantify the relationship of improved productivity to the use of automated tools. We have, however, recorded a decline in resource requirements in the period during which these tools have been installed. Part of this is due to management's increased interest in this subject, as well as improved procedures and tools.

CONCLUSION

There are many disjointed software tools on the market today, and more are emerging daily. Various combinations of these tools will fit unique organizations. We have attempted to outline an approach to the selection of target code units and general types of tools that collectively aid in the maintenance function. A most important conclusion resulting from our experience is that tools cannot be purchased or built and then used indiscriminately. Rather, it takes an administrative activity to identify which code units are best for resource allocation. Then, management has to support these efforts with rational levels of resources designed to "purify" production libraries. Even more pertinently, it requires a high level of management focus to cause the process to occur in an orderly manner. Within the software tools marketplace we anticipate more innovation in the area of automatic restructuring/recoding. It seems inevitable that artificial intelligence (expert systems) may lead the way in this area. One possible way to implement such a scheme would be to create an expert system that is well versed in one of the popular design methodologies (Jackson, Yourdon, etc.), give it access to the path information provided by static analysis tools, then restructure accordingly. Once this can be successfully done, the family of redocumentation tools will become more coherent.

Whatever the case may be, it is probable that tools will continue to play an increasingly visible role in the maintenance of software systems and will require continued management effort to keep them cost effective.

REFERENCES

1. Lientz, B. P., and E. B. Swanson. *Software Maintenance Management.* Reading, Mass.: Addison-Wesley, 1980.
2. McCabe, Thomas J. "A Complexity Measure." *IEEE Transactions on Software Engineering,* SE-2 (1976), pp. 308–320.
3. Elshoff, James L., and Michael Marcotty. "Improving Computer Readability to Aid Modification." *Communications of the ACM,* 25 (1982), pp. 512–521.
4. Jones, T. C. "Measuring Programming Quality and Productivity." *IBM Systems Journal,* 17 (1978), pp. 39–63.
5. Hermann, L. T. "Productivity and Performance Measurement." Paper presented to the American Petroleum Institute (API) Subcommittee on Systems and Programmer Productivity, December 1983, Houston.

MAINTENANCE AND REVERSE ENGINEERING:
LOW-LEVEL DESIGN DOCUMENTS PRODUCTION AND IMPROVEMENT

P.Antonini, P.Benedusi[*] , G.Cantone and A.Cimitile[**]

[*] CRIAI, Localita' Granatello 80055 PORTICI, ITALY, tel(081)482477
[**] DIS, Via Claudio 21, 80125 NAPLES, ITALY, tel(081)7683199

ABSTRACT

Reverse Engineering, Design and implementation of Information Abstractors represent fundamental aspects of a systematic approach to maintenance. It is well known that, at the present state of the art, code analysis cannot guarantee total knowledge of the Design; there is, however, a wide range of possibilities which are still to be covered both on the theoretical and applied levels. This paper deals with the production of Program Low-level Design Knowledge and, in particular, it illustrates a system for the improvement or from scratch production of Jackson or Warnier/Orr documents which are totally consistent with code.   The proposed information abstractor and the related maintenance methodologies have been jointly developed by the DIS ('Dipartimento di Informatica e Sistemistica', University of Naples) and the CRIAI('Consorzio per l'Informatica e l'Automazione Industriale', a trust involved in applied research in information technology and industrial automation); a first application of the information abstractor was carried out in a nationwide software production environment.

Keywords: Maintenance, Reverse Engineering, Information Abstractor, Low-level Design.

1. Introduction.

A practical situation in which software maintainers very often find themselves is that the only available item of a software product is the program code; but even when in addition to this there are products relating to the SLC phases (Software Life Cycle) above those of the coding, the consistency between these and the code is almost always all but non-existent[1,2].

The simple relationship between code and low-level design is in itself emblematic of this situation. Low-level design documents are indispensable for a maintenance operation (both in the phase of comprehension for the software to be maintained, and in the designing and finalization of a maintenance operation). In the absence of these documents the maintainer has to reconstruct them starting from the code.   When these are present, however, simple inspections of the code reveal, in the virtual superimposition of code and design, a situation of the type shown in fig. 1 which is characterized by the presence of 3 areas:

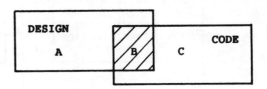

fig.1 Example of virtual overlapping
between code and design of a program

firstly area A, formed of design components that are not present in the code; secondly, an area B of consistency between design and code; and finally, area C, formed of code components which have no equivalent in the design.   Faced by this situation, the maintainers put their trust in walk-through or inspection methodologies which are intended as a manual inspection of code and design documents and their comparison. It is universally acknowledged, however, that these methodologies, even when they are applied to the full and are being continually improved, are inadequate both in terms of quality and costs[7]. It is thus obvious why the maintenance process requires widescale development of research, design and implementation of code analysis software tools if it is to recapture implemented knowledge and, in particular, design knowledge. Hence, the development of reverse engineering and the design and implementation of the information abstractor[11] are crucial factors in this area.   It is well known that, at the current state of the art, code analysis cannot guarantee total knowledge of the design. In the two meaningful papers[3,12], it has been shown that it is impossible to determine "the refinements" from the program code alone:"unrefinements" are only possible with additional knowledge.

In research carried out jointly by CRIAI (Consorzio Campano di Ricerca per l'Informatica e l'Automazione Industriale -a trust involved in applied research in information technology and industrial automation) and DIS (Dipartimento di Informatica e Sistemistica, University of Naples) we have put forward and we are further developing

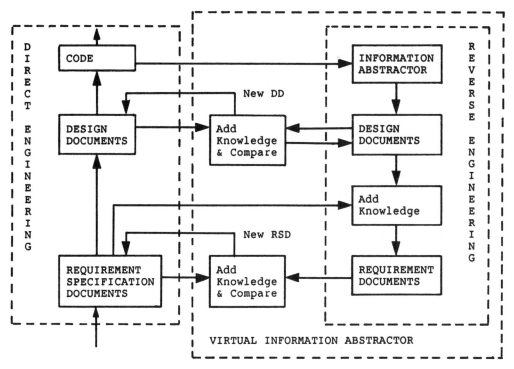

fig. 2 An Information Abstraction process

methodologies and tools based on the scheme shown in fig. 2. The design and implementation of a maintenance operation are typically based on the products of "direct engineering": Code, Design Documents (DD) and Requirement Specification Documents (RSD); the proposed scheme shows the role of reverse engineering in the new DD and RSD production (to help in improvement of the existing ones, to check for completeness and consistency with the code[9], and, finally, for a from scratch production of these documents should there be no existing ones). The information abstractor has a fundamental role to play in that it provides the basis for reverse engineering through automatic code analysis and, in particular, it produces the elementary design elements. With additional knowledge and comparison with any existing DD, the new DD are produced. Further additional knowledge produces a first basis of requirements consistent with the code and the design, while a second operation (additional knowledge) and a comparison with any existing RSD produces the new RSD.

We should now point out that the loop "reverse design documents<-->additional knowledge and comparison" is related to high level design documents production. It is clear that the differences between the virtual information abstractor and a desired information abstractor tool are represented by additional knowledge and comparison: indeed, these require human intervention and can only be supported by simple software aids interactive techniques.

Section 2 gives a list of the main outputs produced by the CRIAI Information Abstractor, and defines two documents in particular (Nesting Tree and Internal Call Graph), that are produced so as to reconstruct the low-level design of a program starting from the source code. Sections 3 and 4 illustrate the rules that allow these IA products to be automatically transformed into Jackson (JSP) and Warnier/Orr (LCP) logical diagrams respectively. Section 5 deals with a program verification and documentation system founded on the IA, which supports both from scratch production and structured maintenance.

2. Low-level Design Document Production.

The first results that were obtained from the CRIAI/DIS joint research concern the production of Low-level Design documents[14]. These were obtained by using a Cobol code information abstractor referring to software products which can be designed as per one of the Jackson[8], Warnier/Orr[13] or PDL[4] methodologies. The process mentioned above is summarized in fig. 3.

At the heart of this process is the information abstractor (IA), which is based on a Static Analyzer and has been implemented and applied to a first block of 1380 programs that were developed by an Italian software company and coded in Cobol.

Most of the IA products were geared to supporting "SLC phase independent" principles and techniques[11]. Some of the IA products are shown in tab. 1; Call graph and Nesting tree are elements

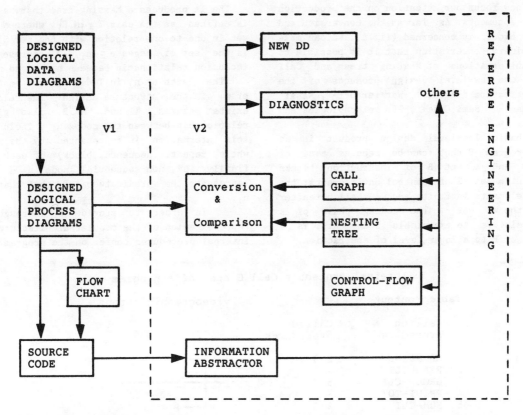

V1 = pre-coding structural verification: control structures versus
                                          data logical structures

V2 = post-coding structural verification: actually implemented versus
                                          designed logical process
                                          structures.

fig.3 Low-level Design Documents production

that are produced by the IA and are used for the reconstruction of new low-level Design Documents (DD). The Control flow graph can also be produced and may be used.

It is to be noted that the IA produced graphs are in themselves important elements for correct maintenance and, in particular, for documentation improvement. Indeed, in the described system and by using the appropriate tools, the graphs are duly represented in videographic form and are used for maintenance operations and white-box post-maintenance testing.

Tab. 1 Some information produced by the COBOL programs information abstractor.

1. Diagnostic documents:
- Signs of unstructuredness
- Violation of coding standards
- Others
2. Low-level Design related documents and information:
- Control flow graph
- Nesting tree
- Internal Procedure Call graph
  (performed procedures)
- Cross references between source
  code instructions, comments
  and Nesting tree
- Others

3. Complexity metrics:
- dimensional metrics: ELOC, decision count, pre-programmed functions count, decision density, function density, comment count, number of nodes in the flow chart and others...;
- structural metrics: structure classes counts (No. of selective, cyclic, serial structures), characteristic polynomial[5], No. of internal procedures, coefficient of structural modularity, percentage of GO TO-free control structures, nesting depth of control structures (maximum, mean), nesting depth of internal procedure calls (maximum and mean perform nesting depth) and others...

Let's now focus our attention on the production of design documents. As far as the conversion and comparison block is concerned (fig.3), we can make the preliminary observation that it is possible to define transformations of Nesting trees and Call graphs in the low-level design products of the Jackson (structure diagrams), Warnier/Orr[10], Nassi-Schneiderman[16], Semi-Code[17], PDL methodologies and vice versa.

The basic low-level design product is an abstract program P that can be seen as a set of predicates and a set B of instruction blocks embedded in a set S of control environments; the type of S elements is finite and we shall hereafter refer to the WR set[15]. The coding phase of a program, relative to executable statements, is a refinement of P to a lower level of abstraction.

The IA produces a Nesting tree that, as in [5,6], is defined as the pair $T \equiv \{N, E\}$, where N is a node set in one-to-one relation with the set $S \cup B$, and E is the set of edges $e \equiv (n_i, n_j)$ representing the inclusion relationship between $n_i \in N$ and $n_j \in N$.

The depth of n_i in T denotes the nesting level of n_i in the structure design. The relation that exists between T and $S \cup B$ also gives the relationship between the nodes $n_{i,k}$ included in n_i; this information is represented by the name n(if, while, repeat, sequence, block) of each node n_i; finally, a non-sequential node $n_i \in S$ also represents the predicate $p \in P$ that characterizes n_i.

In order to provide a thorough overall representation of the modular architecture that the internal procedures confer on the program, the IA

Internal Procedure Call Graph of a program

Table output   videographic output

Calling procedure	Called procedures
1 MAINLINE	2 3 4
2 READ-CLI	–
3 GROUP-CLI	5
4 PRINT-TOT	–
5 SUM-CLI	2

```
        ┌─────2*
1───────┼──3───5───2*
        └─────4
```

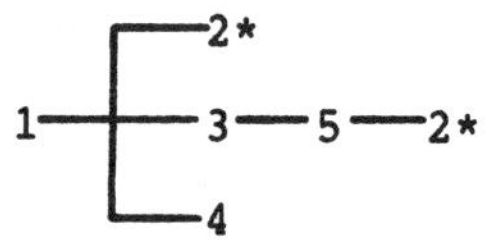

The procedures marked by an '*' are shared "utilities".
Procedure names are paragraph or section names referred to by PERFORM instructions (except for MAINLINE);
procedures are numbered according to the order in which their calling instructions appear in the source code.

Nesting Tree of a program unit

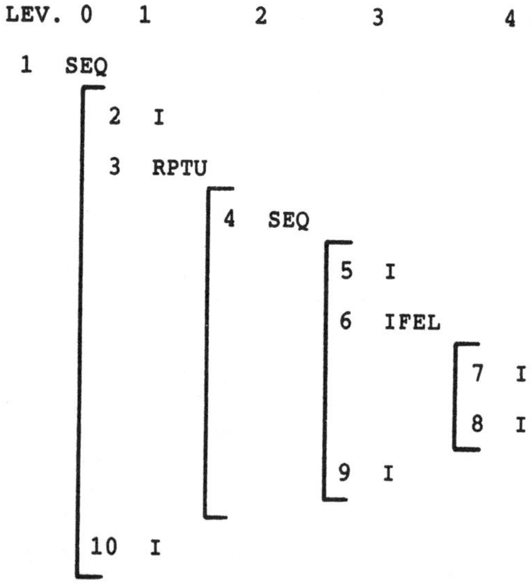

```
LEV. 0      1        2        3        4

 1  SEQ
   ┌ 2  I
   │ 3  RPTU
   │    ┌ 4  SEQ
   │    │    ┌ 5  I
   │    │    │ 6  IFEL
   │    │    │    ┌ 7  I
   │    │    │    └ 8  I
   │    │    └ 9  I
   │    └
   └ 10  I
```

fig.4

generates the Internal Procedure Call graph, in which:
- a node represents an internal procedure, also including the main program;
- an edge between nodes I and J represents the existence in I of one or more instructions that directly call J.

A node with input-degree D>1 represents a "utility" internal procedure called by D different procedures (viz. fig.4).

If we analyze a COBOL program, the IA constructs, for each J unit called by PERFORM, both a C_j node in the call graph and a Nesting sub-tree N_j, and furthermore creates suitable references in the Nesting trees of all the other calling units; for example, a "PERFORM P2" instruction within the P1 procedure is represented by a leaf node l_1 in the nesting tree N(P1), giving l_1 of an attribute which sends straight on to the N(P2) Nesting sub-tree. It is possible to use these cross references between Nesting sub-trees to reconstruct the overall program Nesting, by substituting the called sub-tree in place of the calling nodes.

A simple example of a videographic Nesting tree and Internal Procedure Call graph produced by the IA are given in fig. 4.

We would now like to illustrate the transformation of these graphs into the new DD documents for Jackson and Warnier/Orr Methodologies.

3. Jackson's logic diagrams and Nesting tree.

In the Jackson program development method, the structure diagrams, used for both program and data structures, are formed of 4 types of components: elementary components (which are no further dissected) and the structured components Sequence, Iteration and Selection. As can be seen from fig.5, the elementary components (blocks) correspond to Nesting elementary nodes (type I), while the Sequence and Iteration structures correspond to structure nodes type SEQ and WHDO respectively; the selection structure corresponds to the structure nodes IFTE, IFEL and CASE, according to the number of alternative components. It is possible to see the strong resemblance between Nesting and "schematic logic", the verbal notation used by Jackson[8] for program structures. For documentation purposes the names of the corresponding elements are shown as comments in square brackets in the Nesting tree.

The structural correspondences given in fig. 5 have the function of conversion rules which can be applied either in one direction or in the other.

Fig. 6 gives an example of conversion from Nesting tree into Jackson's diagram and vice versa for an entire program.

4. The Warnier/Orr method and the Nesting tree.

The detailed design of a program as per the Warnier/Orr methodology[13] is based on the following hierarchical diagrams: LOS (Logical Output Structure), LIS (Logical Input Structure) and LPS (Logical Process Structure); the latter is derived from LOS and LIS by applying the rules supplied by Warnier.

The method also allows for Processing Phase Diagrams, when necessary, to process data which is not contained in LIS but which is obtained through one or more intermediate LIS elaboration phases.

In LPS the program is presented as a set of data processing operations, which is sub-divided into a hierarchy of sub-sets with different levels of detail (see fig. 7) and in the form of a tree.

Every set is distinguished by a mnemonic name and a repetition factor.

The elementary sets, which are no further dissected, are the leaves of the tree and correspond to Source Code instruction blocks.

The rules for the ordering of instructions require that every decisional instruction be placed at the end of the block in which it appears.

The control structures allowed in LPS are Sequence, Alternative and Repetition: the latter is always a Repeat-Until, in that Warnier also prescribes the realization of While-Do by means of If-then + Repeat-Until.

The control structures represented in the Nesting tree do not appear explicitly in LPS but they can be easily obtained from the latter by allowing a 2-phase procedure:
1) Splitting of the elementary LPS sets containing decisional instructions so as to isolate every decisional instruction from those preceding it. The following, in particular, contain decisional instructions:
- the block immediately preceding a pair of alternative sets
- the last block in a repetitive set.
2) Aggregation of the decisional instruction to the structure-instructions it controls, as per the rules laid down in fig. 8.

The procedure can be applied backwards to reconstruct the LPS components starting from the corresponding Nesting tree components. Fig. 7 shows a comparison between LPS and Nesting tree from the same program; for purposes of documentation, the usual mnemonic names have been attributed to the sets and nodes which correspond with each other.

As can be seen, every alternative or repetition of set in LPS entails the introduction of a further level of detail in the Nesting tree as a result of the revealing of the structure nodes.

By recursively applying the provided rules to every logic structure it is possible to convert the LPS of an entire program into Nesting tree and vice versa.

1) SEQUENCE

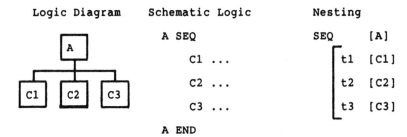

t_i denotes the type of node corresponding to the component C_i; it can be either I, WHDO, CASE, IFTE, IFEL, etc., except for the case C1=C2=C3=SEQ.

2) ITERATION

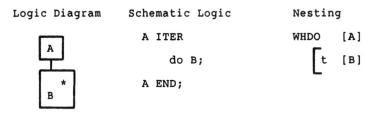

The symbol '*' means '0 or more times'; 't' is the type of B; the conditional instruction is contained in the structure-node WHDO.

3) SELECTION

a. IF-THEN-ELSE

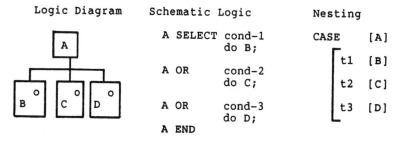

The symbol 'o' means '0 or 1 times'; the selection predicate is contained in the structure-node IFEL or CASE.

b. CASE-OF

fig.5 Jackson's logic diagrams and Nesting Tree

If the program contains PERFORMed procedures, each of these must be supplied with a sub-LPS to which will correspond a Nesting sub-tree, before the coding.

The "straight line" elementary procedures containing neither branch nor PERFORM instructions are an exception to this rule; for these procedures the sub-LPS is reduced to a single non-sublevelled

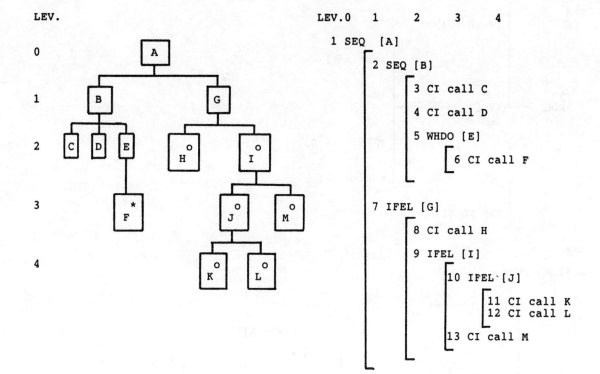

LEV.

LEV.0   1   2   3   4

1 SEQ [A]

    2 SEQ [B]

        3 CI call C

        4 CI call D

        5 WHDO [E]

            6 CI call F

    7 IFEL [G]

        8 CI call H

        9 IFEL [I]

            10 IFEL [J]

                11 CI call K
                12 CI call L

            13 CI call M

Blocks C,D,F,K,L,M are PERFORMED procedures; procedures that have
an internal structure are documented by their distinct sub-diagrams,
each one corresponding to a distinct Nesting sub-tree.

fig. 6 Jackson's diagram and Nesting Tree of a program

elementary set which is represented by an Instruction node (type I) in the Nesting tree.

The conversion rules have been studied so as not to entail the restructuring of the program: i.e., it is not necessary to apply Boehm-Jacopini's theorem to represent an LPS decisional structure through combinations of different types of structures in the Nesting tree.

It is most important to underline this requisite, as otherwise 2 types of inconvenience would be met:
a) the Nesting tree obtained from design LPS might contain decisional nodes representing control instructions which do not exist in the code;
b) the Nesting tree obtained from the source code, once it has been reconverted into LPS, might lead to LPS alternatives which do not correspond to predicates that are actually present in the code.

If a program is designed as per Warnier/Orr, its LPS diagram can always be converted into Nesting tree without the need for restructuring.

The opposite conversion is always possible without restructuring only if the source program both respects the structured programming rules and does not directly codify While-Do structures (e.g. PERFORM..UNTIL) nor Case-Of (e.g. GO TO..DEPENDING ON), in that these are not allowed in LPS.

This hypotesis is reasonable if it is necessary

to verify a code developed by programmers trained in the method and determined to follow it.

In maintenance, however, it is highly probable that one will find programs which, although they are "structured", have been developed and/or maintained without sticking rigorously to the Warnier method. In this case it is still possible to reconstruct a Warnier-like diagram by allowing the notations "(0,N)" in LPS to represent the While-Do structures and multiple alternatives "(+)" for the Case-Of structures.

5. Conclusive remarks for application in structured development and maintenance

Fig. 3 showed the scheme for a verification and documentation system which is applicable both in the development of new programs and in the maintenance of existing programs.

As has been said, the logic diagrams produced in the design phase can be Jackson or Warnier/Orr; according to the method used, the appropriate conversion rules will be chosen from Nesting tree to a Process Logic diagram.

In the passage from design to code, the Warnier/Orr method includes the drawing of the flow chart to which the control graph obtained from the Information Abstractor corresponds: the flow chart is not actually essential in that it is possible to

211

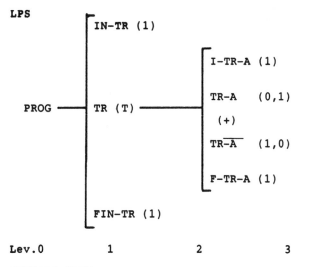

LPS

NESTING TREE

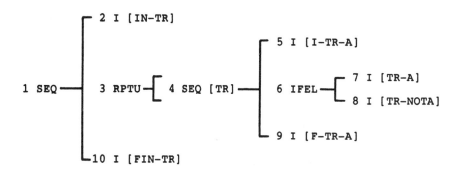

fig. 7   Comparison between Warnier's LPS and Nesting Tree of a program.

pass straight from LPS to Instruction list and pseudocode.

In the case of Warnier/Orr method, we have:
- LOS, LIS, LPS = Designed Logical Structures for Output, Input and Process respectively.
- NEST = actually implemented Nesting tree (from source code)
- NEW-LPS = actually implemented LPS
- ICG = actually implemented Internal Procedure Call Graph (The phase diagrams have been omitted so as not to complicate the scheme in fig. 3).

The Warnier/Orr method does not explicitly include a document similar to the ICG, and so it supplies useful supplementary documentation that is generated automatically.

The V2 verification tool in fig. 3 is currently being implemented and includes:
- a module for the acquisition of LPS from a videoterminal in the form of symbolic expression
- a module for conversion from LPS->Nesting tree and from Nesting tree->LPS.
- a module for comparison between LPS and NEW-LPS, which gives diagnoses.
- a documentation module which produces LPS in graphic form.

The realization of the Information Abstractor has already been achieved.

The comparison module operates by following the criteria:
a) structural identity and b) expansion of structures which are identical up to a certain detail level[9].

In the development of a new program, the verification of structural congruency between design and code is developed in the following steps:
1 - generation of NEST and ICG
2 - Conversion NEST->NEW-LPS
3 - Comparison NEW-LPS/LPS.

In maintenance, every operation on a program entails the following steps:
1 - Analysis of the existing code BEFORE modification, to obtain NEST1 and the corresponding NEW-LPS1 through conversion.
2 - If complete program documentation is not available, and, in particular, if LPS1 is missing, assume as documentation before operation

LPS1=NEW-LPS1

1) Alternative structure.

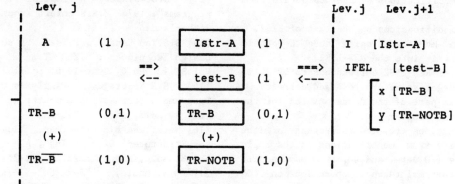

TR-B and TR-NOTB can be either elementary or subdivided into sub-sets, so the corresponding node types can be respectively x=I or x=SEQ , y=I or y=SEQ.

2) Repetition of an elementary set.

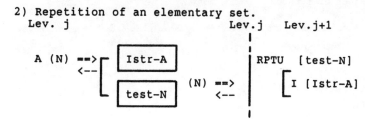

3) Repetition of a non-elementary set.

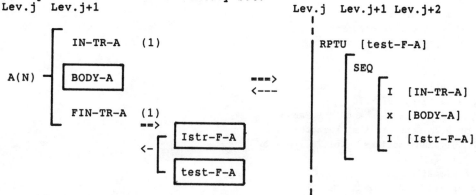

BODY-A must contain al least one repetitive or one alternative structure, so x=RPTU or x=IFEL or x is a sub-sequence of structures.
If x=IFEL, rule n.1 is applied to the sub-sequence (IN-TR-A,BODY-A).

4) Subdivision of a non-repetitive set.

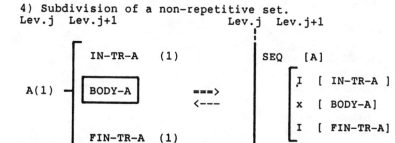

fig.8 Warnier's LPS diagram and Nesting Tree: conversion rules
LPS==> Nesting; Nesting-->LPS.

3 - Design the modifications on LPS1 to obtain from this LPS2.

4 - Codify the modifications on the base of LPS2.

5 - Analyze the modified program code to obtain NEST2 and convert it into the NEW-LPS2.

6 - Check that the NEW-LPS2 corresponds to LPS2, if the outcome is negative return to 4 and correct.

7 - Save LPS2 as part of the documentation for the new version of the program.

The modifications to the structure of the program can arise from modifications in the logic structure of the I/O data, and, so, they may require the design of the maintenance operation on LOS and/or LIS; the scheme in fig. 3 also allows for the verification step V1 between LPS2 and the pair (LOS2, LIS2).

The automation of V1 is the subject of future research.

References

[1] G.Arango, I.Baxter, P.Freeman and C.Pidgeon "TMM: Software Maintenance by Transformation" IEEE on Software, Vol. 3 No. 3, May 1986 pp.27-39.

[2] B.W.Boehm, "Verifying and Validating Software requirements and Design Specification", IEEE on Software, Jan 84 pp. 75-86.

[3] J.M.Boyle and M.N.Muralidharan, "Program Reusability through Program Transformation", IEEE Trans. on Soft. Eng., Vol. SE-10, No.5, September 1984 pp.574-588

[4] S.H.Caine and E.K.Gordon,"PDL: a Tool for Software Design", AFIPS Proc. 1975 Nat.Comput. Conf., vol 44, May 1975, pp. 271-276

[5] G.Cantone, A.Cimitile and L.Sansone, "Complexity in program schemes: the Characteristic Polinomial", ACM Sigplan Notices, Vol.18, March 1983, pp. 22-31.

[6] G.Cantone, A.Cimitile and P.Maresca, "A New methodological proposal for program Maintenance", The Euromicro Journal, Vol.18, Nos 1-5, 1986 pp.319-322.

[7] M.E.Fagan, "Advances in Software Inspection", IEEE Trans. on Soft. Eng., Vol. SE-12, No.7, July 1986, pp.744-751.

[8] M.A.Jackson, "Principles of Program Design", Academic Press 1975, London.

[9] Z.L.Lichtman, "Generation and Consistency checking of Design and Program Structures", IEEE Trans. on Soft. Eng., Vol. SE-12, No.1, January 1986, pp. 172-181.

[10] G.Parikh, "Structured Maintenance:the Warnier/Orr way", Computerworld Sept. 21, 1981, IN DEPTH Section.

[11] C.V.Ramamoorty, V.Garg and A.Prakash, "Programming in the large", IEEE Trans.on Soft. Eng., Vol SE-12, No 7, July 1986, pp. 769-783.

[12] H.M.Sneed, "Software Renewal: A Case Study", IEEE on Software, Vol.1,No.3, July 1984, pp.56-63.

[13] J.D.Warnier, "Logical Construction of programs", 1974 H.E.Stenfert Kroese, B.V. Leiden, Netherlands

[14] S.S.Yau and J.J.P.Tsai, "A survey of Software Design Techniques", IEEE Trans. on Soft. Eng., Vol.SE-12, No.6, June 1986, pp.713-721.

[15] S.R.Kosaraju, "Analysis of Structured Programs", Journal of Computer and System Science, Vol. 9. No.3, 1975 pp.232-255

[16] Nassi and B.Shneiderman, "Flowchart Techniques for Structured Programming", ACM SIGPLAN Notices, Vol.8, No.8, August 1973, pp.12-26.

[17] N.Chapin, "Semi-Code in Design and Maintenance", Computers and People, Vol.27, No.6, June 1978, pp.2-12.

Part 4: Case Studies

In a country as big as the United States, you can find fifty examples of anything.

Jeffrey F. Chamberlain

Can software for the Strategic Defense Initiative ever be error-free?

Reprinted from *IEEE Computer*, Volume 21, Number 11, November 1988, pages 61-67. Copyright ©1988 by The Institute of Electrical and Electronics Engineers, Inc. All rights reserved.

Ware Myers, Contributing Editor

The degree of success of the President's initiative depends heavily on the extent to which its battle management software can be made reliable.

To destroy enemy missiles in their boost phase, in space during their midcourse period, or in the air during their terminal phase will require a worldwide system of sensors, weapons platforms, and communications. Early estimates indicate that the command, control, and communications system binding all these elements together will be based upon the most massive software project ever attempted.

"Because of the extreme demands on the system and our inability to test it [under conditions of operational use], we will never be able to believe, with any confidence, that we have succeeded," asserted David L. Parnas, when he resigned from the SDI Organization's Panel on Computing in Support of Battle Management June 28, 1985. According to Parnas, professor of computer science at the University of Victoria in British Columbia, "Nuclear weapons will remain a potent threat."[1]

"It is much too soon for gloom," countered Frederick P. Brooks, author of *The Mythical Man-Month* and professor of computer science at the University of North Carolina, in an appearance before a congressional committee.[2] "I see no reason why I or any other competent, experienced, better software manager than I am—and there are a lot of them—could not undertake to build such a system."

The House Appropriations Committee, considering funds for SDI, noted that "sizable problems exist in designing and testing software programs for an SDI system."[3] The committee presented nine questions on this theme to the SDI Organization, or SDIO. In his reply Lt. Gen. James A. Abrahamson, USAF, SDIO Director, admitted that no complex system ever built has achieved "perfection."[4] However, many systems—for such critical areas as space operations, military and commercial flying, air traffic control, communications, banking, and medicine—have been "correct" in the sense that the systems were "effective" or "reliable," he added (his emphasis).

In December 1985 the panel from which Parnas resigned concluded that the "computing resources and battle management software for a strategic defense system are within the capabilities of the hardware and software technologies that could be developed within the next several years."[5]

So, there are differences of interpretation and of opinion. One factor the debate has brought out, however, is the critical position of the software in the strategic defense effort. In the panel's judgment, "the anticipated complexity of the battle management software and the necessity to test, simulate, modify, and evolve the system make battle management and command, control, and communication (BM,C3) the paramount strategic defense problem.''

The larger question before us, as Brooks put it in a panel session at the Eighth International Conference on Software Engineering in London on August 30, 1985, is "How good is good enough?''

The problem of "good enough" is that in an exchange of nuclear missiles, if we take 99.9 percent as an effective performance and if 10,000 weapons were directed at us, about 10 nuclear bombs would get through. Of course, that is not a pleasant prospect.

Errors in the software, however, are not identical to leaks in the shield. A software error, for example, may result only in a misplaced element on a readout display. It would be more serious if the system assigned two weapons against one threat when it should have assigned one, Brooks told the Senate committee, but "that is not the kind of thing that one would lose sleep over.''

More serious still would be an error leading to the failure to destroy a target during the boost phase. Still, correct software in later tiers of the system might take out that target. Yet that is a significant error if it leads to overloading the subsequent tiers. The worry is that a few thousand errors in the deployed software would lead to a few hundred significant failures that might finally result in 10 leaks.

The problem of errors

The raw cost of such a system [referring to the SDI software] is therefore less important than the feasibility and methods of finding and correcting errors in it.

—Harold Brown, Secretary of Defense, 1977-81[6]

Errors in large, complex software systems are created in the process of formulating requirements, writing specifications, designing software, and writing code. They are removed by self-checking, walkthroughs, inspections, design reviews, module testing, and integration testing. More errors are created in the course of the reprogramming required to remove earlier errors. Software goes into operational use with some errors remaining. They are gradually discovered when the system malfunctions, and are then corrected, introducing still more errors.

Furthermore, the first release of a large, complex system normally does not exactly satisfy the problems it was created to solve. It must be modified to achieve a

better fit to its problem set, and in the process of modification more errors are created and only some of them are fixed. Next it turns out that the problems themselves are changing, leading to the enhancement of the software. In this process, we are no longer surprised to find out, errors are created and again only some of them are fixed. But always some number of errors, perhaps fairly small, remains to be found when they turn up under some unusual combination of operating circumstances. A system user can never be certain that all of the errors have been found and fixed.

Numbers of errors. The number of errors created is not insignificant. In several studies errors were found to range from 30 to 85 per thousand delivered source instructions.[7]

The variation in the number of errors created depends upon the type of software, the size of the system, the definition of the term "error," the different procedures organizations have for collecting errors, and other factors. For our present purpose the point is there are a lot of errors.

Fortunately, most of them are found and fixed in the course of development and testing, before release. For example, according to Dennis W. Fife of the National Bureau of Standards, delivered software for large systems typically has errors at a rate of one in every 300 program statements, or 3.3 per thousand.

A two-million line system developed and maintained by Bell Communications Research has experienced a range of 0.8 to 1.3 field defects per thousand lines of new and changed source code on three releases per year over a recent four-year period.[8] A Bell Laboratories survey of software faults found that errors typically range from 0.5 to 3.0 occurrences per 1000 lines of program, according to T. R. Thomsen, president of AT&T Technology Systems.[9]

System size. Exacerbating the error problem in the case of a massive system such as SDI is the fact that the number of errors introduced per thousand lines of code increases exponentially with the size of the software system.[10] This finding was based on an analysis of error data from past software projects, but it is also consonant with common sense. One expects proportionately fewer errors in a small, intellectually manageable program than in a large, complex one.

The quantity of software needed by SDI was termed "very large" (order of 10

million lines of code) by the Defensive Technologies Study Team (Fletcher panel) appointed by the Secretary of Defense in 1983 to investigate the feasibility of the SDI concept.[11] Of course, this estimate is little more than a guess as there was no system design at the time it was made. Other guesses have ranged upward to 30 million lines and even 100 million lines. If the low error rate, 0.5 errors per thousand lines, cited by Thomsen is applied to the low estimate, 10 million lines, SDI would contain about 5000 errors at the time it became operational, or even more, allowing for an exponential increase in the quantity of errors.

Bell Laboratories' experience with the only previous large-scale anti-ballistic missile system, Safeguard, suggests that it succeeded in bettering this error rate. The system, developed between 1969 and 1975, consisted of 2,261,000 assembly-language instructions of which 789,000 were real-time software. Approximately 5000 software design problems serious enough to affect "the primary performance objective of the system" were identified and corrected prior to the activation of the system.[12] As an indication of the effort error detection and correction takes, code and unit testing and integration testing of the real-time software consumed 60 percent of the staff resources devoted to this portion of the project.

Following deployment of the system around the Minuteman silos in North Dakota in 1975 a set of demonstration tests at the site revealed only one further serious error. Whether additional errors would have been revealed by long-term operational use cannot be known because the system was decommissioned in 1976, apparently because an opponent could have easily overwhelmed it by increasing the number of attacking missiles beyond its defensive capabilities.

Safeguard was a terminal phase anti-ballistic missile defense system and it was limited by the ABM treaty of 1972 to only 100 interceptors. Consequently, it was much smaller than the SDI system, which will operate over three tiers—boost phase, midcourse, and terminal—and will presumably be capable of coping with some thousands of intercontinental ballistic missiles. Hence it seems reasonable to assume that the SDI software will be many times larger than the Safeguard software and the effort to remove errors will need to be much greater.

Why software is unreliable

I am not a modest man. I believe that I have as sound and broad an understanding of the problems of software engineering as anyone that I know. If you gave me the job of building the system, and all the resources that I wanted, I could not do it. I don't expect the next 20 years of research to change that fact.

— David L. Parnas

Conventional software development methods—the methods in wide use in both industry and the military—are not adequate for building large real-time software systems that must be reliable when first used, Parnas asserted. The conventional method begins with the programmer trying to "think like a computer." It works well on small problems that do not lead into extensive branching and looping.

"As soon as our thinking reaches a point where the action of the computer must depend on conditions that are not known until the program is running, we must deviate from the method by labeling one or more of the actions and remembering how we would get there." Parnas explained.[1] "As soon as we introduce loops into the program, there are many ways of getting to some of the points and we must remember all of those ways. As we progress through the algorithm, we recognize the need for information about earlier events and add variables to our data structure. We now have to start remembering what data mean and under what circumstances data are meaningful.

"As we continue in our attempt to 'think like a computer,' the amount we have to remember grows and grows. The simple rules defining how we got to certain points in a program become more

Attaining 99.9 percent reliability

The number of errors created and later found and fixed has been modeled as a Rayleigh curve.[1] (See Figure A.) The y axis represents errors per month and the x axis, time in months. This curve was projected on the basis of a real-time command and control system of 1 million lines of source code, intended to be roughly representative of one of the subsystems of SDI.

The vertical lines indicate milestones during development and operation:

(1) Preliminary design review,
(2) Critical design review,
(3) First code complete,
(4) System integration test,
(5) User-oriented system test,
(6) Initial operational capability,
(7) Full operational capability (95 percent reliability level),
(8) 99 percent reliability level, and
(9) 99.9 percent reliability level.

For a system of this size and complexity, reaching the 95 percent reliability level, meaning that 95 percent of the errors have been removed, takes about five years. Then about 2.5 years of operation and maintenance are required to reach the 99.9 percent reliability level.

If the other SDI subsystems are independent of this one and of each other, they could be done in parallel, but some additional time would be needed to integrate all of them. If the systems are not completely independent, some of the development would have to be done in serial, perhaps stretching the time to reach 99.9 percent reliability out to 10 years or more.

The cumulative errors out to full operational capability (95 percent reliability) number 6022, and out to 99.9 percent reliability, 6333 (Figure B). At full operational capability 316 errors remain to be found and even at the 99.9 percent point, six errors probably remain. If the entire SDI software system is about 10 times this size, the total number of errors would be in the vicinity of 60,000 and about 60 errors would remain at the 99.9 percent point.

The computation of this error-rate curve is based upon past error data from a limited number of systems. Moreover, the data was not always uniformly defined. Consequently, we do not claim a high degree of accuracy for the projection. Rather the curve is illustrative of the way in which errors are created and removed until finally 99.9 percent of them have been found and fixed.

References

1. Lawrence H. Putnam, Douglas T. Putnam, and Lauren P. Thayer, "Quality in Software is Free (Almost)," *Proc. Int'l Soc. Parametric Analysts*, Seventh Ann. Conf., May 1985, 37 pp.

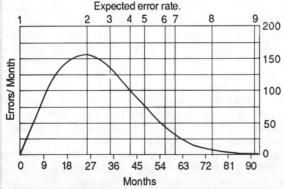

Figure A. Expected error rate. Percent reliability: 7 = 95; 8 = 99; and 9 = 99.9.

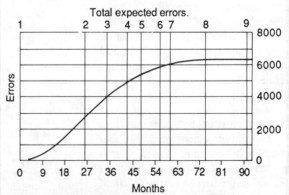

Figure B. Total expected errors. Percent reliability: 7 = 95; 8 = 99; and 9 = 99.9.

complex as we branch there from other points," he continued. "The simple rules defining what the data mean become more complex as we find other uses for existing variables and add new variables. Eventually, we make an error."

In a system such as SDI there will be two further sources of complications, concurrency and multiprocessing, to add to the programmer's thinking load, Parnas pointed out. He concluded that "writing and understanding very large real-time programs by 'thinking like a computer' will be beyond our intellectual capabilities."

SDI especially difficult. All large, complex software systems are very difficult to build, but SDI software has added elements of difficulty, Parnas said at Compcon Spring last March. First, its algorithms must be matched to assumptions about the enemy's target and decoy characteristics. We can never be sure that we have got our algorithms right, because the opponent controls these characteristics and can change them from time to time.

Second, the opponent can arrange to overload the system. To meet strict real-time deadlines, the SDI programs would have to have built-in schedules, computed in advance. These schedules would have to be based upon prior assumptions about the nature of the attack. If the enemy changes that nature, perhaps by directing an unexpectedly large number of missiles at one sector, he could overload those computers, causing them to hang up completely or at a minimum to be incapable of tracking and targeting some share of the missiles.

Third, putting computers and communication links in space is unusually expensive, Parnas noted. Moreover, they are unusually vulnerable. This difficulty is compounded by the need to have redundant elements to enhance reliability and a sufficient number of units to overcome countermeasures. "High reliability can be achieved only if failures of individual components are statistically independent," he added. "For a system subject to coordinated attacks, that is not true."

Product verification. Noting that there are, nevertheless, large programs that work reliably enough to be used, Parnas explained this apparent anomaly by reference to the trial-and-error nature of programming. Programs are not designed to be error-free; they are tested into some degree of reliability and that degree is later enhanced by removing errors during operational use.

Engineers make products reliable by a combination of mathematical analysis, exhaustive case analysis, or prolonged testing, Parnas said. These methods fall short in the case of software. The tools for mathematical analysis work best on continuous functions, he explained. Software is a discrete-state system that cannot be described by these functions.

Another analytical approach is to prove a program, but "the best tools for mathematical verification of software only work on small programs and make approximations that can hide serious errors." Parnas does not expect major improvements in these tools in the SDI time frame.

Our job is to reduce the errors.

What makes the SDI software complex is that it deals with a very large networked real-time, time-critical application whose "threat" environment can only be guessed. Estimates of its size range from 10 million to 30 million lines of executable source code. Most other systems that work in a distributed real-time environment like SDI are very much smaller—under a million lines of code. Only a few systems so far are larger than that. For example, the safety and control system of a nuclear reactor is about one million lines, as is AT&T's No. 5 Electronic Switching System. The Safeguard antiballistic missile software was over two million lines. We simply do not have much experience with systems in the range of millions of lines of code.

In addition to the control software, the sizes of the databases on which such systems work are huge, varying from 10 million bytes to several trillion bytes. Moreover, effective development of such a system requires a software support system (tools, analyzers, dynamic simulators, etc.).

The Fletcher report, the 1983 presidential study that laid the groundwork for the Strategic Defense Initiative, estimates that the system should be capable of 100 million operations per second. It should be reliable enough to survive autonomously for at least 10 years without massive failures. It should have a mean time between failures or crashes of two years.

Hardware reliability. Wing Toy of AT&T Bell Laboratories has shown (in a soon-to-be-published paper) that a reconfigurable triple modular redundant 321 (TMR 321) system—a system with three active processors, two of which can fail without impairing functionality—has a mean time to failure of 208 years. The TMR 321 system has three processors that perform the same computation. If one processor fails (detected by its disagreement with the others), it is taken out of the system for repair. If then one of the two active processors fails, the good processor continues to compute with extensive self-checking. His projection is based on a failure rate per module of less than 10^{-4} (roughly one failure per year), a repair rate per module of 0.125 (roughly eight hours per repair), and a probability of zero for expected recovery from any fault. These figures imply that hardware of this sort is reliable enough for the SDI mission.

Performance. The 100 million operations per second recommended by the Fletcher report could be met by supercomputers like the Cray X-MP. However, this capability is now available only for a ground-based environment. Moreover, space-borne computers generally run one order of magnitude slower than ground-based computers because of environmental considerations. To sustain the required performance, we have to use either multiple computers, running at a slower rate, or we have to design much faster machines, which advances in hardware technology will make possible.

Communications degradation. Before engagement, with communications lines clear, the network would have a high communications bandwidth on the order of 10 million bits per second, according to the estimate of the Fletcher report. Allowing for redundancy to offset noise and enhance security, this bandwidth might be reduced by several orders of magnitude. Then during battle this bandwidth might shrink still further—perhaps to zero—meaning the failure of communications between different entities of the distributed system.

In effect, the SDI network would move from a highly cooperative complex before battle to a loosely coupled data-sharing network early in the engage-

Product verification by exhaustive case analysis is feasible only when the number of cases is small or the product has a highly repetitive structure, he went on. "Software has a huge number of states and no regularity."

Thorough testing is not possible because a large, complex software system has too many input conditions and goes through too many internal states, he said.

Less critical systems than SDI seem to go into operational use at about the 95 percent reliability level, that is, 5 percent of the total errors still remain.[10] The remaining errors are worked out during a "maintenance" phase that may last for months or years.

Presumably SDI would be deployed with some remaining errors and some of them would be found and fixed in the course of in-line, or simulated, operational testing. Unfortunately, full operational use involves a nuclear exchange. "We can't fix it after it fails for the first time," Parnas told the Compcon audience, "because we are all going to be thinking about other things if we are thinking at all."

---

ment, and ultimately perhaps to a set of autonomous nodes, each with sufficient computing power to carry out its functions in isolation from the network. The software capable of reconfiguring the system as it moves through this sequence could be extremely complex, but there is a good prospect for success through research and advances in technology.

Software errors. Studies of the errors experienced in large real-time systems reveal that about 80 percent result from two major sources: requirements and design errors, and a combination of unknown causes and operator errors.

The first category generally results from the failure to state the system requirements explicitly—ambiguity, incompleteness, faulty assumptions, etc. Also, since these large systems take many years to develop, constant changes in the application, the requirements, and the technology take place. These changes create auxiliary changes, leading to the ripple effect and possibly culminating in additional errors.

Unanticipated failures can occur if the problem environment is not fully understood. These difficulties can be overcome by new techniques like rapid prototyping—where the customer can "see" the behavior of the system before it is fully implemented—or by customer participation in the development of the system.

In the SDI application, while we cannot always predict the exact nature of the battle action, we can at least reduce the number of unanticipated failures by carefully examining the assumptions made between the customer, the developer, the maintainer, and the user. Users should know how the system will behave at all times in all modes. Formal methods and knowledge-based systems could be used to support the real-time understanding of the system's behavior so that the operators would not be confused. With better understanding they could react faster and more accurately.

Reducing software errors. While all errors cannot be eliminated, their incidence can be reduced by proper development methodologies, intensive testing, formal validation techniques, and fault-tolerant designs. Software development methodologies are disciplined ways of generating high-quality software with greatly reduced effort. The main emphasis of these are in decomposing the large system into many easily manageable components and producing software with computer-aided tools and analysis procedures. Results in software reliability theory attempt to predict the approximate number of errors in a program and the amount of effort needed to reduce them. Fault-tolerant design techniques reduce the impact of errors by generating correct results using an alternate version of the program if the active version produces an erroneous answer. In one major technique (multiversion development), two or more teams of programmers develop software from the same set of requirements and each version is tested intensively against the others to reduce common-mode errors. The assumption in this technique is that the probability of every team making the same error is very low. Since testing in the actual SDI environment is not possible, simulations and experiments must be conducted in environments approximating the actual.

There has been much discussion of errors in the SDI. As computer and software professionals, it is our job to reduce the frequency of their occurrence.

C. V. Ramamoorthy
University of California, Berkeley

The battle management computing problem

For the very high level of reliability required for a strategic defense system, the central question is how to design this system such that errors are first minimized and then tolerated.
—Eastport Study Group

The SDIO Panel on Computing in Support of Battle Management, also known as the Eastport Study Group, accepted the reality that "all systems of useful complexity contain software errors."[5] The question it addressed in its 30,000-word report was what to do about it. The answers range over system architecture, exploratory development, abundant computing power, testing, fault tolerance, and software research.

Architecture. There is a natural tendency to think of SDI as one vast system—10 million lines of code, thousands of sensors, hundreds of weapons, and so on. Such a system would be fragile and unreliable. There is a further tendency to concentrate on the various weapon possibilities, then on the means to sense the targets, before giving much consideration to the computers, communications, and software that manage the whole.

"If the United States can not build computing systems and battle management software to control the sensors and weapons, then the sensor and weapon characteristics and placement are purely academic," the panel pointed out. In its judgment the Phase 1 contractor studies of system architecture that have already been made focused too much on sensors and weapons and not enough on issues of software complexity and testability.

The panel recommended that SDIO develop an open and distributed architecture. "An army can not and need not coordinate each action of every soldier through the commander-in-chief," it pointed out. "Instead, responsibility and authority are delegated in the chain of command. Similarly, a strategic defense system need not and should not be tightly coordinated.''

To take one example, the panel made a preliminary analysis and simulation of the assignment of weapons to individual missiles during the boost phase under both a centralized and decentralized architecture. It found that the decentralized approach would require about 20 percent more shots to destroy a given number of missiles than a perfectly coordinated system would require. ''The tradeoff is that perfect coordination saves a certain amount of hardware at the cost of increased software complexity and decreased testability,'' it said.

These projects should start out relatively small, at about the 25-manyear level, the panel said. ''Initially, the projects could work with abstractions or simulated approximations of the sensor and weapon characteristics. Each project should be capable of being expanded to a much larger scale exploratory development. As the prototype battle management systems increase in size and capability, the level of realism and detail in the simulations would be increased.''

The prototype programs should be a means to assess the feasibility of a range of battle management software and ultimately should lead into good specifications. Out of these projects should come

(1) ''Develop system architectures in which there is relatively little dependence on coordination or in which the coordination information is used only if available. These architectures are relatively easier to test in parts.''

(2) ''Use simulation extensively, using very high-speed and/or highly concurrent programmable computers that would allow the operational code and algorithms to be tested under very large numbers of battle variations.''

(3) Test components and the system in the actual operating environment with simulated data going to and from the sensor and weapon platforms, since real operation is not possible.

(4) Continue such testing over the life time of the deployed system.

''Hierarchically organized systems lend themselves readily to this type of testing,'' the panel said. Moreover, partitionable systems reduce the vast number of states to be tested. In this connection the application of greater computing power to testing would make it possible to test more states than otherwise.

The prototype programs should be a means to assess the feasibility of a range of management software and ultimately should lead into good specifications.

Moreover, it is obvious when one stops to think that SDI will never be a static system. New models of weapons, sensors, communications links, and computers will appear in periodic releases. Changes will be made to offset enemy countermeasures. The architecture must be formulated as an ''open system'' that can allow the rapid insertion of unanticipated and modified elements, the panel said.

The important point is that software problems—reliability and testability—must be considered in the architectural tradeoff studies, the Eastport Group stressed.

Exploratory development. The panel regarded the ''waterfall diagram'' paradigm, ''the portrayal of a software development project proceeding smoothly and unidirectionally from requirements specification to design specification to coding, testing, and delivery,'' as a misconception of the reality. ''The truth is that these steps can, and often do, feed back into any of their predecessors.''

The panel felt that the design space of possible architectures is ''vast.'' It believes that there are no analytical methods that can assess the feasibility of each architecture. To probe these mysteries, it recommended the construction of several prototype battle management software systems by different organizations.

not only prototype software, but also ''precise definitions of the formulation of the system in terms of modules and the interface protocols among them.''

Computing power. The panel expects hardware technology to continue to increase computing speed and to reduce size, weight, and power. The issue for SDI is how to make effective use of this increasing power. In general, the panel recommended that this massive computer power be used to simplify other tasks and, in particular, not to make the software overly complex in order to compensate for the lack of hardware power.

In the area of software development, for example, the panel believes that greater computing power—even supercomputers or their future equivalents—may allow developers to create new tools and techniques. ''For example, it may be possible to build much higher quality debugging environments or to support much more detailed semantic checkers than are currently available,'' it observed. It may be feasible to exploit the real-time animation of algorithms.

Testing. Confidence in the ability of SDI to work is ''a critical technical point,'' the panel noted. It regards several approaches to the testing problem as promising:

Fault tolerance. The design of hardware to accommodate or to recover from faults is an established field, but the design of fault-tolerant software is less advanced. ''SDIO should place considerable emphasis on the invention, refinement, or evaluation of software design techniques that would allow computing functions to be performed usefully despite hardware faults or software errors,'' the panel recommended.

One such technique sets several independent programming teams to writing a program to the same specification. Then the programs are run together with a decision procedure comparing their outputs. The panel urged larger experiments than have been previously feasible to evaluate this technique, but it warned of the possibility of highly correlated programmer errors in the different programs.

Other techniques include watchdog processes, data structure audits, recovery blocks, runtime checking, and decisions based on probability distributions. Runtime checking, such as placing bounds on variables, is already used, but could be extended further, the panel believes. Basing a decision on a probability distribution limits the degree to which a single fault can propagate. Critical data would be represented not by a single value but by a probability density function.

Software research. In addition to research in the application of massive computing power to software development, to further investigation of testing methods and tools, and to more work in reliability and fault tolerance, the panel outlined half a dozen other areas for research:

(1) *Mathematical proof techniques.* While formal verification methods are limited and advances are likely to come slowly, it is possible that they can be applied to at least some small modules that are critically important.

(2) *Specification languages.* In one class of specification language, as successive levels of detail are added, the programmer has strong assurance that the semantics of the more detailed representation match those of the previous iteration. Another class, the executable specification language, forces the specifier to be precise and to avoid ambiguity, thus reducing errors.

(3) *Parallel, concurrent, or distributed computing.* More systems with these capabilities are becoming available, but the ability to exploit them lags. "SDIO should establish centers for studying algorithmic, compilation, and operating-systems issues in the context of programmable concurrent computer systems with the potential of having fairly general application domains," the panel recommended.

(4) *Development teams.* "The advent of networks of computer workstations, precise specification languages, and other components of advanced software development, creates the possibility of structuring software development teams in entirely new ways," the panel observed. It suggests experimenting with radically structured software development teams, as well as conducting an historical study of past large military software projects.

(5) *Software environments.* High-speed tool-rich environments seem to create a style of program development in which programmers work in new and more effective ways. These environments enable a programmer, for example, to tear a program apart and put it back together in a new structure with less effort than older ways. Study is needed to determine how programming style and more powerful environments can best be exploited.

(6) *Maintenance.* The panel expects a "substantial software maintenance effort," but noted that there has been little research on tools for modifying software systems. It proposes, for example, that methods be developed "to determine and monitor the modules of code that reflect each system requirement, easing the job of accommodating a change to that requirement even if the affected code is dispersed rather than isolated."

There will be errors.

Those who think that software designs will become easy, and that errors will disappear, have not attacked substantial problems.
— David L. Parnas

The whole history of large, complex software development indicates that errors cannot be completely eliminated. The Eastport Study Group has done a brilliant job of analyzing the problem and recommending ways to minimize and tolerate errors. At this time, before the system architecture has been defined, before the research has been done, and before the software development organization has been structured, we cannot know how well the Study Group's recommendations will be implemented.

If the software effort was carried out as well as the efforts previously cited, there would be at least 0.5 errors per thousand delivered source instructions at the time of deployment. If the terminal phase software were to consist of about 800,000 instructions, as the real-time Safeguard software did, and if the boost and midcourse software were comparable, the three would amount to about 2.4 million instructions. That much software would have about 1200 errors at the time it became operational.

It takes a very effective organization to get errors down to that level. The Eastport Group obviously believes that the SDIO software effort must not only take advantage of the best currently known software practices but must learn to use new techniques that SDIO-sponsored research will develop.

Unfortunately, the group "finds it a bit troublesome to be discussing whether radical advancements in software technology would enhance the quality of a new defense system, when we are aware that many of the DoD's biggest software development contractors are presently literally decades behind the state of the art."

Consequently, the group devoted a chapter of its report to program management, offering a number of recommendations designed to get this area up to speed.

Despite the best efforts of all concerned, I conclude that there will be errors and the shield will leak—perhaps only a few warheads, but leaks nonetheless. That leads us back to the original purpose of the Strategic Defense Initiative. If it is to render nuclear weapons "impotent and obsolete," as President Reagan stated in his March 1983 speech inaugurating the concept, then these weapons will still be very much a potent threat. If it is to provide a partial defense, protecting the retaliatory missile silos, assuring the survival of part of the population, and avoiding a worst-case nuclear winter, SDI may accomplish this despite some errors.

But the debate on nuclear strategy has been raging in defense circles for 40 years now and it is beyond the scope of this article to pursue the strategic implications. □

References

1. David Lorge Parnas, "Software Aspects of Strategic Defense Systems," *American Scientist,* Sept.-Oct. 1985, pp. 432-440.

2. Frederick P. Brooks, *Testimony before the Hearing of the Senate Armed Services Committee on Strategic and Nuclear Forces,* Oct. 30, 1985.

3. Letter dated Oct. 18, 1985 from Congressman Robert J. Mrazek of the Committee of Appropriations to Lt. Gen. James A. Abrahamson, USAF, SDIO Director.

4. Letter (undated but apparently in late October, 1985) from Lt. Gen. James A. Abrahamson to Congressman Robert J. Mrazek.

5. Danny Cohen, chairman, Eastport Study Group, Summer Study 1985, Dec. 1985, 70 pp.

6. Harold Brown, "Is SDI Technically Feasible?," *Foreign Affairs,* Vol. 64, No. 3, 1986, pp. 435-454.

7. Barry W. Boehm, *Software Engineering Economics,* 1981, Prentice-Hall, Inc., Englewood Cliffs, N.J., p. 383.

8. Nathan H. Petschenik, "Practical Priorities in System Testing," *Software,* Sept. 1985, pp. 18-23.

9. T. R. Thomsen, letter of Nov. 1, 1985 to Lt. Gen. James A. Abrahamson.

10. Lawrence H. Putnam, Douglas T. Putnam, and Lauren P. Thayer, "Quality in Software is Free (Almost)," *Proc. Int'l Soc. Parametric Analysts,* Seventh Ann. Conf., May 1985, 37 pp.

11. James C. Fletcher, study chairman, *Report of the Study on Eliminating the Threat Posed by Nuclear Ballistic Missiles,* SDI Organization, 1983.

12. W. E. Stephenson, "An Analysis of the Resources Used in the Safeguard System Software Development," *Proc. 2nd Int'l Conf. Software Engineering,* 1976, pp. 312-321.

Reprinted from *IEEE Software*, Volume 1, Number 3, July 1984, pages 56-63. Copyright ©1984 by The Institute of Electrical and Electronics Engineers, Inc. All rights reserved.

Software Renewal: A Case Study

Harry M. Sneed, Software Engineering Service

Error-free software in large applications may be possible only by respecifying the original design—and may be affordable only when automatic tools become available.

The data processing community needs to apply software engineering techniques and tools to real projects to determine their practical usefulness. Such an opportunity was provided by the Bertelsmann Publishing Corporation of Gütersloh, West Germany, during a two year period from 1981 to 1983. This article reports the results of that project and the experience gained from it.

The application

In 1981 Bertelsmann, the world's second largest publishing company, completed a commercial application system for distributing books and other publications throughout the world. The system, which includes ordering, billing, packing, and distributing, runs on line during the day and in batch mode during the night. It is made up of eight subsystems, with more than 1000 modules and 300,000 PL/I source statements. The system was developed with the help of IBM analysts using the HIPO method for design[1] and a decision table generator, Dectab, for coding.[2] The database, which contains some 5000 data items, was constructed using the Adabas database system.[3]

Testing and documenting such a large system proved to be a problem. Due to application size and complexity, the modules needed to be tested individually, but at the time of development no adequate test tools were available. The original documentation, in the form of HIPO charts, was soon outdated as the programs were altered during testing. So great was the difference between the original design documentation, which was never fully completed, and the final programs that the design had to be discarded.

This left the system without a baseline documentation. The only true description of the application was the programs themselves, but these were in a constant state of fluctuation as there were numerous error reports, at the rate of one error per 175 source lines, and user change requests, at the rate of one change per two and a half modules, during the installation phase.

At this critical point, after one year of operation, Bertelsmann decided to try and reconstruct a requirements specification from the programs themselves, and to systematically test the modules with the aid of automated tools. One subsystem of the total system was chosen: the mailing system with 232 modules and some 24,000 lines of PL/I source code. By respecifying, redocumenting and reverifying this one subsystem we hoped to determine whether or not the entire system could be reconstructed in accordance with the principles of software engineering. Like urban renewal, we wanted to find out whether software systems could be economically renovated.

Project strategy

The strategy of the project was to proceed in four stages. In the first stage, the modules were to be statically analyzed and redocumented with the aid of an automated static analyzer. In the second stage, the programs and data structures were to be formally specified using an automated specification tool based on the structured analysis method[4] and the documents produced by the static analyzer. In the third stage, the module test cases were to be written in a test specification language based on the assertion method[5] and executed by a module test system with the objective of achieving 90-percent branch coverage.[6] In the fourth and final stage, the test specification, in the form of assertion procedures, was to be merged with the functional specification of the programs and their data structures to create a production environment for maintenance and further development[7] (Figure 1).

The final result was to be a formal specification of the processes, data objects, and their relationships, as well as a set of test procedures for testing new module versions against the evolving specification.

The process specification was to consist of

- a process description,
- a function tree,
- an input/output diagram for each function,
- a decision table for each group of conditional functions,
- a function tree for each process,
- a description for each function, and
- the assertions on the pre- and postconditions of each elementary function.

The object specification was to consist of

- an object description,
- a data tree,
- a data usage diagram for each data item,
- a description of each data item, and
- the assertions on the input/output domains of each elementary data item.

In addition, the relationships between the processes, between the objects, and between the objects and processes were to be specified in accordance with the entity/relationship model.[8] Finally, there was to be a data test procedure for each of the 78 data interfaces, that is, data capsules, and a module test procedure for each of the 232 PL/I procedures, that is, modules.

The project was planned to last a year and to involve two testers and two specifiers besides the personnel developing the automated tools. As it turned out, this proved to be a gross underestimation, mainly because of the effort required to refine the tools. However, without tools the task of renovation was deemed impossible.

The rationale for employing automated tools was one of sheer economic necessity. A human being can only understand and document a few hundred lines of code per week. With the aid of a tool, this can be increased to several thousand. The ratio is at least one to ten. The same applies to testing. Without the help of a tool, it is not possible to trace the test paths and to document the test coverage. Besides, the tool is what generates the test data and verifies the test results. So it was clear from the beginning that the

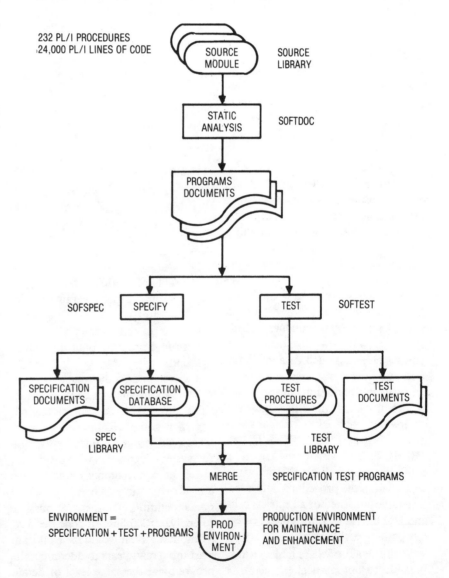

Figure 1. Renovation project strategy.

postdocumentation and the testing of the programs had to be done automatically.

The least help from tools was expected in respecifying what the programs should be doing. But even here a tool was found to be indispensable. The business analysts, who generally are not trained to make precise specifications, were encouraged by the specification tool to be precise and formal. If for no other reason, a specification tool can be justified on this basis. The resulting specification would have been valueless if the discipline enforced by the tool had been missing. In fact, an argument might be made that the lack of discipline on the part of the original developers was a major reason for having to renovate the Bertelsmann system.

Static analysis

The first stage of the project involved the static analysis of the selected programs. This stage proceeded bottom up in three steps: (1) module analysis, (2) program analysis, and (3) system analysis.

The tool for this purpose was Softdoc, a static analyzer for Cobol, PL/I, and assembler programs.[9] Softdoc processed the source code in order to produce four tables for each module: a data description table, a data flow table, a control flow table, and an interface table.

The data description table described the attributes and usage of each data item referenced by the module in question. The data flow table depicted in which statements each data item was used and how it was used, either as a predicate in a condition, an argument, or a result. The control flow table encompassed each PL/I control command, such as PROC, DO-WHILE, SELECT, and IF, including their conditions, as well as all comments contained in the procedure. The interface table consisted of all entries, calls and I/O operations, with their respective parameters (Figure 2).

With the aid of these tables, it was possible to automatically generate a series of documents from the pro-grams themselves, at three different levels of aggregation. At the module level, the following documents were generated:

- a tree of internal procedures and begin blocks,
- an input/output diagram for each internal procedure and begin block,
- a data description list,
- a pseudo code listing,
- a control graph,
- a path analysis report, and
- an intramodular data flow table.

At the program level, the modules of each of the eight programs were aggregated to produce:

- a module tree,
- a calling hierarchy list,
- an input/output diagram for each module,
- an interface description list, and
- an intermodular data flow table.

At the system level, the program tables were aggregated to produce a document of the interprogram relationships. In all, five documents were produced at this level:

Without a tool, it would have taken at least three man years to document the programs at the same level of detail.

- a table of module references,
- an input/output diagram for each program,
- a file reference table,
- an interprogram data flow table, and
- a system data dictionary.

The whole analysis took no more than one week to complete. Altogether some 1624 module documents, 40 program documents, and five system documents were produced, giving an approximately one to one and a half ratio of code to program documentation. Thus, it was possible to analyze 5000 lines of code per day. Without a tool, it would have taken at least three man-years to document the programs at the same level of detail. This showed that for the postdocu-mentation of programs, automated tools are indispensable. There can be no adequate and reliable description of the programs without them. However, it should be noted that the documentation of the programs is no substitute for a requirements specification. This work remained to be done.

Requirement specification

Following the production of the program documentation, it was possible to commence with the respecification of the application. In contrast to the program analysis, the specification proceeded top down. In all, 10 steps were involved (Figure 3):

(1) describing the data objects,
(2) describing the processes,
(3) depicting the object/process relationships,
(4) depicting the user interfaces,
(5) depicting the data trees,
(6) depicting the function trees,
(7) depicting the decision logic,
(8) depicting the data flow,
(9) describing the functions, and
(10) describing the data.

The tool used was Sofspec, a system for the interactive submission of an application using 12 different CRT forms and their storage in a specification database based on the entity/relationship model.[10] Sofspec allows the user to submit the specification in interactive mode under the IBM TSO/SPF monitor in a tabular format. At any time during a terminal session it can be asked to produce a certain specification document, or it can be requested to verify a certain aspect of the specification.

The specification work began by examining the files, databases, and data communication interfaces documented by the static analysis. Data objects could be derived from the file reference table. Each object was defined in terms of its meaning, occurrence, periodicity, space requirements, and description. Processes could be taken from the interprogram data flow table. Each process was also defined in terms of is meaning, occurrence, periodicity, time requirements, and description.

Following the description of the objects and processes, the relationships were defined. The process/object relationships (input, output, I/O) could be taken from the input/output diagrams produced by the static analysis. The Adabas search keys for each access had, however, to be taken from the database design. The object/object relationships (1:1, 1:N, M:1, M:N) were obtained by inverting the process/object relationships. The process/process relationships (predecessor, successor, parallel task, invoker, invokee), that is, the process control flow, could be derived from the system data flow table.

Thus, it proved possible to recreate an abstract conceptual model of the system represented by objects, processes, and their relationships, but only partially from the information obtained from the existing programs. A great deal of information had to be collected from the original designers. This was due to the large semantic gap between the view of the system as a whole, in terms of objects and processes, and the view of the individual programs. The specification process proceeded top down. The fourth and fifth steps were to document the data structures. These were found to be of two types: user interfaces, that is, forms, and data sets. The user interfaces were described in terms of sample forms with references to the variables contained in them. The data sets were defined as data trees in accordance with the Jackson notation using sequence, selection, repetition, grouping, and search key identification.[11] Sofspec supported both notations. The information for the data structuring was taken from the actual listing and CRT panels, as well as from the data dictionary generated through the static analysis of the programs by Softdoc.

In the following two steps, the function structures and decision logic tables were specified from the module tree diagrams and the pseudo code generated by Softdoc. The function trees in Sofspec were also defined in terms of the Jackson methodology. For every repetitive and selective func-

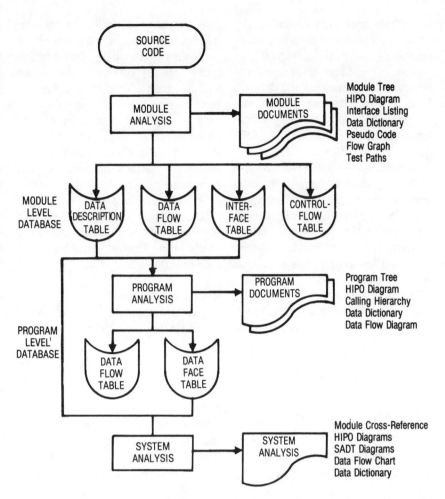

Figure 2. Static analysis with Softdoc.

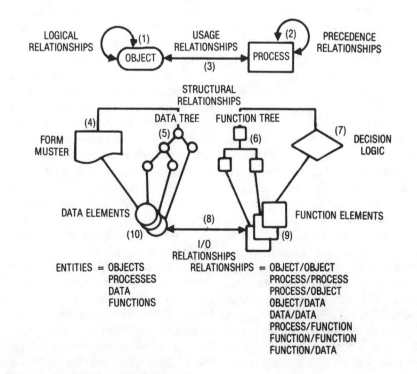

Figure 3. Specification with Sofspec.

tion it was necessary to define the condition. This was done using either a terminal-supported decision table or a decision tree. Later in the documentation the function trees and decision trees, that is, decisions tables, were merged to produce a single specification document, which also included the detailed data flow.

The detailed data flow description was the eighth step. Here the module input/output diagrams derived from the code were used to specify the inputs and outputs of each function. The new data flow diagrams, at the functional level, were then generated by the specification tool.

The ninth step was to describe each function based on the comment block contained in the code. Where the comment blocks were missing, it was necessary to examine the code itself in order to describe the algorithm in

---

There were several deviations between the assumption of the user and the actual construction of the programs.

---

natural language. A function was defined to correspond to a PL/I procedure. These procedures ranged from 50 to a maximum of 500 executable PL/I statements.

The tenth and final step in the respecification phase was actually the first step of the testing phase. Each data element in the system had to be defined in terms of is attributes. These were taken from the Softdoc data dictionary. In addition, the domain of each data item had to be defined. But since this was related to the program test it was postponed until after the test phase.

The task of respecifying the application programs took 17 man-months to complete. This amounted to one man-month of specification per 1400 lines of code. The ratio of program code to specification documentation was on the average of three to one; for example, for every three pages of code there was one page of specification documentation.

When the specification documentation was finished, it was possible to discuss it with the user, who up to this point was not sure what the system was doing. Insofar as the user became familiar with the formal specification techniques, this discussion proved very fruitful. As a result of the discussion, it became clear that there were several deviations between the assumptions of the user and the actual construction of the programs. Because of that it became necessary to revise the specification to accommodate the user's view. This took another four man-months.

Program testing

The final stage of the project turned out to be the most difficult and time-consuming. It entailed testing the programs against the newly constructed specification. Twenty-two man-months were required to specify all of the data, and another six man-months were necessary to conduct the tests themselves. Each module had to be tested independently until at least 90 percent of its branches were covered.

The basis of the test was the program documentation produced by the static analyzer. Among the documents produced were a diagram of the module inputs and outputs and a list of the paths through the module, together with the conditional operands, that is, predicates associated with each path. The person responsible for the test had to analyze each module to determine what inputs would lead to the execution of what paths through the module. They also had to predict which results would occur from each path. A test case table was used to record the inputs and outputs of each path as well as the branches traversed by that path (Figure 4).

Unfortunately, the modules had originally been generated by a decision table generator and then expanded by hand. Thus, they were very badly structured. GOTO instructions were the rule instead of the exception. This made it difficult to trace the paths and predict the results. A module of 300

statements took two man-days to analyze. A module of 600 statements took seven to eight days to analyze. The largest module with some 760 statements took 11 days to analyze. We began to see that the effort involved in defining a program-based test increased exponentially in relation to the number of instructions, the number of decision nodes, and the number of arguments, that is, inputs.

Linear code with sequences of IF and WHILE statements was easier to handle than highly nested code with conditions within conditions and loops within loops. As might be expected, the worst case was that of overlapping GOTOs. Modules with few arguments, especially those with few conditional arguments or predicates, were easier to test than those with many such arguments. All of this further demonstrated that there was a definite relationship between program and complexity—in terms of program length,[12] decision nodes,[13] and data usage[14]—and test effort.

Having designed a test case table for a module, the inputs and outputs were then transformed into an assertion procedure. The assertion language consisted of an IF statement along with four types of assertions: set assertions, range assertions, function assertions, and relational assertions.[15]

Alphanumeric and coded values were usually defined by means of a set assertion. Numeric values were defined as ranges. Address and length information was defined by function. Relationships between input and output values were defined by the relational assertion. The writing of assertions proved to be a simple and easily learned task. The problem was in knowing what assertions to write.

The assertion procedures written were of two types, driver procedures and stub procedures. Driver procedures initialized the preconditions of a module under test and initiated the test cases. After each test case they verified the postconditions of the module. Stub procedures simulated either submodules or files. They verified the outputs and generated inputs to the module under test wherever a call or

I/O operation was performed. In all, over 300 assertion procedures were written with total of some 7000 assertions (Figure 5).

The actual execution of the test lasted less that three months. With two testers working in parallel it was possible to test 20 modules per week, that is, each tester tested approximately two modules a day. This was due to the use of the tool Softest, which compiled the test procedures into test tables, which were then interpreted to test the modules.[16] The testbed was automatically generated. In the testbed all procedure calls and I/O operations were simulated. For coupling the module under test with the test procedures, the module symbol table was used. In this way, the input variables were assigned, and the output variables verified. Concurrently, the paths traversed were traced, the branch coverage registered, and the data flows followed.

After each test a postprocessor produced a series of reports: a test path report, a data usage report, and a branch coverage report. The branch coverage report indicated the coverage ratio and the test branches not tested. Each test was continued until at least 90-percent branch coverage was attained, as prescribed in the contract (Table 1).

In most cases where 90-percent coverage was not reached, it was due to erroneous or incomplete assertion procedures. Modules with more than 500 statements and a highly nested logic proved to be the most difficult to cover. The test had to be repeated as many as 10 times before the adequate coverage was reached. Following each test the assertions had to be adjusted or enhanced to invoke different paths. An average of five to eight test cases were needed to test the smaller modules but as many as 26 test cases were necessary to test larger modules.

Minor errors were discovered in 55 of the 232 modules. These had to be corrected by the responsible programmers before the test could continue. Most of these errors were related and were the result of design decisions. The low level of errors

found was due to the fact that the programs had already been in operation for a year before they were submitted to this test. So most of the critical errors had already been removed. In addition, since the modules had, to a great extent, been generated from decision tables, all the errors were of a common nature and the patterns could be easily recognized. Over 75 percent of the errors were discovered while analyzing the code. The test only documented their existence. The other 25 percent were exposed at execution time by either not being able to reach

DATA	1	2	3
FIELD1	'XXX'	'YYY'	'ZZZ'
FIELD2	100	200	300
FIELD3	−5	0	5
FIELD4	X'FF'	X'F1'	X'FO'
FIELD5	11	10	9
FIELD6	B'0'	B'0'	B'1'

INPUTS

DATA	1	2	3
FIELD11	'XXX'	'YYY'	'ZZZ'
FIELD12	95	200	305
FIELD13	26	10	4
FIELD14	X'FF'	X'F1'	X'FO'
FIELD15	B"1'	B'1'	B'0'

OUTPUTS

MODULE	1	2	3
Y6651	1	1	1
	3	2	5
	7	4	8
	9	6	9
	12	10	11
	15	14	13
	16	17	17
	17		

PATHS

Figure 4. Test case tables.

```
MODULE: V665A, STAT
   ASSERT PRE FIELD1      SET ('XXX−, 'YYY', 'ZZZ');
   ASSERT PRE FIELD2      RANGE (100 + 100);
   ASSERT PRE FIELD3      RANGE (−5:5);
   ASSERT PRE FIELD4      SET (X'FF', 'F1', 'FO');
   ASSERT PRE FIELD5      RANGE (11 − 1);
   ASSERT PRE FIELD6      SET (B'0'(2), '1−);

   ASSERT POST FIELD11    = FIELD1;
   ASSERT POST FIELD12    = FIELD2 + FIELD3;
   ASSERT POST FIELD13    = FIELD5 − FIELD3;
   ASSERT POST FIELD14    = FIELD4;
   ASSERT POST FIELD15    = NOT (FIELD6);

   END V665A;
```

Figure 5. Assertion procedure.

> **Those errors found were almost all on exceptional functions which had not been used in production.**

certain branches or by the control flow following paths other than those predicted. Only three errors were found by violating output assertions. This was probably because the programs had already been exposed to extensive system testing. Those errors found were almost all on exceptional functions that had not yet been used in production. This only underlines the fact that programs do not have to be error free to be useful. It all depends on how they are used.

The total effort of 22 months to test 24,000 lines of PL/I code to find 55 minor errors and three major ones could certainly not be economically justified. The main value of the testing project was in establishing a testbed for future testing. It did, however, demonstrate that systematic module testing on a large scale was feasible, and that with new untested modules it could even be economical, but only if adequate tools are available. The test effort amounted to an average of one man-day per 54 instructions. Considering the fact that this was the first experience with a new test specification language, it should be possible in the future to increase this productivity.

Although we were successful, the move from conventional devel-opment and maintenance practices to systematic software engineering was expensive. The effort cost two thirds of the original cost, and, without the support of highly sophisticated tools, was not economically justified.

In the long run, to reduce costs and make systematic maintenance more attractive, companies will have to invest in developing adequate tools and ways to automatically bridge the gap between programs and their specification. Our work at Bertelsmann convinced us that automation is the only true solution to the maintenance problem. ∎

References

1. "HIPO—A Design Aid and Documentation Technique," IBM Corp., Manual No. GC-20-1851, White Plains, N.Y., 1974.

2. "IBM Decision Table Translator, User-Guide," IBM Form No. 79974, Stuttgart, Germany, 1973.

3. "ADABAS Introduction," *Software AG of North America,* Reston, VA., 1976.

4. T. DeMarco, *Structured Analysis and System Specification,* Yourdon Press, New York, 1978.

5. C. V. Ramamoorthy, S. F. Ho, and W. T. Chen, "On the Automated Generation of Program Test Data," *IEEE Trans. Software Eng.,* Vol. SE-2, No. 4, 1976, pp. 293-300.

6. J. C. Huan, "An Approach to Program Testing," *ACM Computing Surveys,* Sept., 1975.

7. H. M. Sneed and A. Merey, "Automated Software Quality Assurance," *Proc. Compsac 82,* Computer Society Press, Los Alamitos, Calif., 1982, pp. 239-247.

8. P. Chen, "The Entity-Relationship Model: A Basis for the Enterprise View of Data," *AFIPS Conf. Proc.,* Vol. 46, 1977 NCC, Dallas, Tex., 1977, pp. 77-84.

9. G. Jandrasics, "SOFTDOC—A System for Automated Software Analysis

Table 1.
Test coverage measurement.
(Total branches, 17; executed branches, 16; coverage ratio, 94 percent)

MODULE	BRANCH	STATEMENT	LAST TEST	TOTAL TEST
V665A	1	1	3	3
	2	50	1	1
	3	54	1	1
	4	58	1	1
	5	62	1	1
	6	64	1	1
	7	68	1	1
	8	72	1	1
	9	76	2	2
	10	80	1	1
	11	84	1	1
	12	88	1	1
	13	92	1	1
	14	96	1	1
	15	100	1	1
	16	104	(Not executed.)	
	17	108	3	3

and Documentation," *Proc. ACM Workshop Software Quality Assurance,* Gaithersburg, Md., Apr., 1981.

10. Nyary and H. M. Sneed, "SOF-SPEC—A Pragmatic Approach to Automated Specification Verification," *Proc. Entity/Relationship Conf.,* Anaheim, Calif., Oct., 1983.

11. M. Jackson, *Principles of Program Design,* Academic Press, London, 1975.

12. M. Halstead, *Elements of Software Science*, Elsevier Computer Science Library, New York, 1977.

13. T. McCabe, "A Complexity Measure," *IEEE Trans. Software Eng.,* Vol. SE-2, No. 4, Dec. 1976, pp. 308-320.

14. S. Henry and O. Kafura, "Software Structure Metrics Based on Information Flow," *IEEE Trans. Software Eng.,* Vol. SE-7, No. 5, Sept. 1981, pp. 510-518.

15. M. Majoros and H. M. Sneed, "Testing Programs Against a Formal Specification," *Proc. Compsac 83,* Computer Society Press, Los Alamitos, Calif.,.1983, pp. 512-520.

16. M. Majoros, "SOFTEST—A System for the Automated Verification of PL/I and Cobol Programs," *J. Systems & Software,* New York, Dec. 1982.

Harry M. Sneed is the technical manager at Software Engineering Service, a Munich, West Germany, software house. Before joining SES in 1978, he was a systems programmer for Siemens, and before that he was with the Volkswagen Foundation. From 1967 to 1970 he worked as a programmer/analyst for the US Navy Department.

Sneed received his BA and MS degrees from the University of Maryland in 1967 and 1969. He is a member of the ACM and IEEE.

His address is Software Engineering Service GmbH, Pappelstrasse 6, 8014 Neubiberg, West Germany.

Technology transfer in the maintenance environment

by FLORENCE J. BELL

The Equitable Life Assurance Society
of the United States
New York, New York

ABSTRACT

In 1982 The Equitable Life Assurance Society of the United States recognized that software maintenance requires major management attention, and established a maintenance producivity project (MPP). Maintenance was defined as any programming effort that requires at least 25% of a programmer's time to be spent understanding an existing system. Three potential areas were identified for technology transfer: the maintenance function, the maintenance environment, and maintenance metrics. Ongoing programs include cooperation with vendors in developing an integrated environment for the maintenance programmer and manager, a maintenance management handbook, and a maintenance managers' round table. Maintenance is becoming an established and recognized area of specialization for systems professionals at The Equitable.

INTRODUCTION

The Equitable Life Assurance Society of the United States is the third largest mutual life insurance company in the U.S., with assets of more than $45 billion and about $230 billion of life insurance in force. The company installed its first mainframe, an IBM 650, in 1956, and at that time established its systems development department, with a total complement of three people. Twenty-seven years later The Equitable had a total of eight mainframes with over 60 mips capacity, 750 systems professionals, an annual systems budget of $100 million, and an inventory of approximately 350 major systems with 7000 program modules.

In 1974, in keeping with a general decentralization of the company's management, the systems development department was divided into five independent units, whose heads reported to line management. By 1983 there were nine autonomous systems departments. When the systems development department was decentralized, an EDP coordinating committee was formed, composed of the officers who headed each of the systems departments, the head of the data processing department, and the technology officer. The committee was responsible for ensuring that the systems needs of the corporation as a whole were met; specifically that hardware support was available, that well-qualified systems professionals were recruited, trained, and developed, that advances in hardware and software technology and in systems development management were introduced into the company, and that the economies of scale of an EDP installation as large as The Equitable's were not lost through the decentralization.

In 1980 the EDP coordinating committee established an application productivity group (APG) with the charter of technology transfer, specifically to increase the productivity of The Equitable's systems effort by a factor of ten within a period of five years. Within its first two years, the APG introduced interactive computing throughout all systems areas, selected and installed the hardware and operating systems for the interactive testing environment, and established a special interactive testing support organization. The group also introduced the concept of end-user systems development, brought the FOCUS language and database management into the company, and conducted extensive user training.

In 1982, the EDP coordinating committee conducted an off-site planning session to set the direction for future efforts of the APG. At this time, maintenance, methodology, and prototyping were identified as primary areas of concern. Of these, maintenance—which at the beginning of the session had little support—emerged as the top priority, primarily because of an awareness that although maintenance used over half of the systems resources, it had been disregarded in the systems development methodology installed 10 years earlier.

INITIAL SURVEY

Between September and December of 1982, the APG conducted its initial survey of the maintenance effort throughout the company. The purpose of this survey was to define the specific goals of a maintenance productivity project (MPP), to estimate the realizable benefits, and to establish a level of effort and a timetable.

As a first step, the group contracted for the services of Julien Green, a senior consultant with wide systems experience and a thorough knowledge of The Equitable's systems environment. With him, we reviewed current literature and interviewed managers in most of the systems areas to identify the specific needs of The Equitable's maintenance managers and programmers.

The results of this investigation were published in December 1982, and can be summarized under the following headings:

1. Definition of the maintenance function
2. Definition of the maintenance environment
3. Definition of maintenance metrics
4. Project deliverables

Definition of the Maintenance Function

The industry has developed what is now a generally agreed upon terminology in describing maintenance, based upon Swanson's original classification: corrective, adaptive, and perfective maintenance.[1] Corrective maintenance is fixing errors. Adaptive maintenance is changing software to accommodate changes in the computing or business environments without affecting the software's function. Perfective maintenance is enhancing function.

These three quite dissimilar activities have in common the requirement that the programmer spend a considerable portion of time (estimated by Fjeldstad and Hamlen at 50%) in understanding existing materials (code, documentation and procedures).[2] It is this requirement that distinguishes systems maintenance from systems development.

For the purposes of our MPP we define maintenance as any programming effort that requires at least 25% of the programmer's time to be spent understanding an existing system. We believe this is the point at which programmers begin to benefit from maintenance-specific tools, which facilitate the analysis of systems as opposed to their synthesis. If we were to set this cut-off at a lower percentage, we would include some clearly development-type programming, which in a mature EDP environment such as ours usually requires interfacing with, and therefore understanding, existing systems.

We had reviewed other operational definitions used by systems managers; some distinguish small jobs (maintenance) vs. large ones (development); others distinguish modification of existing code (maintenance) vs. the creation of new modules (development); still others, following Barry Boehm,[3] include redesign of less than 50% of existing code (maintenance) vs. redesign of more than 50% (development). We noted however that some small jobs are free-standing, while some large jobs are large precisely because they involve manipulation (i.e., maintenance) of a large existing system; that some projects that require little or no modification of existing systems nevertheless require a major effort in understanding them; and that the redesign of a larger percentage of an existing system requires a greater maintenance effort than the redesign of a smaller percentage.

Accordingly, we concluded that the level of effort required by a technician to understand an existing system is a more fundamental criterion than others that have been proposed. Furthermore, it appears that an operational definition of maintenance from the systems manager's point of view must factor in the cost of understanding code. From this viewpoint, defining maintenance in terms of the effort required to understand existing code makes sense.

Definition of the Maintenance Environment

Our initial survey also identified three components of the maintenance environment, each with its own needs. The first component is the programmers' environment. We found that many tools used in development work were used by maintenance programmers, but that there was a need for tools that addressed the maintenance-specific function of understanding existing code. We also found that, although there were useful maintenance tools, no single product purported to provide an integrated environment—a situation quite different from that on the development side of the house, where it has long been recognized that the greatest productivity gains come not from the sum of the tools, but from the integration of the tools into a structured environment.

The second component of the maintenance environment is the managers' environment. Here we found a need for management tools—packages to assist in estimating programming effort, scheduling and controlling maintenance work, budgeting, and reporting. Again some tools used for development were useful, but some, such as an effort estimator for maintenance work, were not available. In addition there was a need for a description of the sequential steps in maintenance work, and for a checklist with which to determine the accomplishment of each step.

The third component of the maintenance environment is the institutional environment, which encompasses the issues of the image of maintenance, selection and training of maintenance personnel, and career paths for maintenance professionals.

Definition of Maintenance Metrics

Finally, the initial survey identified the need for a good set of maintenance metrics upon which to base rational mainte-

nance decisions. Two types of metrics are needed: First are macro-metrics—used to provide a multidimensional profile of our software inventory. These metrics will allow us to estimate the size, complexity and state of deterioration (or health) of our existing software portfolio, predict the resources needed to maintain our inventory, estimate the cost of maintenance, and identify areas of largest payoff. An example of a macro-metric is the number of man-months required to maintain the "average" program module.

Second are the micro-metrics—used to provide information needed for decisions concerning the maintenance of individual systems. These metrics will serve as a basis for determining when to retire, restructure, or retrofit a system, for measuring productivity trends, for estimating the time and cost of specific maintenance jobs, for preparing an annual maintenance budget, and for evaluating proposed new software tools. An example of a micro-metric is an algorithm to estimate the man-months required to implement a specific program enhancement.

Project Deliverables

Maintenance improvement is an unusually difficult environment for technology transfer. Installed systems cannot be easily adjusted to use a predefined tool or component; nor can an abrupt change of method be implemented by a staff carrying a full load of projects already in progress. A maintenance productivity project does not consist of installing tools, or adopting a methodology, or establishing management policies. Instead, it requires continuing of action on several levels.

Therefore, the initial survey defined our objective as introducing technology transfer into an integrated maintenance environment upon a foundation of sound maintenance metrics. A set of project deliverables for each component of the environment was developed.

These included, for the programmers' environment, a maintenance workbench, i.e., a set of software tools integrated through a common gateway or front end.

Project deliverables specified for the managers' environment were a handbook containing an inventory of the tools in the maintenance workbench, with guidelines for their appropriate use, costs, and expected benefits, a description of the maintenance process, and a milestone checklist; and a set of software tools, probably resident on a personal computer, for estimating, scheduling, controlling, and budgeting maintenance work.

Finally, for the institutional environment, a maintenance managers' round table was recommended. This is a periodic meeting of systems managers to define common maintenance concerns, exchange successful solutions, and channel technical advance. The round table is designed to build a community of interest and to be the main line of communication for technology transfer, for evaluating and integrating tools, for drafting the handbook, and for originating new avenues of investigation.

Strategy

In November 1982, the Application Productivity Group began to address the programmer's environment. There were many reasons why we chose to begin our maintenance project with this activity.

Evaluating and installing software tools is the easiest task for us to work at. Tools pre-exist our efforts, are concrete, and demonstrate measurable results. The APG has had considerable experience in finding, piloting, and evaluating software. Good results are readily realizable through the installation of these tools. Therefore, although we believe that in the long run activities other than the installation and even the integration of tools will prove more important, we started our implementation effort by identifying and evaluating maintenance tools.

Seven types of software tools for the Maintenance Workbench were identified for further investigation. They were retrofitters, restructurers, static code analyzers, interactive debuggers, test data generators, automated documentors, and specialized editors. From among these, we selected a new interactive code analyzer to evaluate and pilot.

INTERACTIVE STATIC ANALYZER BETA TEST

James Martin and Carma McClure had written that "the tool the maintainer most needs is an interactive code analyzer that will help him to understand how the code works, and to predict the side-effects of modification."[4] At the time we completed our initial survey, a vendor was preparing to beta-test an interactive analyzer.

The APG's preliminary evaluations at the vendor's site indicated that the product had powerful functionality. On the basis of this evaluation, The Equitable agreed in February 1983 to be a beta site.

The product loaded COBOL source code to an on-line database, which a maintenance programmer could then access interactively. It presented three views of the program: the structure chart view, which gave the programmer an overview of the design of the program; a source code view, which allowed a programmer to look at selected units of code; and a source code difference view, which presented different versions of the program. In each of these views the programmer could select and trace data flows and control logic. It was at the time the only interactive static analyzer that we were able to find.

Objectives of the Beta Test

The objectives of the beta test were to:

1. Confirm the functionality of the product. Would it effectively trace the logic and data flows of actual production systems, provide accurate flow charts, and compare differences in source code?
2. Determine the quality of the product. How many bugs would be encountered during the beta test, and how seriously would they affect the product's functionality?
3. Evaluate the usefulness of the product in a production environment. Would it provide answers to real maintenance questions, and information actually needed to modify programs?
4. Ascertain training requirements. How long would it take programmers to learn to use the product?

5. Determine the practicality of using the product with programs written for the non-IBM-compatible systems. Could minicomputer programs be analyzed?
6. Evaluate the acceptance of the product by The Equitable's maintenance professionals. If installed, would the product become the systems community's Edsel?
7. Evaluate the support given by the vendor during the beta test. What level of support might we expect when the product was released?
8. Evaluate the system resources required by the product. What effect would its use have on our data centers?
9. Estimate the transfer charges that systems areas would incur for the use of the product. What would it cost to analyze code with it?
10. Estimate the actual productivity gains that could be expected. Would benefits outweigh costs?

Results of the Beta Test

The beta test ran from Feb. 2 through April 15, 1983. During the course of the beta test 100 program modules were analyzed, and approximately 250 hours of interactive testing were logged.

At its conclusion, the functionality of the static analyzer was confirmed. On all other factors, except quality, the product received an acceptable or better rating (Figure 1). However, the vendor withdrew the package.

We learned three major lessons from this experience: First, an interactive static analyzer is a valuable tool, and will be well received by programmers. Since the beta test, whenever programmers evaluate a software tool, they invariably compare it to the analyzer and begin their evaluations, "Well, it isn't a *(product)*, but ... " We found that a static analyzer can reduce the time a programmer spends understanding code by 20–50%. In our environment a 23% reduction in programmer time for this function would have offset the machine charges. We look forward to the day when a viable interactive static analyzer is on the market.

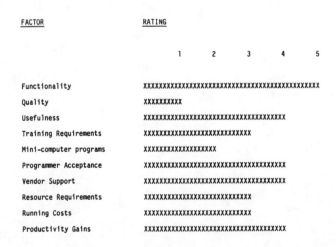

FACTOR	RATING
	1 2 3 4 5
Functionality	XXXXXXXXXXXXXXXXXXXXXXXXXXXXXXXXXXXXXXXXXXXXX
Quality	XXXXXXXXXX
Usefulness	XXXXXXXXXXXXXXXXXXXXXXXXXXXXXXXXXXXX
Training Requirements	XXXXXXXXXXXXXXXXXXXXXXXXXXXX
Mini-computer programs	XXXXXXXXXXXXXXXXXX
Programmer Acceptance	XXXXXXXXXXXXXXXXXXXXXXXXXXXXXXXXXXXX
Vendor Support	XXXXXXXXXXXXXXXXXXXXXXXXXXXXXXXXXX
Resource Requirements	XXXXXXXXXXXXXXXXXXXXXXXX
Running Costs	XXXXXXXXXXXXXXXXXXXXXXX
Productivity Gains	XXXXXXXXXXXXXXXXXXXXXXXXXXXXXXXXXX

Legend: 1. Poor; 2. Acceptable; 3. Satisfactory; 4. Very Good; 5. Excellent

Figure 1—Evaluation of interactive static analyzer

Second, we learned more about evaluating maintenance tools. Although most of our criteria had been defined before the test, others emerged during the weekly review meetings we held with the programmers. It was at these meetings that the distinction between functionality, quality, and usefulness was hammered out. We will evaluate other tools against these criteria, as well as against additional criteria that may apply. We expect other maintenance products to appear on the market in the near future, and we intend to integrate the best of them into our environment.

Third, we conclude that the maintenance workbench is a facility whose time has come. The productivity improvement realized by having static analysis functions available in an interactive harness demonstrated the potential benefits of putting many other maintenance functions in such a harness.

CONTINUING ACTIVITIES

At the time of this writing, The Equitable's maintenance productivity improvement program is progressing along the lines laid out in the initial survey. For the programmers' environment, maintenance tools continue to be evaluated. We are particularly looking at packages that restructure and re-document existing code.

For the managers' environment, a maintenance effort estimator has been developed by another consultant to the project, Howard Rubin, as a component of the ESTIMACS package.[5] The maintenance management handbook is being outlined by Julien Green. For the institutional environment, Nicholas Zvegintzov[6] is working with us as a consultant to coordinate the initial meetings of the maintenance managers' round table.

A new software metrics project has been established. Its team will develop the metrics for maintenance specified by the maintenance productivity project, as well as software development measurements.

CONCLUSION

Software maintenance has been a major systems function at The Equitable for many years. It is now recognized as a function whose contribution to the systems and corporate effort deserves the serious attention of upper management. A maintenance productivity improvement program has been developed, approved, and funded. Maintenance is becoming an established and recognized area of specialization for systems professionals at The Equitable.

REFERENCES

1. Swanson, E. B. "The Dimensions of Maintenance." *IEEE Computer Society, 2nd International Conference on Software Engineering.* Los Angeles, California: IEEE Computer Society, 1976, pp. 492–497.
2. Fjeldstad, R. K., and W. T. Hamlen. "Application program maintenance study—report to our respondents." IBM Corporation, DP Marketing Group, January 23, 1979. Reprinted in: G. Parikh, and N. Zvegintzov. *Tutorial on Software Maintenance.* Silver Spring, Md.: IEEE Computer Society, 1983.
3. Boehm, B. W. *Software Engineering Economics.* Englewood Cliffs, N.J.: Prentice-Hall, 1981.
4. Martin, J., and C. L. McClure. *Maintenance of Computer Programming.* Carnforth, England: Savant Institute, 1982. Reprinted as: *Software Maintenance—The Problem and its Solutions.* Englewood Cliffs, N.J.: Prentice-Hall, 1983.
5. Rubin, H. "Macro and Micro-estimation of Maintenance Effort: the ESTIMACS Maintenance Models." *IEEE Computer Society, Software Maintenance Workshop Record,* Los Angeles, Calif.: IEEE CS, 1984.
6. Zvegintzov, N. "What life? What cycle?" *AFIPS, Proceedings of the National Computer Conference* (Vol. 51), 1982, pp. 561–568.

Part 5: Automated Tools

Machines should work. People should think.

A so-called IBM motto

AUTOMATED CONFIGURATION MANAGEMENT

Alex Lobba

Softool Corporation

Abstract

The purpose of Configuration Management (CM) is to identify all the interrelated components of a body of information and to control its evolution throughout the various phases of its life cycle.

The need for CM is ubiquitous. Among its important applications are: software development and maintenance, document control, problem tracking, change control, and many more.

At present, CM is addressed mostly through manual means which are inadequate and cannot cope with the problem. Automatic CM is an absolute necessity. The purpose of this paper is to discuss the automation of CM and to illustrate the utilization of an automated tool currently in wide use.

The Situation Today

The last few years have witnessed a tremendous increase in the amount of information that is handled by computers, and in the quantity of software being developed. The problem of keeping track of all this information has grown as well. With the aid of computers, information is manipulated at a rate that produces different versions and revisions faster than they can be documented manually.

Configuration Management (herein referred to as CM) is the discipline that addresses this problem. The purpose of CM is to identify all the interrelated components of a body of information and to control and document its evolution throughout the various phases of its life cycle.

The need for effective CM is felt in a wide range of environments and applies to different types of information. From the software developer entangled in the complexity of requirement documents evolving into design documents and then actual code, to those responsible for maintaining all the different versions of the final software product, to the engineering firm trying to keep track of the changes in their computer generated drawings, to the government agency maintaining documents and their amendments, to the government contractor who needs to comply with defined standards ... the list goes on and on.

The Conventional Approach

A manual approach to the problem is unmanageable because it cannot keep up with the speed at which changes take place. Moreover, as the volume of information that needs to be managed increases, the manual approach breaks down. To obtain up-to-date documentation of the status of information requires that the process of making modifications be interrupted; this is clearly unacceptable. Furthermore, manual or semiautomated procedures provide little or no control over who can make changes and where, and over the integrity of information.

The Need

An automated approach to CM is essential in implementing the following major aspects of functionality effectively[1]:

- IDENTIFICATION of all the components of a body of information

- STATUS ACCOUNTING reports to document what changed, when, and who made the changes

- AUDITING the history of components to verify their integrity and compliance with the original specifications

- CONTROL over what changes should be made and incorporated, and over who can access what information.

An automated CM tool should also provide the ability to identify and document changes as they occur, without interfering with the process; thus allowing verification, in real time, that the right changes were made in the right places. It should restrict access to information to selected personnel, and should eliminate the redundant storage of information that is shared by multiple versions or baselines.

In summary, what is required is a tool in which the various aspects and functions of CM are integrated in one consistent environment.

Softool's Change and Configuration Control (CCC™)

The following is a discussion of Softool's Change and Configuration Control Environment (CCC). A software development environment is used as an example to explain CCC's capabilities.

Identification - Structure of Information in CCC

The first function of CM is to be able to identify all the components of a product.

Information in CCC is organized as a hierarchy of data structures, with the DATA BASE at the highest level.

The data base is composed of SYSTEMS. To relate the diagram in Figure 1 (next column) to a typical situation, System 1 might be a manufacturing control system, System 2 might be a simulation program, and System 3 might be an accounts payable or payroll system, and so on.

Each of these systems is composed of one or more CONFIGURATIONS (baselines or versions) of the parent system. For example, Configuration 1 of the manufacturing control system, might consist of production routines, whereas Configuration 2 might be a development version, and Configuration 3 might be an enhanced version of the exact same system being developed to run on machine B rather than machine A.

Each configuration is in turn composed of MODULE data structures. Modules may represent the different routines or programs that make up a specific configuration of a given system, with corresponding TEXT structures to hold each module's source code, object code, and accompanying documentation.

In another situation, it might make more sense to store all the source routines for a given version in text structures under Module 1 and all the accompanying objects for each routine under Module 2.

In any event, a key feature of CCC is the flexibility it provides in both the representation of, and subsequent access to stored information.

Please note that any level in the CCC hierarchy may have text associated with it, providing a convenient mechanism for associating documentation, job control language procedures, macro procedures, test cases, or any other pertinent pieces of information, with an entire level or structure, from the system data structure on down.

Status Accounting and Auditing - Changes

With the internal structure in mind, we will examine how CCC keeps track of and permits users to manipulate changes made to stored information.

Figure 1

Structure of Information in CCC

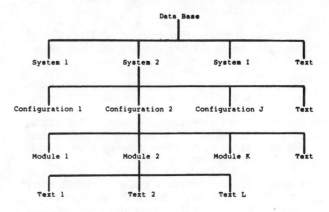

CCC also provides status accounting reports that support the activity of auditing the history of components to verify their integrity.

When a change is made, CCC gives the user an opportunity to enter a change name and a description of the change he or she made, providing a key by which a change, or group of related changes, may be readily accessed and displayed.

For example, a programmer modifying three separate routines to resolve software trouble report (STR) number 65 might name all three changes "STR65". The project manager could then examine, with a single command, all the changes made in order to address STR65.

CCC automatically records who makes a change and when the change is made.

In addition, CCC only keeps track of the actual changes made to a given text structure. This means, for example, that if a programmer changes three lines of a one hundred line program or routine, CCC only saves the three lines that have changed, not a whole new version of the entire 100 lines of information.

This tracking capability of CCC enables a user to maintain a complete audit trail history of all changes made to any structure within the CCC hierarchy. Also, it provides the ability to reconstruct a component as it was at any point in time. In addition to being able to display the actual lines that have been changed in any text component, one is able to generate a number of useful reports based on any one of several change attributes. For example, the following are typical user requests:

. What changes were made by programmer SMITH

. What changes were made to text structure SOURCE1, and by whom

. What changes were made to components of SYSTEMA, After September 27, 1982, at 3:00 PM

. Show me a list of all changes made that have a name of STR65

. Show me the latest version of ROUTINE1, or the version being used on January 23, 1982, at 1:00 AM, etc.

Thus, CCC allows programmers and managers to keep track of all changes, recreate or examine any change made (based on a number of relational criteria), and effectively minimize disk storage by only storing actual changes made to a component structure, rather than storing a whole new copy of the revised structure.

Figure 2 (below) contains a sample change report in which one can see a succinct summary of all the changes made to the component structures of module "SOURCE" in configuration "DEVELOPMENT" of system "SYSTEM1". For each structure, one can see all the versions (e.g., ";1", ";2", etc.), when the changes were made and who made them. Each version is identified by a change name (e.g., STR65).

Figure 2

Configuration Status Accounting Report

```
-  CHANGE REPORT
-
-  STRUCTURE LEVEL:  SYSTEM1.DEVELOPMENT.SOURCE/MOD
-
-  STRUCTURE          DATE;TIME            USER      NAME
-
   DM003/SRC;1        05/02/84;13:20:01    SANDY     STR65
   DM007/SRC;1        05/03/84;15:50:12    SANDY     STR65
   DM007/SRC;2        06/06/84;08:51:20    SANDY     STR18
   DM007/SRC;3        06/09/84;09:04:16    BRUCE     STR76
   DM011/SRC;1        05/03/84;10:34:22    SANDY     STR65
   DM012/SRC;1        05/18/84;09:06:28    BRUCE     STR73
   DM013/SRC;1        05/19/84;12:27:24    BRUCE     STR73
   DM015/SRC;1        04/17/84;11:52:24    SANDY     STR45
```

version number

structure type, in this case SRC stands for source

structure name

Figure 3

Detailed Change Report

```
-  CHANGE REPORT
-
-  STRUCTURE LEVEL:  SYSTEM1.DEVELOPMENT,SOURCE/MOD
-
-  STRUCTURE          DATE;TIME            USER      NAME
   DM007/SRC;3        06/09/84;09:04:16    BRUCE     STR76
-
-  DESCRIPTION
-
   This change was made to accommodate a special graphics device
   (Graphile Mode 13) attached to our compilers.  It was approved
   in Management Request No. M3-42.  It is documented in detail
   in our Internal Memo No. C3-42.
-  ACTUAL CHANGES
-
#1     DELETE 1 LINE BEGINNING WITH LINE 18 :

            ARRAY =   300

#2     INSERT 1 LINE :

18:1        ARRAY = 2500

       AFTER LINE 18:0
```

In Figure 3, an example of a more detailed change report is shown. Here a user asked for a listing of the description and actual changes made in version 3 of text structure DM007/SRC.

Trouble Reports

CCC also provides the ability to keep track of documents such as software trouble reports and engineering change proposals. The first report in Figure 4, contains a listing of the current status of all STR's. In the second report, one can see the complete history of STR number 51. Also, one can selectively ask for a summary description of each change of status, and list the actual contents of each STR document.

Figure 4

```
-  CHANGE REPORT
-
-  STRUCTURE LEVEL:  SYSTEM1.DEVELOPMENT.STR/MOD
-
-  STRUCTURE          DATE;TIME            USER      STATUS
   14/STR;3           04/06/84;09:36:19    BRUCE     FIXED
   77/STR;2           05/03/84;16:14:21    BRUCE     ASSIGNED
   39/STR;2           04/11/84;10:08:28    BRUCE     ASSIGNED
   51/STR;4           05/23/84;14:42:09    BRUCE     CLOSED
-  CHANGE REPORT
-
-  STRUCTURE LEVEL:  SYSTEM1.DEVELOPMENT.STR/MOD
-
-  STRUCTURE          DATE;TIME            USER      STATUS
-
   51/STR;1           04/25/84;11:08:49    BRUCE     REPORTED
   51/STR;2           04/30/84;09:39:06    BRUCE     ASSIGNED
   51/STR;3           05/15/84;16:00:32    BRUCE     FIXED
   51/STR;4           05/23/84;14:42:09    BRUCE     CLOSED
```

Control - Configurations (Baselines)

CCC offers true configuration control:

All components of a given software release or baseline can be organized and managed as a single entity that preserves the relationship between components. Then, all distinct but related releases can be handled as separate units with CCC doing the busy work of managing the changes that define the separate versions.

In addition, CCC provides the capability to operate on configurations as a whole. For example, one can combine the changes made in two separate configurations into a single configuration. CCC will flag any conflicts encountered when combining the two configurations.

Finally, CCC maintains a complete history of exactly what has been changed in moving from the original configuration of a given product to its latest version. The ability to document the changes from baseline to baseline gives full auditing and traceability, thus allowing the user to verify that each component is evolving in a logical and consistent progression from the previous stages.

For the purpose of describing how CCC maintains different versions of components, we have coined the terms "virtual" configurations. What this means to a CCC user is that whenever he or she uses the latest version of a piece of information, it appears as though that person has a complete, up-to-date copy of the information in question. In fact, the user really has only a virtual copy of the baseline configuration.

For example, the production version of a software product contains 20 routines. Configuration 1 of the same product also contains these 20 routines, but 5 of them have been modified to make the system functional under a different host computer. Physically, CCC only stores the changes to those 5 routines under Configuration 1, eliminating the redundancy inherent in duplicating the whole product.

All of this is transparent to the user of CCC.

Access Control and Protection

CCC provides powerful access control features to define who can do what and where (Figure 5 below).

Figure 5

Access Control

. USER-ID AND PASSWORD CONTROL

. THREE TYPES OF USERS:

   Data Base Administrator
   Manager
   User

. ACCESS CONTROL BASED ON:

   Structure
   User
   Class of User

. ENCRYPTION

To ensure that no unauthorized users log into CCC, there is log in user-ID and password control. User-ID and passwords may only be established by a user with data base administrator privileges, and must be correctly entered to gain admittance to CCC upon initial log in.

Furthermore, CCC users are divided into three categories with different degrees of privileges:

. Data Base Administrators

. Managers

. Users

In addition to controlling the access of users to CCC as a whole, CCC provides the capability to limit user access to a specific structure, on a per user, or class of user, basis. Thus, all users of class UPDATER, for example, might only be permitted to log into a development configuration, effectively locking out the corresponding production version from any accidental modification.

Users requiring tighter controls can also request that information be encrypted.

Traits

To determine how data is internally stored, and how difficult it is to access that data, CCC allows the assignment of structure traits.

These traits determine:

. whether a unit of information will be shared among derived configurations (i.e., virtual copy), or its storage will be duplicated (i.e., physical copy)

. whether CCC maintains a complete audit trail of all changes, or only the most recent version of a component

. the degree of compression by which information is stored

. the degree of encryption by which information is encoded.

Conclusion

Keeping track of evolving information is a critical issue with which the current manual methods cannot cope. The automation of configuration management is essential. Softool's CCC provides the high level of automation that is needed in a comprehensive change and configuration control environment.

[1] "Software Configuration Management", An Investment in Product Integrity, by Edward H. Bersoff, Vilas D. Henderson, Stanley G. Siegel

Workspaces and Experimental Databases:
Automated Support for Software Maintenance and Evolution

Gail E. Kaiser*
Columbia University
New York, NY 10027

Dewayne E. Perry
AT&T Bell Laboratories
Murray Hill, NJ 07974

Abstract

We introduce and compare two models of cooperation among programmers during software maintenance. Enforced cooperation is the normal mode of operation when the sheer size of the software maintenance effort makes *laissez-faire* management infeasible. Voluntary cooperation is more common when a small group works together to enhance a small system or modify a small portion of a large system. We describe a tool, Infuse, that provides change management in the context of both models of cooperation. We demonstrate how Infuse automates change propagation and enforces negotiation of conflicts for the enforced model, but provides less restrictive aids for maintaining consistency for the voluntary model.

1. Introduction

The maintenance and evolution of large systems requires cooperation among multiple programmers, but there are very few models and corresponding tools to support this cooperation. We introduce and compare two models of cooperation among programmers doing software maintenance: enforced and voluntary cooperation. We describe a tool, Infuse, that provides change management in the context of both models.

Enforced cooperation among programmers is necessary for software projects involving many (for example, 20 or more) programmers. Maintenance typically consists of a sequence of coordinated, scheduled source code changes each involving a large collection of modules.** Programmers must cooperate to maintain consistency among these modules during the modification and testing process. We present a software engineering environment, Infuse, that automates change management by enforcing such cooperation. Infuse automatically partitions these modules into a hierarchy of *experimental databases*. The partitioning may be determined by the syntactic and/or semantic dependencies among the modules or according to the dictates of project management. Each experimental database provides consistency checking among its modules and provides a forum for the programmers assigned to its modules, or their managers, to negotiate the interactions among the modules. Infuse requires that the modules within an experimental database be consistent with each other before permitting these modules to be merged back into the parent experimental database. This process repeats until the entire collection of consistently changed modules is merged back into the new release of the software system.

Voluntary cooperation is possible for projects involving a small number of programmers (for example, less than 10). Maintenance typically consists of partially ordered sequences of changes made by individual programmers to a small collection of modules, where additional modules are dynamically added to each collection as the programmer deems necessary. Cooperation is required only when multiple changes are made by different programmers at the same time. Infuse automates this more relaxed form of change management by providing a *workspace* in which the programmer makes his changes. Individual workspaces are combined if the programmers choose to coordinate their changes; we are concerned in this paper only with these combined workspaces. Each workspace provides consistency checking among its modules and thus aids the programmers in making sure the changes are consistent

---

* Supported in part by a grant from the AT&T Foundation, in part by a grant from Siemens Research and Technology Laboratories, and in part by a Faculty Award from Digital Equipment Corporation.

** The work described in this paper is independent of any particular programming language. For example, the term "module" applies to both assembler source files and Ada packages.

---

with each other. Infuse also aids the programmers in merging their changes back into the baseline version of the software system.

Infuse supports both experimental databases and workspaces, and both may be used for the same project where warranted. In particular, workspaces may cut across the divisions imposed by the experimental databases to permit flexible modes of cooperation among programmers.

We begin describing the problems of change management during software maintenance. We present Infuse's automated support for enforced and voluntary cooperation and explain how Infuse automates change management using existing programming tools. We compare Infuse to related systems, none of which support an enforced model of cooperation. We conclude by listing our contributions.

2. Changes to Software Systems

Cooperation is required when source code changes to a software system involve the efforts of multiple programmers. In a medium-to-large software project (involving at least 100,000 lines of source code), there are several reasons why maintenance activities are rarely carried out by a single programmer. The sheer volume of the effort may be prohibitive. There may not be any single programmer with knowledge about the modules and the system sufficient to make the changes correctly and rapidly. There may be administrative considerations that make it inappropriate for one programmer from one managerial unit to modify the modules assigned to another programmer reporting to a different manager.

Instead, a group of programmers normally cooperates on a change that involves several modules, particularly a change that cuts across subsystem boundaries. When changes are being made in several modules, it is necessary for the changes to be consistent with each other. The changes must be *syntactically* consistent [15], meaning that the interfaces between the modules must be correct and that the modules can compile and link successfully. Consider the case where module M exports procedure p, where procedure p has two formal parameters of types $t1$ and $t2$. Module N imports procedure p from module M and defines procedure q that calls procedure p; the call is made with two arguments, of types $t1$ and $t2$.

The change to this software system includes modifying procedure p to add a third parameter, of type $t3$. This change requires that module N also be changed, so procedure q calls p with a third argument, which must be of type $t3$. It is necessary for the programmer responsible for module M to communicate this change to the programmer responsible for module N and for the two programmers to coordinate their changes and make sure they are consistent.

When changes are made in several modules, it is also necessary for the changes to be *semantically* consistent [9]. Consider the case where the new parameter of type $t3$ is a pointer to a buffer. Procedure p assumes that procedure q has allocated space for this buffer before calling p. If this has not been done, then procedure p will cause a run-time error when it attempts to write into the buffer implied by its third argument. Assumptions of this kind are not normally reflected in the interfaces among modules, and thus cannot be detected by the compiler linker. It is therefore particularly crucial for the programmers involved to communicate their assumptions and cooperate on making the desired changes in the software system.

Infuse provides the basis for automating two kinds of consistency checking, change simulation and change propagation; both may be applied with either syntactic or semantic consistency. A programmer may request *change simulation* to check for any interface errors [10] introduced by his most recent changes without immediately notifying other programmers of these changes. This permits a programmer to reconsider a change that has undesirable effects on other modules. Change simulation may be performed with respect to only the modules in the programmer's workspace, with respect to only the modules in the programmer's experimental database, or with respect to a baseline version of the software system.

Infuse automatically performs *change propagation* under certain circumstances, discussed below. The tool checks for interface errors among the modules in a workspace or among the modules in an experimental database. For each interface error found, Infuse notifies the programmers assigned to the relevant modules and informs them of the change(s) that introduced the error.

There are three important distinctions between change simulation and change propagation. The first is that Infuse propagates changes automatically while it simulates changes only in response to a programmer's request. The second difference is that Infuse can simulate any change, but propagates only 'committed' changes. The third distinction is in the way that Infuse reports inconsistencies. It reports errors found during change propagation to every programmer whose module was involved in the inconsistency; this permits the programmers to negotiate further changes with full knowledge of any problem areas. In contrast, it reports errors found during change simulation only to the individual programmer who initiated the analysis; this enables the programmer to back out of uncommitted but troublesome changes without entering into negotiation with other programmers.

3. Experimental Databases

An experimental database contains a collection of reserved modules. Modules are placed in a particular experimental database according to some criteria that partition the collection of modules involved in a change. This normally occurs when a planned change (or set of planned changes) in the software system requires coordinated changes in a set of modules. The programmers responsible for these modules are automatically associated with the experimental database.

Experimental databases are hierarchical. The top-level experimental database consists of a virtual copy of the entire software system. The second level experimental database consists of only those modules involved in the change. This database is then partitioned into child experimental databases, where disjoint subsets of the modules are placed in each child. The partitioning is repeated recursively until the experimental database at each leaf contains one or more modules assigned to the same programmer. We refer to a leaf as a 'singleton' experimental database. An example hierarchy (without the base level) is illustrated in Figure 1.

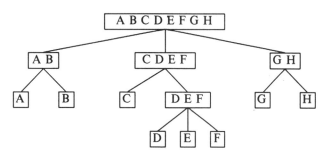

This software system consists of modules A through Z, so the top-level experimental database (not shown) contains each of these 26 modules. Modules A through H are involved in the change, so the second-level experimental database contains copies of A, B, C, D, E, F, G and H. The third level of the hierarchy consists of three experimental databases; the first contains A and B, the second C, D, E and F, and the third G and H. The second of these experimental databases is further subdivided into two experimental databases at the next level. The leaves of the hierarchy each contain a single module.

Figure 1: Hierarchy of Experimental Databases

The hierarchy of experimental databases may be partitioned manually to reflect the management hierarchy of the software maintenance team. Another possibility is to partition, again manually, according to the subsystem organization of the target software system. However, both alternatives often result in higher communication and propagation costs than other methods of partitioning that reflect the interconnections among the modules.

We have developed an approach to partitioning based on the strengths of the syntactic and semantic dependencies among the modules [11]. This approach attempts to minimize the communication and propagation costs, and has the additional advantage that it can be automated. An optimal partitioning would place together in the same subtree of experimental databases those modules whose new changes will interact most strongly. Unfortunately, it is not possible to determine an optimal partitioning *a priori* because the full costs cannot be determined until after the changes have been completed. We propose strengths of dependencies as a good approximation.

The partitioning tool must be embedded within Infuse. However, it is not necessary for an experimental database to interact with the tools used by the programmers to modify their modules. Infuse places no requirements of any sort on these tools. When the programmer completes the changes to his module (or small set of modules), the programmer must give the **deposit** command to notify the experimental database that his part of the overall change is complete.

Infuse invokes an analysis tool to determine whether the module is self-consistent. Self-consistency within a module means that no errors are detected during lexical analysis or parsing and that any symbols that are both defined and used internally are used correctly with respect to their definitions. For example, the front-end of a compiler is easily modified to check syntactic consistency only with respect to a particular module, ignoring consistency with other modules. The deposit of a singleton experimental database is not permitted unless the module is self-consistent.

After all the modules in an experimental database have been deposited, Infuse invokes an analysis tool to propagate changes. The tool checks that the modules in the database are consistent among themselves. Intermodule consistency requires that any symbol defined by one module and used by another is used correctly with respect to its definition. Modules outside the experimental database are not considered. It is not difficult to include external modules in the analysis, but this leads to an information overload and communication difficulties as many error messages are generated due to temporary inconsistencies and other transient conditions. The goal of experimental databases is to limit change propagation to a manageable level.

Infuse checks for three possible results. The first is that the modules are consistent; Infuse automatically deposits the entire experimental database into its parent experimental database. Once all child experimental databases have been deposited, Infuse then analyzes the parent experimental database as it analyzed each of the children.

The second possibility is that the modules are consistent,

but some of the modules in the experimental database must be recompiled due to changes in imported modules. Infuse marks these modules for recompilation, and then deposits the entire experimental database into the parent database as above. It is generally best that recompilation not proceed immediately, since inconsistencies involving these modules may be detected at a higher level of the hierarchy.

The third possibility is that the modules are inconsistent; Infuse informs all the programmers associated with the experimental database about the conflicts. It provides precise information about the localized conflicts for each affected module and appropriate instructions for resolving the conflicts. The programmers or their managers must now negotiate changes to their modules that will resolve the conflict. Infuse does not permit a deposit of the experimental database into its parent until the modules in the experimental database are consistent among themselves.

The relevant programmers choose some subset (perhaps all) of the conflicting modules for an additional set of changes to remove the inconsistencies. This group of modules is then recursively partitioned in the same manner as the original partition into a hierarchy of experimental databases. The root of this new hierarchy is the experimental database in which the inconsistencies were detected, so this new partitioning does not affect the rest of the original hierarchy. This process is illustrated in Figures 2 and 3.

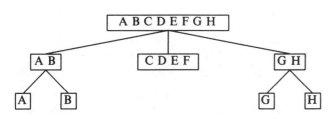

Modules D, E and F were changed and deposited into the experimental database containing only D, E and F. Infuse invoked the analysis tool, which determined that there were no inconsistencies among these three modules. The experimental database was then deposited into its parent, which contains C, D, E and F. Module C had also been changed and deposited into this experimental database.

Figure 2: Deposit into
Parent Experimental Databases

Then the resolution process repeats as if there had been no previous resolution. The modules in the leaf experimental databases are modified again, and deposited again into

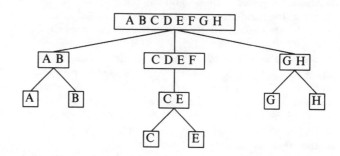

Infuse again invoked the analysis tool, finding a conflict between modules C and E and between modules C and F. Subsequently, the programmers chose to modify C and E (but not D or F) to remove the inconsistency. Infuse creates a new child experimental database containing C and E, which is further partitioned so the leaves of the hierarchy again contain a single module.

Figure 3: Repartitioning into a
Subhierarchy of Experimental Databases

their parent. If there are new conflicts, or if previously detected inconsistencies have not been correctly resolved, then additional negotiation and change must follow.

When part of a hierarchy is deposited, inconsistencies may be detected, requiring repartitioning of the subhierarchy. We call this the 'yo-yo' effect. When the yo-yo effect occurs frequently, particularly within the same portion of the hierarchy, this usually reflects poor communication or a lack of cooperation among the participating programmers. Infuse can be set up to monitor instances of this problem and to notify appropriate managers of the problem.

3.1 Tool Integration and Change Simulation

We have discussed how Infuse operates when the programming tools are not integrated into Infuse, and each programmer must explicitly notify Infuse when his changes are complete by issuing the **deposit** command. This works well for change propagation, but difficulties arise when we apply it to change simulation. The goal of simulating changes is to inform the programmer of any conflicts caused by his changes before the changes have been deposited, while the programmer is still in the context where the change is made. To do this effectively, each modification tool must be integrated into Infuse so that the **simulate** command can be invoked from within the tool.

This is a rudimentary level of 'integration', but it has the significant advantage over non-integration that the programmer can try a small change and immediately find out how it affects the modules in the parent experimental database. Without such integration, the programmer has to leave the modification tool and perhaps sacrifice its internal state to obtain early notification of any problems.

If we add a further level of integration, then Infuse provides more extensive information regarding any problems. For example, Infuse highlights any errors detected in the part of the source code currently being displayed by the modification tool; if this tool supports multiple windows, Infuse pops up a window to display the conflicting source code from other modules. This makes it easier for a programmer to decide whether he wants to commit the proposed change and, if so, to inform other programmers of the effects on their modules.

4. Workspaces

Integration makes it possible for Infuse to inform programmers immediately of conflicts between their module and other modules in the parent experimental database, but it does not help programmers keep track of simultaneous changes being made to other modules. Sometimes it is important for a small subset of the programmers involved in a large change to get immediate feedback about the interactions among the changes to their modules. In these cases, it is appropriate to propagate changes at agreed intervals, such as on demand or after each checkpoint, rather than waiting until all of the modules have been deposited. However, immediately propagating changes does not solve the whole problem, because partitioning does not necessarily place these modules in the same experimental database. These issues motivated the development of workspaces, which support interactive consistency checking among selected modules. Workspaces can cut across the partitioning of the hierarchy of experimental databases, or can be used alone to support changes involving a small group of programmers.

Like an experimental database, a workspace contains a collection of modules. In general, the modules have been placed in the workspace because the programmers responsible for the modules have decided to coordinate their changes to the software system. Figure 4 shows a workspace that cuts across the divisions imposed by experimental databases.

Unlike an experimental database, the workspace must interact with the tools used by the programmers to modify their modules. The tools may include text editors, syntax-directed editors, program transformation systems, *etc*. Infuse does not assume any particular technology for making changes in modules. Each programmer can use his favorite collection of tools, or use the standard collection provided at his site, and there is no need for the modules in the workspace to be modified using the same tools, as long as all these tools are appropriately integrated with

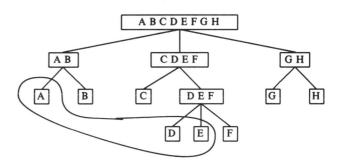

The most crucial part of the change to the software system involves modules A, D and E, so the changes to these modules must be carefully coordinated. Thus a workspace is defined that contains these three modules and provides the three programmers with immediate feedback about interactions among the changes to their modules.

Figure 4: A Workspace

Infuse.

The minimal requirement is that each tool notify the workspace when a modification session terminates; this involves a minor extension to each tool used within Infuse. Many such 'sessions' may be required to complete a change in a module. For example, the end of a session may correspond to a checkpoint, and editing of the same module may continue immediately. A session may involve editing the entire module, or a subunit of the module such as a procedure.

When each modification session ends (or on demand), Infuse invokes an analysis tool to propagate changes. It determines the syntactic and/or semantic changes that have taken place. For example, a theorem prover is an possible tool for semantic analysis. In particular, the Inscape environment [9, 12] provides a notation for specifying the preconditions, postconditions and obligations of each procedure and automatically determines whether all preconditions and obligations have been satisfied by previous and subsequence postconditions, respectively.

Infuse checks for three possibilities. The first is that changes in the module do not affect any other modules in the workspace. In this case, the workspace does nothing except monitor further changes in the module.

The second is that the changes in the module require recompilation of other modules resident in the workspace, but do not require the source code of any of these other modules to be modified. When this occurs, the necessary recompilation is noted for later. There is no need to inform the programmers of such requirements, since Infuse performs these recompilations automatically.

The third possibility is that the changes in the module require source modifications in one or more of the other modules resident in the workspace. This happens when there is a syntactic and/or semantic inconsistency between the changed module and each module that now requires a change. In this case, both the programmer who made the change and the programmer responsible for the affected module are immediately notified of the conflict. Since Infuse propagates changes frequently, it is particularly important to keep the number of modules in a workspace small to restrict the error messages and resulting negotiations among programmers to a manageable level.

4.1 Integration of Analysis Tools

Infuse is most useful when there is a high level of integration between it and the modification tools used by the programmers. For example, notification of new interface errors can take several forms. At the minimal level of integration, Infuse relies on electronic mail messages or simply dumps error messages on the participating programmers' screens. At higher levels of integration, Infuse provides immediate visual feedback and displays the relevant portions of all modules involved in each conflict, enabling the programmers to negotiate changes to their modules as soon as possible.

In any case, the level of detail included in the notification is dependent on the capabilities of the analysis tool(s) used and the level of integration between Infuse and the analyzer(s). The more detail that is provided, the easier it will be for the participating programmers to negotiate changes without confusion. Integration requires that the minimal analysis tool match error messages with textual lines of source code. When the modification tool is a structure editor [4, 13] that shares its internal representation with the analysis tool, this can be improved to attach error messages to portions of the abstract syntax tree.

If the analysis tool is moderately intelligent, in the sense of the intelligent assistants described by Winograd [16], it might suggest how to to fix the problems.

Certain difficulties arise when a conflicting module is involved in several distinct coordinated changes, and thus the module is resident in several overlapping workspaces. Changes made to the other modules in one workspace must not leak to the other modules in other workspaces through the error messages regarding the common module. Infuse prevents this problem by propagating changes to only one workspace at a time. This problem does not arise for change simulation because only the requesting programmer receives the error messages.

5. Related Work

The following tools also propagate changes among modules. However, none support the enforced model of cooperation among programmers necessary for large maintenance projects, since they permit programmers to modify source code at will, in some cases requiring that no other programmer is modifying the same module at the same time. Only one provides an automated forum for change negotiation among programmers.

Make   When requested, the Unix Make tool [3] rebuilds the entire software system. It invokes the tools specified in the 'makefile' on changed files and all files that depend on changed files. Make is normally used to recompile and relink.

Build   The Unix Build tool [2] is an extension to Make that permits various users to have different views of the target software system. A 'viewpath' defines the sequence of directories searched by Make to find the files named in the makefile. Viewpaths are similar to the underlying support for experimental databases.

Cedar   The Cedar System Modeller [7] combines an advanced version of the Make tool with version control. It invokes the tools on selected versions of modules. A distinguished programmer called the 'Release Master' is informed of syntactic interface errors between modules; the Release Master is responsible for communicating with the programmers responsible for these modules.

DSEE   The Apollo Domain Software Engineering Environment [8] also combines Make-like facilities with version control. In addition, DSEE provides a monitoring mechanism that allows programmers and managers to request that they be notified when selected modules are changed.

Masterscope Interlisp's Masterscope tool [14] automatically maintains cross-referencing information among program units. It approximates change simulation by answering queries about syntactic dependencies among program units.

SVCE   The Gandalf System Version Control Environment [5] performs incremental consistency checking across the modules in its database and notifies the programmer of errors as soon as they occur. The consistency checking is limited to detecting syntactic interface errors. SVCE supports multiple programmers working in sequence, but does not handle simultaneous changes.

Smile   The Smile programming environment [4, 6] introduced the notion of an experimental database, but does not support a hierarchy of experimental databases and does not automate partitioning. It both simulates and propagates changes at the syntactic level, and does not permit a deposit of an experimental database until its modules are syntactically consistent among themselves and with the other modules in the main database. However, Smile restricts each experimental database to a single programmer, preventing multiple programmers from cooperating on changes. We have used Smile extensively, and have drawn on that experience in developing Infuse.

6. Conclusions

The primary contributions of this research in software engineering environments are:

- Change management that supports the specific problems of large numbers of programmers maintaining large systems.

- Integration with facilities specific to small group cooperation within large projects.

Acknowledgements

Yoelle Maarek has developed a clustering algorithm for partitioning the change set into hierarchical experimental databases. Bulent Yener is working with us on the implementation of hierarchical experimental databases as an extension of Smile. David Bellanger and David Hanssen provided careful readings and comments on an earlier version of this paper.

References

[1] David R. Barstow, Howard E. Shrobe and Erik Sandewall, eds. **Interactive Programming Environments**. McGraw-Hill, 1984.

[2] V. B. Ericson and J. F. Pellegrin. *Build — A Software Construction Tool*. **AT&T Bell Laboratories Technical Journal**, 63:6 (July-August 1984), 1049-1059.

[3] S. I. Feldman. *Make — A Program for Maintaining Computer Programs*. **Software — Practice & Experience**, 9:4 (April 1979), 255-265.

[4] A. N. Habermann and D. Notkin. *Gandalf: Software Development Environments*. **IEEE Transactions on Software Engineering**, SE-12:12 (December 1986), 1117-1127.

[5] Gail E. Kaiser and A. Nico Habermann. *An Environment for System Version Control*. In **Digest of Papers of the Twenty-Sixth IEEE Computer Society International Conference**, February 1983, 415-420.

[6] Gail E. Kaiser and Peter H. Feiler. **Intelligent Assistance without Artificial Intelligence. Proceedings of the Thirty-Second IEEE Computer Society International Conference**, February 1987, 236-241.

[7] Butler W. Lampson and Eric E. Schmidt. *Organizing Software in a Distributed Environment*. In **Proceedings of the SIGPLAN '83 Symposium on Programming Language Issues in Software Systems**, June 1983, 1-13. **SIGPLAN Notices** 18:6 (June 1983).

[8] David B. LeBlang and Robert P. Chase, Jr. *Computer-Aided Software Engineering in a Distributed Workstation Environment*. In **Proceedings of the SIGSOFT/SIGPLAN Software Engineering Symposium on Practical Software Development Environments**, April 1984, 104-112. **SIGPLAN Notices** 19:5 (May 1984).

[9] Dewayne E. Perry. *Software Interconnection Models*. **Proceedings of the 9th International Conference on Software Engineering**, March 30 - April 2 1987, 61-71.

[10] D. E. Perry and W. M. Evangelist. *An Empirical Study of Software Interface Faults*. In **Proceedings of the International Symposium on New Directions in Computing**, August 1985, 32-38.

[11] Dewayne E. Perry and Gail E. Kaiser. *Infuse: A Tool for Automatically Managing and Coordinating Source Changes in Large Systems*. **Proceedings of the ACM Fifteenth Annual Computer Science Conference**, February 1987, 292-299.

[12] Dewayne E. Perry **The Inscape Program Construction and Evolution Environment**. Technical Report, Computer Technology Research Lab, AT&T Bell Laboratories, August 1986.

[13] Thomas Reps and Tim Teitelbaum. *The Synthesizer Generator*. In **Proceedings of the SIGSOFT/SIGPLAN Software Engineering Symposium on Practical Software Development Environments**, April 1984. **SIGPLAN Notices** 19:5 (May 1984).

[14] Warren Teitelman and Larry Masinter. *The Interlisp Programming Environment*. **IEEE Computer**, 14:4 (April 1981), 25-34. Reprinted in [1].

[15] Walter F. Tichy. *Smart Recompilation*. **ACM Transactions on Programming Languages and Systems**, 8:3 (July 1986), 273-291.

[16] Terry Winograd. *Breaking the Complexity Barrier (Again)*. In **Proceedings of the ACM SIGPLAN/SIGIR Interface Meeting on Programming Languages — Information Retrieval**, November 1973. Reprinted in [1].

AUTOMATED SOFTWARE TESTING — CASE STUDIES

E. Uren, E. Miller, J. Irwin

Software Research, Inc.
625 Third Street
San Francisco, CA 94107-1997

Abstract: Typical Software Research projects are described and numerical results from these projects are given. Levels of productivity are very high provided that a significant level of mechanization can be obtained. SR's use of specialized software tools is described in detail.

Confidentiality Note: We have to keep the names of clients confidential — this is often a main condition of our work -- and have disguised the project summaries extensively. However, in all cases the statistics and the effort levels are reported accurately, as is the general type of product.

INTRODUCTION

We have found four major patterns in the work we are called on to do for clients at the "hi-tech" end of our business. The patterns repeat often enough that we think it will be interesting to current and potential clients to see what the numbers are, so that they can compare themselves with others.

In addition to these patterns, there is substantial common ground across these project types.

The typical situation is that a vendor has a product such as a compiler or operating system under development. The vendor is interested both in detecting errors in the current release or version of the product and in having a procedure for detecting errors. The procedure should be mechanized and should be as simple as possible so that when errors are repaired, the entire product may be retested economically, (this latter procedure is called regression). This will enable the user to verify that the errors have indeed been corrected and that no new errors have been introduced during the repair process.

To detect the errors, a test suite is constructed and since the customer is very eager to see the results of the testing the customer expects the test suite to be applied to the product under study during development of the suite itself. Typically, SR will agree to do this and also to accomodate their eagerness, SR usually sets up electronic mail so that they may get "instant access" to the latest "news " about tests applied and errors detected.

Development of the mechanized procedure for running the test suites was considered to be a process which was unique to each project because environments and test objects appear, at first glance, to be so different. However, as experience with the projects increased, however, it became clear that a general purpose tool could (and should) be constructed.

Project Classes

Test Suite Development: In this category, our purpose is to build the customer a suite for a fixed product. In early discussions with the potential customer, a decision is usually made whether there should be full validation or whether a touch test suite will suffice. A touch test suite consists of a set of programs that collectively exercise all language at least once. Smaller than a full validation suite, it is also far cheaper. It is a compromise between size and required complexity (that one might expect in a full validation), and thoroughness.

Comprehensive Product Testing: In this category, the purpose is to build and apply a complicated mechanized set of tests. The thrust of these projects is to develop a set of tests which provide as complete functional coverage as possible of the product under test. Since the product tends to be complex, the advantages of mechanizing the process of applying the tests become more significant. Consequently, there is considerable effort devoted to constructing the mechanical methods of application. The mechanization process goes hand-in-hand with organizing the tests themselves. This organization in and of itself proves to be a very powerful tool for analysis of the weak and strong components of the product. Generally, the grouping of individual test cases in the suite is oriented towards major functions of the product, and an accumulation of failed test cases in a group will provide a clue to product developers as to how to repair the errors so detected.

Detailed Technical Testing: In this category, we classify compiler or operating system testing. Compilers and operating systems are the foundation upon which which most development work is constructed. Typically, they are widely distributed with the computer hardware, and probably to most programmers, are seen as part of a complete package which happens to comprise both hardware and software. The acceptance of the hardware by the user is indeed "masked" by the "appearance" and performance of the software. Consequently, the vendor considers it crucial to be as fully informed as possible about what these systems can and can not do.

Validation Testing: In this category, we have another type of critical product. Some software products have a particularly important dimension of criticality since they control medical devices which themselves have important impact on the management of health care. They can be of different orders of complexity. At various levels, they provide data used to analyze an individual's state of health and treatment can be prescribed on the basis of results of these systems. Not only do these systems affect human life and the quality of human life, they are also subject to regulation by the Federal Government and they operate in a domain wherein liability assumes a greater and greater importance.

TEST SUITE DEVELOPMENT

Environment Test Suite

Under contract to a foreign company, which was in turn under contract to a (foreign) government agency, SR developed a comprehensive validation suite for substantial extensions to the Unix System V validation suite. This test suite was the first to address validation of an environment, and was targeted to an environment designed for portable common tools.

SR developed the following during about 4 effort-months:

- 157 self-checking test programs.
- 471 tests of 175 commands, calls, drivers and functions.
- Special control program.

The special control program, in addition to executing the tests, reports incrementally on the progress of a group of tests in terms of the pass/fail ratio.

SR provided onsite installation support.

The initial application uncovered 24 errors.

PL/I Touch Test Suite Development

SR developed a touch test suite for the LPI/PL-1 subset G compiler for a major US vendor. This suite tests 204 features of the language. The touch test suite consists of 11,167 lines of PL/I code in 165 programs (and two auxiliary files for one of the programs), 26 scripts, two automated test scripts and 164 baseline files which have been validated manually.

Included in the suite (but not necessary for

"functional coverage") were 8 programs from a widely available PL/I G-subset textbook.

An important feature of the suite was that it was set under SMARTS control (Software Maintenance and Regression System —see Reference 2), so that regression could be just about as automatic as one wished using the two automated test scripts. This is the generalized regression control system referred to previously. The package also included scripts to simplify compiling, loading and executing the test cases should one not wish to use SMARTS.

The programs in the test suite were not self-checking. Instead, SR used another approach. First, all the test output results were accumulated in "baseline" files. Then SR validated the contents of the files to ensure that the contents were correct for the test object in its current state of development. Thus while most of the output was correct because the test object had no errors, in some (perhaps many) instances, the test results were the results of errors. This output was still incorporated into the baseline files. Output from subsequent executions of the test suite during regression could then be compared with the baseline files quite simply using "diff". Clearly, any differences reflected changes in behavior of the test object, which is exactly what the tester was looking for in a regression situation. The goal of the regression test is that correct output remain unchanged and incorrect output be changed, presumably for the better. Under SMARTS, this is always the approach taken.

During development of the suite, SR discovered thirty-one problems serious enough to warrant reporting in formal error reports. The cost of discovery of each error was $500 alone, IGNORING the fact that a test suite, a set of baseline cases and a regression system were delivered.

COMPREHENSIVE PRODUCT TESTING

Assembler Test Suite and Control Program

In this project for a major US vendor, the purpose was to develop both a comprehensive test suite for a new macro assembler and an automated way to apply it, and also to apply the suite to the assembler using the automated procedure. The automated procedure was to allow the user to "browse" through the test set, run individual tests or groups of tests, compare results of runs with previous results, and maintain statistics.

610 test programs were developed and applied, detecting 160 defects. After the client made some revisions to the macro assembler, the tests were re-applied.

The automated procedure developed in this project can be used in other regression situations on other projects. Thus the client has, as a by-product, a new universal tool for regression. Should the client develop another product which requires regression, it is only necessary to define the structure of the tests in a control file, construct the tests and validate the output of the first application in what are called baseline files.

From SR's point of view, development of the automated procedure led SR to completely generalize the process of automated control and produce the SMARTS package. SR had developed so many control programs from scratch that the need was evident. The general purpose qualities of this program were the final step.

To develop the tests and the regression system took one effort-year. The regression system contains 5,400 lines of control file.

System Test Mechanization Project

A major portion of this project was to develop an automated regression system for a client with a quite large, extremely sophisticated, highly user-interactive, product. The product runs on Sun workstations and was designed using object-oriented principles. Interaction with the system used a keyboard as one might expect, but far more emphasis and use was focussed on the use of a mouse. The client had invested substantially (more than 8 figures) in developing the system. There have been many releases and a few versions have been in beta-test for about a year.

Working with the client's programming staff, SR developed a system, integrated into the client's program, which captured key-strokes and mouse movements. Tests may be captured during their first application and played back. This together with the regression system allows the client to automate most of the testing procedure.

Thus the client has an accurate detailed record of what functions the test performed, and there is also a procedure for modifying these test playback files so that test variants may be constructed economically. Performed under control of the regression system, SMARTS, comparisons with the results of prior tests may be made and statistics maintained.

SR developed 210 tests in the process. There were about 650 sub-tests included. In the process of constructing and applying the tests, SR discovered 22 errors.

DETAILED TECHNICAL TESTING

Unix System Testing

The purpose of this project was to apply previously constructed touch tests for Unix utilities, to extend touch tests for the system interface, construct library function tests and to develop and apply tests to assess the computer's kernel-level stability.

The client was a major U.S. computer manufacturer whose new computer model was at about the final

stages of hardware testing.

To assess the computer's kernel-level stability, SR developed a suite of self-checking tests of CPU, memory, disk I/O, serial communications and a CapBak(tm) session simulating a "typical" terminal user. The tests in the stability test suite were parameterized as to size and could be executed in different mixes. Thus instability in terms of test failure or degraded response time was observed in terms of the size and mix of the load on the machine.

There were 141 tests of utility functions testing 665 switches and combinations of 195 Unix base commands, 66 tests of the system interface (with 182 sub-tests) and 87 tests of library functions (with 150 sub-tests). Fifty-one anomalies were detected of which thirty-one proved to be errors in the software.

The stability tests consisted of load tests for the CPU, Disk, communication channel, keyboard and memory. These parameterized tests could be run independently or as a mixture. Test run times ranged from 8 seconds through 37 hours. Five anomalies were detected in this portion.

The control program for the stability tests contained enough general characteristics to be considered the "seed" for SMARTS.

Xenix Touch Testing

Xenix V Software System Test Project

The purpose of this project, for a large U.S. computer manufacturer, was to validate the operation of Xenix V on a variety of the manufacturer's machines. The test suite developed was to be applied to a number and variety of machines in single-user mode, linked together, and to different versions of the operating system.

SR developed touch tests for all XENIX utilities including base commands, software development system commands, and text processing commands. SR also planned and developed full validation tests for the following software device drivers:

>Memory Managment Unit
>80287 Co-processor
>CPU
>Serial Port (including Multiport)
>Parallel Port
>Console
>Clock
>Timer

The statistics for these tests were too voluminous themselves for this document. Suffice to say there were considerably more than 1000 tests. Another point to note is that this project was the last that SR had do without the benefit of either a control program or a regression system. The lack of mechanization meant that running the tests and documenting them accurately consumed substantial manual resources.

SR detected 94 errors in the first application of the tests and 50 in the first of three regressions.

VALIDATION TESTING

Patient Data Management System QC

The purpose of this project was to test a system which permitted medical patients to accumulate periodic readings of certain biological variables without visiting a medical facility. The patient used a portable recording device for this. At fairly regular intervals, the patients' records could be offloaded to a personal computer software system for analysis and storage. The client was a major US supplier of medical equipment. SR developed a system for maintaining the system under strict configuration control; and developed a system for testing new releases thoroughly and economically before distribution to the client's customers. Thus a new release must proceed both under careful configuration control and under examination under the same test situations as previous versions.

To accomplish this, SR developed a set of tests under automatic keystroke capture and playback conditions (using SR's CapBak(tm) system — Reference 1), developed a further set of functional tests, established a Software Incident Reporting System for tracking errors, placed master copies of the code under Unix SCCS control and systematized procedures for making changes to the code smoothly. SR performed detailed coverage analysis on each version of the code using the automated test suite to ensure that the test suite tested the code thoroughly. A variety of errors and anomalies were discovered and repaired as part of the project effort.

Quality Control Printer Testing

This client was under contract to a major U.S. medical equipment supplier to produce hardware and software which would permit the use of a printer as a Quality Control device by producing reports derived from data accumulated in some medical equipment. This medical equipment is, ultimately, the equipment whose operation needs to be checked periodically. When not performing this function, the printer would serve as a printer.

SR's task was to test the software which checked the operation of the medical equipment. SR tested it in a number of ways.

First, SR performed a formal inspection and review of the code, finding 71 anomalies at the modular level and 65 at the system level. Second, it developed a set of 38 functional tests which were applied to instrumented versions of the code compiled on a PC and determined that the coverage levels reached very high levels for both branch coverage and system coverage. SR used TCAT/C and

STCAT/C (References 3 and 4), another set of standard tools for this step of coverage analysis.

Third SR produced another 27 tests and modified the original 38 to have increased numbers of readings. This process required that SR also develop a method for generating test cases.

Fourth, SR developed a validation system for test cases. This system consisted of three parts. One part used the same input as the code under test and computed results and the coordinates of where the results should be plotted on graphs which could be part of the output. Another part extracted the results of the test code's output and presented this data in the same format as the first program's output. A third program could compare the output of the first two parts. That this process worked correctly was formally validated on the output of a sample.

Next, SR placed the test suite under SMARTS control for regression purposes. Regression could not be as automatic as one would like due to fact that the code under test, requires that switches be set and a button pushed before the code executes using the data. Nevertheless, the baseline cases were validated.

Finally, SR applied the test cases to two releases of the software.

Another twenty-two error reports were written; 14 of these were judged serious.

By the end of the project, the defect rate on the latest version was 11 or about 4/KLOC. Of these 11, about 5 were still serious or 2/KLOC. Thus, the complete error detection process reduced the error detection rate by a decimal order of magnitude.

REFERENCES

1) D. Casey, L. Ceguerra, C. Cox, J. Irwin and M. Morrison, "User's Manual for Capbak, Keystroke Capture and Playback System", Release 2.0.9, Technical Note TN-1075, Software Research, Inc, San Francisco, Ca., May 1987.

2) D. Casey, C. Cox, J. Irwin and E. Qualls, "User's Manual for SMARTS, Software Maintenance and Regression Test System", Release 4.1, Teechnical Note TN-1281, Software Research, Inc., San Francisco Ca 94107, May 1987.

3) R.W. Erickson, H. Nguyen, E. Miller, J. Irwin, D. Casey and L. Ling, "User's Manual for TCAT/C (PC Version)", Technical Note RM-1100/2, Software Research Associates, San Francisco, Ca., September 1984.

4) H. Nguyen, "User's Manual for S-TCAT/C PC/DOS Version", Release 4.7, Technical Note RM-1266/1, Software Research Associates, San Francisco, Ca., August 1986.

SOFTWARE MAINTENANCE USING METAPROGRAMMING SYSTEMS

Brian W. Terry and Robert D. Cameron

School of Computing Science, Simon Fraser University, Burnaby,
British Columbia, V5A 1S6, Canada.

Abstract

Metaprogramming systems allow the construction of programs (metaprograms) that operate on programs. This paper introduces the notion of using metaprograms to perform software maintenance activities in a software development environment.

An example metaprogram is introduced to demonstrate ease of use, power and applicability. The authors' experiences in maintaining a large software system are presented and some of the advantages of using metaprograms are outlined.

Introduction

This paper considers the application of metaprogramming systems [3,4] to software maintenance activities. Metaprogramming systems facilitate the construction of programs that treat other programs as data objects. We consider the use of such systems to allow maintenance programmers to construct special purpose (program-specific) tools. This is in contrast to general purpose tools, such as compilers, which are not usually feasible to construct or customize in-house. We would like to bring metaprogramming out of the research and development community and see it used in industrial applications to fill the rather large gap between manual tools (text-editors) and general purpose ones (compilers).

Program-specific metaprogramming is the construction of programs to perform operations on a particular program or collection of programs. Such metaprograms are generally written for program maintenance applications after the construction of the target software. They are usually intended for use only on that software, although parts of the metaprograms may become general utilities for broader application.

A typical situation that we envision is the creation of a 200 line metaprogram to perform some maintenance operation on a 50,000 line target program. The cost of constructing such a metaprogram is minimal compared with the investment in the existing program. One need not be overly concerned about design and efficiency of the metaprogram since it will be used relatively few times and the cost of its execution will be much less than the labour plus machine costs of manually performing any significant task on such a large piece of software.

One example results from the fact that software maintenance is made easier if redundancy is minimized or eliminated. For example consider separate compilation of Pascal programs. Lists of external subroutine declarations must be prepared for inclusion into the calling code. This means that subroutine headers must occur in two places (the precise details of these declarations vary from dialect to dialect). It is more convenient (and error free) to have this externals list generated automatically from the original subroutine declaration. Then changes and additions are made only once. This is an example of a metaprogram that was motivated by a particular system, but also became generally useful.

There are several good reasons for considering the use of metaprograms for software maintenance. Detail changes are automated, removing human error from repetitive tasks, and increasing programmer efficiency. It is inefficient to pay an experienced programmer to sit at a terminal and perform simple repetitive operations. That is what computers are for.

Another advantage is that maintenance work is carried out by editing a metaprogram rather than directly editing the source code. If an attempted maintenance operation does not work out then the metaprogram can simply be changed and reapplied to the original source code. However, if changes are performed directly on the source code then recovering from erroneous changes may be very difficult. After a great deal of work, the maintainer may discover that some or all of the changes are inappropriate. The usual options are to either correct the inappropriate changes or start from scratch. Both approaches are tedious and error-prone compared with re-applying a corrected metaprogram.

The maintenance process may be viewed as understanding and implementing changes. A metaprogram allows changes to be redone as often as required, letting them be determined and implemented one at a time. Thus changes may be experimented with and various alternatives considered without any commitments being made.

This work was supported by the Simon Fraser University Centre for Systems Science and the Natural Sciences and Engineering Research Council of Canada.

Another aspect of maintenance that can be affected by metaprogramming is system configuration and generation. Special purpose processing, source code generation and auxilliary code file generation can be done automatically prior to compilation. This would allow more time to be spent on new problems rather than rediscovering and recovering from old ones.

The metaprogram serves as documentation of changes made. Thus, even if system documentation is not updated or is updated poorly or erroneously, correct and complete information is available on the changes made. In this manner, even the most recalcitrant programmer cannot help but leave traces of what was done.

A problem with the general use of metaprogramming techniques is the lack of availability of metaprogramming systems, and the startup costs. That is, a company that would like to try these techniques will probably have to construct its own system, and evolve its own techniques for using it. The use of grammar-based techniques [3] may make this a bit less expensive since such a metaprogramming system can be used with more than one language. Adding a new language is mostly a matter of writing a grammar for that language although each language will present its own set of implementation difficulties. Also, the metaprogramming process can result in the development of general purpose utilities. Thus the cost of metaprogramming should decrease with time.

An Example Program-Specific Metaprogram

The following example illustrates the basic nature of metaprogramming and how changes required for program maintenance can be implemented automatically using program-specific metaprograms. This example was taken from the use of our own Pascal MPS metaprogramming system [3,4] to maintain itself.

Consider the following maintenance problem.

```
Node = ^NodeCellType;

NodeCellType =
  record
    parent : Node;
    ...(* other fields *)...
  end;
```

Figure 1: The *Node* Data Type Declaration

The data type *Node* partially shown in Figure 1 is to be modified to add a new field named *mutable* as shown in Figure 2. New routines will be added to the system for manipulation of this field. However, the default value of this field is to be *true* and all routines currently in the system should be modified to set the value to *true* when they create *Node* objects. The problem, then, is to find all such locations and add the appropriate field assignments. The solution to this maintenance problem is conceptually simple, but difficult to implement with the standard tool for software maintenance, the ubiquitous text editor. All locations at which *Node* objects are created can be found by locating all calls to the Pascal predefined procedure *new* which have a *Node* type variable as their first (and

```
Node = ^NodeCellType;

NodeCellType =
  record
    parent : Node;
    mutable : boolean (* new field added *);
    ...(* other fields *)...
  end;
```

Figure 2: Modified *Node* Data Type

possibly only) parameter. At such locations an assignment of *true* to the *mutable* field of the variable can then be inserted. Although this solution can easily be expressed in syntactic terms, it would be very difficult, if possible at all, to express these changes in the textual terms used by a text editor.

Using a program-specific metaprogram, however, this solution can be readily implemented. Figure 3 shows a Pascal MPS procedure which can be applied to each statement in the program to effect the required maintenance operation.

```
procedure FixStmt (stmt : Node);
  var ptrType, vrbl, assig, newStmt : Node;
begin
  if ProcedureCallQ (stmt) then
    if SameWords
        (CoerceIdentifier (ProcedureNameOf (stmt)), Str ('new'))
      then begin
        ptrType :=
          LookUpVarType
            (NthElement (ArgumentsOf (stmt), 1));
        if IdentifierQ (ptrType) then
          if SameWords (CoerceIdentifier (ptrType), Str ('Node'))
            then begin
              vrbl :=
                MakeComponentVar
                  (MakeReferenceVar
                    (NthElement (ArgumentsOf (stmt), 1)),
                  MakeIdentifier (Str ('mutable')));
              assig :=
                MakeAssignment
                  (vrbl, MakeIdentifier (Str ('TRUE')));
              newStmt :=
                MakeCompoundStatement
                  (List2 (StatementList, stmt, assig));
              Replace (stmt, newStmt)
            end
      end
end;
```

Figure 3: Maintenance Procedure for Individual Statements

In this procedure, the statement is first checked to determine if it is a procedure call to a procedure named *new*. If so, the program-specific assumption (valid for our system) is made that this occurrence of the name *new* does denote the standard procedure of that name and not a locally defined procedure. Next the type of the first argument to the procedure is determined using the utility for symbol look-up *LookUpVarType*. If and only if the specifier of this type is the identifier *Node*, a location for modification has been found (this is another valid program-specific assumption). When such a location has been found, the *new* procedure call is replaced by a compound statement consisting of a list of two statements: the original procedure call and an assignment to the *mutable* field of the object allocated by the call to *new*. Although the use of the compound statement to bracket the two statements is sometimes redundant, it allows for simpler metaprogramming and can be eliminated afterwards by a standard utility that removes redundant **begin**-**end** pairs.

Making use of this *FixStatement* procedure, all the statements of a given program unit can be modified appropriately with the *FixBlock* procedure shown in Figure 4.

```
procedure FixBlock (blk : Node);
begin
    ScanStatements (BodyOf (blk), FixStmt, continue)
end;
```

Figure 4: Maintenance Procedure for Blocks

The key to this procedure is the *ScanStatements* utility which applies a given procedural parameter (its second argument) to all statements encountered in a recursive traversal of its first argument (which must be a statement or statement-list). This scanning process continues as long as the variable which is the third parameter to *ScanStatements* remains *TRUE*; it does so throughout in this example.

Similarly, the appropriate modifications can be made throughout all nested blocks in the entire program using the *ScanNestedBlocks* utility of Pascal MPS. The arguments to *ScanNestedBlocks* are similar to those of *ScanStatements*. The first argument must be a Pascal block. The second is a procedural parameter which is to be applied to all the blocks encountered in a recursive traversal of the first argument. As long as the third argument remains *TRUE*, the scanning process will continue. The code of the main program to implement all these changes is shown in Figure 5.

```
begin
    InitializeMPS;
    mainProg := ParseInput (Progrm);
    continue := TRUE;
    ScanNestedBlocks (BlockOf (mainProg), FixBlock, continue);
    PrintSyntagm (output, mainProg)
end
```

Figure 5: The Example Main Program

This example illustrates both the problems and potential benefits of software maintenance using program-specific metaprograms. Using a text editor, a software maintainer could start to work right away, manually making modifications at the appropriate locations one-by-one. Using the program-specific metaprogram, however, involves the psychologically daunting overhead of perhaps 15 minutes coding time and two or three edit-compile-run cycles. Nevertheless, once the metaprogram has been implemented, all the changes required throughout the program can be made immediately, with confidence that changes are made at all and only locations where they are required and that all the changes are made

uniformly. Furthermore, it seems that there is a fair potential for developing metaprogramming tools and techniques to reduce the time needed to implement program-specific metaprograms. In comparison, a software maintainer manually making these changes manually with a text editor could take far more than 15 minutes, depending on the size of the system; confidence in the completeness and the correctness of these changes will also diminish with the size of the system.

Maintaining a Large System

We were recently faced with the common problem [1,2] of generating and supporting versions of large systems (specifically our MPS metaprogramming system) in different environments. This problem will recur many times since MPS is still very much a research system in a state of development. That is to say that we are still playing with its internals.

MPS was initially implemented in UBC Pascal on the Michigan Terminal System (MTS). Other research required MPS to be available on systems running Berkeley Pascal/UNIX, and possibly in a personal computer environment in the near future.

We were faced with two maintenance problems: first, translation between two (or more) dialects of Pascal on different operating systems, and second, that the source system code is still in flux. Thus any method used to port MPS must be repeatable, and relatively immune to source code changes. "Repeatable" would seem to require a metaprogram of some type, since manual changes are not viable for this.

Two different sorts of metaprograms are being used to address these problems. The first one is a Pascal dialect translator, and the other is a source code generator. The source code generator is very program specific, but the dialect translator promises to turn into a general purpose utility.

The dialect translator takes UBC Pascal MPS readable source code and does whatever operations are required to make it run on the target system. There are several interesting problems in getting MPS to do this. They stem from the fact that all dialects and operating systems are not created equal.

One of the problems with Pascal is that it was designed as a language to teach programming and not as a general purpose language; hence the proliferation of superset dialects. The MPS system's Pascal grammar attempts to stay as close to standard Pascal as possible. The result of this is that some dialect features are inexpressible within MPS. It might be useful if the MPS grammar was in some sense a union of all dialect grammars. However, some features of different dialects may prove to be mutually exclusive. Also, the MPS grammar would require modification every time one of the dialects changes. These problems have motivated us to find other ways of coping with the problem.

Difficulties occur at both ends of the metaprogram. That is, the source program must be completely MPS-parsable, and the output text program must be able to compile and run in the target environment. This means that there is some information about the source program necessary to the generation of the result program that cannot be stored as part of the source. We circumvented this by constructing a *configuration file* for each source program file. The configuration file contains all of the extra information required by the dialect translator. For example, names of external declaration files, the target environment, and the syntactic class of the input file are included in the configuration file. Syntactic class (program, subroutine list, etc.) is used because system parts may not all be kept as complete programs, and the MPS parser has to be told what to expect.

Output difficulties were handled by a flexible pretty printer that alternated between converting printing portions of the parse tree and the information contained in the configuration file. An example of the sort of difficulty encountered here is the different methods by which files are included in the source program. MTS uses a "$CONTINUE WITH" construct which is completely independent of the UBC Pascal compiler while the Berkeley Pascal compiler uses a "#include" preprocessor statement. Neither of these is part of the Pascal grammar. They cannot, therefore, be represented in the parse tree, and must be handled outside of it.

Another minor difficulty results from very different operating system environments. Differences in the I/O interface and facilities available (such as access to an interactive text editor from within the program) may be outside of the language domain itself. For example, the existence of OS facilities and their names and operations will vary from system to system and are not really part of any Pascal dialect. Coping with these problems may be possible within a metaprogram but may also require operations that amount to a redesign and reimplementation of large sections of code rather than just a simple transformation. Much work remains to be done here but our current method of handling these sorts of problems is to tuck the offending section of code into a separate subroutine (or set of subroutines). A new version is then implemented manually for each separate target environment and the appropriate version is included when the system is generated.

Not all of our solutions are pretty, but so far we have encountered nothing that could not be dealt with in some fashion. It must be stressed that handling two dialects with one grammar is a contradiction in terms. MPS is much more tractable on problems using only a single dialect.

The source code generator was much more straightforward as we did not need to construct anything that was not expressible in Pascal. This program generates specialized routines that make use of more general purpose subroutines. However, not all of the specialized routines were derivable from just the information contained in the general purpose routines' code. Thus there is a question of where and how this extra information is to be kept. Regardless of how this is dealt with, the information is tied to the source code and might be considered a property of it. This suggests the existence of code sections that must be processed in some consistent and unique manner. This had the effect of forcing

us to rearrange the source structure (what code was in what file, etc.) of MPS and resulted in a cleaner overall organization. It would seem that the use of metaprogramming techniques on an existing system can serve to point out design inadequacies that might not otherwise be apparent since they may have real as well as esthetic significance.

Development of Utilities

During our work with MPS, we encountered several situations where specific pieces of code could be made more general, amortizing the cost of constructing them over several metaprograms. As time went on, and the number of these utilities increased, it became easier to construct new metaprograms and the motivation required to do so decreased. This is an important consideration, since there is sometimes considerable inertia in getting started metaprogramming.

One of the things that is done frequently when metaprogramming is performing an operation over a set of syntactic structures. That is, something must be done to each subroutine or to each statement in a block, etc. The structure of a routine to do this sort of operation is the same regardless of the particular operation to be performed. Thus, a little work in generalizing the code resulted in a class of procedures called *scanners*. These procedures take an operation (through a procedural parameter) and a syntactic structure, and apply the operation to each appropriate element of the structure. For example **ScanNestedBlocks** (see figure 5) applies the provided operation **FixStmt** to the provided program's subroutine blocks (and recursively to their subroutine blocks) and then to its own block. We have constructed these for all appropriate syntactic structures and they have proven quite useful in speeding up the metaprogramming process.

Another example is the dialect translator mentioned above. It was originally intended for use with MPS, but as it handled more of the changes required, it became clear that it could be used for general porting operations. Of course, it is not (and may never be) complete, but as more and more programs are ported with it, inadequacies should decrease. This sort of utility has the advantage that not all programmers have to become familiar with all dialects. A programmer writes in the source dialect and translation is automatic and invisible. This is in contrast with other techniques for dialect translation [5] that merely filter out sections of code that are not required, and thus force all programmers to know all dialects.

Conclusions

A promising technique for software maintenance is the in-house use of metaprogramming systems for the construction of specialized software tools and program-specific metaprograms. We have found that program-specific metaprograms can be used to implement powerful automatic editing operations that are repeatable, safe, fast and comprehensive.

Maintenance metaprograms were reasonably easy to construct. The costs of writing metaprograms should amortize over several projects as special purpose metaprograms find more general application, and the amount of programming required for a particular metaprogram decreases. Also, as more utilities are constructed and as metaprogrammer abilities and confidence increase, maintenance operations that were formerly considered too complex or costly to consider may be undertaken.

An examination of the specific maintenance problems and requirements of industry would be useful and their input is encouraged.

References

1. Arango, G., Baxter, I., Freeman, P., and Pidgeon, C. "TMM: Software Maintenance by Transformation." *IEEE Software*, May 1986, 27-38.

2. Boyle, J. M., Muralidharan, M. N. "Program Reusability through Program Transformation." *IEEE Trans. Softw. Eng.*, **10 1**, (Sept. 1984), 574-588.

3. Cameron, R. D. and Ito, M. R. "Grammar-Based Definition of Metaprogramming Systems." *ACM Trans. Program. Lang. Syst.*, **6 1**, (Jan. 1984), 20-54.

4. Cameron, R. D. "Multi MPS Reference Manual." (draft) School of Computing Science, Simon Fraser University, September 1986.

5. Sorens, M. J. "A Technique for Automatically Porting Dialects of Pascal to Each Other." *SIGPLAN Notices*, **21 1**, (Jan. 1986), 58-63.

Conclusion

When thinking about software maintenance, I am reminded of something Yogi Berra, an American baseball player, a great catcher and hitter, once said, "If the people don't want to come out to the ball park, nobody's going to stop them." The same thing could be said about software maintenance: if nobody uses software maintenance, nobody's going to stop them. Well, the key words are "stop them."

Managers of Information Systems have to learn that the practice of software maintenance is critical. Code that is not maintained or tested can, and has, brought organizations to their knees.

As I conducted literature searches to find articles to include in the tutorial, I was overwhelmed by the amount of excellent research being conducted on software maintenance. It was difficult to choose papers. I hope no one is offended because their paper was not included. This list is intended to be representative, not exhaustive.

Wilma Osborne, National Bureau of Standards, and Charles Richter, MCC Software Technology Program, provided editioral comments. They were greatly appreciated.

Annotated References

There are hundreds of articles being published on software maintenance. It would be unrealistic to try and include all of them in this tutorial, therefore I have included fifty annotated references.

Since there are several references that come from foreign publications, I have included the names and addresses of several companies that can provide copies of any of the articles for a small fee.

Engineering Information, Inc.
Document Delivery Service Rm. 20
345 East 47th Street
New York, NY 10017
(212) 705-7131

NERAC, Inc.
Attn: Document Dept.
One Technology Dr.
Tolland, CT 06084
(203) 872-7000

Information on Demand
P.O. Box 1370
Berkeley, CA 94701
(415) 644-4500

The Information Specialists
2490 Lee Boulevard
Cleveland, OH 44188
(216) 321-7500

"Look at Support," *Computer Management*, July-Aug. 1984, p. 11.

When purchasing software, it is important to consider the technical support offered. Software maintenance can cost twice as much as the software package. Purchasers need to determine whether the seller of the software is committed to their products.

Altmann, J., "New Tools Allow Better Budgeting," *MIS Week*, Vol. 9, No. 6, Feb. 8, 1988, pp. 19-21.

Blue Cross and Blue Shield of South Carolina wins *MIS Week's* solution of the month award. The award is for their use of Sage Software's APS Development Center to streamline their budget process. The programmer productivity tool was chosen

primarily for its flexibility rather than for ease of use.

Baker, C.T., "Effects of Field Services on Software Reliability," *IEEE Transactions on Software Engineering*, Vol. 14, No. 2, Feb. 1988, pp. 245-259.

The inherent reliability of a program and certain characteristics of a software service organization are the basis for a program's reliability when many copies are run in a multisite environment.

A small number of parameters that determine the relevant characteristics of the service organization are identified. Two software reliability models are used to achieve this.

Bassett, Paul, "Frame Based Software Engineering," *IEEE Software*, Vol. 4, No. 4, July 1987, pp. 9-16.

Extensive COBOL frame experience has been accumulated since the mid 1970s. The source of potential gains has inspired Norma Industries Ltd., a Toronto based group of manufacturing concerns, to develop and install more than 20 million lines of custom COBOL in thousands of programs for different application. The programs are composed of 30 I-O frames, screen and report frame generators, and one custom specification frame per program. The specification frames are of pivotal importance and contain less than four percent of the total COBOL coding. A mathematics of software engineering is needed. The frame technique is an empirical example of a construction system that clarifies some fuzzy area, such as waste of construction and modification.

Benmergui-Perez, M., "Maintenance-It Is Not a Sexy Job But More of Us Should Do It: Experts," *Computing Canada*, 1985, pp. 1-2.

Software engineering experts agree that there are great rewards for the programmer involved in software maintenance. Companies are looking for programmers who can do maintenance work both economically and efficiently. Most companies use a hit and miss approach to software maintenance. The external contracting of maintenance may be a viable alternative for a company.

Black, G., "US Government Cuts Software," *Computer Weekly*, No. 959, April 18, 1985, p. 1.

A paper called "Management of the US Government Fiscal Year 1986" calls for U.S. Government departments to cut software maintenance costs by twenty five percent. Old software is costing a great deal in maintenance. New projects in the automation area will also be required to show a ten percent return on investment.

Brocka, B., "Measuring Software Quality," *Government Data Systems*, Vol. 14, No.1, Jan. 1985, pp. 44-45.

The difficulty in the determination of quality of computer programs is directly related to the number of executable lines of source code. Weak documentation, insufficient requirements, and underdeveloped testing procedures contribute to the quality problem. Furthermore, good programming seems just as much an art as a science, and reliable quantitative evaluation of something involving so much creativity and imagination does not promise to be easy.

Buei, E., "Software Quality and Jungian Psychological Type," *Proceedings of the 10th Anniversary COMPSAC 1986,* IEEE Computer Society Press, Los Alamitos, Calif., Oct. 8-10, 1986, pp. 177-178.

Software quality is affected by several factors, including programmer's styles of working and the ways in which programmer team members interact with users and with one another. The author who has previously described the framework of Jungian psychological type, suggested ways in which managers and team members might use this framework to examine their work and communication styles to improve their teamwork.

Cavano, J. and F. Lamonica, "Quality Assurance in Future Development Environments," *IEEE Software*, Vol. 4, No. 5, Sept. 1987, pp. 26-34.

The nature of software quality assurance, including coverage inspection, quality control, quality improvement, quality by design, and quality metrics is examined. The aspects of developmental environments that impact the quality issue are discussed. SQA functions, traditionally performed manually or not at all, that will be integrated in future software developmental environments are discussed; they are quality planning, quality specification, data collection, quality analysis, traceability and change effect analysis, automated documentation, and project management.

Collofello, J. and J. Buck, "Software Quality Assurance for Maintenance," *IEEE Software*, Vol. 4, No. 5, Sept 1987, pp. 46-51.

The role of maintenance in protecting quality as a system evolves is discussed. The results of a study that shows how maintenance can be made a part of software quality assurance are presented.

Conner, R., "Happy Birthday COBOL-But after 25 Years Your Age Is Showing," *Computerworld Australia*, Vol. 6, No. 50, June 15, 1984, pp. 35-39, 41.

The COBOL language was developed twenty-five years ago and has had an overall negative influence on data processing. It was designed by a committee established by the Department of Defense. Because of a need to keep compilation time to a minimum, COBOL is technologically lacking. It is portable and machine independent, and also difficult to maintain.

Desmond, J., "MIS Managers Advised to Group Software Changes," *Computerworld*, Vol. 19, No. 19, May 13, 1985, pp. 14.

According to Fainina Konotorivich, senior consultant for Alexander Grant and Co., software maintenance can be eased in MIS departments, which should issue new releases of enhanced applications. By using this method, software changes can be grouped rather than making changes one at a time.

Esmond, J., "Softtalk: Programming by the Rules," *Computerworld*, Vol. 19, No. 20, May 20, 1985, pp. 41,45.

The author suggests that programs that are written using proper rules are easier to maintain than programs written in a haphazard manner using no rules. In a test of programming techniques by both novice and expert programmers, it was discovered that a novice spends 75 percent of his time coding and only 10 percent analyzing programs. By sharp contrast, an expert will spend as much as 30 percent of his time analyzing a program and 55 percent of his time writing code.

Feuche, M., "Attention is Being Generated by Complexity Metric Tools," *MIS Week*, Vol. 9, No. 9, Feb. 29, 1988, pp. 27-29.

There is a growing interest among the MIS (Manager of Information System) in a new category of software packages that use complexity metrics techniques to help optimize application development and maintenance. Complexity metrics measure the difficulty with which individual programs or entire software libraries can be understood, tested, debugged, and maintained. Particular characteristics are measured such as the number of decision points in code written for an application. These products include Inspector for Language Technology, PC-Metric from Set Laboratories, and Pathvu from Peat Marwick-Catalyst Group. Complexity metrics tools can be used for such applications as evaluating the quality and understandability of software or the requirements for reverse engineering. The tool's effectiveness is questioned by many industry experts.

Fiderio, J., "Defect-Free Maintenance a Priority as DP Focus Shifts," *Computerworld*, Vol. 20, No. 17, pp. 54-55.

William E. Perry, executive director of the Quality Assurance Institute, discusses software maintenance. Perry is an advocate of software maintenance programmers and favors defect-free maintenance. The role of managers and software maintenance methodologies are discussed.

Forney, R., R. Race, and R. Nashleanas, "A Strategic Approach: The Use of Tools," *Journal of Systems Management*, Vol. 34, No. 6, June 1983, pp. 29-31.

The traditional job-shop approach to software maintenance is inefficient and unproductive because programmers spend 60 percent of the time familiarizing themselves with the code and only 40 percent working on it. Some effective software tools are static and dynamic analyzers, formatters, code splitters, documentators, and test data generators. Grouping types of problems together is another way to improve programmer productivity.

Garrett, A., "Emerging Remedies for an Old Headache," *Computing (U.K.)*, May 23, 1985, pp. 16-17.

Data processing managers use considerable amounts of resources in maintaining programs already in use. Programming staff shortages make it difficult to cope with maintenance. In the future, production center environments with mainframes and fourth-generation languages will be used to increase productivity. British Airways' annual software maintenance bill is over one million pounds sterling. One-fourth of its 470 programmers do maintenance work. British Airways maintains systems in three areas; reservation systems written in assembler, finance and engineering, and decision support.

Gilb, T., "Increasing Software Productivity," *Data Processing*, Vol. 25, No. 7, Sept. 1983, pp. 16-20.

Productivity should be measured against goals set by a company. The net effect of a solution based on the results should be the ultimate yardstick. The two categories a software package should be measured against are functions and attributes. Also, user-friendliness, security, and resources (such as time and cost) are all points to consider when setting goals.

Gill, P., "Tools Ease Time-Consuming Tasks of Maintenance, Documentation," *Information Week*, No. 96, Dec. 15, 1986, pp. 21-25.

Although software maintenance and documentation can be aided with administrative project-management packages, dedicated programs offer several advantages, including the ability to accept input as it is written; to allow the data to be manipulated into charts, graphs, and indexes; and to track how often particular verbs and statements occur. About 45 such programs for the IBM 370 environment are available, mainly for COBOL applications, and some for assembly source-code applications. Several IBM software maintenance and development tools and alternatives to IBM products from several software publishers are examined, including Documentor from Information Builders, SyDoc from SyncSort, CA-Job from Computer Associates International, and Chart3800 from Glasscom Systems.

Gillin, P., "Spaghetti Code Glut Spawns Program Restructuring Services," *Computerworld*, Vol. 19, No.4, Jan. 28, 1985, pp. 1,10.

There are thousands of spaghetti code programs in use throughout the business world which were probably written in COBOL ten to twenty years ago. Service firms are now emerging that will take an old, patch work program and rewrite it in structured format that will function exactly like the old one. Since the program has been restructured, it is easier to maintain. A firm called Language Technology provides such a service for 50 cents per source line.

Gorelik, A. and Ushkova, "Supporting Program Portability and Reliability in Programming Languages," *Programming Computer Software*, Sept-Oct 1986.

This article was translated from Progammirovanie (USSR). The properties of programming languages that either enable or impede writing portable, reliable programs are examined. The languages being analyzed are Fortran 66, Fortran 77, PL/1, Algol 68, Pascal, C, Ada and the new standard Fortran, tentatively called Fortran 8x.

Grey, O., "Making SDI Software Reliable Through Fault-Tolerant Techniques," *Defense Electronics (USA)*, Vol. 19, No. 8, Aug. 1987, pp. 77-80, 85-86.

Speculation continues over whether the strategic defense initiative's (SDI) software can ever become error-free. It is unlikely that the estimated 10 million lines of code will be completely free of errors. The application of software fault-tolerance can make the software reliable enough for deployment within a reasonable time. Fault-tolerance design approaches can help modularize it and provide a high level of operational confidence. The cost of software over the life of a system can exceed the initial system cost by as much as 1000 percent. As software continues to dominate system cost and its use in safety-critical systems increases, the effects of "bugs" become a more serious problem.

Grossman, F., "Debugging with the 80386: Notes on Real Mode Debugging With the 386," *Dr. Dobbs Journal of Software Tools for the Professional Programmer*, Vol. 13, No. 2, Feb. 1988, pp. 18-24.

The Soft-ICE debugger from Nu-Mega is a tool designed for Intel 80386. This debugger includes most hardware-aided debugger features. Soft-ICE makes use of several protected mode functions such as paging, virtual 80386 mode, I-O privilege level, and breakpoint registers, to offer real-time hardware-level breakpoints and related functionality. The creative application of 80386 protected mode operation will provide most hardware-aided debugger features with the convenience of a software debugger.

Gruman, G., "Process Programming: A Seductive Danger?" *IEEE Software*, Vol. 4, No. 3, May 1987, pp. 91-94.

Process programming versus human intellectual activity was the issue under discussion at the Software Engineering Conference in Monterey, California. Leon Osterweil of the University of Colorado at Boulder analyzed the advantages of process programming which, he said, seeks to automate and formalize the software process. The task is "to start with a process description and end up with a problem solver," Osterweil claims. Meir Lehman of the Imperial College of Science and Technology in London made the point that people have to make the decisions as to what is correct. He conceded that process programming is useful if the steps are algorithmic, but he added that it represents a threat because it can convey a false sense of understanding. Bob Balzer of USC pointed out that if the programming process is put in a mechanical realm, human activity is free to pursue the decision-making issues.

Gullo, Karen, "Automating COBOL Support Is the Cause Celebre in Is Shops," *Datamation*, Vol. 24, No.1, Jan. 1, 1988, pp. 19-21.

New programming tools for automating the maintenance of old COBOL "spaghetti" code are attracting the attention of Fortune 1000 companies that have begun to recognize the value of support and maintenance in getting the most out of applications. One such program is Recorder, which turns spaghetti code into structured code by reducing a program to its simplest form and running a new abstract of the syntax tree through a COBOL generator.

Jackson, R., "Software Engineering for Safety" *IEE Colloquium on "Electrical Safety of Medical Equipment,"* Jan. 9, 1987, pp. 4/1-4/5.

As more diverse applications for microprocessors are found, the consequences of failures become more serious and the need for safe and reliable software is more urgent than ever before. The definition of reliability of software is the probability that the software will perform correctly for some specified period. Safety is more difficult to define. It depends on reliability, but the definition must also take into account the probability of a hazardous situation arising because of software failure.

"Data Processing: A Management Paradox," *Journal of Systems Management*, Vol. 34, No. 5, May 1983, pp. 21-23.

Software maintenance has not experienced productivity improvements to support both new development and maintenance. As a result, organizations have had to increase staff. Although an organization's greatest expense is in maintenance, the least effort at cost reduction is also in maintenance. To address this issue requires focusing management attention on anticipating maintenance problems and on modifying existing systems to make them maintainable.

Kafura, D., "The Use of Software Complexity Metrics in Software Maintenance," *IEEE Transactions on Software Engineering*, Vol. SE-13, No. 3, March 1987, pp. 335-344.

Seven different software complexity metrics are compared to the experience of maintenance activities on a medium-sized software system. The three different versions of the program that evolved over a three-year period are described and an on-going full-scale revision of the system is discussed. It is shown that the growth in system complexity resulting from software metrics corresponds to the general maintenance tasks performed in each version, that metrics were able to find the improper integration of functional enhancements made to the system, that complexity values of system components found by the metrics correspond to programmers' understanding of the system, and that the usefulness of software metrics was evident by the discovery of a poorly structured component of the system in the (re)design phase.

Knight J. and N. Leverson, "An Empirical Study of Failure Probabilities in Multi-Version Software," *FTCS Digest of Papers, 16th Annual International Symposium on Fault-Tolerant Computer Systems*, IEEE Computer Society Press, Los Alamitos, Calif., July 1-4, 1986, pp. 165-170.

N-Version programming is being used in existing crucial systems and is being considered for others. The assumption of independence of version failures in *N*-Version systems is not born out in practice, which makes modeling of reliability quite difficult. The estimation of the software reliability depends on the reliability of the individual versions and their interaction. This has been modeled, but in practice, little is known about how programs will fail in practical multiversion systems. Experimental results are presented with several cautions to their interpretation.

Leech, C., "An Introduction to Quality Assurance in the Information Processing Industry," *Software World*, Vol. 16, No. 1, pp. 7-8.

It is estimated that of all software products delivered, only 3 percent work, the other 97 percent is either late, over budget, or does not meet specifications. The quality assurance standards used by most technologies are missing from the information processing industry. Quality assurance is defined as the "degree of excellence" dependent upon correctness, reliability, maintainability, cost, and schedule. The product life cycle includes "phases" that are always the major areas of risk in a project. The quality assurance engineer must oversee the following activities in the software life cycle: project management, technical control, definition, specifications, implementation, and configuration management. Each one of these topics is discussed in detail in a configuration series of articles by the author.

Littman, D., J. Pinto, S. Letovsky, and E. Soloway, "Mental Models and Software Maintenance," *Journal of Systems and Software*, Vol. 7, No. 4, Dec. 1987, pp. 341-356.

Understanding how a program is constructed and how it functions are significant components of the task of maintaining or enhancing a computer program. We have analyzed videotaped protocols of experienced programmers as they enhanced a personnel database program. The analysis suggests that there are two strategies for program understanding, the systematic strategy and the as-needed strategy. The programmer using the systematic strategy traces data flow through the program in order to understand global program behavior. The programmer using the
as-needed strategy focuses on local program behavior.

Martin, R. and W. Osborne, "The Ideal Maintainer: A Profile," *Data Management*, Vol. 22, No. 3, March 1984, pp. 39-40.

The characteristics, which range from flexibility to experience, of the ideal software maintainer are addressed. The maintainer must be able to work with users as well as application programmers.

Murneo, Neil, "DOD Writing New SDI Software Policy Directive," *Government Computer News*, Vol. 7, No. 6, March 18, 1988, p. 33.

Department of Defense studies from various agencies indicate there are no adequate models for the development, production, testing, and maintenance of software for the Strategic Defense Initiative (SDI). The directive will integrate the software policies in the three armed services as those policies relate to SDI. The directive will implement some of the recommendations of a report from the Defense Science Board.

Nirmal, B., "Structured Approach to Solving Systems Problems," *Journal of Systems Management*, Vol. 35, No. 3, March 1984, pp. 26-27.

Programmers and analysts can solve unexpected systems problems more quickly with a structured approach to debugging. A set of five questions to ask isolates the problem, then successive elimination is used to find the specific problem.

O'Flaherty, T., "Maintenance Plans and Strategies," *Computerworld*, Vol. 20, No. 7A, Feb. 19, 1986.

Software maintenance activities typically consume 50 to 70 percent of programming resources in large data-processing operations. The nature and definition of software maintenance are vague. Maintenance is divided into three categories: cases of either total or partial nonperformance, extensive or isolated failure to meet specifications, and making enhancements beyond specifications. Some major flaws in maintenance operations involve the lack of strategic planning and the failure to keep analytical records of maintenance activities. The nature of business operations today demands that maintenance be considered an integral part of all business activities, affecting all business issues rather than a problem relegated to the DP environment.

Parikh, G., "Micro, Mainframe Software Maintenance Issues Similar," *Computerworld*, Vol. 19, No. 17, April 29, 1985, pp. 24.

The steps for maintenance of programs developed in-house for microcomputers are examined. It is important to include technical reviews and code walkthroughs during the development process. Also, it is important to maintain documentation during the development process. Programmers and technicians should be educated in maintenance practices. It is important to recruit competent maintenance programmers.

Peralman, D., "What to Do When You Find a Software Bug," *Popular Computing*, Vol. 3, No. 3, Jan. 1984, pp. 140, 142.

Since software packages generally do not carry a warranty, they cannot be returned when a bug appears. Suggestions are given on what to do when a software bug occurs. The bug can be carefully studied and its behavior carefully catalogued, it may even be possible to eliminate it by using a new procedure. Other remedies include contacting the dealer or manufacturer for help, consulting a user group, or joining in a group complaint to the manufacturer to increase leverage.

Perry, W.E., "A Plan of Action for Software Maintenance," *Data Management*, Vol. 23, No. 3, March 1985, pp. 44-45.

Much of the programming backlog is in software maintenance. The solutions to this are a better attitude toward maintenance and a well thought out plan, which must take into account an organization's resources and must heighten productivity as well as leave maintenance in the hands of a software maintenance group. A plan submitted at the DPMA's Second Annual Single Software Maintenance Conference contained five objectives: selection of a single authority, development of goals, use of the maintenance release made method, calculation of the cost benefit of maintenance, and quality control. All facts of the plan must be implemented simultaneously.

Perry, W., "Modernized Code Extends Dated Program's Life," *Information Systems News*, June 27, 1983, pp. 21,22.

How to maintain hundreds of obsolete programs is a major problem for information systems managers. There are only two options: (1) to maintain the status quo and to install changes as they are requested or (2) to modernize the code. The second is the preferred solution.

Powerm, Kevin, "Development Disguised as Maintenance, Feds Warn," *Government Computer News*, Vol. 6, No. 3, Feb. 13, 1987, pp. 76-77.

The National Bureau of Standards and the Office of Management and Budget reported that costs listed as software maintenance are hiding "enormous" software development costs. The recent meeting of the Interagency Committee of Information Resources Management, revealed a need for a standard definition of software maintenance and tighter controls of information resources. "MIS managers need to be less short-sighted on thinking that each problem needs a separate solution and systems should be chosen for their transportability and maintainability," said officials. The conclusion was that improving computer systems and giving agencies tools to make system changes would help federal agencies to more efficiently maintain systems.

Robichaux, Paul, "What's Behind Those Maintenance Charges?" *Canadian Datasystems*, Vol. 20, No. 3, March 1988, pp. 71-73.

It is easy to accept the inevitable maintenance of hardware, but theoretically software should work forever. This theory causes many DP managers to question the annual software maintenance charges of 15 to 30 percent of the purchase price levied by publishers. The basic element of software support is problem resolution, in which problems relating to software implementation or use are answered; product currency, in which software is kept updated as hardware enhancements are delivered; and product enhancement, in which the software itself is changed to meet the needs of the user.

Rosenbaum, D., "Social Security's Near Data-Disaster," *Information Systems News*, Dec. 12, 1983, pp. 1, 20.

The United States Social Security Administration has let its computer shop become a well known and acknowledged shambles. Opening an account and getting a number takes as long as four to six weeks. Although the hardware is old, the problem is mainly lack of EDP leadership. The solution will cost about $600 million.

Scherer, M., "Unsafe Software-The Missing Security Perspective," *Computer Security Journal*, Vol. 3, No. 1, Summer 1984.

Unsafe software is software that does not work correctly, software that creates hazards in its operating environment, or software that no one really understands. The greater degree of customizing of software, the greater the potential for problems. In software engineering, a hierarchical approach should be taken to recognize potential software hazards. Effective countermeasures to unsafe software involve the software, the user, and the vendor in a process analogous to first-aid.

Shor, D., "Better Software Manuals," *Byte*, Vol. 8, No. 5, May 1983, pp. 286, 288, 290-294.

Most software buyers shop for the program that has the most attractive, readable, and understandable manual. Computer stores are also looking for well written manuals since they will have to spend much less time supporting the program. When writing such manuals, active verbs should be used rather than the passive. A checklist is provided as a simple method of evaluation.

Snyders, J., "The Benefits of Programmer Productivity Software," *Infosystems*, Vol. 32, No. 6, June 1985, pp. 59-64.

Programmer productivity software can help users convert to new systems, modify old systems, and even train new programmers. Case studies are cited where these products were used with a significant savings in time. Debugging

software products, which include compilers and assemblers, are useful programming tools currently available.

Swanson, E., B. Burton, and M. Cynthia, "The Use of Case Study Data in Software Management Research," *Journal of Systems and Software*, Vol. 8, No. 1, Jan. 1988, pp. 63-72.

Among the problems of software engineering are its effective organization and management. The case study method, which presents a number of challenges in data collection, analysis, and sharing is particularly suited to research on such problems. Direction in meeting these challenges is given by maintenance of an illustrative multiple-case study of application software maintenance, which combines quantitative and qualitative data. Research context and design, the data collection process, and approach to analysis and synthesis, and the sharing of data and results are discussed.

Tayntor, C., "In Defense of the Maintenance Programmer," *Infosystems*, Vol. 32, No. 1, Jan. 1985, pp. 78.

Because their work is routine and non-creative, maintenance programmers lack the status of development programmers. Maintenance work is essential to the company and the skills are not necessarily at a lower level. Maintenance programmers must be able to decipher someone else's often unstructured programs, comprehend the entire design, work with little or no documentation, work in a limited amount of time, and work with several projects at one time.

Wess, B., "Artificial Intelligence Techniques Speed Software Development," *Mini-Micro Systems*, Vol. 17, No. 11, Sept. 1984, pp. 127-128, 130.

Expert systems tools and concepts can help systems integrators develop and maintain commercial DP systems. Information architects combined COBOL, PROLOG, and fifth-generation AI language to develop a customized, transaction-processing program for an unspecified distribution company.

Index

Macro CM, 118

Macro level CM, 119

Macro level of change control, 120

Macro Model, 23,24,30,35

Macro-metrics, 234

Maintainability analysis tool, 19

Maintainability, 3,8,12,20,15,16,21,46,78,138,139,175,
187,189

Maintainable software, 2

Maintenance activity, 19

Maintenance by Abstraction, 20

Maintenance Configuration Control Board (MCCB), 74,75,
77,78

Maintenance costs, 4,98,175

Maintenance environment, 232,234

Maintenance expenditures, 101,102

Maintenance function, 174,202,232

Maintenance implementation, 95

Maintenance management handbook, 236

Maintenance measurement, 92

Maintenance metaprograms, 257

Maintenance metrics, 191,232,234

Maintenance phase, 44

Maintenance plan, 95

Maintenance practices, 17

Maintenance problem, 180

Maintenance procedure for blocks, 255

Maintenance procedure for individual statements, 254

Maintenance productivity project (MPP), 232,233

Maintenance programmer, 115

Maintenance work, 63

Maintenance workbench, 235,236

Maintenance, 15,16,17,26,30,33,62,64-66,86,88,94,96,106,
143,156,157,166,173,176,177,179,187,205,223,
233,234,242

Maintenance-specific tools, 233

Major release, 73,77,78

Management discipline, 72

Management information systems (MIS), 166

Management of design libraries, 120

Management viewpoint, 80

Management, 17,39

Managers of information systems (MIS), 85,88

Managers of information systems, 259

Manual documentation, 196

Manuals, 107

Martin, James, 235

Masterlist (ML), 128

Mathematical proof techniques, 223

Matrix management, 71-73

MCC metric, 84

McCabe's Cyclomatic Complexity (MCC), 79,80,83

McCabe's measure of cyclomatic complexity, 167

McClure, Carma, 235

McKee, James, R., 173

Measure of software risk, 157

Measurement of risk, 157

Melton, Austin C., 23

Metaprogram, 256

Metaprogramming systems, 253,257

Metaprogramming tools, 255

Metaprogramming, 254,255

Methodology, 81,233

Metric, 8,46

Metrics summaries, 135

Metrics, 18,19,40,42,44,48,114,132

Michigan terminal system (MTS), 255

Micro change process, 120

Micro CM discipline, 121

Micro CM management, 119

Micro CM, 118-120

Micro-metrics, 234

MIL-STD-1679, 139,140

Miller, E., 249

Mode of analysis, 68

Model of maintenance activities, 24,35

Models, 16

Modifiability, 187,191

Modification tools, 246,247

Modification, 64,66,107,108,115,120,188,198,218,234,246

Modified waterfall chart, 118

Modular decomposition, 188,189

Modularity, 140,142,146

Module exposure, 160

Module fault potential, 159

Module hierarchy charts, 204

Module risk assessments, 162

Module stability, 19

Module symbol table, 229

Module test system, 224

Module, 144

Monitoring, 112

Monitoring/evaluation, 12

Moquin, Bert, 122

Motivation, 82

MPS, 256

MTS, 256

Multiple regression technique, 94

Multiple regression tests, 29

Multiprocessing, 220

Murine Metric Set (MMS), 140

Murine, Gerald E., 137

Mutable, 254

Myers, Ware, 217

Narrow, Bernard, 110

Nassi-Schneiderman, 208

Navlakha, Jai, 79

NCC cost model, 92,95

About the Author

David Longstreet is a 1983 graduate of Texas A&M University, where he studied economics and electrical engineering. He has worked for Control Data Corporation, Software Maintenance, Inc., and, most recently, U.S. Sprint Corporation. He has held positions as an engineer and as a systems analyst.

He provides technical editing for IEEE and Que Publishing. He is a member of the Association of Computer Machinery and the IEEE Computer Society. Furthermore, he is an avid fan of baseball, especially of the Kansas City Royals. David and his wife Margaret make their home in the Kansas City area with their two children, Joseph and Rachel.

IEEE Computer Society

IEEE Computer Society Press Publications

Monographs: A monograph is an authored book

Tutorials: A tutorial is a collection of original materials prepared by the editors and reprints of the best articles published in a subject area. They must contain at least five percent original material (15 to 20 percent original material is recommended).

Reprint Books: A reprint book is a collection of reprints divided into sections with a preface, table of contents, and section introductions that discuss the reprints and why they were selected. It contains less than five percent original material.

(Subject) Technology Series: Each technology series is a collection of anthologies of reprints, each with a narrow focus on a subset of a particular discipline, such as networks, architecture, software, robotics.

Submission of proposals: For guidelines on preparing CS Press Books, write Editor-in-Chief, IEEE Computer Society, P.O. Box 3014, 10662 Los Vaqueros Circle, Los Alamitos, CA 90720-1264 (telephone 714-821-8380).

Purpose

The IEEE Computer Society advances the theory and practice of computer science and engineering, promotes the exchange of technical information among 100,000 members worldwide, and provides a wide range of services to members and nonmembers.

Membership

Members receive the acclaimed monthly magazine *Computer*, discounts, and opportunities to serve (all activities are led by volunteer members). Membership is open to all IEEE members, affiliate society members, and others seriously interested in the computer field.

Publications and Activities

Computer. An authoritative, easy-to-read magazine containing tutorial and in-depth articles on topics across the computer field, plus news, conferences, calendar, interviews, and new products.

Periodicals. The society publishes six magazines and four research transactions. Refer to membership application or request information as noted above.

Conference Proceedings, Tutorial Texts, Standards Documents. The Computer Society Press publishes more than 100 titles every year.

Standards Working Groups. Over 100 of these groups produce IEEE standards used throughout the industrial world.

Technical Committees. Over 30 TCs publish newsletters, provide interaction with peers in specialty areas, and directly influence standards, conferences, and education.

Conferences/Education. The society holds about 100 conferences each year and sponsors many educational activites, including computing science accreditation.

Chapters. Regular and student chapters worldwide provide the opportunity to interact with colleagues, hear technical experts, and serve the local professional community.

Other IEEE Computer Society Press Texts

Monographs

Analyzing Computer Architecture
Written by J.C. Huck and M.J. Flynn
(ISBN 0-8186-8857-2); 206 pages

Desktop Publishing for the Writer: Designing, Writing, Developing
Written by Richard Ziegfeld and John Tarp
(ISBN 0-8186-8840-8); 380 pages

Integrating Design and Test: Using CAE Tools for ATE Programming
Written by K.P. Parker
(ISBN 0-8186-8788-6 (case)); 160 pages

JSP and JSD: The Jackson Approach to Software Development (Second Edition)
Written by J.R. Cameron
(ISBN 0-8186-8858-0); 560 pages

National Computer Policies
Written by Ben G. Matley and Thomas A. McDannold
(ISBN 0-8186-8784-3); 192 pages

Physical Level Interfaces and Protocols
Written by Uyless Black
(ISBN 0-8186-8824-6); approximately 272 pages

Protecting Your Proprietary Rights in the Computer and High Technology Industries
Written by Tobey B. Marzouk, Esq.
(ISBN 0-8186-8754-1); 224 pages

Tutorials

Advanced Computer Architecture
Edited by D.P. Agrawal
(ISBN 0-8186-0667-3); 400 pages

Advanced Microprocessors and High-Level Language Computer Architectures
Edited by V. Milutinovic
(ISBN 0-8186-0623-1); 608 pages

Advances in Distributed System Reliability
Edited by Suresh Rai and Dharma P. Agrawal
(ISBN 0-8186-8907-2); 352 pages

Computer Architecture
Edited by D.D. Gajski, V.M. Milutinovic, H. Siegel, and B.P. Furht
(ISBN 0-8186-0704-1); 602 pages

Computer Communications: Architectures, Protocols, and Standards (Second Edition)
Edited by William Stallings
(ISBN 0-8186-0790-4); 448 pages

Computer Graphics (2nd Edition)
Edited by J.C. Beatty and K.S. Booth
(ISBN 0-8186-0425-5); 576 pages

Computer Graphics Hardware: Image Generation and Display
Edited by H.K. Reghbati and A.Y.C. Lee
(ISBN 0-8186-0753-X); 384 pages

Computer Graphics: Image Synthesis
Edited by Kenneth Joy, Max Nelson, Charles Grant, and Lansing Hatfield
(ISBN 0-8186-8854-8); 384

Computer and Network Security
Edited by M.D. Abrams and H.J. Podell
(ISBN 0-8186-0756-4); 448 pages

Computer Networks (4th Edition)
Edited by M.D. Abrams and I.W. Cotton
(ISBN 0-8186-0568-5); 512 pages

Computer Text Recognition and Error Correction
Edited by S.N. Srihari
(ISBN 0-8186-0579-0); 364 pages

Computers for Artificial Intelligence Applications
Edited by B. Wah and G.-J. Li
(ISBN 0-8186-0706-8); 656 pages

Database Management
Edited by J.A. Larson
(ISBN 0-8186-0714-9); 448 pages

Digital Image Processing and Analysis: Volume 1: Digital Image Processing
Edited by R. Chellappa and A.A. Sawchuk
(ISBN 0-8186-0665-7); 736 pages

Digital Image Processing and Analysis: Volume 2: Digital Image Analysis
Edited by R. Chellappa and A.A. Sawchuk
(ISBN 0-8186-0666-5); 670 pages

Digital Private Branch Exchanges (PBXs)
Edited by E.R. Coover
(ISBN 0-8186-0829-3); 400 pages

Distributed Computing Network Reliability
Edited by Suresh Rai and Dharma P. Agrawal
(ISBN 0-8186-8908-0); 368 pages

Distributed Control (2nd Edition)
Edited by R.E. Larson, P.L. McEntire, and J.G. O'Reilly
(ISBN 0-8186-0451-4); 382 pages

Distributed Database Management
Edited by J.A. Larson and S. Rahimi
(ISBN 0-8186-0575-8); 580 pages

Distributed-Software Engineering
Edited by S.M. Shatz and J.-P. Wang
(ISBN 0-8186-8856-4); 304 pages

DSP-Based Testing of Analog and Mixed-Signal Circuits
Edited by M. Mahoney
(ISBN 0-8186-0785-8); 272 pages

Fault-Tolerant Computing
Edited by V.P. nelson and B.D. Carroll
(ISBN 0-8186-0677-0 (paper) 0-8186-8667-4 (case)); 432 pages

Gallium Arsenide Computer Design
Edited by V.M. Milutinovic and D.A. Fura
(ISBN 0-8186-0795-5); 368 pages

Human Factors in Software Development (2nd Edition)
Edited by B. Curtis
(ISBN 0-8186-0577-4); 736 pages

Integrated Services Digital Networks (ISDN) (Second Edition)
Edited by W. Stallings
(ISBN 0-8186-0823-4); 404 pages

For Further Information:

IEEE Computer Society, 10662 Los Vaqueros Circle, P.O. Box 3014,
Los Alamitos, CA 90720-1264

IEEE Computer Society, 13, Avenue de l'Aquilon, 2,
B-1200 Brussels, BELGIUM

IEEE Computer Society,
Ooshima Building, 2-19-1 Minami-Aoyama,
Minato-ku, Tokyo 107, JAPAN

Interconnection Networks for Parallel and Distributed Processing
Edited by C.-L. Wu and T.-Y. Feng
(ISBN 0-8186-0574-X); 500 pages

Local Network Equipment
Edited by H.A. Freeman and K.J. Thurber
(ISBN 0-8186-0605-3); 384 pages

Local Network Technology (3rd Edition)
Edited by W. Stallings
(ISBN 0-8186-0825-0); 512 pages

Microprogramming and Firmware Engineering
Edited by V. Milutinovic
(ISBN 0-8186-0839-0); 416 pages

Modeling and Control of Automated Manufacturing Systems
Edited by A.A. Desrochers
(ISBN 0-8186-8916-1); 384 pages

Modern Design and Analysis of Discrete-Event Computer Simulations
Edited by E.J. Dudewicz and Z. Karian
(ISBN 0-8186-0597-9); 486 pages

New Paradigms for Software Development
Edited by William Agresti
(ISBN 0-8186-0707-6); 304 pages

Object-Oriented Computing--Volume 1: Concepts
Edited by Gerald E. Peterson
(ISBN 0-8186-0821-8); 214 pages

Object-Oriented Computing--Volume 2: Implementations
Edited by Gerald E. Peterson
(ISBN 0-8186-082108); 214 pages

Office Automation Systems (Second Edition)
Edited by H.A. Freemand and K.J. Thurber
(ISBN 0-8186-0822-6); 324 pages

Parallel Architectures for Database Systems
Edited by A. R. Hurson, L.L. Miller, and S.H. Pakzad
(ISBN 0-8186-8838-6); 478 pages

Programming Productivity: Issues for the Eighties (Second Edition)
Edited by C. Jones
(ISBN 0-8186-0681-9); 472 pages

Recent Advances in Distributed Database Management
Edited by C. Mohan
(ISBN 0-8186-0571-5); 500 pages

Reduced Instruction Set Computers (Second Edition)
Edited by W. Stallings
(ISBN 0-8186-8943-9); 448 pages

Reliable Distributed System Software
Edited by J.A. Stankovic
(ISBN 0-8186-0570-7); 400 pages

Robotics Tutorial (2nd Edition)
Edited by C.S. G. Lee, R.C. Gonzalez, and K.S. Fu
(ISBN 0-8186-0658-4); 630 pages

Software Design Techniques (4th Edition)
Edited by P. Freeman and A.I. Wasserman
(ISBN 0-8186-0514-0); 736 pages

Software Engineering Project Management
Edited by R. Thayer
(ISBN 0-8186-0751-3); 512 pages

Software Maintenance
Edited by G. Parikh and N. Zvegintzov
(ISBN 0-8186-0002-0); 360 pages

Software Management (3rd Edition)
Edited by D.J. Reifer
(ISBN 0-8186-0678-9); 526 pages

Software-Oriented Computer Architecture
Edited by E. Fernandez and T. Lang
(ISBN 0-8186-0708-4); 376 pages

Software Reusability
Edited by Peter Freeman
(ISBN 0-8186-0750-5); 304 pages

Software Risk Management
Edited by B.W. Boehm
(ISBN 0-8186-8906-4); 508 pages

Standards, Guidelines, and Examples on System and Software Requirements Engineering
Edited by Merlin Dorfman and Richard H. Thayer
(ISBN 0-8186-8922-6); 626 pages

System and Software Requirements Engineering
Edited by Richard H. Thayer and Merlin Dorfman
(ISBN 0-8186-8921-8); 740 pages

Test Generation for VLSI Chips
Edited by V.D. Agrawal and S.C. Seth
(ISBN 0-8186-8786-X); 416 pages

VSLI Technologies: Through the 80s and Beyond
Edited by D.J. McGreivy and K.A. Pickar
(ISBN 0-8186-0424-7); 346 pages

VLSI Testing and Validation Techniques
Edited by H. Reghbati
(ISBN 0-8186-0668-1); 616 pages

Reprint Collections

Dataflow and Reduction Architectures
Edited by S.S. Thakkar
(ISBN 0-8186-0759-9); 460 pages

Expert Systems: Software Methodology
Edited by Peter Raeth
(ISBN 0-8186-8904-8); 476 pages

Logic Design for Testability
Edited by C.C. Timoc
(ISBN 0-8186-0573-1); 324 pages

Microprocessors and Microcomputers (3rd Edition)
Edited by J.T. Cain
(ISBN 0-8186-0585-5); 386 pages

Software (3rd Edition)
Edited by M.V. Zelkowitz
(ISBN 0-8186-0789-0); 440 pages

VLSI Technologies and Computer Graphics
Edited by H. Fuchs
(ISBN 0-8186-0491-3); 490 pages

Artifical Neural Networks Technology Series

Artificial Neural Networks: Concept Learning
Edited by J. Diederich
(ISBN 0-8186-2015-3); 140 pages

Artificial Neural Networks: Electronic Implementation
Edited by Nelson Morgan
(ISBN 0-8186-2029-3); approximately 192 pages

Artificial Neural Networks: Theoretical Concepts
Edited by V. Vemuri
(ISBN 0-8186-0855-2); 160 pages

Software Technology Series

Computer-Aided Software Engineering (CASE)
Edited by E.J. Chikofsky
(ISBN 0-8186-1970-8); 110 pages

Communications Technology Series

Multicast Communication in Distributed Systems
Edited by Mustaque Ahamad
(ISBN 0-8186-1970-8); 110 pages

Robotic Technology Series

Multirobot Systems
Edited by Rajiv Mehrotra and Murali R. Varanasi
(ISBN 0-8186-1977-5); 122 pages